RED PETROGRAD

REVOLUTION IN THE FACTORIES
1917–1918

SOVIET AND EAST EUROPEAN STUDIES

Editorial Board

The National Association for Soviet and East European Studies exists for the purpose of promoting study and research on the social sciences as they relate to the Soviet Union and the countries of Eastern Europe. The Monograph Series is intended to promote the publication of works presenting substantial and original research in the economics, politics, sociology and modern history of the USSR and Eastern Europe.

SOVIET AND EAST EUROPEAN STUDIES

Books in the series

This book explores the   ife
in the Russian capital
control of their wor'   igh
to June 1918, wh   h
not primarily c
Revolution, t
produc
conflic.

Having discussed the structure and composition of the factory workforce in Petrograd prior to 1917 and the wages and conditions of workers under the old regime, Dr Smith shows how workers saw the overthrow of the autocracy as a signal to democratise factory life and to improve their lot. After examining the creation and activities of the factory committees, he analyses the relationship of different groups of workers to the new labour movement, and assesses the extent to which it functioned democratically.

The central theme of the book is the factory committees' implementation of workers' control of production. Dr Smith rejects the standard Western interpretation of this movement as 'syndicalist', showing that its ideological perspectives were close to, but not identical with, those of the official Bolshevik party. Essentially, workers' control was a practical attempt to maintain production and to preserve jobs in a situation of deepening economic chaos. On coming to power in October, the Bolsheviks envisaged an expansion of workers' control, and the committees pressed for nationalisation and workers' management. The collapse of industry and the reluctance of employers to continue their operations, however, convinced the Bolshevik leadership that workers' control was inadequate as a means of restoring order in the economy, and they subordinated the committees to the trade unions in 1918.

Dr Smith assesses the extent to which the Bolsheviks' capacity to carry out a genuinely revolutionary programme was limited by their own ideology or by the economic and social conditions in which the revolution was born. Throughout, he places the struggle in the factories in the context of an international and comparative perspective. The book will thus appeal not only to historians of Russia and the Russian Revolution, but also to students of labour history and of revolutionary theory.

S.A. SMITH is Senior Lecturer at the University of Essex. He studied at the Universities of Oxford, Birmingham, Moscow and Beijing.

RED PETROGRAD

REVOLUTION IN THE FACTORIES
1917–1918

S. A. SMITH

Senior Lecturer in History, University of Essex

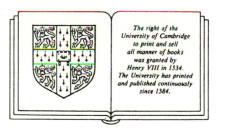

The right of the
University of Cambridge
to print and sell
all manner of books
was granted by
Henry VIII in 1534.
The University has printed
and published continuously
since 1584.

CAMBRIDGE UNIVERSITY PRESS

CAMBRIDGE

LONDON   NEW YORK   NEW ROCHELLE

MELBOURNE   SYDNEY

Published by the Press Syndicate of the University of Cambridge
The Pitt Building, Trumpington Street, Cambridge CB2 1RP
32 East 57th Street, New York, NY 10022, USA
10 Stamford Road, Oakleigh, Melbourne 3166, Australia

First published 1983
First paperback edition 1985

Library of Congress catalogue card number: 82–12885

British Library Cataloguing in Publication Data
Smith, S. A.
Red Petrograd: revolution in the factories,
1917–18.—(Soviet and East European studies)
1. Leningrad—Politics and government
2. Russia—Politics and government—1894–1917
3. Soviet Union—Politics and government—1917–1936
I. Title   II. Series
947′.45   DK265.8.L/

ISBN 0 521 24759 4 hard covers
ISBN 0 521 31618 9 paperback

Transferred to digital printing 2003

CE

To my mother and father

Contents

vii

Acknowledgments

This book began life as a Ph.D. thesis undertaken at the Centre for Russian and East European Studies at the University of Birmingham. I wish to thank everyone there for providing a stimulating atmosphere in which to work, especially Professor Moshe Lewin, now of the University of Pennsylvania, who provided much of the inspiration for this work when it was in its early stages. I would like to express my warm thanks to Maureen Perrie, also of CREES, who supervised the final stages of this work. I am most grateful to the British Council for granting me an exchange studentship to Moscow University in the academic year 1976–7, and to Professor V. Z. Drobizhev of the Faculty of History, who gave me advice and hospitality. I would like to record my indebtedness to the librarians of INION and the Lenin Library in Moscow, the newspaper room of the BAN Library in Leningrad and, above all, to Jenny Brine, librarian of the Baykov Library, CREES.

I would like to thank the University of Essex for granting me study leave during the Autumn term of 1979, and all my colleagues in the History Department for providing a congenial atmosphere in which to teach. Mary McAuley, Geoffrey Crossick, Geoffrey Hosking and Rose Glickman all made helpful comments on parts of this book in an earlier form. Professor Yoshimasa Tsuji of Waseda University read the whole manuscript, and made many useful criticisms. I am grateful to all of them, though none bears any responsibility for any errors that remain. Finally, I would like to say thank-you to all my friends in Birmingham, Moscow, Leningrad, Colchester and elsewhere, who offered me the personal support without which I could not have written this book. Special thanks to Bob Lumley, Kevin Halliwell, Karl Goswell, Elia Michael, Peter Baxter and, above all, Philip Jakes.

Introduction

Revolutions are centrally about the breakdown of state power, the elimination of old political elites and institutions, and the ultimate reconstitution of a new state power and a new elite.[1] The history of revolutions is thus, intrinsically, a political history, and the history of the Russian Revolution of 1917 is no exception. It begins in February with the overthrow of the tsarist autocracy, continues with the 'dual power' of the Provisional Government and Petrograd Soviet, culminates in the Bolshevik seizure of power and eventuates in a one-party dictatorship. Yet revolutions entail more than the collapse of state power: they engender a whole-scale restructuring of social relations. Only recently, have historians begun to pay attention to the profound changes which took place in the society, culture and economy of Russia during the revolutionary years. The manifold transformations of social relations were dependent on the collapse of state power, but they in turn shaped the processes whereby centralised, bureaucratic state power was reconstituted. Power was thus directly at issue in all the multiple changes which rent the fabric of tsarist society, and it is for this reason that any 'social history' of the Russian Revolution cannot but also be a political one.

The present study is concerned with the relationships between class power as it was manifest in the world of work and the broader processes of the Russian Revolution. It seeks to explore the impact of the revolution on factory life in Petrograd during 1917 and the early part of 1918. Its central theme is the struggle of workers to abolish the autocratic order of the tsarist factory, their efforts to establish workers' control of production, and their groping attempts to reorganise life in the factory. This study is not primarily concerned with tracing the emergence of a revolutionary political consciousness among Petrograd workers, and thus the events, political parties and personalities which dominate other accounts of the revolution recede into the background of the present study.[2] Nevertheless, in deliberately foregrounding the activities of workers around work and production, it is hoped to shed new light on the wider political developments of 1917, in particular, by demonstrating that the sphere of production was itself an important arena of political as well as economic conflict.

Although the separation of the economy and polity is a particular feature of modern capitalist society, the unequal distribution of power within production is crucial to the maintenance of class power in society at large. If one defines power as the capacity of a group to control the physical and social environment and to thus make its interests prevail over those of other groups, then it is clear that management and workers do not enjoy equal power within the production process.[3] The two sides of industry do not have equal access to and control over resources and sanctions, be they material or ideological. In 1917 the unequal distribution of power within production was a central concern of Petrograd workers, and their struggle for greater power in industry had major implications for the balance of class forces in society at large and for the eventual consolidation of a new state power.

This perspective has implications for the way in which we analyse working-class activity in 1917, for it means that we must jettison any simple dichotomy between the 'economic' and 'political' struggles of workers, i.e. between struggles which take place within the sphere of production and those which take place on the terrain of the state. In Marxist discourse this dichotomy appears in the guise of the Leninist distinction between 'trade-union' and 'Social-Democratic' struggles. Although he was not absolutely consistent in this view, Lenin tended to argue that the spontaneous struggles of workers for the improvement of wages and working conditions could only generate a 'trade-union' consciousness, the chief characteristics of which are sectionalism and economism, and that only through the intervention of a revolutionary party could workers develop a revolutionary awareness of capitalist society.[4] The experience of 1917 suggests that this rigid dichotomy is in need of modification. In that year, in a context of economic crisis and acute class conflict, the attempts of workers to defend their living standards and to preserve jobs led them, to a large extent 'spontaneously', to see in the revolutionary options offered by the Bolsheviks the 'natural' solution to their immediate problems. Moreover, the Leninist thesis overlooks issues of power and control within production. In most work-situations there is resistance by workers to the authority of the employer, so that, in the words of Carter Goodrich, the 'frontier of control' is constantly shifting.[5] An orthodox Leninist might argue that such conflicts over job-control are but a variant of economistic struggles, since they encroach on, but do not transcend, managerial authority. Yet even at their most defensive, such conflicts testify to the desire of workers to impose their definitions upon the work-situation. The experience of 1917 again suggests that when the power of the state is relatively ineffective, defensive struggles by workers to control production can quickly become offensive struggles to take power from management, and that these struggles have profound implications for the balance of power within society as a whole. The present study suggests that it was the struggles of workers in the world of work, and the activities of work-based organisations, such as the factory committees and trade unions, which were of central importance in promoting revolutionary consciousness in 1917. This is not to suggest that consciousness developed solely on the basis of the experience of work. In 1917 revolutionary feeling grew in response to the wide range of problems that faced the Russian people – problems of war, governmental ineptitude and the crisis in the countryside. Nor is it to suggest that revolutionary consciousness grew in a purely 'spontaneous' fashion. Bolshevik agitation played a crucial part in articulating this consciousness. Nevertheless the Bolsheviks did not themselves create revolutionary feeling; it developed primarily out of attempts by workers to grapple with problems of survival.

This study concentrates almost exclusively on factory workers in Petrograd. It ignores important groups such as railway workers, transport workers, workers in public utilities, postal and telegraphic workers, shop workers, construction workers, domestic servants, small artisans and others. This is not because these workers were defined *a priori* as somehow less 'proletarian' than factory workers. It was decided to concentrate on factory workers, partly to keep down the length of the book, and partly because factory workers did constitute the major element within the industrial labour force and within the labour movement in Petrograd in 1917. Perhaps something should be said to justify the inclusion of printers in the category 'factory workers'. It is true that of the sixty-four print works (*tipografii*) in Petrograd for which we have information, twenty-seven employed less than fifty workers; but even if one excludes the huge State Papers print works, which employed 5,784 workers, the average print works still employed 136 workers, so it was more of a 'factory' than a small workshop.[6] It should not be supposed that factory workers, in any sense, constituted a homogeneous social group. They were divided among themselves by industry and trade, degree of proletarian-isation, skill, sex, age etc. These divisions are important in under-standing the dynamics of the labour movement in 1917, and are explored in Chapters 1 and 8.

A word should be said about periodisation. The first two chapters discuss the structure of the working class, and life in the tsarist factory before February 1917. The main body of the text (Chapters 3 to 8) is concerned with developments between February and October, but since the main theme of the work – the attempt of workers to take control of their working lives – continues beyond October, it was decided to pursue the analysis into the middle of 1918, though in a less detailed way than for 1917. The account thus stops at the point when the Bolsheviks decided to nationalise industry at the end of June 1918, but this is more a convenient finishing point, than a real historical break, for it was some time before workers' control of production disappeared, and some time before nationalisation was a reality.

The capital of Russia is called by St Petersburg when referring to the period before 18 August 1914. On that date the tsarist govern-ment, in a fit of anti-German fervour, changed the name of the city to the less German-sounding Petrograd. This study follows suit. When referring to the period beyond Lenin's death in 1924, the city is called by its modern name of Leningrad. This study uses old-style dates of the Julian calendar until 14 February 1918 (i.e. 1 February 1918), which was the date when the Bolshevik government changed to the Gregorian calendar. All dates thereafter are given in the new style. Except in quotations, measures of weight have been translated into metric units. The currency of rubles and kopecks is abbreviated to 'r.' and 'k.'.

1

A profile of the Petrograd working class on the eve of 1917

PETROGRAD: THE CITY AND ITS INDUSTRY

Petrograd was a city of sharp contrasts. It was the capital of the Russian Empire, yet closer culturally to Western Europe than to the rest of Russia. It was at once a city of elegant grandeur, lauded by Pushkin, and a city of eerie squalor, abhorred by Dostoevsky. Petrograd was both symbol of tsarist power and of popular revolt. Here the Imperial Court headed an army of 70,000 civil servants; here in 1905 the first Soviet had headed a general strike. Along the avenues and canals of the city centre stood palaces, splendid emporia, banks and company offices. Across the river stood bleak tenements and teeming factories. Not a stone's throw from the University and the Academy of Sciences thousands of people lived in appalling ignorance and misery. Petrograd was home to rich and poor, to a thriving revolutionary underground and to the Holy Synod, to the liberal opposition and to the Black Hundreds. Here in February 1917 a revolution erupted which was to have world-shattering reverberations.

In 1917 Petrograd had a population of 2.4 million, making it the fifth largest city in Europe.[1] The Russian Empire had about 182 million inhabitants, less than a fifth of whom lived in towns.[2] Petrograd was by far the largest city in the Empire; between 1897 and 1914 its population had grown from 1.26 million to 2.21 million – a very high rate of growth, compared to the average for the country as a whole.[3] This growth was largely due to the immigration of peasants from the countryside. Every year thousands of peasants flocked to the city in search of work – some to stay for a short while, others to settle permanently. In 1910, no fewer than 68% of the population had been born outside the city.[4]

The huge scale of peasant migration to St Petersburg gave the city's population a distinctive demographic structure. The birth-rate in the capital was low by Russian standards, though high by Western European standards.[5] The death-rate was lower than the national average, but this was deceptive, since in almost every age-group it was actually higher than average. Only the preponderance of young adults in the population depressed the overall death-rate. Even so, mortality in St Petersburg was extremely high by European standards. The large proportion of young adults in the city was paralleled by very small proportions of children under 10 and of people over 50. This reflected the tendency for children to be brought up in the countryside, and for older people to retire there. Since greater numbers of men than women left the countryside in search of work, there was an imbalance in the population in favour of males, though the proportion of women grew rapidly after 1900. Finally, a majority of both men and women were single. The marriage-rate in St Petersburg was low both by Russian and European standards, and late marriage was the norm. These distinctive demographic patterns suggest that the 'typical' inhabitant of St Petersburg on the eve of the First World War was, therefore, a single, male peasant in his twenties.

The census of 1910 provides the fullest information on the social structure of St Petersburg. This classified the city's population of 1,881,000 by social estate (*soslovie*), revealing that 7.2% were nobility, 0.5% clergy, 4.1% honorary citizens, 0.7% merchants, 15.5% 'lower middle class' (*meshchane*) and 68.7% peasants.[6] This latter category included most wage-earners. Workers comprised about 27% of the capital's population, and consisted of 234,000 factory workers; 77,000 white-collar workers in commercial and industrial enterprises (*sluzhashchie*); 52,000 transport workers; 25,000 in the catering trade and 41,000 who worked in public utilities and city organisations. In addition, there were about 260,000 servants in private or public employment and 58,000 artisans. Financial and industrial business-men comprised less than 1% of the population, and there were about 21,000 owners of small businesses, including shops and restaurants.[7]

In 1914 Petrograd was the foremost financial and industrial centre in a country where two-thirds of the population still engaged in agriculture. The city's banks controlled the metallurgical and coal industries of the South, the oil industry of Baku, Urals copper, Siberian gold, Ukrainian sugar, Turkestan cotton and Volga steamships.[8] By 1917 the assets of Petrograd's private commercial banks amounted to three-quarters of the entire assets of Russia's commercial banks.[9] These banks financed the major industrial companies of the capital, most of which were concentrated in the metalworking and engineering sector. The Discount and Loan bank, for example, financed the Nobel-Lessner engineering group, the American-Russian rubber company and the Skorokhod shoe company.[10] Since two-thirds of the assets of Russian commercial banks were foreign-owned, foreign capital played a crucial part in Petrograd industry.[11] In 1917, however, only fifteen firms in the capital were owned outright by foreign companies.[12] The industry of Petrograd was distinguished not so much by its dependence on foreign capital as by its dependence on the state.

Underpinning the economy of the city was a tight nexus of large monopolies, finance capital and government orders. From the industrial crisis of 1900–3 onwards, companies began to form syndicates in order to exercise monopoly control over the market.[13] This process of monopolisation was given a sharp boost by the First World War, which made Petrograd the main centre of armaments production. By 1917 sixty of the largest firms in the capital were organised into syndicates or trusts. During the war, the government farmed out orders for ammunition and some types of ordnance to these syndicates. The Russian-Asiatic bank organised a War Industries syndicate which distributed orders to the Baranovskii engineering company, the Russian Optical Company and the Russian Company for the Manufacture of Shells and Military Supplies. Snaryadosoyuz, a private syndicate comprising six firms, produced shells directly for the Artillery Administration. The transport-engineering syndicates Prodparovoz and Prodvagon were treated by the Ministry of Communications more or less as official government contractors. S.N. Vankov headed a state-capitalist organisation which produced three-inch shells directly for the Artillery Administration by sub-contracting orders to four large companies in Petrograd.[14]

As well as providing orders for the major private companies, the state directly owned several large enterprises in Petrograd. From its foundation in 1703, St Petersburg had been a major centre of government-sponsored industry. By 1917 there were 31 state-owned or state-controlled enterprises in the city and the surrounding region, which provided a large part of the cartridges, revolvers, machine-guns and other types of ordnance required by the army and navy. Ten enterprises were run by the Artillery Administration, the largest of which were: the Pipe works (*Trubochnyi zavod*) with a workforce of 18,942 in January 1917; the Cartridge works (*Patronnyi zavod*) with some 10,000 workers; the Okhta explosives works with 10,200 workers; the Sestroretsk works, situated 34 km from the capital, which had 6,228 workers. In all, 53,000 workers were employed by the Artillery Administration. In addition, a further 36,000 workers worked in five large factories run by the Naval Ministry. These included the Obukhov works, which employed 12,954 workers in January 1917; the Izhora works at Kolpino, which had 8,902 workers; the Baltic shipbuilding works, which had 7,645 workers. The rest of the state enterprises were made up of miscellaneous ports, arsenals and railway workshops.[15] In 1917 there were also two large companies which were state-controlled, though not state-owned. These were the massive Putilov works, with its workforce of around 30,000, and the Nevskii shipbuilding company, which employed more than 6,000 workers. In 1916 the government sequestered both firms, by appointing new boards of management, although each continued to be privately owned.[16]

In both state and private sectors, Petrograd industry was remarkable for its advanced technology. From the start of industrial 'take-off' in the 1890s, most branches of industry in the capital were highly mechanised. This was a response to the high labour-unit costs in Russia, which reflected low labour-productivity, the cost of raw materials and marketing, and the relatively restricted market for sales.[17] After 1907 Petrograd was caught up in the 'Second Industrial Revolution', which saw the emergence of new industries, such as chemicals, the rise of mass production, the restructuring of the labour process and the invasion of workshops by electric power. By 1914 Petrograd industry had attained a high level of technological sophistication.[18] Its largest firms lagged little behind those of America and Western Europe. The Putilov works exchanged technical information and patents with the Schneider, Armstrong-Whitworth, Paul Girault and A.G. Duisberg companies.[19] There was, however, considerable variation in technological level between different factories and different industries: machine-tool construction and machine construction, for example, were somewhat archaic, compared to the electro-technical and engine-building industries.[20]

The technical efficiency of Petrograd industry was put to stringent test by the war and, on the whole, was not found wanting.[21]

Enterprises were reorganised and re-equipped, and massive amounts of capital were injected into them. Mass-production techniques were introduced in the armaments factories and in some machine-contruction plants. The conversion of private factories to production of shells, hand grenades, detonators and mortars was very successful. Production of guns was less successful, but adequate. Most engineering industries coped well, but could not always meet demand. Production of engines increased and simple machine-tool production expanded both quantitatively and qualitatively. Production of automobiles and aircraft was established, but production of precision instruments remained weakly developed.[22]

Industrial output in the capital doubled between 1914 and 1917. In 1916 Petrograd factories fulfilled military orders worth 1.5 million rubles. In the metalworking industry, 81% of enterprises and 98% of the workforce worked on war orders.[23] Until the later part of 1916, therefore, in spite of some weaknesses, Petrograd industry managed to satisfy the voracious appetite of the Russian war machine. Thereafter, it found it increasingly hard to maintain output in the teeth of declining supplies of fuel and raw materials and growing chaos in the transport system.[24]

On the eve of the Russian Revolution, the structure of industry in Petrograd was altogether remarkable, unparalleled except in Germany. Petrograd represented an island of technologically sophisticated state-monopoly capitalism in a country whose mode of production still consisted in the main of rudimentary capitalist and pre-capitalist forms, albeit under the overall dominance of large capital. The economy of the city was being convulsed by a colossal boom which was entirely a consequence of the slaughter daily taking place at the Front. War, however, could not go on for ever. This was an economy living on borrowed time: as soon as the mighty powers had glutted themselves with carnage and destruction, the economy of Petrograd would deflate like a pricked balloon. No end to the war was as yet in sight, but already the signs of imminent collapse were on the horizon.

THE SIZE AND DISTRIBUTION OF THE FACTORY WORKFORCE IN 1917

Between 1890 and 1914, the number of factory workers in St Petersburg grew from 73,200 to 242,600.[25] Between 1914 and 1917, it

grew by 150,000 to reach 392,800 – or 417,000, if one includes the
factories situated on the outskirts of the city.[26] About one-third of the
workforce of the city and its suburbs, i.e. 134,464 workers, worked in
state enterprises.[27] At the beginning of 1917, the factory workers of
Petrograd represented about 12% of Russia's 3.4 million industrial
workers.[28] During the first half of that year, the number of workers in
the capital continued to grow – possibly by as much as 10%. From the
summer onwards, however, the workforce began to contract, as
economic crisis set in.[29]

The huge expansion of the Petrograd workforce between 1914 and
1917 took place almost entirely in industries producing for the war
effort. In the metal industry the workforce grew by 135%; in
chemicals by 99% and in clothing by 44%. In textiles the workforce
remained constant in size, and in the food, printing and paper
industries the workforce shrank.[30] By 1917 the distribution of the
Petrograd workforce by industry was as follows:

Table 1.

Branch of Industry	Number of enterprises	Number of workers	% of total workforce
Metalworking	379	237369	60.4
Textiles	100	44115	11.2
Chemicals	58	40087	10.2
Printing and Paper	218	26481	6.8
Food	70	15773	4.0
Woodworking	81	6754	1.7
Leather and footwear	50	12627	3.2
Minerals	32	3900	1.0
Miscellaneous	23	5722	1.5
TOTAL	1011	392828	100.0

Source: Z. V. Stepanov, *Rabochie Petrograda v period podgotovki provedeniya oktyabr'
skogo vooruzhennogo vosstaniya* (Moscow, 1965), p.29.

The most astonishing feature of this table is the extraordinary
predominance of metalworkers. Whereas metalworkers had comprised only one-third of the Petrograd workforce in 1908, nine years
later they comprised almost two-thirds.[31] In the same period
textileworkers grew in number, but dwindled as a proportion of the
workforce from 22% to 11%.[32]

Russia was renowned for its large factories. In 1914 54% of workers

Table 2: *% Distribution of workers in Petrograd according to size of enterprise*

Year	Enterprises of under 50 workers	Enterprises of 51 to 100 workers	Enterprises of 101 to 500 workers	Enterprises of 501 to 1000 workers	Enterprises of over 1000 workers
Average for 1901–1905[1]	6.7%	8.1%	31.8%	15.5%	37.9%
1906[2]	7.0%	7.2%	31.3%	18.6%	36.5%
1910[2]	6.8%	7.3%	31.0%	19.4%	35.5%
1914[2]	5.6%	5.6%	24.8%	14.8%	49.2%
[1913][3]	[5%]	[5%]	[20%]	[15%]	[55%]
1917[4]	3.0%	3.2%	15.9%	10.0%	67.9%

1. These figures are based on enterprises under the Factory Inspectorate in the whole of St Petersburg province.
   Source: S.N. Semanov, *Peterburgskie rabochie nakanune russkoi revolyutsii* (Moscow, 1966), p.37.
2. These figures are based on enterprises under the Factory Inspectorate in the whole of St Petersburg province.
   Source: A. I. Davidenko, 'K voprosu o chislennosti i sostave proletariata Peterburga v nachale XX veka' in *Istoriya rabochego klassa Leningrada*, issue 2 (Leningrad, 1963), pp.98–9.
3. The figures in square brackets are based on private and state enterprises in the city.
   Source: E.E. Kruze, *Peterburgskie rabochie 1912–1914g.* (Moscow, 1961), p.71.
4. The figures are based on private and state enterprises in the city and its suburbs.
   Source: A.G. Rashin, *Formirovanie rabochego klassa Rossii* (Moscow, 1958), p.105.

in Russia were employed in factories of over 500 workers, compared to 32.5% in the USA.[33] Concentration of production was largely a response to the shortage of skills and to low labour productivity. In Petrograd in 1917 there was an average of 409 workers per enterprise – 40% more than the average for Russian industry as a whole.[34] Such a high degree of concentration of the workforce made Petrograd quite unique in the world. No fewer than 70% of workers were employed in factories of over a thousand, and two-thirds of this number worked in thirty-eight huge enterprises, each of more than 2,000 workers.[35] It is apparent from *Table 2* that the trend towards concentration of plant size was a long-term trend which was merely intensified by the war. In the metal industry concentration was especially high, and an average of 2,923 workers worked in each of the 72 largest metal works of the capital and its suburbs.[36] Textile production was somewhat smaller in scale, but 78% of textileworkers worked in 25 mills with an average workforce of 1,372.[37] This suggests that concentration in large units cannot have been the key factor promoting the greater militancy of metalworkers *vis-à-vis* textileworkers in 1917, since both groups worked in factories which by Western European standards were extremely large.

The concentration of factory workers in large units of production was paralleled by their concentration in particular areas of the city. James Bater has shown that residential mixing rather than residential segregation of social classes was the norm in St Petersburg up to 1914.[38] The poor were to be found throughout the city, even in the wealthy, central-city districts of Admiralty and Kazan, where they tended to live in the cellars and garrets of buildings. In a socially more mixed district, such as Vasilevskii Island, the poor inhabitants of the Harbour district and of Malyi and Srednyi Prospekts lived cheek-by-jowl with the officials and intelligentsia of Bol'shoi Prospekt. Most factory workers, however, lived close to their place of work and were concentrated in the areas where industry was. In 1917 18% of workers lived on Vyborg Side, where the metal factories were located, and this figure rises to 25%, if one includes the adjoining suburban districts of Lesnoi and Polyustrovo. Some 20% lived in the Narva and Peterhof districts, where the giant Putilov works lay; 14% lived on Vasilevskii Island; 11% in Nevskii district and 10% on Petrograd Side.[39] In social terms the proletarian districts were worlds apart from the aristocratic districts of the city centre, but in geographical terms they were very close to one another. From Vyborg Side one had only to cross the Alexander II bridge to arrive at the Central Law Courts, and from there it was but a stone's throw to Nevskii Prospekt. The contrast in the living conditions of rich and poor was glaringly apparent in St Petersburg, because of both social mixing and the proximity of working-class and upper-class districts. Class divisions were more visible than in Western European cities, where suburbanisation and residential segregation had long been under way. This must have been a factor promoting class consciousness among the workers of St Petersburg.

The appalling statistics on mortality bear stark testimony to the reality of class division in the city. In 1915 the death rate per thousand in the working-class areas of Vyborg, Narva and Kolomenskaya was, respectively, 24.8, 22.8 and 26.5; in the Admiralty, Kazan and Liteinaya districts it was 8.7, 11.2 and 11.7.[40] About a quarter of all babies born in the capital died before the age of one. For those who survived, the biggest killers were tuberculosis, pneumonia, typhoid, spotted fever, smallpox, stomach and intestinal diseases.[41] In 1908 an epidemic of infectious diseases accounted for a staggering 47% of all deaths.[42] Such epidemics were a constant hazard, owing to the contamination of the water supply and the heavy pollution of the river Neva.

Living conditions in the proletarian districts were sordid and filthy. In 1920 42% of homes were without a water supply or sewage system.[43] Rubbish in the streets and open cesspools posed a grave danger to health. No proper roads or pavements existed in working-class areas, which meant that public thoroughfares turned into quagmires of mud during the winter. Street lighting was extremely bad or non-existent. Open spaces were few. Overcrowding was rife. The chairman of the Vyborg duma sanitation committee claimed that local residents had less space than those buried in the nearby cemetery.[44] Throughout the city an average of 3.2 persons lived in each room in single-room apartments, and 3.4 persons in each cellar; this was double the average for Berlin, Vienna or Paris. Around the Putilov works there sprawled a fetid slum; here an average of 4.1 people lived in each rented room. In the third ward of Aleksandr-Nevskaya district the corresponding figure was 4.6.[45] The majority of workers thus lived in cramped rooms, often damp and inadequately ventilated.

Although the standard of rented accommodation was frightful, it was by no means cheap. Rents in Petrograd were among the highest in Europe. In the decade up to 1914 they rose by 30% on average, and then doubled or trebled during the war.[46] Exorbitant rents reflected the desperate shortage of accommodation in the city, which had been a problem since the 1860s, owing to the massive influx of immigrants. According to S.N. Prokopovich's survey of 1908, only a quarter of workers could afford to rent a flat of one or two rooms, and those who could, usually sub-let a part of it. About 70% of single workers and 40% of workers with families lived in shared rooms. Many single workers made do with just a bunk, which they shared with workers on other shifts.[47] It was common for peasant workers to live as an *artel'*, sharing rent and living expenses and organising shopping and cooking collectively. In 1912 150,000 people lived in shared rooms, and during the war the number increased.[48] In Petrograd only a small proportion of workers lived in barracks accommodation or on factory premises (7% in 1918). This was in contrast to factories in rural areas where such accommodation was common.[49]

THE SOCIAL COMPOSITION OF THE PETROGRAD WORKING CLASS

Peasant workers and 'cadre' workers

Since the industrial labour force in Russia was recruited overwhelmingly from the countryside, the working class had a peculiar 'peasant' character which distinguished it from most Western European working classes, whose roots were more urban and artisanal. Whether one can even speak of a 'working class' in Russia before 1917 is still a matter of historical controversy, a controversy which goes back to the debates in the last quarter of the nineteenth century between Russian Narodniks and Marxists.

Crudely speaking, one can discern two groups within the workforce. The first consisted of peasants who worked in industry, but who still retained strong ties with the countryside. The second consisted of workers who lived solely by wage work and who were fully committed to factory life. Soviet historians call this latter group 'cadre' workers. They comprised either peasants, who had settled in the towns and severed their ties with the land, or second-generation workers who had been born into working-class families. Historical controversy revolves around two related problems. The first concerns the relative weight of each of these two groups within the labour force, i.e. the extent to which peasant workers outnumbered 'cadres'. The second concerns the extent to which a process of proletarianisation was under way, whereby more and more workers were cutting their links with agriculture and coming to identify with the industrial working class.

Between 1910 and 1917 the proportion of immigrants in the population of Petrograd rose from 68% to 73.6%.[50] The overwhelming majority of these were peasants, forced from the land by acute land scarcity, indebtedness and chronic poverty, or attracted to the big city by the prospect of making a better life for themselves. Many peasants came to the city with the intention of staying for only a short time, although in 1910 seasonal migrants, i.e. those who came during the winter months and returned to their villages in the summer, comprised only 10% of peasants in the capital.[51] Many more came with the intention of staying until they had earned enough money to make the family farm once more a viable undertaking.[52] Many, however, came with the intention of starting a new life and settling in the city. In 1910 25% of peasants had lived in the capital for ten years or more, and a further 25% had actually been born there.[53] Thus only about half the peasant population were recent arrivals to the city.

Peasants who migrated to Petrograd came from provinces distant from the capital, whereas in Moscow they came from contiguous areas. Most came from the non-black-earth central provinces and from the north-western provinces, particularly from Tver', Pskov, Vitebsk, Novgorod, Smolensk, Kostroma, Vilna, Yaroslavl' and Ryazan'. Only 9% came from Petrograd province itself.[54] It was common for peasants from the same locality to work in the same factory, for it was difficult to get taken on at a factory unless one had inside connections. At the Baltic works, for example, many workers came from Tver' province, and in the boat shop most came from Staritskii *uezd* within that province, since the foreman was a native of the area. At the Triangle works there were large numbers of workers from Vasilevskii *volost'* in Tver' *uezd*, Tver' province.[55]. Peasants from the same locality (*zemlyaki*) tended to work together and often lived together as an *artel'*. *Zemlyak* networks, however, did not necessarily insulate the peasants from new cultural pressures, but served instead to ease their transition into an urban-industrial environment. These networks were sometimes important means of organising labour protest, and in 1917 formally-organised *zemlyachestva* sprang up which played an important role in politicising peasant workers and soldiers.[56]

It is difficult to determine the number of workers who had close ties to peasant society, not just because of the paucity of data, but also because the concept of a 'tie' to the countryside is a nebulous one. Many workers who had worked for years in industry, and who had no association with farming, may have felt a vague kinship with the peasants, a spiritual 'tie' to their place of birth. This, however, would hardly warrant our categorising them as 'peasant workers'. Nor were familial ties with peasant society necessary evidence that a worker was not fully proletarianised. Many who had dug up their rural roots in early life would still have parents or relatives in the countryside. Only if workers had immediate family dependants in their native village – a wife or child – could they properly be considered 'peasant workers'. Even then, it was only if this familial tie had an *economic* underpinning that such workers were 'peasant workers' in the fullest sense. For in the last analysis, it was the ownership and cultivation of land, either directly or indirectly, which most crucially characterised a 'peasant worker'. In an attempt to estimate the proportion of 'peasant workers' in the factory workforce, therefore, two variables have been examined: firstly, the number of workers sending money to relatives in the countryside; secondly, and more importantly, the number of workers who owned and farmed land.

In 1908 the economist S.N. Prokopovich undertook a survey of 570 mainly skilled metalworkers in St Petersburg. This revealed that 42% of married workers and 67% of single workers sent money to the countryside.[57] Although a smaller proportion of married workers than single workers sent money to relatives, married workers tended to send a bigger portion of their earnings than single workers. A survey of St Petersburg textileworkers in 1912 showed that single women sent home 6.5% and single men 8% of their earnings, whereas married workers sent 28%.[58] One youth explained that he sent money regularly to his family 'so that my father will not summon me back to the countryside'.[59] A contemporary worker, P. Timofeev, wrote that the unskilled low-paid workers would often starve themselves in order to send as much as a fifth or a quarter of their earnings back home, but as their earnings were so miserably low, these savings could not substantially ease the plight of their rural dependants. If an unskilled worker managed to get a better job, preferably paid on piece-rates, he would start to find the tie with the countryside irksome, since visits home were costly. He would try, therefore, to bring his family out of rural poverty to live in the town. The skilled, well-paid worker would tend to do likewise.[60]

Table 3: *Proportion of workers in Leningrad who owned and farmed land*

	% of total who owned land	% of total who farmed land	% with no land
1918	16.7% (17.2)[1]	9.5% (10.8)	83.2% (82.8)
1926	11.8%[2]	4.4%	88.2%
1929	9.8%[3]	–	91.2%

Sources:
1. Ts.S.U., *Trudy*, XXVI, no. 2, pp. 118–19. My calculations. The figures in brackets are those in V. Z. Drobizhev et al., *Rabochii klass sovetskoi Rossii v pervyi god proletarskoi diktatury* (Moscow, 1975), p. 97.
2. S. Krasil'nikov, 'Svyaz' leningradskogo rabochego s zemlyei', *Statisticheskoe Obozrenie*, 4 (1929), pp. 107-8. This is my recalculation of the figures for single and married workers.
3. A. G. Rashin, *Sostav fabrichnogo-zavodskogo proletariata* (Moscow, 1930), p.25. This is my recalculation of the figures for the proportion of textileworkers and metalworkers with land.

The proportion of workers in 1917 who owned land is difficult to estimate. The 1918 industrial census is the source closest to that year, but it covers only 107,262 workers in Petrograd – less than a third of the 1917 workforce. This was because the census was taken at a time when factory closures and the promise of land in the countryside had led to a gigantic exodus of workers from the capital. Consequently, the figures from the 1918 census (see *Table 3*) should be treated with caution, since it is reasonable to assume that those workers who held land in the countryside in 1917 would have gone back to it before the census was taken. Those workers surveyed by the census were asked not only whether they still owned land, but also whether they had owned land prior to the October Revolution. 16.5% of the workers said that they had held land prior to October 1917, and 7.9% had farmed it.[61] This was considerably lower than the national average, for the census revealed that 31% of workers, nationally, owned land. Despite the fact that the 1918 census almost certainly underestimates the extent of land-ownership among Petrograd workers in 1917, especially among single workers (see *Table 4*), information from the 1926 and 1929 censuses suggests that the underestimation was only slight.

Using data from Prokopovich's 1908 survey of metalworkers and from the 1918 and 1926 censuses, *Table 4* provides further evidence that only a small minority of workers owned land, and only a minority

Table 4: *% of workers who owned land*

	% single workers who:		% married workers who:	
	owned land	farmed land	owned land	farmed land
1908[1]	50%	32%	33%	12%
1918[2]	12.5%	7.3%	13.7%	6.6%
1926[3]	21.3%	6.6%	8.8%	3.7%

Sources:
1. S. N. Prokopovich, *Byudzhety peterburgskikh rabochikh* (St Petersburg, 1908), p.7.
2. Drobizhev et al., *Rabochii klass sovetskoi Rossii*, p.95.
3. Krasil'nikov, 'Svyaz' s zemlei', p.107.

of these actually farmed it. It shows too that single workers were more likely to own land than married workers. This is probably due to the fact that the majority of peasant migrants to the capital were single. If they married, they would be under pressure to choose either to try to make a living on the land, or to sell up and move as a family to the town.

The censuses of 1918, 1926 and 1929 give some information on land-ownership among metalworkers and textileworkers (see *Table 5*). It emerges from this table that metalworkers were no less attached to the land than other groups of workers. The 1929 census figures proved to be an embarrassment to the Stalin government, since they disclosed that there were more land-owners among the 'vanguard' of the proletariat, the metalworkers, than among the 'backward' textileworkers. An even more interesting finding emerged from this census. Figures showed that the proportion of land-owners was

Table 5: *% of total workforce who owned land*

	metalworkers	textileworkers
1918[1]	18.7%	18.6%
1926[2]	10.2%	11.6%
1929[3]	12.4%	4.4%

Sources:
1. Drobizhev et al., *Rabochii klass sovetskoi Rossii*, p.98.
2. Krasil'nikov, 'Svyaz' s zemlei', p.108.
3. Rashin, *Sostav fab. zav. prol.*, p.30.

Table 6: *% of workers owning land who began work:*

	Leningrad textileworkers	Leningrad metalworkers
prior to 1905	8.0%	17.5%
between 1906 and 1913	4.6%	14.6%
between 1914 and 1917	3.6%	12.3%

Source: Rashin, *Sostav fab. zav. prol.*, p.30.

highest among groups with the longest service in industry (see *Table 6*). It is thus apparent that long service in industry did not necessarily erode the tie with the countryside. Yet workers who had worked in industry for twenty-five years were obviously 'proletarian', regardless of the fact that they owned land. This is borne out by a further finding of this census, which showed that a quarter of workers who owned land had been born into working-class rather than peasant families.[62] This suggests that by itself land-ownership is not an adequate index of proletarianisation.

Tables 3, 4, 5 and 6 all attest that the proportion of workers in Petrograd who owned land declined significantly over time. Further evidence that the working-class was becoming increasingly proletarianised is found by examining data on the numbers of hereditary workers, i.e. workers one or both of whose parents were themselves workers, and data on the numbers of settled workers, i.e. on average length of service in industry.

According to the 1918 census, 20% of metalworkers and 24.8% of textileworkers had one or both parents a worker.[63] The 1929 census correlated the social origin of Leningrad metalworkers and textileworkers with the year of their entry into industry. Whilst these data are scanty, they point clearly to an increase over time in the proportion of workers in Petrograd born into working-class families and a corresponding decline in the proportion born into peasant families (see *Table 7*).[64]

The data on length of service in industry is sparser and more difficult to interpret. Soviet historians usually assert that it took about five years for a worker new to industry to become a fully-fledged proletarian. It is, of course, impossible to estimate with scientific precision the length of time which it took a peasant to become socialised into factory life. It may have taken as long as ten years for a

Table 7

Year of entry into industry	Proportion of total sample who entered industry in the period:		Born into working class families (%)		Born into peasant families (%)	
	textile-workers	metal-workers	textile-workers	metal-workers	textile-workers	metal-workers
before 1905	22%	22%	44.5	43.1	52.7	52.0
between 1906 and 1913	18%	17.9%	53.8	52.2	42.2	42.0
between 1914 and 1917	10.4%	11.8%	56.2	56.9	39.6	37.3

Source: Rashin, *Sostav fab. zav. prol.*, pp. 19, 21.

peasant to overcome his rustic habits of work, the instinctive rhythm of hard and slack work, the dislike of close routine and his longing for the freedom of the outdoors.[65] For a young worker, however, it certainly would have taken far less time. One must therefore be cautious in interpreting the data.

In 1908 a survey of 5,720 metalworkers showed that 28% had worked less than two years in industry; 34% between two and five years and 39% five or more years. In the large factories with a workforce of more than a thousand, however, the proportion of workers with five or more years of service rose to 53%.[66] These figures suggest that a majority of workers were new to industry, yet this need not mean that the labour force was obviously 'peasant' in character. We know that it took very little time for some peasants to submit to the cultural pressures of town life and factory work. In view of this, Soviet historians may well be right to allow only five years as the average period it would take a worker to become acculturated to industrial and urban life, but the problem is very under-researched.

The preceding review of data on land-ownership and second-generation workers clearly reveals that a process of proletarianisation was taking place among the workers of St Petersburg. The proportion of 'cadre' workers in the workforce was increasing, owing to the decay of ties with the land and the growing number of hereditary workers. It is, however, more difficult to try to quantify the proportion of 'cadre' workers on the eve of the war. The data on land-ownership and sending money to the countryside suggest that, at most, a third of workers had real economic links with peasant society, but these were not the sum of 'peasant workers'. In addition, there were peasants who had only just arrived in industry and who would soon lose contact with the countryside, but who had not yet acclimatised to factory life. In the five years up to 1914, nearly 85,000 workers entered the factories of the capital, so that on the eve of the war about one-third of the total factory workforce had entered industry within the previous five years.[67] One can perhaps hazard that in 1914, 'peasant workers' and new workers (not all of whom were peasants) together comprised nearly half the factory workforce. Cadre workers, therefore, i.e. those who had severed their ties with peasant society and who had considerable industrial and urban experience, were probably in a slight majority.

The war led to a decline in the proportion of 'cadre' workers in the industrial workforce of the capital. This was caused partly by conscription, and partly by the massive influx of new workers into the factories. Throughout Russian industry about 400,000 to 500,000 (or 20% to 25% of the 1914 workforce) were conscripted into the army.[68] In Petrograd the proportion was much less, since workers there were needed to produce for the war effort. Leiberov and Shkaratan estimate that about 40,000 industrial workers in Petrograd were conscripted – or 17% of the 1914 workforce.[69] Those conscripted were mainly young workers without a great deal of experience of industry. Fully-proletarianised 'cadre' workers usually had some skill and so were less affected, since their skills were in desperately short supply. In later mobilisations, however, known militants and strike leaders were drafted into the army as punishment for participation in industrial and political protest. Leiberov and Shkaratan estimate that as many as 6,000 workers may have been conscripted on political grounds.[70] They conclude, nevertheless, that the 'cadre' proletariat was preserved during the war. The proportion of 'cadres' within the workforce was reduced not so much by conscription, as by the influx of new workers caused by the wartime expansion of production. Between 1914 and 1917 the workforce of Petrograd grew by 150,000; making allowance for the 40,000 who were conscripted, this means that some 190,000 workers must have entered industry. These comprised four main groups: male and female peasants; working-class women and youth; rural artisans and urban petit-bourgeois (*meshchane*); and evacuees. About 68,200 women came into Petrograd industry during the war, bringing the total number of women workers

to 129,800 by 1917. If one assumes that the 31,800 workers who were
under the age of eighteen in 1917 had entered industry during the
war, then the total number of female and young recruits was about
100,000.[71] Many of these may have been from working-class families
where the male breadwinner – husband, father or brother – had been
sent to the Front, and was thus no longer able to support the family. A
majority, however, were almost certainly from the countryside.
Although there are no statistics on the social origin of newcomers to
industry, it has been estimated that between one-half and three-
quarters of the newcomers were from the peasantry.[72] About 25,000
to 30,000 recruits to Petrograd industry were drawn from the rural
and urban petit-bourgeoisie.[73] When the war broke out, many small
traders, shopkeepers, landlords, porters, domestic servants, artists
and others took jobs in munitions factories in order to escape
conscription. A check on reservists at the Putilov works in August
1917 led to the 'voluntary' departure of 2,000 workers, described as
'book-keepers, shop-owners, tailors, artists, jewellers, corn-
chandlers, coopers, landlords, and cafe-owners'.[74] There were various jingles about such workers which were current in the factories
during the war:

> Once he was a yardkeeper
> > sweeping footpaths,
> Now he's in the factory
> > making shrapnel.[75]

Leiberov and Shkaratan estimate that such workers comprised 5% to
7% of the factory workforce in Petrograd.[76]

    Between 40,000 and 50,000 recruits were workers evacuated from
the Baltic provinces and Western parts of Russia. Some twenty
factories were evacuated from Riga – with a combined workforce of
over 6,000 – and about twenty-five from Lithuania.[77] In addition,
many Polish workers were removed to the capital. There were around
5,000 Poles at Putilov in 1917. Relatively few Chinese, Korean,
Central Asian or Persian workers came to Petrograd, although scores
of thousands were drafted into the mines of the Donbass, Urals and
Siberia, but there were several hundred in the state enterprises of the
capital.[78] If the 1918 industrial census is reliable for 1917, then 15.8%
of the factory labour force in Petrograd were non-Russians in 1917,
though by no means all of these had come to the capital during war.
The largest group were Poles (who comprised 5.8% of the total

labour force),followed by Latvians and Lithuanians (2.6%), Finns (2.3%), Germans (0.5%), Jews (0.3%) etc.[79]

Leiberov and Shkaratan conclude that if one subtracts the 190,000 workers who came into industry during the war from the total factory workforce in 1917, one is left with the number of 'cadre' workers – between 200,000 and 220,000 (assuming that most evacuees were 'cadre' workers). This leads them to conclude that a majority of the factory workforce in Petrograd in 1917 – 50% to 52% – were 'cadres'. But this assumes that by 1917 all those workers who had been working in industry in 1914 were 'cadres'. This seems an unwarranted assumption, in view of the fact that at least 40% of the workforce in 1914 had either less than five years' experience in industry or were peasant workers. Making some allowance for this, therefore, it is likely that by 1917 'cadres' no longer comprised a slight majority of the workforce, as they had done in 1914, but had shrunk to perhaps as little as 40% of the total workforce.[80]

Sexual and age divisions

By January 1917 129,800 women worked in the factories of the capital.[81] This compared to 83,000 domestic servants, mostly women, who worked in dire conditions for shockingly low wages.[82] Perhaps 50,000 women worked in offices and similar establishments, and a similar number worked in shops and in the wholesale and retail trade.[83] Other women worked in the clothing trade and in various kinds of workshops and sweatshops. The proportion of women in the factory labour force rose from 20.8% in 1900, to 25.7% in 1913 to 33.3% in 1917 (see *Table 8*). The war thus led to a big increase in the number of women in Petrograd industry, though this was not as large an increase as in Russian industry as a whole, where the proportion of women soared from 26.6% in 1914 to 43.2% in 1917.[84]

The Petrograd textile industry had the highest proportion of women workers. After the 1905 Revolution millowners had deliberately increased the number of women employees. In 1907 the annual report of factory inspectors noted: 'the increase in the application of female labour is particularly sharply reflected in the cottonweaving industry, where women weavers have ousted men. The reasons for this are as before: their greater industry, attentiveness and abstinence (they do not drink or smoke), their compliance and greater reason-

Table 8: *Sexual and age breakdown of Petrograd workforce*

Branch of Industry	Year	% of workers			% increase of women and youths 1913–17
		men	women	youths	
All branches	1913	66.2	25.7	8.1	7.7
	1917	58.5	33.3	8.2	
Metalworking	1913	91.2	2.7	6.1	18.1
	1917	73.1	20.3	6.6	
Woodworking	1913	96.9	1.1	2.0	25.1
	1917	71.8	20.7	7.5	
Textiles and Sewing	1913	32.0	57.0	11.0	13.3
	1917	18.7	68.6	12.7	
Food	1913	51.8	40.7	7.5	29.6
	1917	22.2	66.0	11.8	
Leather and shoes	1913	71.1	20.5	8.4	24.8
	1917	46.3	42.8	10.9	
Chemicals	1913	56.1	41.6	2.3	9.3
	1917	46.8	46.7	6.5	
Minerals	1913	76.2	16.7	7.1	17.2
	1917	59.0	20.6	20.4	

Source: Stepanov, *Rabochie Petrograda*, p.34.

ableness in respect of pay'.[85] The textile workforce was composed mainly of young single women. A survey of 7,000 textileworkers in Petrograd in 1918 revealed that 18% were aged 17 or under; 17% aged 18 to 20; 28% aged 21 to 30; 18% aged 31 to 40; and 19% aged 41 and over. 69% of women were under the age of 30 compared to 39% of men, most of the latter being boys under 17.[86] Amongst the male textileworkers, who comprised only 13% of the total, 70% were married, 2% widowed and 28% single. Amongst the women, however, only 33% were married, 11% widowed and 56% single. This reflected the large share of young girls in the industry, and also the fact that the marriage rate had gone down as a consequence of the war. This was particularly striking among women textileworkers aged 20 to 30. In 1909, 74% of this group were married, whereas nine years later, only 49% were.[87]

By 1917 more women in Petrograd worked in the metal industries than in textiles – approximately 48,000 as against 30,000. The proportion of women in the metal industries rocketed from 2.7% in 1913 to 20.3% (see *Table 8*). These women worked in mass-production factories producing cartridges, shells, shrapnel, etc. Some 18,000 women worked in the 'chemicals' industry, of whom over 10,000 were employed at a single plant – the giant Triangle rubber-works, which produced everything from galoshes to gas masks. A further 10,000 women were employed in the food and tobacco industries. Finally, about 5,000 women worked in the leather industry, including 3,000 at the Skorokhod shoe factory which made boots for soldiers. All these jobs had one thing in common, they were unskilled and badly-paid. The distribution of women in factory jobs thus reflected the fact that the sexual division of labour within the patriarchal peasant household had been transposed into a factory setting.[88]

Prior to the war, the employment of children was less widespread in the capital than in Russian industry generally. In 1914 about 8% of the workforce under the Factory Inspectorate in St Petersburg consisted of youths aged 15 to 17. In addition, about 2,000 children aged 12 to 15 were employed in porcelain and glass factories, printshops and other small enterprises.[89] In the course of the war the number of young workers in Petrograd grew, but less than the national average. The number of under-18s rose from 22,900 to 31,800, but their proportion within the factory labour force remained about the same (see *Table 8*). Although the proportion of young workers was the greatest in the textiles, food and leather industries, young workers were most numerous in the metal industries. It was this industry which provided a base for the youth movement in Petrograd in 1917.

The labour force in Russia was remarkable for the low proportion of middle-aged workers and the almost complete absence of elderly workers in its ranks. In 1900 23% of St Petersburg factory workers were aged 16 to 20; 52% were aged 21 to 40; and only 12% were older than 40.[90] The First World War dramatically changed this age balance. The fullest data on this question are provided by the industrial census of 1918, but because of the collapse of industry in the first half of that year, these data can be applied to 1917 only with some caution. The census showed that among male workers, 4.2% were under 15; 6.3% were 16 to 17; 6.5% were 18 to 20; 41.7% were 21 to 39; 38.4% were 40 to 59 and 2.9% were 60 or more.[91] This represented an enormous increase in the proportion of over-40s and a significant decline in the proportion of workers aged 21 to 40. This was an obvious consequence of conscription. Among women workers,

2.7% were under 15; 7.8% were 16 to 17; 18.4% were 18 to 20; 52.7% were 21 to 39; 17% were 40 to 59 and 1.3% were 60 or over. Women workers thus had a younger age profile than men in 1918, with a bigger proportion of under-21s and a far smaller proportion of over-40s.[92]

In 1918 60% of industrial workers in Russia were married or widowed. This compared to 63% of male and 46% of female metalworkers in Petrograd in the same year.[93] Late marriage was the norm: 45% of male and 48% of female workers aged 21 to 30 were unmarried in Petrograd in 1918.[94] Among the more highly-paid groups of workers, the marriage-rate and average family size were greatest. A survey of metalworkers in 1908 showed that 46% of those earning less than 1.50r. a day were single, compared to 21% of those earning more than 2.50r. a day.[95] In 1918 married male workers in Petrograd had an average of 2.4 dependants, but skilled metalworkers had 3.7.[96] Whereas in 1897 only 30% of married metalworkers had lived with their families, in 1918 three-quarters of skilled fitters in Petrograd did so.[97] In that year 71% of all married workers lived with their families – an important indication of the extent to which workers had broken ties with the countryside since 1897.

One Soviet anthropologist has suggested that women had a higher status in the working-class family than in the peasant family, and that there was a more equal division of labour within the former than the latter. She cites as evidence the opinion of M. Davidovich, surveyor of St Petersburg textileworkers, who wrote in 1909: 'While the woman hurries straight home from the factory to the children, the husband goes off to market and to the shops to buy provisions for supper and next day's dinner . . . in his spare time the husband must always look after the children.'[98]

Yet there is a good deal of other evidence to suggest that domestic labour remained as much the responsibility of the woman in the 'proletarian' family, as it was in its peasant counterpart. A. Il'ina, writing in the journal of the textileworkers, *Tkach*, gives this agonising description of the lot of the working mother:

Having finished work at the factory, the woman worker is still not free. While the male worker goes off to a meeting, or just takes a walk or plays billiards with his mates, she has to cope with the housework – to cook, to wash and so on . . . she is seldom helped by her husband. Unfortunately, one has to admit that male workers are still very prejudiced. They think that it is humiliating for a man to do 'woman's' work [*bab'yu rabotu*]. They would sooner their sick, worn-out wife did the household chores [*barshchinu*] by herself. They would rather tolerate her remaining completely without leisure – illiterate and ignorant – than condescend to help her do the housework. And on top of all these yokes and burdens, the woman worker has still the heavy load of motherhood . . . Today for a working class woman, having a baby is no joy – it's a burden, which at times gets quite unbearable.[99]

For single women who left their families, factory work may have brought a measure of economic independence,[100] but for married women, the burdens of being a housewife and mother, as well as a wage-worker, were onerous in the extreme. Low wages, together with the obligation to perform unpaid domestic labour, made married women economically dependent on the wages of their husbands.

Skill divisions

The definition of 'skill' is a thorny problem. Skill refers to the quality of work: a skilled job demands greater precision, dexterity and mental exertion than an unskilled job. Skill differences are rooted in the labour process – in the physical and intellectual requirements of particular operations within the process of production. Some writers have argued that it is possible to measure skill by comparing the length of training necessary for different jobs.[101] The problem is, however, that while skills do have real existence in the requirements of a job and in the capabilities of the worker, they are also partially determined by class struggle. Workers' organisations can 'artificially' create skills, by restricting access to particular jobs; they can control the institutions and practices whereby skills are acquired, transmitted and recognised.[102] Because skill determination is a site of class struggle, the usefulness of criteria such as length of apprenticeship or relative wage levels as 'objective' measures of skill must be fairly limited.

The origins of the St Petersburg metal industry go back to the first quarter of the eighteenth century, but the modern metallurgical and metalworking industries came into existence only in the 1890s. From the first, they were machine-based industries, fairly advanced in technology, but still dependent on the manual skills of craftsmen. The sociologist, Alain Touraine, has distinguished three phases in the organisation of work: the first was the old system which relied on craftsmanship and required only universal machines, such as lathes, not limited to the production of a single product; the second saw the break-up of a job into its component parts, the development of mechanisation and the feeding of machines by unskilled workers; the third phase is the phase of automation, where direct productive work by human beings is eliminated.[103] One could say that in the decade prior to 1917 the metalworking industry of Petrograd was moving from the first to the second of Touraine's phases.

Skilled craftsmen (*masterovye*) played a crucial role in the labour process in the metal industry of Petrograd. Highly-skilled workers, such as instrument-makers, pattern-makers, milling-machine operators, electricians, platers or engravers, performed complex precision work, working independently from technical drawings and using sophisticated measuring instruments. Beneath them were many skilled workers who were fully trained and who could work from technical drawings, but whose work was not especially complex or precise. These included most fitters (*slesari*), turners (*tokari*), electricians, mechanics, planers, mortisers, etc.[104] These highly-skilled and skilled men (there were no women in these trades) were directly involved in production: the rapidity of their reflexes, their visual, auditory and tactile sensibilities were crucial to the operation of the machine or tool. They were deeply knowledgeable of their work, used to taking decisions about their work, used to thinking for themselves and to exercising control over their jobs. They were respected by other workers and by management for their manual and intellectual skills. As such, they were not unlike craftsmen at Armstrong-Whitworth, the Schwarzkopf works in Berlin or at Fiat-Centro in Turin.

One should not imagine, however, that the skilled metalworker in St Petersburg was a 'labour aristocrat'. Some of the most highly-paid men did constitute a small 'aristocracy', but the average skilled man was far removed from the craftsman one might associate with the British 'new model' unions of the mid-nineteenth century. Firstly, Petersburg metalworkers were not organised into exclusive craft unions, capable of controlling entry to the trade, of imposing standard pay and conditions and of regulating workshop matters through 'custom and practice'.[105] Secondly, metalworkers did not serve a formal five- or seven-year apprenticeship. A survey of fitters at the Putilov works in 1918 showed that 67% had served an apprenticeship, averaging 3.3 years and starting at about the age of 15 or 16; 32% had trained on the job as assistants to craftsmen (*podruchnye*), for 4.5 years on average.[106] Thirdly, unlike British engineers in the nineteenth century, the metalworkers of St Petersburg did not rely so exclusively on manual skill: they operated up-to-date drilling machines, turret lathes, vertical boring mills, self-acting planing machines and horizontal milling machines. There were, of course, still turners who were masters of the parallel lathe, but there were many who worked automatic lathes which required them only to assemble parts, measure their dimensions and sometimes to regulate tools. Similarly, there were traditional fitters, who fitted parts with a file and scraper, ran the bearings and assembled all the parts themselves, but limit-gauges were already dealing a blow to their skills. The skilled metalworkers of St Petersburg were thus distant from British 'labour aristocrats', but neither were they yet the 'mass-production' workers of the modern assembly plant.

The *masterovye* of the metal trades were distinguished by their craft consciousness. Many worker-memoirists remark on this. A.M. Buiko, who worked at the Putilov works at the turn of the century, recalled:

In those days it was felt that if a worker did not master his trade, did not become a good craftsman, then he was not a proper fellow. This point of view had its roots in the days of *kustarshchina*, when old craftsmen regarded unskilled workers as a casual element in their midst. A worker who had not mastered his trade was scornfully called a 'master at earning his bread'

If a young man began a conversation with an older skilled fitter or turner he would be told: 'Learn first how to hold a hammer and use a chisel and a knife, then you can begin to argue like a man who has something to teach others.' For many years we had to put up with this. If you wanted to be an organiser, then you had to know your job. If you did, then they would say of you – 'He's not a bad lad – he works well and he's got a smart brain when it comes to politics.'[107]

A. Buzinov, who worked at the Nevskii works as a foundryman, remembered:

Every branch of production, and even each craft [*tsekh*], infects the worker with professional or craft patriotism. He sings the virtues of his own trade [*remeslo*] and spits on all the rest. Metalworkers felt themselves to be aristocrats among the rest of the working class. Their profession demanded more training and so they looked down on weavers and others, as though they were inferior bumpkins – today they are at the mill, tomorrow they go off to plough the land. Everyone recognised the superiority of metalworkers, with all the advantages that that implied ... The oddness of textileworkers hit me in the eyes. Many of them still wore peasant clothes. They looked as though they had wandered into the town by mistake and tomorrow would find their way back to their native village. Women predominated among them and one never lost an opportunity to pour scorn on them. Alongside the textileworkers, the metalworkers appeared to be a race apart, accustomed to life in the capital and more independent ... The more I grew into the factory family [*zavodskuyu sem'yu*], the more it became clear just how much variety there was even within one factory. Soon I began to feel that the workers in the engineering shop – fitters and turners – looked down on me. Later I realised that workers in the 'hot' shops – the foundry, the rolling-mill and the forge – had a low status. Then for the first time I saw that the people there were heavy and awkward in speech and gait. In each face, through the deep tan of the furnace, coarse features were clearly visible, which seemed to say that strength, not wit, was what was required in their work. I soon realised that next to the most experienced foundryman, even a poor fitter seemed an educated, thinking man.[108]

In these two passages one sees the classic elements of craft ideology: the pride of the craftsmen in the mastery of their trade;[109] the esteem they enjoy because of their knowledge of processes and materials and their manual dexterity; their condescension towards labourers and unskilled workers; their disdain for the peasants and their boorish way-of-life; their scorn of callow youth; their oppressive attitudes towards women; their measuring a person's moral integrity – indeed their political credibility – in terms of their mastery of their trade. Such craft pride was to take a knock, as the position of these skilled workers was undermined by technological change.

Most skilled workers were to be found in the machine-building and engineering sectors of the metal industry. Less skilled workers were to be found in metallurgical sectors, and in the so-called 'hot' shops of the large metal works. In a mammoth enterprise, such as the Putilov works, where there were 41 different workshops in 1917, the division between 'hot' shops, such as the foundries, the 'Martin' shop (named after the Siemens-Martin process of open-hearth steel-making), the crucible shop or rolling mills, and the 'cold' shops, such as the pattern shop, the machine shops, the gun or gun-carriage shops, was crucial. In the 'hot' shops the work was extremely arduous and most of the workers were peasants. The worker P. Timofeev described the work of an unskilled labourer (*chernorabochii*) in such a shop:

The chief characteristic of the work of a *chernorabochii* is that it is shockingly hard. It is one of the meanest, roughest, heaviest jobs which one finds in the factories. Apart from sheer muscle-power, nothing significant is required – neither literacy, skill, nor even simple quick-wittedness, since the gang-leader or senior *chernorabochii* will provide this. To carry iron, to load and unload wagons, to lift two hundred *pudy* of cast iron, to fetch and carry all kinds of heavy weights, to dig and prop up pits – these are some of the tasks of the *chernorabochii*. But his chief task is to be able to survive on seventy kopecks a day, to support a family, or from time to time to send ten or fifteen rubles to the countryside.[110]

The years after 1908 saw the emergence of a new layer of semi-skilled workers in the metal industry – mainly machine-operators of one kind or another. The appearance of semi-skilled workers was bound up with the introduction of new technology and the reorganisation of production. After 1909 the economy picked up, there was limited introduction of assembly lines, standardised calibres and interchangeable parts. At the Putilov works a shipyard was built, a new turret shop and gun shop were constructed, the factory was fully electrified and cranes began to be used for loading furnaces.[111] Other factories began to implement F.W. Taylor's techniques of 'scientific management'. By 1917 Russia was, after the USA, the country where scientific management was most widely applied.[112] The outbreak of war in 1914 gave a big boost to the transformation of work processes and work organisation. The whole-scale introduction of mass-production processes substantially changed the skill profile of the metal workforce, greatly expanding the ranks of the semi-skilled.

The influx of peasants and women into semi-skilled jobs potentially threatened the position of the *masterovye*. Yu. Milonov, a leader of the metalworkers' union, described the process thus:

The technology of production during the war was characterised by the broad application of automatic machines. The whole of war production was done on them ... This caused sharp changes in the professional make-up of workers in the metal-working industry. Alongside a reduction in the number of skilled, specialist *masterovye* as a result of the numerous mobilisations, the number of workers operating machines increased. And so the metalworkers' unions which arose after the February Revolution differed in their occupational make-up from the unions in the pre-war period. No longer did *masterovye* predominate in them, but the unqualified workers.[113]

Petrograd metalworkers were experiencing what in the British context was called 'dilution', i.e. the introduction of semi-skilled workers into jobs formerly done by skilled male workers, but also 'dilution' in the sense of a decrease in the specific weight of fully-proletarianised elements within the workforce. James Hinton has shown that in the British engineering industry, craftsmen whose status and privileges were still intact when the war broke out – mainly those on Clydeside and in Sheffield – led a class-wide offensive against 'dilution'. C. Goodey has suggested that 'dilution and de-skilling were almost as much at issue in Petrograd as they were on Clydeside'.[114] Yet what is surprising about the Russian experience is

precisely the absence of any militant opposition from the *masterovye*.
I. Gordienko, who worked as a moulder at the Lessner works, wrote:

During the time of my short absence, big changes took place. The turning
shop was filled with machines (mechanical assembly lines and vices) and new
workers, including many women, youths and the sons of those who could
afford to buy them out of the army. *The mood of the cadre workers was
indifferent.*[115]

This indifference to 'dilution' was probably the result of several
factors. First, the extent of 'dilution' should not be exaggerated. Some
rather doubtful calculations by S.G. Strumilin purport to show that
the average skill-level in the Petrograd metal industry fell by 17%
during the war, and by 12% among fitters and turners.[116] Secondly,
it is unlikely that skilled metalworkers were *directly* displaced by
semi-skilled women; the latter went into new sectors of production. In
the short term the opportunities for many craftsmen increased, owing
to the massive expansion of production. Thirdly, although working
conditions deteriorated and the intensity of work increased, the
Petrograd metal industry was one of the few industries in Russia
where real wages increased between the autumn of 1914 and the
winter of 1916, owing to the fact that the skills of the metalworkers
were in critically short supply. Together these factors helped blunt
opposition to 'dilution'.

In spite of some wartime de-skilling, the proportion of skilled
workers in the metal industry remained higher than in other
industries in 1917. The only data on skill-composition relate to 1918,
and must thus be treated with caution, in view of the tremendous
changes which took place in 1918 as a result of the rapid demobilisation of the war industries. Classifying the 21,792 metalworkers in
Petrograd enterprises of more than 500 workers according to the skill
categories used by the metalworkers' union. Strumilin calculated that
22.7% were highly skilled; 23.1% were skilled; 21.1% were semi-
skilled and 29% unskilled.[117] Even after wartime changes, the most
numerous occupational category in the industry remained that of
'fitter', a relatively unspecialised craftsman, who could turn his hand
to several jobs.

The skill structure of the textile industry was far less differentiated
than that of the metal industry. Skilled workers comprised only 6% of
the workforce. They were nearly all men, who performed fine
spinning and weaving and specialised carding operations. The
overlookers and mechanics were also mainly men. Semi-skilled

workers comprised 72% of the workforce. These were mainly women who tended jennies and fly-frames or operated power looms. About 20% of the workforce were classed as unskilled, who comprised mainly young girls and boys who worked as 'piecers', bobbin-tenders, heddlers, twisters, sorters and cleaners of raw wool or cotton.[118]

In 1917 there were 19,400 workers employed in the different branches of the printing industry of Petrograd.[119] During the war the number of printers had fallen by over 3,000, and the proportion of women in the industry had grown from 23% to 35%.[120] Although all large and many medium-sized print-works were mechanised to some extent, the print trade relied predominantly on manual skill. Typesetters comprised over a third of the workforce. Their skills and wages varied considerably, but as a group they were distinguished from other trades, such as paper-feeders, pressmen, machinists, lithographers or binders, by their high earnings, by the control which they exercised over their jobs, and by the fact that they regarded themselves as a cut above other workers in the industry. Newspaper compositors and the *aktsidentnye*, who did specialised and complex compositing, were better-paid than the *strochnye*, who typeset books.[121] Typesetters often worked in a *kompaniya* (company) in order to expedite a particular job as quickly as possible. They would organise the work among themselves and appoint a steward (*starosta*) to supervise discipline, hours and wages. The *kompaniya* enjoyed a high degree of job-control and was not subject to close supervision by management. The wages which could be earned by a member of a *kompaniya* were extremely high – 150 r. a month in 1916, as opposed to the 50 r. earned by an average typesetter – but it was not high wages *per se* which made the typesetters of the *kompaniya* into an 'aristocracy' so much as their position within the authority-structure of the enterprise and the distinct cultural world which they inhabited. According to Tikhanov, himself a printer, 'the *kompaniya* was a state within a state; no one knew what it did, and it did not care to know about anybody else'.[122] Most typesetters were born in the city. Many came to work on bicycles, wore starched shirts, went to the theatre and horse-races and generally tried to maintain a 'good tone'. Others drank heavily and sometimes ended up penniless in the doss-house.[123] The typesetters enjoyed close personal relations with their employers, many of whom were themselves former printers. Employers addressed their staff as 'Mister', and gave long-service medals and civic honours to loyal employees. The print trade was thus one of the few industries in which there was a sizeable 'labour aristocracy'.

The 1897 census revealed that only 21% of the total population of European Russia was literate. This was mainly because of the appallingly low level of literacy in the countryside – 17% compared to 45% in the towns.[124] The spread of schooling in the next two decades helped boost the rate of literacy, so that by 1920 a third of the population was literate, including 42% of men and 25.5% of women.[125] In St Petersburg the rate of literacy was the highest in the country. As early as 1900, 70% of the population aged six or over was literate; by 1920 this had risen to at least 80%.[126]

Working-class literacy was higher than the average for the population as a whole. By 1918 89% of male workers and 65% of females in Petrograd were literate, compared to 79% and 44%, respectively, of workers in the country as a whole.[127] Working-class literacy was heavily influenced by sex, age and occupation. A survey of 3,998 textileworkers in Petrograd in 1918 showed that only 50% were literate, but 74% of men were literate compared to 45% of women.[128] Younger women, however, were more literate than older women (see *Table 9*).

A survey of 12,000 metalworkers in Petrograd in the same year revealed that overall literacy was 88%: 92% among men and 70% among women. 81% of women under 20 could read and write, compared to 48% of women aged 40 to 50, and 26% of women over 50. Only a quarter of metalworkers aged 55 or over were literate.[129] A survey of 724 skilled fitters at Putilov showed that literacy was as high as 94.7%,[130] but in the boiler-plate shop at the Baltic shipworks in April 1917, no fewer than 12 out of 93 *masterovye* (13%) marked a petition demanding the removal of the shop director with a cross instead of their signature, which suggests that literacy among skilled fitters at Putilov may have been exceptionally high.[131]

A majority of workers in Petrograd in 1917 had had some kind of schooling. Primary education made great strides in Russia in the decades prior to the war, but in 1911 still only a third of Russian boys aged 7 to 14 and 14% of girls of the same age were attending school.[132] In St Petersburg primary education was more widespread, and between 1906 and 1916 the number of primary school pupils doubled to reach 62,418, while the number of secondary school pupils rose to 10,480.[133] Although most working-class boys and some working-class girls attended school at some time, only a tiny minority ever completed their primary education. In 1914 a mere 22% of children

Table 9: *The relationship of age and sex to literacy among textileworkers in Petrograd in 1918*

Age group	Male	Female	Both
under 20	83%	67%	69%
21-30	86%	45%	48%
31-40	83%	22%	33%
41-50	68%	9%	31%
over 50	54%	1%	24%

Source: *Vestnik professional'nykh soyuzov*, 2 (1918), p.9.

in St Petersburg stayed the full course of primary school.[134] Strumilin estimated that on average most factory workers had had three to four years' schooling, but most women would have had less.[135] Parents were under great economic pressure to send their children out to work, and once children were set on at the factory, it was difficult for them to continue their education. Even where they worked a six-hour day, and where some provision was made for evening classes, few youngsters had the stamina to begin to study after a hard day's work. In any case, although the ability to read and write was an important prerequisite to becoming a skilled worker, length of factory experience, rather than length of schooling, counted for more in getting a skilled job.[136]

CONCLUSION

Combined and uneven development of capitalism in Russia left its mark on the working-class itself. The economy of Petrograd was an articulated system of advanced and rudimentary forms of capitalist production under the dominance of state-monopoly capital. A majority of wage-earners in the capital worked in factory industry, mainly in vast, technologically-sophisticated enterprises, run by private capital or by the state. In 1917 the city's industry was geared totally to the war, and the overwhelming majority of its workers produced for the war effort. In an economic sense, the city was one of the most modern in the world, but in a social and political sense Petrograd was decades behind other world cities. It was still a city of peasants, and the huge scale of peasant migration brought the infrastructure of the city to the point of collapse. The city fathers proved unable to meet the challenge, since the incubus of tsarist absolutism had stifled civic initiative. The result was staggering levels of death and disease, massive overcrowding, and appalling squalor and poverty.

The workforce was recruited from the peasantry and lacked urban and artisanal traditions. The fact that many workers had a peasant culture and mentality did not necessarily inhibit their participation in labour protest: indeed, their grievances as industrial workers may have been fed by deeper peasant discontents.[137] Moreover we shall see that Russian workers experienced the horrors of early industrialisation in the particular political context of autocracy. They thus grew up acutely aware of the 'political question', particularly susceptible to radical political ideas, and not so responsive to reformist, economistic or craft ideologies.[138]

Within the industrial workforce there were important social divisions, according to degree of proletarianisation, skill, sex and age. Social differentiation within the working class was probably greater than in the working classes of the West, though wage and skill hierarchies may not have been so steep.[139] For the working class did not yet reproduce itself, and there was thus a crucial cleavage between 'cadre' workers and peasant workers. In Petrograd this cleavage may have been losing its significance in the decade prior to the war, but the influx of peasants into the workforce during the war reinforced its salience. Overlaying this division, however, were other divisions between skilled and unskilled, male and female, old and young workers. These divisions had their autonomy, and in the specific conjunctures of the revolutionary process of 1917, could become 'over-determined'.[140] Nevertheless, one can think of the working class in Petrograd in 1917 as being roughly divided into two: on the one hand, were peasant workers, women workers and workers new to industry, who comprised around 60% of the workforce; on the other, were older, proletarianised, skilled, male workers. We shall see that these two groups had a different relationship to the organised labour movement and to revolutionary politics in 1917. Chapter 8 explores the interaction of these two groups and the modalities of their revolutionary development.

2

The tsarist factory

The power of the tsarist autocracy did not rest on its ability to maintain ideological hegemony among the Russian people. Although it sought to procure the consent of the governed, the government was constantly compelled to resort to force. This was nowhere more apparent than in the sphere of industrial relations. Although working-class unrest exercised the tsarist administration from the 1870s onwards, it tried to ignore the existence of a 'labour problem', preferring to promote a strategy of paternalism, judiciously mixed with repression.[1] Anxious that harsh exploitation of workers might push them in a revolutionary direction, the government entreated employers to show greater solicitude towards their employees, and offered workers a measure of legal protection. In 1882 and 1885 laws restricting female and child labour were passed; in 1885 a Factory Inspectorate became fully operative, and the following year hiring practices were regulated; in 1897 the working hours in private factories were limited to eleven-and-a-half hours a day.[2] Even the experiments in 'police socialism', which were radical by the standards of the autocracy, especially the Zubatov scheme of 1901, were motivated more by paternalism than by commitment to the reform of industrial relations.[3] The autocracy remained adamant that workers should not be permitted to organise collectively in defence of their interests. Where labour unrest occurred, it was seen as a deliberate subversion of the peace, and was dealt with accordingly by the police or troops. Workers had few illusions in the neutrality of the state, since police intervention to crush strikes revealed the identity of interests between employers and the authorities.[4] During the 1905

Revolution, there was a shift towards a more liberal industrial relations policy, as witnessed by the limited legalisation of the trade unions.[5] Thereafter the regime reverted from its unhappy liberal mode to the more homely paternalist one. Once more, strikes and unions became unlawful, and workers brave enough to participate in them risked the knout, jail or exile.

At factory level employers relied mainly on the 'stick' rather than the 'carrot' to run their enterprises. In all countries repressive methods of labour discipline were typical of the first phase of industrialisation, and Russia was no exception.[6] Draconian forms of discipline, however, were as much a reflection of the political culture of Russia as of capital's need to socialise labour into the norms of factory life. The violent exercise of management power within the factory mirrored the violent exercise of power without.

The 1886 law made it obligatory for every factory to have a written code of rules which were printed in the wage book of each worker. These rules covered every aspect of factory life. Some were designed to combat labour turnover, lateness and absenteeism, others to create a docile workforce which would not offer collective resistance to management. At the Northern Cotton Mill, paragraph 25 of the factory rules laid down that workers might not meet together in the shops, leave work before time, shout or fight, show disobedience or disrespect to management, play games or read newspapers, bring in or take out items without the director's special permission, bring in vodka or alcohol, smoke in unauthorised places, go near or touch machines in operation, go through the boiler room or engine room, send apprentices or other workers to buy things without the permission of the manager.[7] At the nearby New Cotton-Weaving Mill the rules stated: 'Workers must not express demands whilst in the shops nor go in a crowd to complain at the office. Each worker must go personally with his complaint to the manager.'[8] Infringement of factory rules usually entailed a fine deducted from one's wages and, occasionally, a beating or even dismissal.

During the 1905 Revolution the autocratic structure of power within the factories was partially dismantled, under the pressure of a mass strike movement.[9] The beating of workers ceased, and the searching of workers as they left the factory – a ritual of degradation much resented – virtually disappeared.[10] After 1905 these practices were revived. Fines once more became ubiquitous, but the great majority were now exacted for bad workmanship rather than for infraction of factory rules.[11] In some factories employers sought to modify the system of coercion by introducing incentive schemes. American bonus systems were in operation in sixteen factories by 1908 – a sign that the real subordination of workers within the labour process was being achieved.[12] Right down to 1917, however, despite growing interest in scientific management, factory administrations ruled by fear rather than by material or moral incentives.

The tsarist enterprise was administered in a strictly hierarchical fashion. At the top was a board of directors, which in state enterprises consisted of naval and army officers. Below them were section managers, followed by shop managers and their assistants, and finally by foremen (*mastera*) and their assistants (*podmaster'ya*). In most factories the system of administration was still a 'craft' one, i.e. a decentralised system in which the foreman took most decisions.[13] The foreman had an office in the workshop and was responsible for hiring and firing workers, for fixing time and piece-rates and for supervising the distribution and execution of work. He ruled the workers' lives in a direct way, and was regarded as occupying the bottom rung of the management ladder.[14] His assistants were usually promoted from among the skilled workers; they helped the foreman carry out his tasks and reported any breach of workshop regulations by the workers. There was some doubt as to whether they were part of the management hierarchy, but in 1910 the metalworkers' union refused them membership on the grounds that they were.[15] In large shops in the metal works there might be *desyatniki* or *starshie* interposed between the foreman's assistants and the workers: the former were in charge of a group of ten or so workers; the latter were gang-masters in charge of a *partiya* of perhaps fifteen workers. The *starshie* formed a 'labour aristocracy', for they earned up to three times as much as the average member of the *partiya*, who was often an apprentice. They were, however, considered to be part of the workforce rather than management.[16] In the years up to the war, the larger enterprises of St Petersburg moved towards a more bureaucratic system of administration, characterised by detailed centralised planning, communications-processing departments and the proliferation of specialised clerical, technical and supervisory personnel.[17] This shift was registered in a reduction in the functions of the foreman. Where bonus systems were introduced, rate-fixers began to fix wage-rates instead of foremen. Similarly, draughtsmen and technicians, instructors, inspectors and quality-controllers took over other aspects of the foreman's job.[18] The foreman's tasks thus became largely super-visory.

Sluzhashchie were an extremely heterogeneous social category. The term is best translated as 'salaried employees', since it embraced clerical and technical staff in industrial and commercial enterprises and in government and public institutions; but it also referred to non-productive workers in the service sector, such as shopworkers and transport workers. Rashin estimated that in 1917 there were 250,000 clerical and technical staff employed in Russian factory industry,[19] and as many as a fifth of these may have worked in the factories of Petrograd.[20] They were overwhelmingly concentrated in the metalworking, chemicals and electrical industries, where the ratio of workers to *sluzhashchie* in 1918 was, respectively, 6.6, 4.3 and 2.4, compared to 25 in the textile industry.[21] *Sluzhashchie* occupied a contradictory class location.[22] In many ways they were similar to manual workers, since they sold their labour-power, often for wages below those of skilled workers, and had little real power in the enterprise. Some, such as draughtsmen, were close to the skilled workers by virtue of the work they did. Yet although they may have been 'objectively' close to manual workers, subjectively, most *sluzhashchie* felt separate from them. They were at the bottom of the administrative hierarchy, but they depended on that hierarchy for their livelihood. Although separated by a great distance from senior management, they never lost hope of rising to an exalted position. They preferred to try to improve their lot by seeking promotion, rather than by organised defence of their collective interests, and because they frequently performed semi-administrative functions, they tended to adopt a management viewpoint.[23] Management, moreover, actively encouraged *sluzhashchie* to be antagonistic towards the workforce.

For the workers on the shop floor, it was not so much the tyranny of the directors which was resented, as the petty despotism of the lower ranks of the management hierarchy. The foremen, supervisors, engineers all exercised their power in the same arbitrary way, untrammelled by any notions of workers' rights. It is thus not surprising that workers who lacked any broad conception of the social system should have identified their main enemy not as the factory owner, but as the low-level administrators who were the bane of their everyday working lives. Strikes to remove foremen and their assist-ants were endemic prior to 1917, and demands for polite treatment by administrative staff figured prominently in strike demands. In January 1905, for example, strikers at the Baltic shipworks raised twenty demands, including ones for an eight-hour day, a ban on overtime and a review of piece-rates. Three demands concerned 'dignity' issues: specifically, a demand that management deal honestly with workers without resorting to deception; a demand that foremen and their assistants treat the workers 'as people and not as things'; and a demand that Mikhail Denisov be fired for being rude and insolent when hiring *chernorabochie* off the street.[24] Commenting on the importance of 'dignity' issues, the worker Timofeev said 'the workers value proper treatment . . . and if they get it, are often ready to put up with many of the darker aspects of their conditions and the discomforts of their work'.[25]

CONDITIONS OF WORK

Conditions of work in Petrograd's factories before 1917 were exceedingly miserable. Employers paid little heed to standards of safety and hygiene and provided few facilities for their workforces. There were decent factories, such as the foreign-owned Parviainen and Siemens-Schukert works, but these exceptions merely underlined the general awfulness of conditions elsewhere. Conditions were notoriously bad at two factories subject to the Naval Ministry in the Okhta district. In December 1912 an explosion occurred at the Okhta explosives factory which killed five workers and injured more than fifty. The director, General Somov, did his best to prevent the Social Democratic deputies in the Duma from undertaking an investigation into the accident. 'Such accidents do happen', he argued, 'and will go on happening. I for one never enter the factory without first making the sign of the cross.'[26] He proved to be correct in his forecast, for in April 1915 a further explosion occurred in the melinite shop of the explosives works, which blew up two workshops and eight houses killing 110 people and injuring 220.[27] A woman described conditions in the melinite shop where 3,000 women worked: 'In the part where they do the washing and spraying, the air is so suffocating and poisonous that someone unused to it could not stand it for more than five or ten minutes. Your whole body becomes poisoned by it.'[28] On 31 March 1917 yet another explosion occurred at the Okhta explosives works which killed four workers and injured two. A few days later a worker from the factory told the conference of representa-

tives from factories under the Artillery Administration: 'We are
working on top of a volcano. The whole factory is overloaded with
explosives, bombs and shells ... but the administration says it's not
their responsibility and refers us to the Artillery Administration.'[29]
Conditions at the Okhta works were notoriously bad – women who
worked there could be identified by their yellow skins – but they were
not exceptional. At the Putilov works there was no ventilation in the
gun shop or galvanising shop, where workers handling acid were
given no protective clothing.[30] In the gunpowder department of the
Admiralty works, noxious fumes, lead and antimony dust caused
vomiting and pulmonary disease among the workers. The manager of
the department described conditions thus: 'great congestion, a mass
of machines, burning oil, night work, poor diet and the excessive
intensity of work caused by piece-rates have resulted in general
exhaustion, acute anaemia and a huge number of lung and heart
diseases'.[31]

Petrograd had the highest industrial accident rate of any region in
Russia. In 1913 there were 14,300 accidents reported to the Factory
Inspectorate, and rates were highest in the metalworking industry,
especially in state factories, and in textiles.[32] During the war the
accident rate increased. At the Putilov works, up to September 1914,
there was an average of fifteen accidents per month; thereafter this
increased to twenty-one. At the Lessner works there were 180
accidents in 1914 and 312 in 1915.[33] This increase in the rate of
industrial accidents was linked to a general increase in the rate of
illness among factory workers caused by more overtime, greater
utilisation of female and child labour, speed-ups, insanitary conditions and worsening diet. Between 1913 and 1917 the rate of sickness
and injury in Petrograd factories increased between one-and-a-half
and two times.[34] In 1914 the number of cases of sickness and injury at
the Metal works was 60.3 per 100 workers; by 1915 it had risen to
118.4. At the Putilov works the corresponding figures were 64.3 and
98.2.[35]

Insurance provision for workers who were injured at work, or who
fell sick, was grossly inadequate. Between 1901 and 1904 workers in
state enterprises secured sickness and injury benefits. In private
industry individual employers were liable after 1903 to pay similar
benefits, but it was difficult to prove their liability.[36] Up to 1912
workers in the state sector were better protected than their counterparts in private industry – not least, because they also qualified for

long-service pensions. The Insurance Law of 1912, however, put them at a disadvantage *vis-à-vis* workers in private industry, since it did not apply to the state sector.[37] This law provided sickness benefit, but not invalidity or unemployment benefit, for about a fifth of all industrial workers in Russia.[38] Workers donated 2% of their wages into the fund, and employers paid a sum equal to two-thirds of the total contribution made by the workers. The size of benefit paid was half to two-thirds of the normal wage of a married man and a quarter to a half that of a single worker – not a lot, given soaring inflation.[39] Medical funds (*bol'nichnye kassy*) were set up to administer the distribution of benefits, and were run jointly by workers' and employers' representatives. By 1917 there were 80 medical funds in Petrograd, with a membership of 176,000.[40] Nineteen of the better-organised funds set up four clinics during the war.[41] The Bolsheviks played an active part in the funds, using them partly as a front behind which to organise working-class resistance.[42]

As late as 1914 Russian workers still worked significantly longer hours than their Western-European counterparts. The 1905 Revolution had reduced hours noticeably, in spite of the fact that it had been defeated precisely at the moment when the demand was raised for the immediate legalisation of the eight-hour day. In 1905–6 the average working day in Russia was ten hours, or sixty hours a week, but this figure does not include overtime, which was widespread.[43] During the Years of Reaction, although pressure for a shorter working day declined, the average working day appears to have shrunk slightly. By 1913 Russian workers worked an average of 9.7 hours a day, excluding overtime; in St Petersburg the average stood at 9.54 hours.[44] There was considerable variation by industry however. Workers in the food and paper industries tended to work the longest hours – around twelve hours a day – followed by textile workers.[45] In 1914 most workers in Petrograd worked about ten hours a day and seven hours on Saturdays. In addition, overtime working was widespread, except where shift systems were operative, such as in the metallurgical enterprises. Overtime was frequently compulsory and often paid at the standard rate.[46]

In 1913, according to Strumilin, 270 days were worked each year in Russian industry – twenty to thirty fewer than in Britain, Germany or the USA.[47] This was due to the large number of religious holidays enjoyed by Russian workers. In St Petersburg, however, some 290 or more days were worked each year – an index of the 'modernity' of the industry of the capital. This meant that the number of hours worked each year, as well as each week, was gruellingly long by Western European standards.

During the war working hours increased substantially in Petrograd, owing to its central importance to the war effort. In January 1917 the average working day in Petrograd was 10.1 hours, compared to 9.9 hours in Russia's private industry.[48] Overtime working was greatly extended in the capital, and in 1915 restrictions on night work for women and children were lifted. There was considerable variation between industries, with the longest hours in metalworking, textiles and leather.[49] In the metal industry workers in the 'hot' shops worked an eight-hour day, since the work was so exhausting; skilled workers in the 'cold' shops worked ten to eleven hours, and *chernorabochie* worked up to fourteen hours.[50]

THE STANDARD OF LIVING DURING THE WAR

On the eve of the First World War wages in Russian industry were significantly lower than those in Western industry.[51] Strumilin estimated that in 1913 the average Russian factory-worker earned 283 rubles per annum, but that when one took into account wages received in kind – as welfare provision, housing, etc. – this rose to 295 r, or about 25 r a month.[52] In St Petersburg in the same year, cash wages were about 40% higher than the national average, but the cost of living in the capital was also considerably higher.[53] In human terms, these wages spelt chronic poverty. Prokopovich estimated that one needed about three times the average annual wage to support a family in the city.[54] How therefore did workers manage?

The largest portion of a worker's budget was spent on food. In 1908, 49% of a married worker's income and 37% of a single worker's income was spent on food. In 1912 in textileworker families where the mother worked outside the home, 52% of income was spent on food, compared to 60% where the mother worked in the home. In poorer textileworker families as much as two-thirds of income was spent on food.[55] A survey of the budgets of members of the works committee at the Baltic shipyard in 1917 showed that 60% of income was spent on food and lighting. The second largest item of expenditure for working-class families was accommodation. Prokopovich's survey revealed that the majority of workers lived in partitioned rooms. Single workers spent 15% of their income on rented accommodation and married workers 21%.[56] Among textileworkers, single women spent 16% of their income on accommodation, compared to only 8% spent by single men. Families where the mother was at home spent 19% of their income on accommodation, compared to 12% spent by families where the mother worked outside the home.[57] In 1917 members of the Baltic works committee spent 14% of their income on accommodation.[58] The third largest item of working-class expenditure was clothing. Workers dressed shabbily. Men wore a dark shirt or blouse, with a standing collar buttoned to the side, a rough woollen jacket and trousers tucked inside high boots. In winter they wore very heavy, coarse cloth coats, a dark cap with a patent leather visor or a fur hat. Shirts and ties were unknown, except among skilled workers who wished to look respectable. Women wore a long skirt, a cotton blouse, a cotton kerchief, or in winter a woollen one, but no hat.[59] According to Prokopovich's survey, single workers spent 14% and married workers 12% of their income on clothing.[60] Single male textile workers spent 10% of their income on clothing and single females 17%. In textileworker families 15% or 16% of the budget was spent on clothing.[61] In 1917 the Baltic works committee members spent 12% of their income on clothing.[62]

The outbreak of war unleashed rampant inflation. It is very difficult to produce an index of the rise in prices, partly because of regional variations, and partly because of the discrepancy between official prices and market prices. M.P. Kokhn produced what is probably the most conservative national price index for the war years. He estimated that if one takes the index of prices in 1913 as being equal to 100, then it reached 221 at the end of 1916, and 512 by the end of 1917.[63] There is no comprehensive price index for Petrograd, but patchy data suggest that prices in the capital followed the national pattern, starting to rise as soon as war broke out and then rocketing from the second half of 1916 right through 1917 and into 1918.[64] The prices of basic subsistence items were two to three times their pre-war level by the end of 1916, and at least four times this level by the middle of 1917.[65] To compound the problems of survival, in the autumn of 1915 and again in the winter of 1916, flour, meat, sugar and butter vanished from the shops, and people were forced to queue for long hours to buy bread.

Wages rose rapidly during the war, partly due to the rise in the cost of living, and partly to the fact that more overtime was being worked. The national average wage in enterprises subject to the Factory

Inspectorate rose from 257 rubles (1913) to 322 r. (1915) to 478 r. (1916). In defence enterprises average annual earnings rose from 393 r. (1913), to 594 r. (1915), to 912 r. (1916).[66] According to data from the 1918 Industrial Census, average earnings in Petrograd doubled between 1914 and 1916, from 405 r. to 809 r. per annum.[67] Given the rising cost of living, what did these wage increases mean in real terms?

There seems little doubt that, nationally, real wages fell during the war – very slowly during 1914 and 1915, and then increasingly rapidly as 1916 wore on. The crucial importance of defence industries in the capital meant that Petrograd was probably the only area in Russia where overall real wages rose throughout industry until the winter of 1916. Thereafter, however, real wages began to fall rapidly, and by the time of the February Revolution were probably 15% to 20% below the level of 1913.[68]

There were enormous variations in the wage movements of different industries. In only two Petrograd industries – metals and chemicals – did real wages increase between 1913 and 1916.[69] In all other industries they fell – a fall that was particularly dramatic in the case of printers, formerly the highest-paid industry. This meant that compared to other industrial groups, metalworkers were better off in 1916 than in 1913. In 1913 average earnings in the Petrograd metal industry were 63% higher than in textiles, 49% higher than in food and 42% higher than in chemicals. In 1917 the ratios were respectively 106%, 109% and 51%. This pattern holds true for Russian industry as a whole.[70] The 30% of the Petrograd labour force who worked in textiles, printing, food, woodworking, leather and minerals were thus not only worse off in real terms as a result of the war, but also worse off relative to the high-wage metal industries.[71]

It is difficult to determine how the war affected the wages of different categories of workers in the metal industry. Firstly, there were almost 300 different occupations within industry, and rates for the job varied between factories. This variation, combined with the different skill-composition of individual factory workforces, meant that average wage-levels between factories could vary considerably. Average wages in the private sector of Petrograd's metal industry were higher than in the state sector – 127 r.50 k. a month compared to 114 r.27 k. in August 1916.[72] Within each sector, however, inter-factory variations could be very great. In January 1917 average monthly earnings at the Obukhov works and the Baltic works – both run by the Naval Ministry – were, respectively, 171 r. and 86 r.[73] A second problem arose from the fact that complex piece-rate systems were the norm in the majority of factories. These assigned groups of workers a basic hourly rate (*tsekhovoe*), and then determined a sliding scale of bonuses which linked output to time saved. Workers disliked these bonus systems, since they were difficult to understand. Piece and bonus systems meant that those skilled workers on the highest hourly rates did not always earn the highest monthly earnings; sometimes semi-skilled machinists might earn as much or more than them. A further complication is added by the fact that, in addition to standard bonus schemes, a special war-bonus came into operation in Petrograd factories in October 1915 for good timekeeping.[74]

Bearing these problems in mind, one can generalise as follows. For a layer of very skilled workers, whose skills were in short supply, it was possible to earn extremely high wages during the war. At the Putilov works the daily earnings of such groups as caulkers and moulders rose dramatically. Other skilled groups, such as metal-rollers and mortise-makers, however, experienced a relative decline.[75] It is almost certainly the case that the differential between the highest and lowest earnings in the metal industry widened during the war, but it is more difficult to say whether the differential between the earnings of skilled and unskilled workers in general increased. Strumilin argued that the position of *chernorabochie, vis-à-vis* skilled workers, improved during the war – largely on the basis of a study of wages at the Parviainen works, which paid among the highest wages in Petrograd.[76] Evidence from the Putilov, Obukhov and Metal works, however, suggests that in most factories differentials between skilled and unskilled workers widened.[77] Generalising from the rather exiguous data, it seems that the majority of metalworkers improved their real earnings up to the winter of 1916–17, but that the unskilled generally failed to keep abreast with inflation. From the winter of 1916, a sudden acceleration in price rises, brought about by food shortages, led to a sharp fall in the real wages of all metalworkers, and this was an important cause of the February Revolution.

One final point needs to be made about the wages of women workers during the war. Women were concentrated in low-paid jobs, and where they did the same jobs as men, rarely got equal pay. The print trade was an exception to this, but there few women did the same jobs as men. In 1914 adult female wages were on average half those of adult males; young boys earned about 40% of the adult male wage and young girls earned about a third.[78] In spite of the increased demand for female labour during the war, women's wages fell in relation to those of men. Between 1914 and the beginning of 1917, the ratio of men's wages to women's wages throughout Russian industry increased from 1.96 to 2.34.[79] In Petrograd certain women who worked in armaments factories on piece-rates may have earned tolerable wages, but in 1916 the overall wage of women in the metal industry was only 40 r. a month, compared to the average wage of 105 r.[80] In the textile industry a semi-skilled jenny-operator earned 49.3 r. a month in January 1917, which represented 90% of her real wage in July 1914; she now spent 63% of this on food compared to 57% prior to the war.[81] In the printing industry women earned a pittance of 20 to 25 r. a month.[82] For these women, therefore, the war brought them from poverty to the brink of destitution.

To conclude, one can say that from the outbreak of war until the winter of 1916–17, the wages of a slight majority of workers in Petrograd improved, although this improvement came about largely as a result of increased labour-intensity and a deterioration in working conditions. For a large minority however – at least a third – the already low wages of 1914 failed to keep pace with the rise in prices, and by February 1917 they were teetering on the verge of starvation.

THE STRIKE MOVEMENT DURING THE WAR

The wartime wage-increases in Petrograd were not granted by the employers out of the kindness of their hearts; they had to be fought for. Although it is not the purpose of the present work to describe the labour movement during the war, a short account of the wartime strike movement must be given in order to provide background to the preceding analysis of wage movements, and as a preface to the next chapter, which describes the response of Petrograd's factories to the February Revolution.

After the outbreak of war the government toyed with the idea of 'militarising' labour by fixing wages, prohibiting strikes and transferring workers to sectors where they were required. The Duma and employers' organisations resisted the idea, since they resented state interference in industry and were sceptical of its efficacy. Workers whose conscription into the army was deferred, so that they might work in defence industry, were prevented from changing jobs.[83]

Soldiers and sailors were sent to the factories to do the most unpopular jobs under military discipline, and received rates of pay lower than those of civilian workers. It is important to bear in mind the military discipline of the defence factories when analysing the pattern of wartime strikes.

Table 10 is based on work by the Soviet historian, I.P. Leiberov, and provides a comprehensive breakdown of the strike movement in Petrograd during the war.[84] Leiberov follows the Factory Inspectorate and Okhrana in classifying strikes as either 'economic' or 'political'. This classification should be treated with caution. The bulk of strikes in each category are unproblematic: most 'economic' strikes concerned wages, hours or conditions; and 'political' strikes took place on occasions such as the anniversary of Bloody Sunday, or to protest against government plans for the militarisation of labour, the threatened execution of Kronstadt sailors or the arrest of the Workers Group of the War Industries Committee. Some strikes involved both economic and political demands. Leiberov classifies these as political, so there is a bias in the table towards overstating the number of political strikes. Finally, one should remember that the economic/political distinction refers to the *demands* of the strikers rather than to the strikers' motives. It might have taken a certain level of political consciousness to go on any kind of strike during the war, at a time when the press, public opinion, and even socialists like Plekhanov, considered strike action to be treasonous. One thus cannot impute types of consciousness to workers on the basis of this table.

The table shows unambiguously that the outbreak of war in August 1914 defused the insurrectionary mood which had been building up in the working-class areas of Petrograd during the preceding six months. A wave of patriotic support for the war, combined with repression by the authorities, led to the virtual disappearance of strikes until July 1915. The few small, badly-organised strikes which did occur were provoked by management attempts to cut wage-rates. The few political strikes during the first year of the war – to protest against Bloody Sunday and the trial of the Bolshevik Duma deputies – were organised by socialists, and involved tiny numbers of workers.[85] The tide began to turn in July 1915, when a successful wage strike by New Lessner workers prompted similar strikes in other metal works on Vyborg Side. News of the massacre of striking textileworkers in Ivanovo-Voznesensk led to political strikes

Table 10: *Number of strikes in Petrograd, 1914–1917*

Month	Political Strikes			Economic Strikes		
	No. of strikes	No. of strikers	No. of working days lost through strikes	No. of strikes	No. of strikers	No. of working days lost through strikes
1914						
July 1–18	–	160,099	–	–	580	–
July 19	26	27,400	48,540	16	10,942	76,914
August	–	–	–	–	–	–
September	1	1,400	280	3	905	1,180
October	–	–	–	2	160	42
November	2	3,150	1,260	3	785	785
December	–	–	–	2	1,020	1,240
1915						
January	14	2,595	2,488.5	2	115	565
February	6	340	183.5	2	120	85
March	–	–	–	6	461	311
April	–	–	–	7	4,064	9,988
May	10	1,259	899	7	2,571	1,607
June	–	–	–	9	1,141	531
July	–	–	–	29	17,934	33,965.5
August	24	23,178	24,574.5	16	11,640	15,879
September	70	82,728	176,623.5	13	7,470	12,730.5
October	10	11,268	34,911.5	21	13,350	69,031.5
November	5	11,020	6,280	19	6,838	7,509.5
December	7	8,985	5,624.5	26	13,284	15,261
1916						
January	68	61,447	64,566	35	16,418	37,749.5
February	3	3,200	170	55	53,723	220,026.5
March	51	77,877	386,405.5	16	11,811	81,162.5
April	7	14,152	87,019	48	25,112	47,758
May	3	8,932	2,282	42	26,756	125,496
June	6	3,452	3,062.5	37	15,603	72,191.5
July	2	5,333	60,025	27	20,326	26,004
August	4	1,686	2,761	18	6,259	10,934.5
September	2	2,800	2,400	33	24,918	84,783.5
October	177	174,592	452,158.5	12	15,184	12,912
November	6	22,950	8,283	24	18,592	30,204.5
December	1	1,000	25	7	8,798	29,835
1917						
January	135	151,886	144,116	34	24,869	59,024.5
Feb. 1–17	85	123,953	137,508	14	19,809	62,647
TOTAL	1,044	826,593	1,652,446.5	585	380,978	1,148,354

I. P. Leiberov, 'Stachechnaya bor'ba petrogradskogo proletariata v period pervoi mirovoi voiny (19 iyulya 1914g.–16 fevralya 1917g.)', *Istoriya rabochego klassa Leningrada*, issue 2 (Leningrad, 1963), pp.166, 177, 183.

in August, again based on militant metalworking factories on Vyborg Side, such as Lessner, Aivaz, Baranovskii, Nobel and Parviainen. These strikes, together with protests against rising food-prices, so alarmed the police that sweeping arrests of worker-activists were made between 29 August and 2 September 1915. This repression provoked protest strikes among metalworkers on Vyborg Side, at Putilov and in other districts, mostly under leftist slogans, but some pledging support to the Duma and calling for the creation of a responsible Ministry.[86]

Between August 1915 and August 1916 there was a big increase in the number of strikes. Many workers celebrated the anniversary of Bloody Sunday in January 1916, and February witnessed the largest number of economic strikes of any month during the war. Unrest centred on the Putilov workers, where demands for a 70% wage-increase became widespread. In spite of a lockout at the factory, and the drafting of 2,000 militants into the army, significant wage-rises were achieved. Some 70,000 workers at the beginning of March came out in support of the *Putilovtsy*, and a strong anti-war mood developed The crushing of these strikes led to a decline in the movement during the summer of 1916.

In the autumn of 1916 the strike movement exploded on a scale unprecedented since June 1914. The roots of the unrest lay in acute food shortages and rising prices, but three-quarters of the strikes between September 1916 and February 1917 voiced political opposition to the autocracy and the war. On 17 October workers on Vyborg Side marched to the Finland station singing the Marseillaise. Significantly, they were joined by soldiers from the 181st infantry regiment, who were quartered in the area and who had been the target of Left Socialist Revolutionary (SR) and Bolshevik propaganda. The arrest of the insurgent soldiers spread the strike and caused the authorities to bring Cossacks and mounted police into the proletarian areas. After news came through of the threat to execute revolutionary sailors in Kronstadt, more factories went on strike so that by 28 October, 77 factories had stopped work for clearly political reasons. A lockout was imposed at fifteen factories and 106 militants were arrested, but the interruption of supplies to the Front forced the government to climb down for the first time since war broke out.[87.]

In the first six weeks of 1917 stoppages, go-slows[88] and strikes occurred in response to plummeting real wages and shortages of bread. The increased failure-rate of the economic strikes reflects the fact that workers in small enterprises were entering into struggle for the first time. On 9 January, 132 enterprises struck to commemorate Bloody Sunday. The success of this demonstration encouraged the Workers' Group of the War Industries Committee to redouble its efforts to persuade workers to put pressure on the Progressive Bloc in the Duma. The authorities reacted by arresting eleven of the sixteen members of the Workers' Group on 27 January. On 14 February, 58 factories obeyed the summons of the Defencist labour leaders to strike. Within the next week a large strike broke out at Putilov in support of wage-increases, which provoked a lockout on 22 February. This proved to be an important step in the immediate run-up to the general strike which precipitated the overthrow of the autocracy.[89]

If one examines the factories which participated in the wartime strike movement, it is possible to group them into three 'divisions', according to the extent to which they participated in strikes.[90] In the first, most strike-prone division was a group of private metal works in the Vyborg district, making munitions, weapons and engineering products. The territorial proximity of these factories, together with the fact that they were medium-large rather than vast, facilitated the coordination of strikes. The workforce of these factories had grown rapidly during the war, often tripling in size; the New Lessner, Nobel and Puzyrev works were exceptions to this. Nevertheless, in spite of an influx of new workers, a core of skilled, experienced workers remained intact. These workers were members or sympathisers of the Bolshevik party. This is borne out by the fact that after February 1917, it was these 'first division' factories, such as Aivaz, Baranovskii, Vulcan, Nobel, New Lessner, Phoenix and Puzyrev, which were the first to swing to the Bolshevik party. Exceptions were the Dinamo, Old Lessner, Erikson, New Parviainen and Promet works, which at first supported the Mensheviks and SRs, but none of these was slow to go Bolshevik in 1917.

The second division of factories consisted, firstly, of private metal-works of a rather specialist kind, less engaged in the production of munitions. Here the pattern of wartime growth was less uniform than in the first division, though all combined an intact core of 'cadre' workers with a majority of new workers. Bolshevik activists were less in evidence here, and these factories tended to be rather slower in coming to support the Bolsheviks in 1917, though they were by no means as slow as state enterprises. It has been suggested that young workers were important in leading the wartime strike movement, particularly those of urban origin.[91] While the activism of young workers in 1917 is not in doubt, an analysis of strike-prone factories during the war does not suggest that the presence of young workers was a factor of paramount significance. It is true that the two most strike-prone state enterprises, the Baltic and Putilov shipyards (both in the second division), had high proportions of young workers, as did the Metal works. Other factories in the second 'division', however, such as Renault, Rozenkrantz, Langenzippen, Wagon-Construction and Siemens-Schuckert, had very few. The last-named factory is of particular interest in this regard, since its sister factory, the Siemens-Halske works, had a much higher percentage of young workers (20% compared to 7%) but a low level of strike activity during the war. A second group within the second 'division' consisted of cotton-spinning and weaving mills, such as Sampsionevskaya, Leontiev, Nevka, Okhta and Pal'. These factories employed mainly women, but as they did not expand during the war, the women would have been workers with industrial experience. The textile strikes were in pursuit of economic demands, and there is no evidence of a Bolshevik connection.

The third 'division' was more varied, consisting mainly of metal works, some textile mills and a few wood or leather factories. State enterprises, such as the Nevskii shipbuilding works, the Obukhov works, Franco-Russian works and Arsenal, fell into this category. Military discipline discouraged strike action in state factories, as did the 'defencist' Mensheviks and SRs, who were strong in this sector. If one compares the state factories which did participate in the strike movement with vast state munitions works, such as the Pipe or Cartridge works, which did not, then it is clear that in the latter, the minority of 'cadre' workers was engulfed in a sea of workers new to industry, and was thus unable to mobilise them into organised activity. Moreover the 'cadres' in these vast state enterprises tended to be stalwarts of the Workers' Group of the War Industries Committee, and thus ill-disposed to take strike action during wartime. This rather cursory analysis of strike-prone factories suggests that factories were most likely to go on strike, firstly, if there was an organised Bolshevik cell in the enterprise and, secondly, if there was a core of proletarianised men or women with some experience of strikes, sufficiently numerous and cohesive to organise new workers. We shall see that in 1917 new workers were quite capable of being militant, without any help from 'cadre' workers, but during the war this does not seem to have been the case.

3

The February Revolution: a new dispensation in the factories

On 23 February 1917 thousands of housewives and factory women, angry at the bread shortage, surged onto the streets, ignoring pleas from labour leaders to stay calm. By the next day, 200,000 workers in Petrograd were on strike. By 25 February, huge armies of demonstrators were clashing with troops, and a revolution had commenced. On 27 February, the critical point was reached, when whole regiments of soldiers began to desert to the insurgents. The same day, the worthy members of the Duma refused to obey an order from the Tsar to disperse, and instead set up a Provisional Government. Meanwhile the Petrograd Soviet of workers' and soldiers' deputies came into existence, thereby creating an extraordinary situation of 'dual power'. By 3 March it was all over: the Tsar had abdicated and Russia was free.[1]

The toppling of the Romanov dynasty inspired workers with euphoria. They returned to their factories determined that the *ancien régime* would be swept aside in the workplaces, just as it had been swept aside in society at large. They resolved to create, in the place of the old 'absolutist' order, a new 'constitutional' order within the enterprises. They set to work at once by tearing up the old contracts of hire, the old rule books, and the vicious blacklists. Just as the agents of the autocracy had been driven from the police stations and government offices, so the workers set about expelling those who had been most identified with the repressive administration of the factories. Throughout the factories of Petrograd workers clamoured for the removal of all members of the management hierarchy who had made their lives miserable under the *ancien régime*, who had behaved tyrannically, who had abused their authority, who had taken bribes or acted as police informers.[2] Sometimes administrators were removed peacefully, sometimes by force. At the Putilov works, the director and his aide were killed by workers and their bodies were flung in the Obvodnyi canal; some forty members of management were expelled during the first three 'days of freedom'.[3] In the engine-assembly shop, Puzanov, quondam chief of the factory's Black Hundreds, was tossed in a wheelbarrow, red lead was poured over his head, and he was ignominiously carted out of the factory and dumped in the street. In the brickyard of the same plant, A.V. Spasskii, the foreman, was deprived of his duties by workers for:

(i) rude treatment of workers,
(ii) forced overtime, as a result of which such incidents occurred as when the worker, S. Skinder, having worked overtime, collapsed at midnight of exhaustion and had to be taken to hospital . . .[4]

At the Baltic shipyard at least sixty members of the administration were demoted, transferred or carted out of the factory in wheelbarrows.[5] At the Cartridge works up to 80% of technical staff were expelled and the factory committee refused them leave to appeal to a conciliation chamber.[6] At the Admiralty, New Admiralty and Galernyi Island shipyards forty-nine technical employees were expelled by general meetings of the workers. Management insisted that each employee had the right to appeal to a conciliation chamber, but the chamber was forced to accept the *fait accompli*.[7] At the Pipe works the director and fourteen senior managers were temporarily relieved of their duties by the factory soviet.[8]

The purge extended to private factories. At the Thornton textile mill women workers chased thirty factory police from the premises.[9] At the Baranovskii engineering works twenty-five members of the administration were fired by the workers, eighteen of them being carted from the factory for having acted like 'hangmen' in the past.[10] After long disputes, twelve members of management at the Skorokhod shoe factory and sixteen at the Tentelevskii chemical works were dismissed at the insistence of the respective workforces.[11] The reasons why workers compelled the removal of administration were multifarious. At the Triangle works on 5 March, a general meeting of shop stewards agreed that 'all foremen who are disorganising production by hiding tools, etc. must not be allowed into work. We ask comrades to inform the soviet of workers' deputies of this.'[12]

At the Nevskii shipyard a list was drawn up of twenty-five foremen and their assistants who had abused their authority in the past. The Menshevik-dominated factory committee forbade the expulsion of these people until their cases had been examined by a conciliation chamber. In only one shop – the boiler room – did the workers refuse to accept the factory committee decision. On 30 March the factory committee allowed those threatened with dismissal to return to the factory pending appeal. One case which came before the conciliation chamber concerned the manager of the metallurgical section, who had come to the Nevskii works in 1908 as a foreman. He had openly boasted that he would 'sweep out of the workshop all the sedition remaining from 1905', he had collected information on the politics of the workers, established a network of informers and forced the workers to work unpaid overtime. The conciliation committee found that there was no case to answer against him, but so great was the hatred felt by the workers towards him that the chamber was powerless to make them take the foreman back.[13] The inability of conciliation chambers to settle cases of expulsion by peaceful arbitration was a general phenomenon. At the Kersten knitwear factory the conciliation committee recommended the reinstatement of all but one of the administrators expelled by the workers. On 16 March, for example, it announced:

We are convinced that V.V. Zhuchaevich is a nervous irascible character who cannot restrain himself in the way that moral tact dictates. However we consider that the charges made against him of contemptuous cruelty, of humiliating workers and, in particular, of giving promotion only to his fellow Poles, are totally without foundation.

The chamber found in relation to another worker that 'the charge of rude, shameless abuse of women workers is not supported by the testimony of witnesses and therefore we consider it unproven'.[14] In neither of these cases was the committee able to overcome the opposition of workers and secure the reinstatement of the personnel.

Carting administrators out of the factory in a wheelbarrow was a well-established form of protest in the Russian labour movement. Prior to 1917 the working class had had precious few institutional means at its disposal with which to defend its interests. In the absence of formal means of defensive organisation, workers devised other, informal, ways of defending themselves. One of these was to dump a particularly hated administrator in a wheelbarrow and cart him out of the factory. To contemporary leaders of the organised labour movement this form of action was seen as little more than an expression of blind rage, but it had a deeper symbolism. 'Carting out' was a symbolic affirmation by workers of their dignity as human beings and a ritual humiliation of those who had deprived them of this dignity in their day-to-day working lives. Ironically, it was the employers' newspaper, *Torgovo-Promyshlennaya Gazeta*, which came closest to recognising this symbolic dimension when it commented that 'carting out' had the same significance in the factory as did tearing off an army-officer's badges of rank.[15]

The expulsion of the old administration was but the negative side of democratising factory life. The positive, and far more important side consisted in creating factory committees to represent the interests of the workforce. Factory committees sprang up mushroom-like in the vertiginous days of the revolution. The apparent 'spontaneity' with which they appeared is something of an optical illusion, for there was a strong tradition within the Russian working class of electing stewards (*starosty*) to represent workers before management. This tradition had its origins in the countryside, where villagers were accustomed to elect a headman to represent them. In the factories, the workers elected *starosty* not only to represent them in conflicts with the management but to carry out such apparently trivial activities as collecting money to buy oil for the icon lamps in each workshop.[16] In 1903, in a vain attempt to palliate working-class anger at its refusal to countenance formal trade-union organisation, the government sought to institutionalise the *starosty*, as a rudimentary form of labour representation. The 1903 law permitted workers to propose candidates for the job of *starosta*, from whom management would then make a final choice. The powers of the *starosta* were strictly circumscribed, for he could not seek to modify the contract of hire and he enjoyed no legal protection.[17] Workers disliked the law, for *starosty* were rarely able to give decisive leadership in working-class struggles since they were too vulnerable to victimisation by employers and by the state. The factory-owners of St Petersburg also disliked the law, since they saw in it a dangerous precedent.[18]

It was the 1905 Revolution which signalled the immense possibilities of shopfloor organisation. As the general strike swept across the country, *starosty* and strike committees developed dramatically as organs of working-class self-activity and self-expression. In the autumn, 'factory commissions' proliferated, which adumbrated the factory committees of twelve years later. These commissions began to take charge of all matters affecting the internal life of the factory, drawing up collective wage agreements and overseeing the hiring and firing of workers. In the print-trade an astonishing development took place in the spring of 1906, when 'autonomous commissions' were created. Although printshop owners sat on these commissions, they comprised a majority of workers elected by the entire workforce, and were responsible for drawing up the internal rules of the printshop, seeing to their implementation and for the hiring and firing of workers.[19] After 1907, however, few autonomous commissions, factory commissions or *starosty* survived. During the 'Years of Reaction', workers found it almost impossible to maintain representative institutions.

The invigorating experience of 1905 was not forgotten by worker militants. From time to time after 1910 individual factories tried to revive the *starosty*. At the Phoenix engineering and Sestroretsk arms works, *starosty* existed intermittently right down to 1917.[20] During the war, the elected members of the medical funds (*bol'nichnye kassy*) and the worker members of the War Industries Committees functioned, to some extent, as workers' representatives. Attempts by the latter to revive the *starosty* came to grief, although they did re-emerge in a handful of factories in 1916 (the Aivaz, Erikson and Pipe works). Nevertheless class-conscious workers kept alive the memory of electing shopfloor delegates to represent their interests during the grim years between the two revolutions. Once the police apparatus of tsarism had been smashed, they set about building on the *starosta* tradition.

The new factory committees were the offspring of older elective institutions. In many enterprises the committees were initially called '*sovety starost*', or 'stewards' committees'. In some factories, like the Pipe works, the Siemens-Halske or New Admiralty works, a stewards' committee and a factory committee existed side by side. At the New Admiralty works, the committee had the job of overseeing factory management, whereas stewards represented the workers in individual shops and settled any conflicts which arose.[21] At the Triangle rubber works, a 'soviet of workers' deputies' (i.e. factory committee), dominated by the SRs, existed in fierce rivalry with a stewards' committee, whose executive was led by Bolsheviks.[22] In general, factory committees were elected by the whole workforce and had general responsibilities of 'control' (supervision and inspection) throughout the enterprise; the stewards' committees consisted of representatives of each workshop and dealt with wages and workshop-conditions. In many enterprises, stewards' committees changed their name to factory committees in the course of the spring.

Organisations similar to the Russian factory committee arose in many countries during the First World War. In the British engineering industry, particularly on Clydeside and in Sheffield, a powerful shop-stewards' movement emerged to combat 'dilution' and the militarisation of industry engendered by the war.[23] In Germany, the revolutionary shop stewards (*Obleute*) in the metalworking industries of Berlin, Hamburg, Leipzig, Halle and elsewhere, led struggles against the class-collaborationist policies of the leaders of the Free Unions, which spilled over into anti-war demonstrations, support for the Independent Social Democrats (USPD) and, finally, into the workers' and soldiers' councils (*Räte*). During the German Revolution of 1918–19 it was the young semi-skilled workers in the large metal-works of the Ruhr and Halle who were most active, although skilled craftsmen in the iron and steel industries of older industrial areas, such as Remscheid and Solingen, played a prominent role.[24] In Italy 'internal commissions' (*commissioni interne*) in the metal and engineering industries of Milan and Turin evolved from organs of arbitration into defenders of shopfloor autonomy against the reformist bureaucracy of the metalworkers' federation (FIOM) and, finally, into the mighty workers' councils which led the factory occupations of the '*Biennio Rosso*' of 1919–20.[25]

These movements had much in common. They were shopfloor movements, based in the metalworking and armaments industries, led by skilled workers who were opposing the effects of war-mobilisation on their industries. In crucial respects, however, the movements were very different from one another. 'Dilution' was less of an issue in Russia than in Britain, and so it cannot be considered a key cause of the emergence of the factory committees. In Germany and Italy much of the momentum behind the council movement came initially from the struggle by rank-and-file workers against the sclerotic trade-union bureaucracy, but in Russia this clearly was not a factor, since trade unions were virtually illegal, and since there had never existed within tsarist society the economic and political space for a successful reformist strategy to be pursued by an oligarchical trade union leadership.

In the aftermath of the February Revolution it was in the state sector of Petrograd industry that factory committees most firmly established themselves. Here, in the first weeks of March, the

committees in effect took over the management of the state enterprises, achieving a degree of power which made factory committees in
the private sector look weak by comparison. Given the fact that state
enterprises had not been in the van of labour struggles before
February 1917 why did they suddenly become such an important
base of the factory committees?

It has been suggested that the committees developed out of the
traditions of job-control exercised by skilled craftsmen.[26] There is
much truth in this, for the committees were set up by skilled workers
who understood how production worked, who were literate and who
were used to organising themselves. On the eve of the war, however,
job-control was not as highly developed in Russia as, for example, in
Britain, partly because modern technology had dispensed with the
skills of the traditional craftsman, and partly because in the West
job-control was premissed on forms of craft organisation which were
illegal in Russia. Nevertheless the process of rationalisation and
de-skilling which was going on in Petrograd industry, particularly in
the state sector, had caused skilled workers to feel extremely insecure,
and the February Revolution allowed them to combat that insecurity
by forming new organisations.

There was also an important political motive for the establishment
of the factory committees. Paradoxically, the activities of the
committees were boldest precisely in those enterprises where Bolshevik agitation and strike-militancy had been least in evidence during
the war. The state enterprises were strongholds of defencism, and it
was, in the main, defencist workers who spearheaded the creation of
factory committees. The crucial reason why factory committees took
over the running of state enterprises was to ensure that production for
the war effort was not jeopardised. Nevertheless it would be wrong to
conclude that the political motive of those who created the committees was simply a conservative, pro-war one. They were also
motivated by revolutionary ambitions, albeit of a democratic kind.
For although skilled workers in the state enterprises had been among
the better-off sections of the working class during the war, they had
had grievances aplenty. They had suffered greatly as a result of the
intensification of labour, brought about by the mobilisation of the war
industries, and they had also been subject to a military discipline
which their comrades in the private sector had been spared. They
thus had experienced in a very direct fashion the repressive nature of
the tsarist state, and when the latter was overturned in February,

militants in the state sector saw this as a signal for a root-and-branch overhaul of factory administration. Fearing precisely such an overhaul, many of the naval and army officers who ran the state enterprises fled during the revolution, and so on their return to work, militants faced not only the task of creating a radically new structure of administration, but also the urgent task of maintaining production for the Front.

In the absence of management, the factory committees took responsibility for running the state enterprises by setting up 'executive committees', comprising workers' representatives, engineers, technicians and, in some cases, members of the old administration. At the Cartridge works, the executive appointed Captain V.D. Meshcherinov temporary director, and set up two commissions: one consisting largely of technical staff, to deal with urgent practical business; the other consisting of workers to deal with the formation of a new administrative structure and the strengthening of internal order.[27] At the Sestroretsk arms works the stewards' committee appointed a new director and technical director, and set up a revolutionary committee to oversee production.[28] At the Pipe works a committee, consisting of five members of the factory soviet and four members of the former administration, took charge of production, wages and the security of the factory.[29] At the Okhta explosives works the committee simply declared itself the new administration. Later, reporting on the early weeks of its activity, the committee noted that: 'because of the novelty of things, the committee got lost in its business for a time. The immediate tasks of the committee were unclear, so it took on not only the task of controlling the factory administration, but the duties of the latter.'[30] Thus, for a few weeks in March 1917 the factory committees found themselves virtually in charge of state enterprises. This situation was not to last, but the experience was crucial in giving birth to the idea of 'workers' control of production'.[31]

On 13 March factories run by the Artillery Administration met to discuss what demands they should put on the Administration. They resolved to demand an eight-hour day, a minimum wage, and payment for the days they had spent toppling the Romanov regime.[32] This proved to be the first of a series of meetings of factory committee representatives and officials of the Artillery Administration. An Organisation Bureau, consisting of delegates from different enterprises, was set up to coordinate the work of the factory committees in the Artillery sector. Its members were moderate Bolsheviks and radical SRs, in the main.[33] At about the same time, the factories run by the Naval Ministry also began to organise. On 18 March factory committee representatives met to discuss the condition of workers in naval enterprises and to demand the democratic reorganisation of the council responsible for the industry.[34] Regular meetings began to take place, to which the directors of the naval enterprises came after 26 April. The workers' leaders at these meetings were overwhelmingly defencist in their politics.

At the beginning of April, 28 delegates from the naval enterprises met to discuss the role of the factory committees. They were addressed by a member of the Petrograd Soviet Executive Committee, G.E. Breido, a Menshevik and former member of the Workers' Group of the War Industries Committee. He denounced the attempts of some factory committees to run the naval enterprises by themselves, arguing that the committees should confine themselves to 'control' (i.e. supervision) of the activities of management.[35] A heated discussion ensued concerning the boundaries of such 'control'. At the Obukhov works, the committee reserved to itself the right to make enquiries of management and to inspect accounts. At the Izhora works, the workers had elected a new administration, and the committee had set up a commission to improve the technical side of production. 'Control' had gone furthest at the Baltic works, where the administration had been elected by the workers, and where the committee participated in management to the extent of keeping the financial accounts. Breido severely censured the Baltic arrangement, expressing a preference for the minimalist programme of the Obukhov works.[36]

On 15 April representatives from factories under the Artillery Administration and Naval Ministry met together to discuss further the role of the factory committees. Both sectors had already discussed this matter, and several important problems had emerged. The first of these concerned the desirability of 'self-management', i.e. of the factory committees actually running the state enterprises lock, stock and barrel, as they were doing at the Gun works, Okhta explosives, the Cartridge and the Baltic works. At the first meeting of Artillery Administration representatives in March, the delegate from the Cartridge works had urged 'self-management by workers on the broadest possible scale'.[37] The majority of delegates at the conference, however, whilst cursing the 'ancient fetters which have bound the workers in state enterprises so tightly to the authorities by means of military discipline', rejected the idea of the committees usurping the place of the official administration. In their resolution, the delegates declared: 'Until such time as full socialisation of the national economy, both state and private, shall occur, workers shall not take responsibility for the technical and administrative-economic organisation of production, and shall refuse to take part in the organisation of production.'[38] The first meeting of representatives of Artillery Administration enterprises had thus repudiated 'self-management', and declared for an official administration to be responsible for production, complemented by a factory committee to be responsible for all other aspects of the internal order (*vnutrennyi rasporyadok*) of the enterprise.

The joint conference of 15 April confirmed that the factory committees should take no responsibility for production. It proceeded to try to define the responsibilities of the factory committees more closely, by drawing up a constitution for the committees. This called for 'collegial management' in the enterprise, which it defined as meaning that: 'committees of workers' representatives . . . shall direct and manage the whole life of the factory'.[39] Yet how the committees were to exercise 'directing and managing' functions, and still abstain from actual management, was unclear. The draft constitution assigned total responsibility for matters of 'internal order', such as the regulation of wages, hours and hiring and firing, to the committees, and complete responsibility for administrative, economic and technical matters to the official administration. This apparently simple division of labour was complicated, however, by the fact that the committees were to have powers of 'control' over the administration.[40] The nature of this 'control' was to be 'informational' (*osvedomitel'nyi*), rather than 'responsible' (*otvetstvennyi*), and entailed the committees having representatives on all administrative organs for purposes of information, and access to all official documents and accounts, without thereby assuming any responsibility for production. This constitution appears to have been a compromise designed to satisfy both the radical delegates who, if they could not have 'self-management', wanted 'responsible' control, and those moderate elements who would have preferred to drop the idea of 'control' altogether. In the ensuing weeks, particularly after the enactment of a law on factory committees on 23 April, the moderate workers' leadership of the naval factories largely succeeded in clipping the wings of the committees, confining their activities to those of a purely 'trade-union' type, and jettisoning any notion of 'control'.[41]

A further problem concerned the extent to which the principle of election should apply within state enterprises. In almost all factories, workers had insisted in the wake of the February Revolution on electing their foremen and other members of the shop administration. In a few factories, such as the Baltic and Izhora works, all levels of administration were elected by the workforce in early March, reflecting strong rank-and-file feeling that a completely elected administration was necessary if workplace democracy were to be meaningful.[42] The constitution ratified by the joint conference on 15 April carefully skirted this issue, but, in effect, came out against a fully-elected administration. It spoke of directors, shop-directors and engineers being 'accepted with the agreement of the factory committee', and of the workers' right to 'object' (*otvod*) to those who could not guarantee normal relations with the workers.[43] It was this right to 'object', rather than to elect, which became rooted in factory-committee practice.

In the course of March, the councils running the Artillery Department and Naval Ministry were democratised. They proceeded to appoint new administrations to all state enterprises, and thereupon the factory committees ceased to play a direct role in management. In most naval enterprises, the factory committees henceforth exercised only minimal control over the administration, though more ambitious control was practised at the Baltic and New Admiralty works. In Artillery Department enterprises workers' control was more systematic, though it varied in scope from modest (Putilov) to far-reaching (Military-Horseshoe and Arsenal works). Nevertheless, throughout the state sector, a degree of workers' control continued to exist which was not matched by factory committees in the private sector until the summer and autumn of 1917.

In the private sector, the factory committees functioned essentially as 'trade-union' organisations in the spring of 1917. It was several months before proper trade unions began to function, and the committees were at the forefront of the battles to achieve an eight-hour day and to improve wages. Before examining these struggles, however, it is worth noting one area in which the factory committees transcended the 'normal' sphere of trade-union activity from the first. This was in the realm of 'control' of hiring and firing workers.

After the February Revolution, one of the first demands posed by workers was to 'control' the hiring and firing of workers. At the Phoenix engineering works the shop stewards' committee insisted that no worker be hired without the knowledge of the committee 'in view of the fact that undesirable elements may get in, such as looters, former servants of the old regime or people convicted of theft and other unworthy deeds'.[44] At the Okhta explosives works the committee established control of hiring and firing 'so that there'll be no patronage and people will be recruited according to a worked-out plan, and not fired at the whim of an individual'.[45] At the Tentelevskii chemical works the committee proposed to management that 'as a general rule, no worker may be hired, dismissed or transferred from one job to another without preliminary consultation with the factory committee'.[46] At the Putilov works, the Baltic, the Admiralty works and elsewhere, factory committees managed to reinstate workers, fired from their jobs during the war for strike and antiwar activity.[47]

It is probable that the motive behind these demands was as much a concern with job-security as a concern with limiting management power, but it was regarded by employers as an intolerable challenge to their right to manage. To them, the demand to control hiring and firing represented the wedge which would crack the unitary authority of the employer in the enterprise and open the way to a terrifying form of 'dual power'. They resisted it ferociously, and it is thus not accidental that the first of the Minister of Labour's circulars designed to curb the power of the factory committees, issued on 23 August, should have aimed to stop committees from interfering in hiring policy (see Chapter 7).

THE EIGHT-HOUR DAY

Having failed to achieve an eight-hour day in 1905, the workers returned to the factories in the second week of March determined that this time things would be different. The demand for the immediate introduction of an eight-hour working day was top of the agenda for workers at the Putilov works, the Metal works, Cable works, New Lessner, Skorokhod and many other factories. Most of these factories implemented the eight-hour day immediately, often without the formal agreement of the employers. The workers argued that the

eight-hour day was necessary not merely to diminish their exploitation, but also to create time for trade-union organisation, education
and involvement in public affairs.[48] Many workers expressed doubts
lest a reduction in the working day adversely affect production for the
war effort. At the Cartridge works the workers agreed: 'to recognise
the eight-hour day as basic . . . but in view of the imminent danger, to
try by all means to support our brothers at the Front and to work more
than eight hours without question – up to twelve hours or more – if
necessary'.[49] At the Nevskii shipbuilding works the factory 'soviet of
workers deputies', which comprised two Mensheviks, two Bolsheviks
and one SR, met with the director on 6 March to discuss the
eight-hour day. The director argued that it was impossible to
introduce an eight-hour day in the foundries and engineering shops
for technical reasons, and that it was practicable only for mechanised
shell production. The soviet agreed that 'any disruption of the
existing technical system at the factory will involve a decrease in
productivity and so we must begin work at the normal time, but take
the eight-hour day as basic and consider any hours worked over that
to be overtime'.[50] Although the Menshevik-dominated factory committee took exception to the 'tactlessness' of the factory soviet in
deciding this question without consulting them, they affirmed its
correctness.[51] Most factories took a similar position at this time: they
introduced an eight-hour day, but were prepared to work overtime in
support of the war effort.

Employers were reluctant to agree to the eight-hour day, and in
some areas put up a good deal of resistance to it. In Petrograd,
however, most were in a more conciliatory frame of mind, although it
was the pressure of the workers which pushed them into making this
concession so speedily. The Menshevik and SR leaders of the Soviet
believed that the political gains of the revolution should be consolidated before economic demands were put forward, but they were
ignored by the workers. As soon as factory committees began to
implement the eight-hour day unilaterally, the Society of Factory and
Works Owners (SFWO) entered into negotiations with the Soviet
regarding a reduction in working hours. On 10 March the two sides
agreed to the eight-hour day, the recognition of factory committees
and the establishment of conciliation chambers in the factories.[52] On
14 March the SFWO sent a circular to its members calling on them to
recognise the eight-hour day as an 'historically necessary measure',
'capable of ensuring the future spiritual development of the working

class, by providing time for self-education and trade-union organisation, and of establishing correct lawful relations between labour and capital'.[53]

The introduction of the eight-hour day led to a diminution of the average working day in the Petrograd area from 10.2 hours to 8.4 hours.[54] In the metal industry it decreased from 10.4 hours to 8.6 hours; in chemicals from 9.6 hours to 9.1 hours; in textiles from 9.5 hours to 8 hours; in the paper industry from 11.6 to 9.8 hours; in woodworking from 9.8 to 8.2 hours and in the food industry from 10.2 to 8.6 hours.[55] In non-factory industries, particularly in shops and small workplaces, the standard working day continued to be well in excess of nine or ten hours, owing to the poor organisation of the employees and to the fact that an eight-hour day was not legally binding on employers.[56] Overtime working continued to be widespread after February. In almost all factories, however, labour organisations insisted on their right to control the operation of overtime working. At the 1886 Electric Light Company the factory committee agreed to overtime only in case of accidents, urgent repair work or the absence of key personnel.[57] Elsewhere factory committees pressured management to take on extra workers instead of extending overtime working. From the first, there were a few factories which refused to work overtime on principle, regardless of the war. At the Nevskaya footwear factory the factory agreed at its very first meeting to abolish overtime 'for ever'.[58] At the Promet armaments factory the Menshevik-dominated factory committee voted 20 against 12 in favour of continuing overtime, but a general meeting of 3,000 workers overwhelmingly overrode its decision.[59] Women workers, in particular, were adamant that an eight-hour day meant precisely that. A complete ban on overtime was called for by women in Moscow district of the capital on 7 March and by laundrywomen on 19 March.[60] At the Vyborg spinning mill the average number of hours worked by male workers fell from 11.4 hours in January 1917 to 8.7 hours in July – including one hour's overtime. The hours worked by women workers, however, fell from 10 hours to 7.8 hours, with almost no overtime.[61] Women's refusal to work overtime sprang from the fact that domestic labour consumed so large a proportion of the time not spent at the factory.

As the first signs of economic crisis appeared later in the year, the labour leaders took up the fight against overtime. At the Third Conference of Trade Unions in June, the Bolshevik leader of the metalworkers' union, V. Schmidt, urged: 'At the present time, the eight-hour day is only a norm of payment and has not actually been put into practice. Overtime is done everywhere, but it must be allowed only in exceptional circumstances with the agreement of the unions.'[62] The woodturners' union tried to limit the amount of overtime, but not always without opposition from its low-paid members.[63] The same was true of the printers' union which took a firm stand against overtime working because of the worrying level of unemployment in the print-trade.[64] This policy had considerable success later in the year as closures and redundancies increased. By October there was very little overtime working in Petrograd.

WAGE STRUGGLES

In addition to a significant reduction in working hours, workers gained large wage increases as a consequence of the February Revolution. They returned to the factories in March determined that the overthrow of tsarism should signal a dramatic change in their working lives. A deputy from the Narva district told the Petrograd Soviet on 5 March: 'Surely political freedoms are meant to help workers live like human beings. They should guarantee the minimum conditions of human existence – the eight-hour day and the minimum wage. Freedoms are useless if the old conditions persist.'[65] He was undoubtedly expressing a general opinion, for everywhere workers began to raise demands for large wage-rises, payment for the days spent toppling the Romanov dynasty, and a minimum wage. Although the demands raised by different factories tended to be the same, the struggle to achieve them was conducted on an extremely localised basis. In the absence of trade unions, it was the factory committees which led the wages battles, but in some factories there was very little organisation – merely a free-for-all, in which workers unused to traditions of organised wage negotiation sought to improve their wages by the only method they knew – direct action. The result was considerable variation between factories in the level of achievement of the struggles.

At the Skorokhod shoe factory, which employed 1,508 men, 2,687 women and 705 young people, workers engaged in a militant, but relatively organised, battle for better wages. On 9 March the factory committee demanded: management recognition of the committee; an eight-hour working day; a dinner break of one-and-a-half hours; a minimum daily wage of 5 rubles for men, 2 r.50 k. for women and 2 r. for youths; the continuation of a war bonus introduced in 1915; the abolition of payment for one's own materials; double pay for overtime; a joint commission to examine wage-rates; payment for the February Days; payment for deputies to the Soviet; the dismissal of undesirable elements and control of hiring and firing. Management refused to countenance a 47-hour week, but agreed to 48 hours; it resisted with particular stubbornness the demands concerning minimum wages, at first agreeing only to a 20% increase; it agreed to overtime only at time-and-a-half; it refused to abolish fines and insisted on the retention of the system whereby workers bought their own ancillary materials; it agreed only to the factory committee's right to be informed of hiring and firing and to its right to request the removal of an administrator. Management refused to pay members of elected organisations but offered 300,000 rubles towards the cost of a canteen.[66] Almost immediately, it was forced to back down on hours, fines and payment of elected representatives, once it became clear what was happening in other factories. The wage demands were referred to a conciliation chamber, which recommended a 40% increase in the minimum wage. The director, A.K. Gartvig, agreed to this, and promised 10,000 r. to the renascent leatherworkers' union. The workers' representatives in the conciliation chamber expressed satisfaction with his magnanimity, but they had not reckoned with the workers on the shopfloor. On 20 March the latter stopped work and a crowd began to abuse the director. After some ugly negotiations, during which the workers complained that the director 'behaved provocatively and used unprintable language',[67] Gartvig made some amazing concessions, including a minimum wage of ten rubles for men and the abolition of piece-rates.[68] This did not prevent the workers from forcing Gartvig to resign in May, ordering him to clean his apartment before he left![69]

In the textile industry the revolution gave vent to a rash of wage demands, some of which were pursued through explosive, confrontations with management, others through patient, even resigned, negotiation. At the two Nevskaya spinning mills women comprised 81% and 90%, respectively, of the two workforces. No factory committee existed at either mill until the end of March, and women drew up extremely moderate lists of 'requests' which they put to management on a shop-by-shop basis. The most ambitious demands were those drawn up by women in the scutching-room at the Koenig mill, who requested of the English director, Harvey, that they be not asked to sweep the floor after they had finished work (refused); that machines be stopped for an hour each day for cleaning and oiling (refused); that new workers be put on the same rate as older ones ('What will the older women say?'); that women be paid six weeks' maternity leave (referred to medical fund); that they receive equal pay with men on the same job (no reply); that they be entitled to retirement and injury pensions (no reply).[70] The plaintive tone of the Koenig women's entreaty was not typical of the majority of workers, nor was the obtuse intransigence of the English management typical of employers as a whole.

The month of March saw a plethora of small-scale, short, sometimes sectional struggles for higher wages. The most effective were those which were organised by factory committees, but 'spontaneous' outbursts of direct action were by no means ineffective in this period. Most employers were prepared to make far-reaching concessions under pressure, so very few disputes developed into strikes proper. At the Osipov leather works a strike broke out on 8 March, and at the Cable works a strike took place from 16–21 March, a comparatively long time by the standards of this period – but such strikes were exceptional.[71] The result was considerable variation in the level of wages between different factories, industries and occupational categories. This makes it difficult to generalise about the size of the wage rises achieved in the spring of 1917.

During the course of March, monthly earnings rose by between 35% and 50%, and continued to rise over the next two months.[72] In the absence of global data, one can only estimate that by July monthly earnings were double or treble their January level (see *Table 11*).[73] Average hourly earnings rose much more than this, in view of the change from a ten to an eight-hour day and the reduction in overtime. The latter changes meant that by July the unit-costs of employers were perhaps as much as four to five times the level of the previous year.[74] Yet one should not assume that all workers benefited at their employers' expense. In order to keep abreast of inflation, workers had to at least double their monthly earnings, and by no means all of them managed to do so.

How did the wage-rises of spring 1917 affect the relative positions of skilled and unskilled and male and female workers? *Table 11* suggests

Table 11: *Petrograd workers grouped according to wages in January and June 1917*

Monthly earnings in rubles	Sample of metalworkers						Skorokhod shoe factory				Nevka woollen mill			
	% of men		% of women		% males aged 16–18		% of males		% of females		% of males		% of females	
	Jan.	June	Jan.	June	Jan.	June	Jan.	June	Jan.	June	Jan.	June	Jan.	June
under 60 rubles	8.8	–	–	–	31.7	1.6	9	1.1	54.2	0.5	–	–	83.6	–
60–89	10.4	0.7	54.2	11.9	28.0	12.5	17.7	1.5	36.5	1.7	62.4	–	16.3	–
90–119	17.1	3.9	37.4	31.9	25.6	25.0	32.6	1.9	7.2	7.4	18.0	–	–	81.8
120–149	15.2	7.1	6.9	35.6	8.5	14.1	26.8	4.6	1.0	10.3	8.8	–	–	17.6
150–179	12.6	6.7	0.8	11.1	6.1	6.3	9.1	3.7	0.6	76.7	7.3	–	–	–
180–209	8.5	9.1	0.8	7.4	–	20.3	2.8	5.5	0.1	3.0	2.9	49.0	–	0.5
210–239	7.8	10.8	–	2.2	–	12.5	1.0	14.8	0.04	0.3	–	29.4	–	–
240–269	7.0	12.4	–	–	–	4.7	0.5	51.0	–	0.1	0.4	14.4	–	–
270–299	4.3	11.5	–	–	–	1.6	0.06	9.5	–	0.04	–	3.7	–	–
300–329	2.5	11.4	–	–	–	1.6	–	2.7	–	0.08	–	1.4	–	–
330–359	2.3	9.5	–	–	–	–	–	1.2	–	–	–	–	–	–
360–389	1.2	5.0	–	–	–	–	–	1.3	–	–	–	–	–	–
390–419	1.8	3.0	–	–	–	–	–	0.7	–	–	–	0.1	–	–
420–449	0.4	7.0	–	–	–	–	–	–	–	–	–	–	–	–
450 or more	–	2.0	–	–	–	–	–	–	–	–	–	–	–	–
Total number of workers	1313	1451	131	135	82	64	1551	1628	2277	2470	205	214	1970	2000

Table based on:
A.P. Serebrovskii, *Revolyutsiya i zarabotnaya plata metallicheskoi promyshlennosti*, Petrograd, 1917, p.9.
I.A. Baklanova, *Rabochie Petrograda v period mirnogo razvitiya revolyutsii, mart–iyun', 1917g.*, Leningrad, 1978, p.3.

71

that the wages of the low-paid rose proportionately more than did those of the better-off. This is borne out by evidence from other factories. At the Parviainen works the hourly rate of a turner rose by 59% between February and May, compared to a 125% rise in the rate of an unskilled worker.[75] In the thirty paper mills of Petrograd, male wages increased by 214% in the first half of 1917, compared to 234% for female wages and 261% for young people's wages.[76] The diminution in wage-differentials was the result of conscious policy on the part of factory committees to try to improve the dire situation of unskilled workers, women workers and youth. However, the improvement in the relative earnings of the low-paid was not true of all factories. From *Table 11* it appears that at the Nevka spinning mill men's wages increased more than those of women. And at the Vyborg spinning mill the average hourly rates of male workers rose by 368% between January and July, compared to 327% for adult women, 335% for male youths and 321% for female youths. Moreover better-paid workers of both sexes achieved proportionately bigger increases than the poorer-paid.[77] This suggests that in factories where workers were not well organised, groups fought for themselves on a sectional basis. In the textile industry, where factory committees were weakly developed at this stage, attempts to implement a collective wages policy, biassed in favour of the low-paid, were few. Women in the industry, generally lacking the bargaining power of the minority of skilled men, were the inevitable victims of this situation.

The demand for a minimum wage for the low-paid was valiantly fought for by workers' organisations. At the Metal works negotiations between the works committee and management over a minimum wage became deadlocked, and a member of the committee proposed that skilled workers should supplement the wages of the unskilled out of their own pay-packets until the matter was settled: '... We must show our true mettle. Are we the same as the exploiting bourgeois, or are we just a bit more aware and willing to help the *chernorabochie?* Let us, the *masterovye,* lend a hand to our starving, ragged comrades.'[78] At the Putilov shipyard management and workers agreed to assign 20% of the annual wages bill to help the lowest-paid, pending a settlement of the minimum wage.[79] The workers' section of the Soviet took up the pressing question of a minimum wage at its meetings of 18 March and 20 March. Representatives from fifty of the largest enterprises described the sorry plight of the poorly-paid, which had come about as a result of inflation. The Menshevik, V.O. Bogdanov, complained about the number of partial, sectional conflicts in the factories and the 'continued misunderstanding' between capital and labour, to which the delegate from the Putilov works retorted angrily:

> It is the duty of the Soviet to examine our position, to look at all rates and standards, to revise them and create a tolerable existence for us, and not be surprised that we raise demands ... When the workers arose from their toiling slumber, they demanded just wages, they put forward just demands, but the employers cried: 'Guards! They are robbing us!'[80]

The workers' deputies in the Soviet agreed that a minimum wage of five or six rubles a day should be made legally binding on employers, but the SFWO proposed a minimum of 3 r. 20 k. for men and 2 r. 50 k. for women.[81] The matter was then referred to the Central Concilia- tion Chamber, at which the workers' representatives argued for a daily minimum of five rubles for men and four for women. The employers' representatives at first resisted this, but then conceded it, recognising that 'from the political point of view, we are now living through a time when strength lies with the workers'.[82] This minimum was formally announced on 22 April, but the announcement sent few workers into raptures. It was clear that this minimum was already inadequate in the face of soaring prices.[83]

A final word should be said about piece-rates. Piece-rates were deeply disliked by many workers under the old regime. In 1905 the metalworkers had pressed for their abolition, as had the printers in 1907.[84] In the ensuing years, however, piece-rates had become ever more widely established as the normal method of payment. After the February Revolution workers clamoured to eliminate piece-systems. In the metal works of the private sector, factory committees appear to have had some success, at least temporarily, in getting piece-rates abolished.[85] In the state sector, especially in enterprises run by the Naval Ministry, there seems to have been less pressure for their abolition, and they remained in force.[86] In the print-trade, the union pressed for an end to the system whereby typesetters were paid according to the number of words they set, and called for a guaranteed minimum wages.[87] They seem to have been fairly successful. Once the crisis in labour discipline became apparent, however (see Chapter 4), most unions agreed in principle to the restoration of piece-rates.

MANAGEMENT STRATEGY AFTER THE FEBRUARY REVOLUTION

In the tsarist era the capitalist class in Russia was characterised by economic strength and social and political weakness. This arose from the fact that large capital achieved dominance in the economy in the 1890s, not by challenging the political power of the landowning elite, but by relying on the economic and political protection of the autocratic state. The industrial and commercial bourgeoisie thus never really developed into a political force capable of challenging the old order. It was to prove a far less dynamic social class than the proletariat, and this social weakness was mirrored in its internal divisions and in its underdeveloped sense of class identity.

The capitalist class in Russia was not monolithic. Several fractions can be distinguished within it, according to industrial and regional base, degree of dependence on foreign capital, degree of dependence on the state, differences in industrial and commercial policy and differences in political outlook. The biggest fraction of the capitalist class was also the most genuinely Russian, and consisted of those entrepreneurs of the Moscow region whose wealth derived from textiles and other light industries, and who were independent of foreign and government finance.[88] The Moscow entrepreneurs tended to pursue a conservative economic policy, but a liberal policy in the political arena; they played a minor role in the opposition movement of the Third Duma and supported the Progressive Bloc during the war.[89] This political liberalism sharply distinguished the Muscovites from the more reactionary fractions of capital, such as the mineowners of the Donbass and Krivoi Rog, the semi-feudal bourgeoisie of the Urals metallurgical industry and the oil magnates of Baku, all of whom depended heavily on foreign capital.[90] In this respect, the latter were similar to the strongest fraction of the capitalist class – the industrialists and financiers of St Petersburg, who derived their wealth from banking and the metalworking industries and were heavily dependent on state orders and foreign investment. Because of its dependence on the government, the St Petersburg bourgeoisie was far less active in the social and political arena than its Moscow counterpart.

Although the St Petersburg capitalists were obsequiously servile towards the government prior to 1914, the war put their loyalty to severe strain. The Moscow industrialists dominated the War Industries Committees (set up to take responsibility for military supplies after the defeat of the army in the summer of 1915), but some entrepreneurs in Petrograd became increasingly sympathetic to the committees. Alienated by its inept pursuit of the war and by the scandalous intrigues of the Rasputin clique, most entrepreneurs in Petrograd were not sorry to see the passing of the Imperial government in February 1917.

The mood of a majority of industrialists after the February Revolution was one of anxious hope. They were confident that the Provisional Government could establish a liberal parliamentary regime which would represent their interests, but they were also acutely aware that the *ancien régime* had been liquidated by means of a popular movement, which, they feared, could easily get out of hand, and thus endanger the objective of a liberal capitalist system. The paradoxical character of the February Revolution – a 'bourgeois' revolution, undertaken by workers and soldiers – brutally exposed the social weakness of the bourgeoisie, once the crutch of the tsarist state had been knocked from under it. At a national level, the bourgeoisie was weak in numbers, internally divided, lacking in class consciousness, politically inexperienced and badly organised. The prime task for the capitalist class, therefore, was to organise to promote its interests more effectively and to exert pressure on the new government.

In Petrograd the main employers' organisation was the Society of Factory and Works Owners (SFWO). This had been founded in 1897 and represented all the major firms in the capital. By 1917 it represented 450 mainly large factories, employing a total workforce of 280,000. It had seven sections – for metalworking and engineering, chemicals, textiles, paper, wood, printing and for miscellaneous industries.[91] The first number of the SFWO journal in 1917 defined the Society's tasks as 'to search for new ways to develop Russian industry within the framework of capitalism' and to ensure that 'free citizen industrialists and free citizen workers find a common language'.[92] In April a new council and presidium were established, and city district sections were set up; these did not prove successful, and in summer the SFWO was reorganised along industrial lines.[93] The weakness of the SFWO was due not so much to defective organisation, as to the inherent difficulties in enforcing a common policy on all members. In spite of the fact that firms who went against SFWO policy risked heavy fines, there were often good business reasons why firms should break ranks. In view of the failure to create a unified employers' organisation in Petrograd, it is not surprising that attempts to create a national organisation came to grief, and that a host of sectional organisations proliferated, each representing different fractions of industry and commerce.[94]

In terms of its industrial relations policy, management in Petrograd factories was faced with a choice of two strategies after the February Revolution. On the one hand, lacking moral authority in the eyes of the working class and inured to a quasi-feudal system of industrial relations, it could attempt to suppress labour unrest and restore the *status quo ante*. This was the strategy chosen by employers in the Urals and Donbass. On the other hand, deprived of the support of the autocracy and confronted by a labour force in ferment, management could make real concessions in the hope of inaugurating a system of Western-style labour relations. In Petrograd they chose the latter, and thus committed themselves to dismantling the system of industrial relations based on coercion, in favour of one based on mutual recognition, negotiation and collective bargaining. A circular from the SFWO to its members on 15 March reads:

Relations between employers and workers have changed radically; speedy, energetic work is needed to initiate a new order in the factories and to re-establish normal work on defence as rapidly as possible.[95]

In practical terms, this meant making four key concessions: firstly, immediate and sizeable wage increases; secondly, the eight-hour day; thirdly, recognition of factory committees and trade unions, and, fourthly, the establishment of conciliation chambers.

This programme coincided felicitously with that of the Provisional Government. The latter set up a Department of Labour within the Ministry of Trade and Industry, which was headed by A.I. Konovalov. He declared that the government's aim was to 'establish proper relations between labour and capital, based on law and justice'. On 29 March he announced that the priorities of the government in the sphere of labour relations were: firstly, the development of trade unions; secondly, the creation of conciliation chambers, factory committees and labour exchanges; thirdly, legislation on labour protection, working hours and social insurance.[96] This programme had the backing of the SFWO, but it was considered dangerously socialistic by the mineowners of the Urals. Later, after opposition began to build up, the government's zeal for reform proved surprisingly half-hearted. It refused, for example, to enact a law on the eight-hour day, setting up a commission to study the 'complexity' of the problem instead. This was a portent of the paralysis which was to overcome the labour policy of the Provisional Government.

Conciliation chambers were the centrepiece of the system of 'constitutional' industrial relations to which both the SFWO and the Provisional Government aspired. Conciliation chambers had first appeared in the years 1905-7, particularly in the printing and construction industries. They died out during the Years of Reaction and did not emerge again until the end of 1915, when they were revived by the progressive wing of Moscow industrialists and by the Workers' Group of the War Industries Committee. Conciliation chambers were strongly resisted at this time by industrialists in Petrograd, who considered them to be fetters on their freedom of action.[97] The February Revolution soon changed their minds and they became staunch advocates of arbitration in disputes.

The Menshevik and SR leaders of the Petrograd Soviet were as anxious as the SFWO to set up machinery for arbitration and for the avoidance of unofficial action by rank-and-file workers. In the agreement between the two bodies of 10 March, it was stated that conciliation chambers should be set up 'for the purpose of settling all misunderstandings arising out of labour–management relations'. They were to consist of an equal number of elected representatives from both workers and management and were to reach decisions by joint agreement.[98] In the event of agreement not being reached, the dispute was to be referred to a Central Conciliation Chamber. *Izvestiya*, the paper of the 'conciliationist' leadership of the Petrograd Soviet, explained the significance of this agreement on conciliation as follows: 'The wartime situation and the revolution force both sides to exercise extreme caution in utilising the sharper weapons of class struggle such as strikes and lockouts. These circumstances make it necessary to settle all disputes by means of negotiation and agreement, rather than by open conflict. Conciliation chambers serve this purpose.'[99]

In the early months of the revolution the conciliation chambers were very busy, playing an important role in mediating in wages negotiations. As the unions began to consolidate themselves, however, the significance of the chambers waned.[100] From the first, many workers regarded the conciliation chambers with suspicion, since they appeared to repress the reality of class struggle and to compete with the factory committees. The general situation was not favourable to the harmonious resolution of disagreements between workers and employers, and where class tension was acute, the conciliation chambers tended to be impotent. The most striking example of this was the general failure of conciliation committees to achieve the reinstatement of managers and foremen expelled from their jobs by the workers.[101]. It is thus not surprising that as early as March, dissenting voices should have been heard at a convention of factory-owners in Vyborg district, warning that 'the conciliation chambers cannot justify the hopes placed in them, since they do not enjoy the necessary confidence of the workers and lack a firm foundation'.[102]

It is now barely possible to understand why employers should have conceived the factory committees to be part of their scheme for a 'constitutional' system of industrial relations. At the time, however, there seemed good grounds for thinking that factory committees would encourage order in the factories, by acting as safety-valves for the explosive build-up of shopfloor grievances. It is clear from the agreement made between the SFWO and the Soviet on 10 March that industrialists saw the factory committees as an updated version of the *starosty*. In a circular interpreting the agreement, the SFWO emphasised the need for workers to make a 'careful choice of people who are able to maintain good relations between the two sides'.[103] A week later a further circular was sent out informing employers that 'working hours spent by these people (i.e. deputies, *starosty*, members of the factory committee, and so on), in fulfilling the duties laid down, must be paid at the normal, i.e. average, daily rate'.[104] Until the autumn most employers financed the factory committees and, in return for their support, expected them to operate in a manner that was acceptable. The SFWO therefore put pressure on the Provisional Government to define the powers of the factory committees by law.

The labour department of the Ministry of Trade and Industry agreed to set up a commission under Professor M.V. Bernatskii to draft such a law. The commission received submissions from the labour department of the Petrograd Soviet and from the SFWO, and tried to find a compromise between the two. It resisted pressure from the SFWO to give employers the right to remove members of the factory committees, specifying that this might only be done by a conciliation committee. The final law followed the proposals of the Petrograd Soviet fairly closely, though it did not make factory committees responsible for safety or deferments of conscription as the

Soviet had suggested.[105] On 23 April the law was promulgated by the Provisional Government. It provided for the setting up of factory committees to represent workers' interests *vis-à-vis* management on questions such as pay and hours; to settle disputes between workers; to represent workers before the government and public institutions and to engage in educational and cultural work.[106] The law thus defined the functions of the factory committees narrowly: it made no mention of 'control', whether of hiring and firing or of any aspect of production. The aim of the government, as in the legislation on conciliation committees, was not to stifle the factory committees, but to institutionalise them and quell their potential extremism by legitimising them as representative organs designed to mediate between employers and workers on the shopfloor.[107] Some employers were disgruntled by what they believed to be the excessive liberalism of the legislation, but most tried to put it into operation. Workers, however, were not prepared to have their hands tied by the new law. Most factory committees in Petrograd were already operating on a much broader mandate than that allowed for by the law, and so they simply ignored it. In the naval enterprises of the state sector, however, the law was used as the excuse for reducing the functions of the factory and port committees to those of a 'trade-union' type. In many parts of Russia, the law proved to be a stimulus to workers to set up factory committees for the first time.

It is easy in retrospect to mock the guarded optimism of the employers in March and April, but at the time it was not unreasonable to hope that with the granting of substantial concessions, working-class unrest would subside. For some time in April, things did look hopeful.[108] By May, however, the omens indicated that the policy of compromise, favoured as much by the Soviet Executive Committee as by employers, would prove as bankrupt in the sphere of industrial relations as it would in the sphere of politics.

4

The structure and functions of the
factory committees

THE STRUCTURE OF THE FACTORY COMMITTEES

The bigger a factory, the more likely it was to have a factory committee.[1] The most comprehensive data on this question do not, at first sight, appear to bear out this contention, for if one groups the delegates to the First Conference of Petrograd Factory Committees (30 May–3 June), according to the size of the factory from which they came, it emerges that the biggest proportion of delegates came from medium-sized factories of 100–500 workers, rather than large ones.[2] If, however, one compares the number of factories of a given size, represented at the conference, to the total number of factories of that size in Petrograd, then it becomes clear that a direct correlation exists between the size of an enterprise and the likelihood of its being represented.[3] Thus 100% of factories with a workforce of more than 5,000 (18 in number) were represented at the First Conference, whereas less than 5% of factories with 50 workers or less were so. 200 workers seems to have been the critical size, for over half the factories of that size or larger sent delegates to the conference. In enterprises of less than 200 workers, it seems that workers were either less interested or less able to set up committees. There is evidence that, notwithstanding the fact that factory owners were obliged by law to recognise the committees, some small employers prevented their workers organising such committees. At the tiny Glazer leather workshop, the nineteen workers formed a committee in March, but its members were fired by the boss and, as a result, the committee collapsed.[4] Even at the relatively large Kan printworks, with a workforce of 850, committee members were victimised, and the committee survived only because of support from the printers' union.[5]

The size of factory committees varied considerably.[6] The April conference of representatives of state enterprises recommended that in a factory of 500–1,000 workers, the committee should comprise 11–13 members; that in one of 3,000–6,000, it should consist of 13–15 members, and so on.[7] It was envisaged that the committee would be supplemented either by a network of shop stewards or by shop committees. These norms of representation were ratified by the Second Conference of Petrograd Factory Committees (7–12 August).[8] The size of factory committees seldom conformed to this pattern. At the Admiralty shipyard 800 workers elected a committee of 24 members. At the Obukhov works, 12,900 workers had a committee of 12 members, supplemented by 40 *starosty*.[9] At the Baltic shipyard the works committee originally consisted of 103 members, but proved so elephantine that it had to be cut down to 40.

In large enterprises, the works committee was supported by a structure of workshop committees. The Putilov works was one of the first enterprises to set up shop committees, although, interestingly, it had been late in establishing a factory committee. This seems to have been due to the fact that the giant enterprise so dominated the life of the Narva–Peterhof district of Petrograd, that the local soviet of workers' and soldiers' deputies at first functioned as a committee of the Putilov works.[10] In addition, it seems that the non-party and Menshevik majority of the Narva soviet were hostile to the idea of a separate works committee at Putilov, feeling that it might operate as a rival centre of power.[11] Elections to a works committee were eventually held between 10 and 14 April, and six Bolsheviks, six non-party persons, one Menshevik-Internationalist, two SRs, one anarchist and five whose political affiliation was unknown were elected.[12] On 24 April, the new works committee issued detailed instructions on the setting up of shop committees, prefaced by the following remarks:

In view of the fact that the practical business of organising shop committees is a new affair, it is necessary that these committees, which look after life at the grass roots, should display as much independence and initiative as possible. The success of the labour organisations in the factories fully depends on this. By becoming accustomed to self-management [*samoupravlenie*], the workers are preparing for that time when private ownership of factories and works will be abolished, and the means of production, together with the buildings erected by the workers' hands, will pass into the hands of the working class as a whole. Thus, whilst doing the small things, we must constantly bear in mind the great overriding objective towards which the working people [*rabochii narod*] is striving.[13]

This passage, which is typical of working-class discourse at the time, cannot be interpreted as reflecting a spirit of shop sectarianism; it rather expresses a commitment to grass-roots democracy and to self-activity which is characteristic of 1917. Nor can it be viewed as a concession by the works committee to rank-and-file pressure for shop autonomy. The rest of the declaration makes clear that the motive for setting up shop committees is largely practical, i.e. the works committee cannot deal with the huge volume of business facing it, and is thus farming out all business concerning individual shops to the shop committees. There is no intention of encouraging federalism – still less, anarchy: the declaration spells out unequivocally that shop committees are subordinate to the works committee.[14]

Nearly forty shop committees were set up at the Putilov works. Their tasks were defined as being to defend the workers of the shop; to observe and organise internal order; to see that regulations were being followed; to control hiring and firing of workers; to resolve conflicts over wage-rates; to keep a close eye on working conditions; to check whether the military conscription of individual workers had been deferred, etc.[15] At the Baltic shipyard, the functions of the shop committees were similarly defined. They were to consider all socio-economic matters and demands aimed at improving the workers' lot, although final decisions on such matters rested with the works committee; they were empowered to warn people, including management, if they were violating factory regulations or working carelessly or unconscientiously; they were to represent workers before management; they were to suggest ways of increasing production and improving working conditions; they had the right to request from management all memoranda and information concerning their shop; they were to settle conflicts between workers or between the workers and the shop management; they were to carry out the decisions of the labour organisations and ensure that all wage agreements were implemented.[16]

Western historians have placed considerable emphasis on the local, decentralised aspect of the factory committee movement, but their depiction of a diffuse, centrifugal movement, harnessed after October into centralist channels, is in need of qualification. For whilst the committees were characterised by greater decentralisation and local autonomy than the trade unions, from the first, there were pressures towards centralisation and higher-level coordination within the movement. Centralisation was not imposed from above by a triumphant Bolshevik government, it arose from below, at the behest of the committees themselves.

As early as the beginning of March the communications and organisation commission of the Izhora works committee was established to 'coordinate the actions of the workers' committee with the actions of other workers' committees'. Coordination with other factories was discussed by workers at the Atlas engineering works on 4 March, and at San Galli the works committee quickly established contact with other works committees.[17] In April, the Chief Committee of representatives of factory committees in state enterprises was inaugurated.[18] At the beginning of May factory committees in the Nevskaya yarn company set up a body 'for joint organisation and practical work', and a week later workers at the six textile factories in the Voronin, Lyutsh and Cheshire group formed a central committee 'for close contact and information about the operations of each factory'.[19]

Simultaneous with this process of inter-factory coordination went a process of coordinating factory committee activities in each district of the capital. The first district council of factory committees was created on Vasilevskii Island on 29 March. Workers at the Arsenal and at Old Lessner proposed the setting-up of a district council of factory committees on Vyborg Side but nothing seems to have come of it, for the council did not get off the ground until 4 September.[20] A more successful council was set up in Nevskii district in May, which represented 34 factory committees. In general, however, the attempt to establish a district level of factory committee organisation came up against various obstacles, causing the Second Conference of Petrograd Factory Committees (7th August) to propose that the middle-level organisation of factory committees be on the basis of branch of industry rather than geographical district. It proved even harder to organise on an industrial basis, and the Third Conference of Petrograd Factory Committees (5–10 September) once again pronounced in favour of territorial organisation and urged all districts to form district councils of factory committees.[21] By October fully operational district councils existed in Nevskii, Peterhof and Vasilevskii districts and others were beginning to function.[22]

These district councils gave help to individual factory committees in the practical work of workers' control and in settling disputes. Some had control commissions which supervised the administrative, financial and technical sides of production; others had commissions which distributed fuel and raw materials, and others dealt with the demobilisation of industry, i.e. the transfer to civilian production.[23] On the whole, however, the district councils of factory committees cannot be counted a success. In contrast to the trade unions, where city-district organisation was of crucial importance, district organisations of the factory committees seem to have been fairly redundant. The bulk of factory-committee business related to the individual factory, and was of no concern to neighbouring factories. Where broader coordination of forces was necessary, this seems to have been best achieved at city level, rather than at city-district level.

The supreme expression of the centralising tendency within the factory committee movement was the Petrograd Central Council of Factory Committees (CCFC), which was set up in June after the First Conference. From its inception, the CCFC was a bulwark of Bolshevism, consisting of nineteen Bolsheviks, two Mensheviks, two SRs, one *Mezhraionets* (the so-called Interdistrict Group of Social Democrats of which Trotsky became leader after his return from the USA in May 1917), and one syndicalist.[24] In its early days, the CCFC was involved mainly in diverting threatened factory closures and in wage disputes. It then settled down to the task of coordinating workers' control of production.[25] Its members sat on government economic organs – in particular, the supply committees and the Factory Convention – but refused payment for their work, on the grounds that this would make them state officials.[26] By October, the CCFC had the following commissions: communications and personnel, economic, finance, literary and editorial, agitation, conflict; the following departments: technical-production control and demobilisation, administrative-financial control, raw materials and metals supplies, fuel supplies, energy; and the following sections: evacuation, agricultural equipment for the countryside, cultural-educational, instruction. Some 80 people worked in these different commissions, departments and sections.[27] In view of the enormous scope of its work, there are no grounds for saying, as does Solomon Schwarz, that the Bolsheviks deliberately obstructed the economic work of the CCFC, using it instead for the political ends.[28] If the CCFC failed in its central aim of restoring order to the economy via workers' control, this was not through lack of trying, but because the odds were stacked massively against it.[29]

At the grass roots, too, factory committees quickly developed an enormous volume of business and were forced from the first to create commissions to deal with specific areas of work. At the 1886 Electric Light Company the new committee set up three commissions on 2 March: a commission of internal order, which received notices from management saying what needed to be done, and then organised the execution of this work; a food commission and a militia commission. On 26 April a further two commissions were created: an education commission and a commission of enquiry into disputes between workers.[30] The works committee at the Nevskii shipyard had six commissions, including a militia commission responsible for the security of the factory, a food commission, a commission of culture and enlightenment, a technical-economic commission responsible for wages, safety, first-aid and internal order, a reception commission responsible for the hiring and firing of workers, and finally, a special commission which dealt with the clerical business of the committee. At the Baltic shipyard the works committee had seven commissions, and at the Izhora works ten commissions operated.[31] At the Metal works no less than 28 different commissions existed, involving some 200 workers, in addition to the sixty shop stewards.[32] At the Putilov works, some 400 workers were involved in the commissions of the works committee.

Factory committees dealt with every aspect of life, as an examination of the minutes of any factory committee will reveal. In the first two weeks of its existence the committee at the 1886 Electric Light Company dealt with matters as diverse as food supplies, the factory militia, arbitration of disputes, lunch breaks, overtime and the factory club.[33] In a typical week the committee of the gun shop at Putilov dealt with the hiring of workers, wear-and-tear of machinery, wage-fixing, financial help to individual workers and the experiments of a worker-inventor trying to invent a new kind of shell.[34] Much factory committee business was of a fairly trivial kind. On 28 July the Baltic works committee discussed what to do with a consignment of rotting fish. On 29 September the New Admiralty works committee discussed whether or not to buy scented soap for use in the factory.[35] Precisely because of this concern with the detail of everyday life at the factory, however, the committees were considered by the workers to be 'their' institutions – far closer to them than the unions or the soviets, and consequently more popular. Workers did not hesitate to turn to the committees for help and advice. The wife of a worker at the Sestroretsk arms works turned to the works committee when her husband threw her out, although the committee was unable to do much.[36] Rather than attempt to describe the work of the committees in all its breadth, the rest of this chapter deals with five specific areas in which most factory committees were active.

FACTORY COMMITTEES AND THE ORGANISATION OF
FOOD SUPPLY

One of the most urgent problems facing the factory committees was that of food supply. This had become a growing problem during the war, for since 1914 the area under seed had shrunk owing to the fact that 14 million peasants had been conscripted into the army. In addition, peasants were no longer marketing as much grain, since there were fewer manufactured goods to buy.[37] Moreover the distribution of such grain as was marketed, was hampered by growing disruption of the transport system. In Petrograd grain shortages became particularly acute in the winter of 1916, and this was a major cause of the February Revolution. In the spring of 1917 grain supplies improved, after the Provisional Government established a grain monopoly and set up a State Food Committee and local food committees to organise supplies.[38] By July, however, the food situation in the capital was again grave. By the beginning of August there was only two days' bread supply left in Petrograd. The situation improved as the harvest was brought in, but the harvest was not a particularly good one, and attempts by the government to induce peasants to sell more grain, by doubling fixed prices, had only a limited effect. By the beginning of October, grain supplies were lower than ever; meat stocks were depleted, and livestock was dying off owing to lack of animal-feeds. Sugar, milk and most other staple commodities were in dangerously short supply. To make matters worse, chaos on the transport system was aggravating the food shortages. On 14 October there was only three-and-a-half days' supply of grain left in the capital, yet 13,000 tonnes were stranded on the railways and canals outside the city limits. The food in 1,200 wagons at the Nikolaev railway depot had to be thrown away after it went rotten while waiting to be unloaded.[39]

In 1916, according to data collected by Dr Gordon, the average worker in Petrograd ate between 800 and 1,200 grams of bread each day, 400 grams of potatoes or 200 grams of kasha, a little milk, a few onions and no meat.[40] In February 1917 citizens of the capital were rationed to 500 grams of bread per day, and in summer rationing was extended to a kilo of sugar, 200 grams of buckwheat, 600 grams of fats, 800 grams of meat and 20 eggs per month.[41] There was not enough food in the capital to meet these rations. According to official ration estimates, some 4,000 tonnes of meat were required *each week* in Petrograd, but in the *month* of May only 885 tonnes were delivered. By October the bread ration had been reduced to 300 grams per day and a further reduction to 200 grams was imminent. These rations represented only what people were allowed to buy at official prices, but many could no longer afford to buy food even at fixed prices. Buying food on the open market was out of the question, since food prices had soared into the stratosphere. People were thus competing for an ever-diminishing stock of food, the price of which was rising ever higher. Queues were to be seen everywhere. The Ministry of Internal Affairs noted that queues 'have in fact turned the eight-hour working day into a twelve- or thirteen-hour day, because working-class women and men go straight from the factory or workplace to stand in queues for four or five hours'.[42] The inevitable result was that workers were eating far less. Nationally, Strumilin estimated that the calorie intake of workers was down by 22% on the 1913 level, but in Petrograd things were worse. Binshtok estimated that a worker doing medium to hard work needed more than 3,000 calories a day and that in Petrograd in the summer of 1917 such a worker consumed about half of this amount.[43]

The democratically-elected central and district food committees dealt with the supply of rationed products, but a host of different popular organisations threw themselves into the grim business of staving off hunger. The consumer cooperative movement was less developed in Russia than in western Europe, but it grew rapidly in the course of 1917. In February 1917 there were 23 workers' cooperatives in Petrograd, run mainly by Mensheviks. During 1917 membership grew from 50,000 to 150,000.[44] The worker cooperatives worked closely with district soviets, trade unions and factory committees in procuring food and in organising its distribution. At the Okhta explosives works the committee set up a works canteen to serve 2,500 cheap meals each day; it also ran two shops and a bakery, looked after 80 pigs and a fish-pond and grew potatoes.[45] At the Cable works the food commission of the works committee ran a canteen which produced 1,200 dinners a day.[46] At the Pipe works no fewer than 110 workers were actively involved in procuring and distributing food. In months of particularly acute food-shortage, such as May, July and

October, some factory committees attempted to buy food independently.[47] The Izhora works committee bought fish and potatoes
from local peasants, and the Putilov works committee sent thirty-nine
workers into the countryside to try to purchase food.[48] At the Putilov
works, tension ran particularly high. When meat suddenly
appeared in local restaurants in the Peterhof district, starving
workers from Putilov attacked members of the district cooperative
society and sacked food shops. Only prompt action by the works committee and district soviet prevented the spread of disturbances.[49]

Such initiatives by grass-roots organisations were utterly puny
compared to the colossal scale of the food crisis. This simply got worse
through the winter of 1917–18, until mass starvation drove hundreds
and thousands out of the capital. Nevertheless one day's dinner
meant a great deal to a hungry worker, and the fact that the factory
committees did all in their power to provide such meals, immeasur-
ably enhanced their prestige in the working class.

FACTORY COMMITTEES AND LABOUR DISCIPLINE

The deterioration in the diet of workers was one cause of the decline in
productivity in industry in the course of 1917. By early summer the
gross output of Petrograd Factory industry had fallen dramatically.
This was a consequence largely of the shortages of fuel and raw
materials, partly of the reduction in working hours and partly of a
decline in labour productivity. The causes of the latter were a subject
of sharp dispute. The colossal expansion of output during the war had
placed acute strains on the infrastructure of industry; machinery was
worn out, stocks were depleted, organisation within the enterprise
was breaking down. These were key factors behind the decline in
labour productivity, but it was also abundantly clear that labour
intensity had dropped sharply. Workers were making less effort to
produce, but whether this was because they had less energy, since
they were eating less, or whether it was because they were less
disciplined, was unclear.

As early as March, there were signs that the abolition of punitive
sanctions for infringing workshop regulations was leading to problems of indiscipline among the workforce. In the second week of
March, the 'soviet of workers' deputies' at the Pipe works declared:

We believe that production has declined because many workers, on various
pretexts, are avoiding work and ignoring the instructions of foremen and
others responsible for output.

The soviet declares that it will take every measure against those who neglect their duties, including dismissal. A council of *starosty* is being set up to watch over the course of work, to resolve questions affecting relations between workers and also relations between workers and management ... The council of *starosty* in each shop will act in full accord with the administration of the shop, on whom lies full responsibility for output.[50]

A group of anarchist workers promptly reacted to this statement on 13 March:

The soviet of workers' deputies of the Pipe works, instead of making concrete proposals and raising questions for discussion by the general meeting, issues orders and threatens us with punishment, including the sack, if we do not carry them out ... Formerly, we were slaves of the government and of the bosses, but now there is a new despotic government in the shape of our elected representatives, who, in a touching display of unity with the management, are executing the police task of supervising the conduct and work of the workforce.[51]

In May the mainly SR shop-stewards' committee at the Franco-Russian works rejected management complaints about a deterioration in labour discipline, but promised that its technical-economic commission would investigate. The latter came to the unwelcome conclusion that 'the workers have become undisciplined and do not want to work'. In consequence, the stewards agreed by 61 votes, with none against and four abstentions, to recommend a return to piece-rates.[52]

Absenteeism was a particular problem. A survey by the Ministry of Trade and Industry showed that the turn-out of workers to work in March 1917 was 6.6% below the January level, and 11.4% below in the metal industry.[53]. In January about 10% of the workforce at Putilov were absent for various reasons; by September, this had risen to 25% and by November to 40% of the workforce.[54] In July a general meeting of the gun shop at Putilov condemned certain young workers who were deliberately breaking their machines; the shop committee began to fine and even dismiss workers for slackness or absenteeism.[55] By September, a crisis of labour discipline extended throughout the Putilov works. A Menshevik worker at the plant reported to the district committee of his party:

There is not even a shadow of discipline in the working masses. Thanks to the replacement of professional guards by soldiers, who are not quite familiar with the rules for letting workers in and out of the factory, thefts have become more frequent recently. The number of instances of workers being drunk is also increasing. But what is most terrible, is the sharp fall in the productivity of labour. Just how low this is, is shown, for example, by the fact that formerly 200 gun-carriages were produced each month, but now at most there are 50 to 60. The situation is complicated by purely objective factors, the most important of which is the shortage of fuel and materials, and also the fact that many people of doubtful qualifications have entered the workforce. The Putilov works is in debt to the state to the tune of about 200 million rubles and is hurtling towards the abyss. It is already in a catastrophic state.[56]

The Menshevik district committee, after discussion, passed the following resolution:

(1) Putting aside all party strife, the conscious workers must develop self-discipline in order to give a shining example to the mass of the workforce; (2) Measures must be taken, even of a repressive character, such as imposing fines, in order to eliminate carelessness and an unserious atitude towards work; (3) The introduction of piece-rates must be sought. This latter measure, although contradicting the party programme, is necessary, for the time being, as the only radical measure which will raise productivity.[57]

Factory committees tried to create a moral climate in which workers would voluntarily develop a collective self-discipline at work. They issued countless exhortations to work conscientiously, many of which were coloured by defencist political sentiments in the spring of 1917. At the New Parviainen works, at Putilov, the Franco-Russian works and the Admiralty works general meetings passed resolutions which condemned negligence at work, and called for self-sacrifice in the interests of the revolution.[58] From the first, however, it was clear that ideological exhortation and moral suasion could not by themselves ensure that inexperienced workers, suddenly liberated from despotism, would work assiduously. Certain formal sanctions had to be enforced.

Factory committees drew up new internal regulations and set penalties for infraction of these. Often such penalties were stiff. At the 1886 Electric Light Company the committee announced on 16 March that 'all abuses and individual actions which undermine organisation and disrupt the normal course of work will be punished as follows: such workers will be suspended from work for two weeks and their names will be made known to the workers of Petrograd through the press'.[59] The committee, which had seven Bolshevik, two Menshevik and two SR members, fired a peasant worker on 23 May for absenteeism and drunkenness.[60] At the Nevskaya cotton mill the largely Menshevik committee warned that any worker stopping work before time would be 'punished without mercy'.[61] At the Koenig mill a general meeting on 25 May agreed that 'in order to reduce absenteeism and carelessness, a worker should receive strict censure for a first offence, one ruble fine for a second (the fine to go to a workers' newspaper) and dismissal for a third offence'. After three warnings a woman was sacked for 'bad behaviour'.[62] As the year wore on, more and more factories tightened up labour discipline. On 15 September the Voronin, Lyutsch, and Cheshire cloth-print factory agreed to reintroduce periodic searching of workers in view of the alarming increase in stealing.[63] On 3 October the workers' organisations at Izhora decided that 'every order of the foremen, their assistants and senior workers must be unconditionally carried out ... In all cases of doubt about the validity of an order, you must immediately inform the shop committee, without any arbitrary opposition or resistance to carrying out the order.'[64]

There are several comments to be made on the factory committees' activities in the sphere of labour discipline. In the first place, these activities ill-accord with the image of the committees dominant in the Western literature, which projects them as chaotic, anarchic, elemental organisations hell-bent on undermining capitalist production. Secondly, although in most cases disciplinary measures were agreed by a general meeting of the workforce, and not just by the committees, the latter did have responsibility for implementing disciplinary measures. The committees were dominated by skilled, experienced, relatively well-paid workers who were used to making 'effort bargains' with the employers, even if they were never as committed to the notion of a 'fair day's work for a fair day's pay' as were their British counterparts.[65] The new wartime recruits, in contrast, had no such experience of 'effort bargaining', and it is thus not accidental that problems of indiscipline appear to have been particularly common among women and young workers. In their efforts to inculcate discipline among the less-experienced workers, the committees could easily appear to be a privileged layer of workers dominating the less privileged – a new management to replace the old.

Finally, it was often asserted by enemies of the Bolshevik party that they had 'poisoned the psychology of workers' that workers became 'corrupted by sheer idleness'.[66] In fact, the Bolshevik-dominated factory committees seem to have been just as concerned as committees dominated by moderate socialists to maintain labour productivity – even before October. It is true that in the spring of 1917 some of the concern to uphold discipline was motivated by a political concern to maintain output for the war effort, but Bolshevik opposition to the war did not lead them officially to encourage workers to disrupt production or refuse to work. The difference between the Bolsheviks and the moderate socialists lay in the fact that the Bolsheviks linked demands for labour discipline with demands for workers to have a greater say in production. As Yu. Larin so eloquently put it in the Bolshevik press: 'Whoever talks of the necessity of labour discipline and does not demand workers' control of capitalist enterprises is a hypocrite and a windbag.'[67]

FACTORY COMMITTEES AND THE CAMPAIGN AGAINST DRUNKENNESS

Heavy drinking was deeply rooted in the popular culture of Russia. In the towns, especially, working men tended to spend their few leisure hours drinking. A survey of 1909 revealed that 92% of workers in St Petersburg drank alcohol.[68] In 1908 5.4% of the income of a married male metalworker was spent on drink and tobacco, and single male textile workers spent as much as 11% of their income in this way.[69] Women workers, however, spent hardly anything on alcohol, and married women had to fight hard to prevent their husbands squandering their wages on vodka. Several worker-memoirists recall how wives would stand outside the factory on pay-day in order to catch their husbands before they had a chance to spend their wages at the local bar.[70] During the 1905 Revolution, women textile workers launched the Popular Campaign against Drunkenness in Nevskii district. This initially elicited the scorn of male workers, but soon factory meetings were passing resolutions against vodka.[71] The campaign, along with other temperance campaigns by the Church and middle-class organisations, had few lasting effects.

Although per capita consumption of alcohol was higher in some European countries than in Russia, in the years preceding the First World War (1909–13), consumption in Russia rose steadily.[72] It was partly in response to this, that the government introduced prohibition in 1914. The ban on liquor had an immediate effect, in that the number of registered cases of alcoholism fell by nearly 40%.[73] In Petrograd the sale of wine and beer was forbidden in December 1914, and in 1915 there was a drop in the number arrested for being drunk and disorderly. As the war dragged on, however, and as the diet of workers deteriorated, so the sale of alcoholic substitutes, particularly methylated spirits, increased.[74]

After the February Revolution, alcohol became more freely available. In the first heady months of spring, there seems to have been little public concern about alcohol, but from May contemporaries began to warn of a disturbing increase in heavy drinking. In that month the Executive Committee of the Petrograd Soviet deplored a recent wave of drunkenness.[75] At the Okhta explosives works, concern was expressed at the incidence of drunkenness in the factory, particularly among workers making trotyl.[76] At the Atlas metal works, the committee of *starosty* claimed that insobriety was rife:

They drink methylated spirits, varnish and all kinds of other substitutes. They come to work drunk, speak at meetings, bawl inappropriate exclamations, prevent their more class-conscious comrades from speaking, paralyse organisational work, and the result is chaos in the workshops. Thanks to alcoholism, class-conscious workers are being suffocated; they don't have the strength to work, when every step they take brings them up against some obstacle. But what is more shameful is that some class-conscious, advanced [*peredovye*] workers are now taking part in this vile activity.[77]

Whether there was an objective increase in the scale of drunkenness or simply an increased awareness about the problem is unclear. Certainly all workers' organisations appear to have developed a heightened sensitivity to the problem of working-class insobriety.

On 23 May the Baltic works committee decided that any elected workers' representatives who were found drunk would immediately be relieved of their duties; two promptly were.[78] The Sestroretsk works committee suspended an adjuster in the box shop for drunkenness, and dismissed two workers in the machine shop for stealing two quarts of methylated spirits from the laboratory.[79] Factory committees elsewhere deprived workers of their wages for being drunk, and in serious cases dismissed them.[80] On 10 October the Nevskii district council of factory committees proposed high fines for drunkenness and card-playing, the proceeds of which were to go to orphan children.[81] Trade unions too fought against drunkenness. The conflict commission of the metalworkers' union upheld a decision at the Triangle works to impose fines on workers who appeared drunk at work.[82] The Petrograd Council of Trade Unions ratified the sacking of a worker at the Siemens-Halske works for repeated drunkenness.[83] This tough action by labour organisations cannot have had much effect, however, for the October uprising set off an orgy of mass drunkenness.

The campaigns against drunkenness and labour indiscipline within the labour movement were inspired by a passionate belief that workers should live in a new way now that the old order had been cast aside. At the Nevskaya cotton mill on 20 March, the factory committee appealed to the women workers, who comprised 81% of the workforce, to cease being rude to one another, to stop fighting and quarrelling, stealing and going absent without cause.[84] Such aspirations to live in a new way were fed by the well-springs of the culture of the skilled craftsmen, in particular by deep-rooted notions that work was an honourable 'calling' which conferred dignity and moral value on the worker.[85] On 23 May, for example, a general meeting of the gun shop at the Putilov works decided to dismiss Yakov Smirnov, a worker in the militia who had been caught stealing, 'for bringing into disrepute the calling of the honest worker'.[86] 'Courts of honour' (*sudy chesti*) existed at the Shchetinin aeronautics works and at the State Papers print-works.[87] At the Triangle works, the conciliation chamber had the task of investigating disputes concerning 'honour, morality and personal dignity'. This notion of 'honour' was pivotal to the morality of the skilled craftsmen, and since they dominated the labour movement, it was their morality which set the tone for the working class as a whole. It was partly in an effort to raise the 'mass' to their level, that the leaders of labour organisations established commissions for 'culture and enlightenment'.

FACTORY COMMITTEES AND CULTURAL POLICY

It was axiomatic for all socialists to the right of the Bolshevik party in 1917 that workers did not possess a level of culture adequate to establishing their hegemony throughout society. This was a favourite theme of the Menshevik-Internationalist group headed by Maxim Gorkii, which published the daily newspaper *Novaya Zhizn'*. Gordienko, a moulder at the New Lessner works and treasurer of the Vyborg district soviet, recalled a visit to Gorkii's home in 1917 where he met Sukhanov and Lopata. Gordienko and his workmates began to argue the need for a socialist revolution, at which Lopata pointed out of the window to a group of soldiers sitting on the lawn. 'See how they've been eating herrings and have thrown the bones into the flower-bed. It's with people like them that the Bolsheviks want to make a socialist revolution.'[88] In 1922, Sukhanov reiterated this argument in his *Notes on the Revolution*. Lenin was incensed by the work, commenting:

You say that the creation of socialism demands civilisation. Very well, But why should we not at once create such prerequisites of civilisation amongst ourselves as the expulsion of the landlords and Russian capitalists and then begin the movement towards socialism? In what books have you read that such alterations of the usual historical order are inadmissible or impossible? Remember that Napoleon wrote: 'On s'engage et puis on voit'.[89]

This is precisely the argument which the Bolsheviks put to their critics in 1917, although its reiteration by Lenin in 1923 was less than ingenuous since, by this time, the Bolsheviks had become deeply anxious about the social and political problems posed to the soviet regime by the cultural level of the workers and peasants. Lenin himself constantly complained of the 'semi-asiatic lack of culture, out of which we have not yet pulled ourselves' and 'the piles of work which now face us if we are to achieve on the basis of our proletarian gains even a slight improvement of our cultural level'.[90]

The problem of improving the educational and cultural level of the working class was already a central concern of the new labour organisations in 1917. This concern was expressed in an appeal by the Putilov works committee which called on Putilovtsy to enrol in evening classes:

Let the idea that knowledge is everything sink deep into our consciousness. It is the essence of life and it alone can make sense of life.[91]

Some time later the committee urged:

Questions of culture and enlightenment are now most vital burning questions ... Comrades, do not let slip the opportunity of gaining scientific knowledge. Do not waste a single hour fruitlessly. Every hour is dear to us. We need not only to catch up with the classes with whom we are fighting, but to overtake them. That is life's command, that is where its finger is pointing. We are now the masters of our own lives and so we must become masters of all the weapons of knowledge.[92]

The factory committees were quick to set up 'cultural-enlighten- ment commissions' in March 1917. The activities of these commis- sions covered a wide area. At the Admiralty works the commission took charge of the factory club, renovating its premises and arranging a programme of lectures.[93] At the Baltic works the education commission sponsored theatrical entertainments; arranged for women workers to be given some teaching by women students from the Bestuzhev courses; gave financial help to the apprentices' club and to a school for soldiers and sailors; oversaw the running of the factory club and bought portraits of the pioneers of the labour movement in Russia.[94] At the Sestroretsk works the commission gave the house and garden of the former director to local children as a kindergarten, reorganised the technical school and forbade apprentices to leave it before they had completed their technical education.[95] At the New Parviainen works the factory committee sponsored poetry readings by Ivan Loginov, an accomplished worker-poet.[96] At the Metal works the committee sponsored a wind band, a string orchestra and a band of folk instruments.[97] At Rosenkrantz, management gave the committee 10,000 rubles towards the cost of a school; here Olga Stetskaya ran a literacy class, where she taught workers to read by writing Bolshevik slogans on the blackboard in big letters.[98]

One of the areas in which factory committees, trade unions and political parties were particularly active was in setting up workers' clubs. Such clubs had arisen in St Petersburg during the 1905 Revolution, and about twenty were in sporadic existence between 1907 and 1914, catering mainly for young, single, skilled and reasonably educated men.[99] During the war most of these clubs closed down. After the February Revolution, managements at the Phoenix and Erikson works gave large donations towards re-establishing them.[100] On 19 March, workers at Putilov founded a club with a small library and buffet. Soon it had 2,000 members and a management committee, comprising Bolsheviks, Mensheviks and SRs. The club defined its aim as to 'unite and develop the working-class public in a socialist spirit, to which end are necessary general knowledge and general development, resting on basic literacy and culture'.[101] On Vasilevskii Island a club named New Dawn was founded in March which soon had 800 members. As well as lectures, the club organised a geographical expedition to Sablino, a steamer excursion to Shlissel'burg for 900 people, a brass band concert and an entertainment for workers at the Pipe works.[102] The opening ceremony to inaugurate the Gun works club consisted of a recital by workers of arias from Mussorgsky operas and a performance by the works band of the Internationale and the Marseillaise. The club housed a library of 4,000 books, a reading room, a small theatre and a school. Evening classes were held in literacy, legal affairs, natural sciences and mathematics.[103] By the end of 1917, there were over thirty clubs in Petrograd, including ones for postal-workers, tram-workers, Polish workers and Latvian workers.[104]

Workers' clubs had sponsored amateur dramatic societies among the workers of St Petersburg prior to 1914. These staged plays by Ostrovskii, Tolstoy, Gogol, Hauptmann and lesser-known playwrights. Workers liked realistic plays about everyday life, with which they could identify directly. They disliked religious or didactic plays, plays about peasant life, fantasy or foreign plays.[105]. After the February Revolution working-class theatre took on a new lease of life. At Putilov the works committee took over the factory theatre, formerly in the charge of the administration.[106] In Sestroretsk local workers staged *Hamlet*, Shaw's *Candida* and a play by Maeterlinck, but Larissa Reisner, later famous for exploits in the Red Army, lived in Sestroretsk at the time and complained about the number of crude, tendentious 'class' plays which they performed.[107]

A rather cheerless moralism infected some of the cultural work of the labour movement. Such work aspired to the noble purpose of developing class consciousness and political awareness, not to entertain. The theatre group at the Nobel works, for example, defined its aim thus:

We exist not to amuse [*razvlechenie*] but to foster spiritual growth, to enrich consciousness ... to unite individual personalities into one gigantic class personality. All that does not serve the development of Humanity is vain and empty. We want theatre to become life, so that in time life will become theatre.[108]

There was a widespread belief within the labour movement that education and amusement were mutually exclusive. Within the youth movement, for example, there was a fierce battle between the non-party *Labour and Light* group, whose 3,000 members went in for dances and shows, interspersed with educational events,[109] and the Union of Socialist Working Youth, whose zealots scorned the '*tantsul'ki*', and defined their aim as 'the preparation of developed, educated fighters for socialism'.[110] A similar conflict occurred in the workers' clubs, which tended to shun frivolous pursuits in favour of political meetings and lectures. The Putilov works club held eight lectures in the first three months of its existence on such themes as 'The Constituent Assembly', 'On Socialism', 'On Cooperation' and 'The Trade Unions and War'.[111] These proved to be very popular, attracting an average audience of 710, but more and more complaints were heard that workers, especially women, were sick of an unrelieved diet of politics, and wanted more entertainment, sporting activities and events for children.[112] Such murmurings of discontent were articulated by Mensheviks at the first proletkult conference, 16–19

October; they were denounced by the proletarian puritans for seeking to divert workers from the struggle for power.[113]

Related to this conflict was a conflict between those who saw working-class education as politically neutral – mainly moderate socialists – and those who saw education as geared to the objective of socialist revolution. On 19 July representatives from 120 factory committees met members of the agitation collective of the Petrograd Soviet to discuss educational work. A Menshevik member of the collective, Dement'ev, criticised political meetings as a means of education, arguing that they merely served to inflame the passions of workers. Factory committee representatives were furious at this, and the resolution passed by the meeting proclaimed that 'the cultural enlightenment activity of the factory committees must be revolution-ary-socialist and must be directed towards developing the class consciousness of the proletariat'.[114] One can perhaps here detect the seeds of the later Civil War controversy between those, like Lenin, who argued that 'we must take the entire culture that capitalism has left behind and build socialism with it',[115] and the advocates of Proletkult, who argued that bourgeois culture could not simply be 'adopted' or 'acquired' by the proletariat, but had to be rejected or radically reworked as part of the development of new, proletarian culture.[116]

FACTORY MILITIAS AND RED GUARDS

The February Revolution witnessed the whole-scale dismantling of the repressive apparatuses of the tsarist state. Police stations and prisons were burnt to the ground; up to 40,000 rifles and 30,000 revolvers were seized.[117] The overturned police force was replaced by two rival militias – a civil militia, organised into district and sub-district commissariats, and a workers' militia, brought into being by groups of factory workers. Between 28 February and 1 March workers of Rozenkrantz, Metal works, Phoenix, Arsenal and other factories formed the first Vyborg commissariat of the workers' militia.[118] In the Harbour district of Vasilevskii Island the Cable works committee at its first meeting on 1 March agreed to set up a militia, 'for now the people itself must protect the locality'. It asked for 270 volunteers over the age of 18, including women, to serve in the militia.[119] Throughout the factories of Petrograd, workers were elected or volunteered to serve in these militias in order to maintain law and order in the locality, protect life and property and register inhabitants.[120] The factory committees established militia commissions and appointed commissars to oversee the militiamen. The latter did not leave their jobs permanently to serve in the local workers' militia, but served according to a rota drawn up by the factory militia commission. At the Metal works 470 workers served in the Vyborg workers' militia between March and July, but only ten served for the whole period.[121] At the Arsenal, Cartridge, Radio-Telegraph, Siemens-Schuckert and Siemens-Halske works, factory committees lost no time in demanding that management pay workers serving in the militia at the average wage.[122] Reluctantly, most employers agreed to do so.

From the first, there was rivalry between the workers' militias and the civil militias, which were subject to the municipal dumas. On 7 March, the Soviet Executive Committee decided that the workers' militias should be absorbed into the civil militia.[123] Only the Bolsheviks denounced this decision, but they echoed the feelings of many workers at the grass roots.[124] The Cable workers declared: 'This attack [on the workers' militias], begun by the bourgeois municipal duma, provokes our deep protest. We suggest that at the present time, when the democracy is faced with a struggle for a democratic republic and a struggle against the vestiges of tsarism and the constitutional-monarchist aspirations of the bourgeoisie, the workers' militia should be placed at the head of the popular civil [*obyvatel'skoi*] militia.'[125]

In areas where strong commissariats of the workers' militia existed, they managed to resist absorption into the civil militia. At the end of March some 10,000 militiamen, out of a total of 20,000, were organised into specifically workers' militias.[126] As the civil militia came to control most districts of Petrograd, however, increasing pressure was put on the workers' militias to dissolve. The city and district dumas urged factory owners to stop paying the wages of militiamen, in order to force them to become full-time militiamen employed by the local authority (at much lower rates of pay than they were getting in the factories) or to go back to their jobs in the factories. This campaign seems to have had some success, for by the end of May there were only 2,000 workers left in exclusively workers' militias.[127] In the same period, however, the number of civil militia fell from 20,000 to 6,000, so members of the workers' militias still comprised about a third of the total.

On 27 May a conference of Petrograd workers' militias took place

which heaped obloquy on the Soviet Executive Committee and the
municipal dumas for their efforts to integrate the workers' militias
into the civil militia. The conference claimed that they intended to
impose on the populace 'a police force of the Western-European type
which is hated throughout the world by the majority of the people, the
poorer classes'.[128] The conference agreed to Bolshevik proposals for
the reorganisation of the workers' militia 'as a transitional stage
towards the general arming of the whole population of Petrograd'.[129]
Many factory committees came out in support of the decisions of the
conference, insisting that employers continue to pay the wages of the
workers' militias. These included committees consisting mainly of
Mensheviks and SRs, such as those at the Baltic and Admiralty
works.[130]

From the first, there were tiny armed groups of workers, calling
themselves 'Red Guards,' who differed somewhat from the workers'
militias, in that they saw their function as exclusively to protect the
gains of the revolution.[131] On 17 April a meeting of worker militiamen
elected a commission, made up of two Bolsheviks and three Mensheviks, to draw up a constitution for a city-wide organisation of Red
Guards. This commission explained that the Red Guard would be 'a
threat to all counter-revolutionary attempts from whatever quarter,
since only the armed working class can be the real defender of the
freedom which we have won'.[132] Certain factory committees also
called for the setting-up of factory Red Guards. On 16 April the
Renault metalworkers, in one of the first resolutions calling for a
soviet government, demanded 'the organisation of a Red Guard and
the arming of the whole people'.[133] On 22 April 6,000 workers at the
Skorokhod shoe factory declared: 'Dark forces ... threaten to
encroach on the foundation of free Russia. Since we wish to protect
the interests of the toiling masses, as well as general state interests
(which can only be defended by the people themselves), we declare
that we will call on the Soviet to assist us in obtaining arms to organise
a Popular Red Guard of 1,000 people.'[134] Red Guards were set up at
the New and Old Lessner, Erikson, Aivaz and New Parviainen works,
i.e. in that minority of factories where Bolshevik strength was already
great.

On 26 April the Peterhof district soviet called on workers to enrol in
the Red Guards, but warned: 'Only the flower of the working class
may join. We must have a guarantee that no unworthy or wavering
people enter its ranks. Everyone wishing to enrol in the Red Guard

must be recommended by the district committee of a socialist party.'[135] Two days later, the Vyborg district soviet announced that it intended to transform the two district workers' militias into a Red Guard, whose tasks would be:

(a) to struggle against counter-revolutionary, antipopular intrigues by the ruling class;
(b) to defend, with weapons in hand, all the gains of the working class;
(c) to protect the life, safety and property of all citizens without distinction of sex, age or nationality.[136]

On 28 April 156 delegates from 90 factories, most of whom belonged to no political party, attended a conference to discuss further the creation of a Red Guard.[137] The Soviet Executive condemned the conference as a 'direct threat to the unity of the revolutionary forces'. The Mensheviks blamed it on agitation by 'Leninists' and said that the attempt to create Red Guards revealed a deplorable lack of confidence in the army.[138]

Although the number of Red Guards may have grown slightly during May and June, the Soviet Executive successfully blocked plans for the creation of a city-wide network of Red Guards.[139] Because of the political difficulties involved in openly organising Red Guards, the radicals appear to have rechannelled their energies into the workers' militias. On 3 June the second conference of workers' militias elected a Council of the Petrograd Popular Militia. This consisted of eleven members, including an anarchist chairman, seven Bolsheviks and at least one Left SR.[140] It was this Council, rather than the embryonic Red Guards, which played a key role in events leading up to the July Days – the attempted uprising against the Kerensky government by workers and soldiers. On 21 June the Council hastily summoned a meeting of workers' militias to discuss the ejection of anarchists from Durnovo villa, two days previously. The meeting fiercely denounced the role played by the civil militia in this incident and resolved to 'defend the elective basis of the popular militia of revolutionary workers and soldiers by every means, up to and including armed action'.[141] Over the next couple of weeks the Council whipped up a furore among the workers of Vyborg Side at the purportedly anti-democratic and counter-revolutionary activities of the municipal dumas, arguing that 'a blow against the militias is a blow against the revolution'. In agitating for an armed demonstration against the government at the beginning of July, the Bolsheviks on the Council acted quite outside the control of the party Central Com-

mittee. The Red Guards as such kept a low profile during the July
Days.

The fiasco in which the July Days ended provided the government
with the opportunity for which it had been waiting. It took action
against the far left, extirpating not only the Council of the Popular
Militia, but all the remaining independent workers' militias. The
factory committees were compelled to recall all workers serving in
such militias and force them to choose between going back to their
benches or enrolling in the civil militia for a paltry salary of 150 r. a
month.[142] The July Days thus spelt the end of the workers' militias,
after an adventurous five months' existence.

The workers' militias were a major achievement of the February
Revolution, which guaranteed workers' power in the factories and in
society at large. Workers, in general, never accepted that there were
'bourgeois' limitations on the February Revolution. For them it was a
popular-democratic revolution, which was potentially threatened by
the bourgeoisie. It was crucial that workers organise independently to
defend the democratic gains of the revolution, and it was thus
inconceivable that the workers' militias should be absorbed into a
civil militia under the control of the middle classes. The experience of
the militias illustrates the impossibility of drawing neat distinctions
between the military, economic or political 'aspects' of the workers'
movement. The militias were closely linked to the factory committees
and underpinned workers' power in production. Later, the campaign
to establish Red Guards became intimately bound with the campaign
to establish workers' control of production: the armed workers'
movement represented not only the defence of workers' control of
production, but an attempt to extend workers' control into the public
sphere. Fundamentally, it was the experience of trying to impose
workers' 'control' over the gains of the February Revolution which,
perhaps more than anything else, served to radicalise the politically
conscious minority of workers. The shock of seeing the Soviet
Executive trying to bring an end to the independent existence of the
workers' militias shattered their faith in the moderate socialists, for it
was seen as tantamount to sabotaging the gains of February.
Conversely, it was the Bolsheviks' willingness to support the militias
and workers' control in production which won them growing support.

5

Trade unions and the betterment of wages

CRAFT UNIONISM AND INDUSTRIAL UNIONISM

Trade unionism in Russia was a very different animal from trade unionism in the West. There the organised labour movement was more powerful than in Russia – in terms of membership, organisational resources, industrial muscle and political influence – but a by-product of the strength of the Western labour movement had been the emergence of a bureaucratic leadership which, to some extent, stood as an obstacle to working-class militancy. As early as 1911, Robert Michels had analysed the apparently inexorable tendency for a conservative oligarchy to emerge in both socialist parties and trade unions, as a function of increasing size and organisational complexity, but it was only with the outbreak of war in 1914 that the full implications of this development were revealed.[1] In return for the accolade of government recognition, Western European union leaders abandoned any pretensions to transforming society, and agreed to support their government's policy of *Burgfrieden*, or civil peace. They thereby subordinated the interests of the working class to the higher interests of the *Union Sacrée*.

In Russia trade unionism emerged out of the 1905 Revolution. The first proper trade union to be founded in Russia was the Moscow printers' union, set up illegally in 1903. Between 1906 and 1907 trade unions flourished, but during the 'Years of Reaction' they came in for considerable persecution. They revived again in the years 1912–14, but the outbreak of war again led to their suppression.[2] In March 1917, therefore, labour leaders faced the enormous task of constructing a trade-union movement more or less from scratch; paradoxically, this was to work to the advantage of revolutionary socialists. In

Germany and Italy, when semi-revolutionary situations emerged in
1918–19 and 1919–20, the trade-union and socialist leaders were so
inured to the gradualist pursuit of improvement within the existing
system, that they proved constitutionally incapable of heading the
insurrectionary popular movements, and instead played a crucial role
in restabilising the bourgeois order.[3] In Russia, however, the absence
of an entrenched labour bureaucracy enormously facilitated the
development of a revolutionary socialist labour movement.

In February 1917 eleven unions maintained a shadowy existence in
the Petrograd underground: they were tiny, illegal and much subject
to the depredations of the police. A further three unions – of printing
employees, pharmacy employees and shop assistants – existed
legally, but were as tiny as the illegal unions and almost as
ineffective.[4] After the February Revolution trade unions quickly
re-established themselves. In the first two weeks of March about
thirty were refounded. Militants who had been active in the earlier
periods of union construction of 1905–8 and 1912–14 called meetings
of workers in different industries to re-form the unions, which were
advertised in the socialist press. On 11 March a thousand textileworkers assembled to elect twenty representatives (half of them
women) to take on the task of reconstructing the union.[5] The next day
nearly 2,000 metalworkers met to elect an organisation commission,
to which mainly Mensheviks were elected.[6] Workers in small enterprises had to band together in order to form a group large enough to
elect a deputy to the soviet and, in so doing, they used the occasion to
resuscitate a trade union. This was one reason why the first unions to
get off the ground were those in small-workshop industries, such as
tailoring, hairdressing, gold-, silver- and bronze-smithery and
joinery.[7] In the larger factory industries factory committees initially
promoted workers' interests, and it was thus a couple of months
before the larger industrial unions began to function properly.

The metalworkers' union was particularly slow to get off the
ground. It did not function on a city-wide basis until the middle of
April. Prior to this, metalworkers' unions functioned at district level.
The Bolsheviks organised a union in Narva district, which had 11,000
members by the end of April, and all but one of the district board were
Bolsheviks. Mensheviks set up the Vyborg district union, which by
the end of April had 5,000 members, and they were balanced equally
with the Bolsheviks on the district board. Mensheviks dominated the
Moscow-district union, which had 7,500 members; SRs dominated

the Nevskii district board. Bolsheviks were instrumental in organising unions in Petrograd district, the First and Second City districts, Kolpino and Sestroretsk. By the time the different districts amalgamated into a city union they had 50,000 members.[8] The slowness of the metalworkers to organise at a city level was principally a function of size, reflecting the difficulties of organising so vast an industry. It seems, however, to have also reflected a certain 'district patriotism', which had been something of a problem in 1905, when it had taken until April 1906 to weld the district unions of metalworkers in St Petersburg into a city-wide organisation. This preference for organising on a district, rather than city basis, seems to have arisen from a distrust of trade-union bureaucracy.[9]

From the beginning of May the major unions of factory workers in Petrograd grew spectacularly. According to figures published in 1928, which are almost certainly exaggerated,[10] the membership of the major factory-based unions in Petrograd was as follows:

Table 12

Union	Membership on 1 July 1917	Membership on 1 October 1917
Metalworkers	82,000	190,000 (140,000)
Textileworkers	28,000	32,000 (32,658)
Printers	–	25,328 (25,100)
Paperworkers	–	6,400 (5,200)
Cardboardmakers	–	2,000 (3,100)
Woodworkers	15,000	20,500 (20,500)
Leatherworkers	15,750	16,708 (16,708)
Foodworkers	–	13,000 (13,250)
Tobaccoworkers	–	14,000 (14,000)
Chemicalworkers	–	- (17,200)

Source: Professional'noe dvizhenie v Petrograde v 1917g. (Leningrad, 1928), pp.341–3. The figures in brackets in column three are the official Ministry of Labour figures for Petrograd membership on 1 October 1917. See *Delo Naroda*, 174, 7 October 1917, p.4 and *Professional'nyi Vestnik*, 3/4, 15 October 1917, p.21. I have not used the table in Stepanov, *Rabochie Petrograda*, p.50, as his figures seem to be altogether too high.

By October there was a total trade-union membership of about 390,000 in Petrograd, including non-factory workers such as shop-

workers, catering workers, postal and railroad workers. Throughout
Russia as a whole there were about two million trade-union members
– about 10% of wage-earners of all kinds.[11]

In Britain and the USA in the nineteenth century, craft unions had
proved to be the dominant form of trade-union organisation.[12] They
developed out of the collapse of broader-based unions, such as the
General National and Consolidated Trade Union in Britain and the
Knights of Labor in America.[13] These craft unions were exclusive
unions of skilled men, which tended to ignore the needs of the mass of
factory workers, many of whom were women and children in the
textile industry. In the last two decades of the nineteenth century
trade unionism had begun to expand in France and Germany. Here
industrial unionism proved more resilient. Although the CGT in
France and the Free Unions in Germany were still dominated by
coalitions of skilled trades, they were more easily able to incorporate
factory workers than their Anglo-American counterparts.[14] It was
partly with an eye to this experience, that trade-union leaders in
Russia chose industrial, rather than craft forms of organisation,
though in a context where industry was dominated by factory
production, rather than small-workshop production, industrial
unionism made obvious sense. Although Russian trade unions
recruited mainly skilled and artisanal workers in 1905, by 1912–14
they were beginning to attract broader layers of factory workers.[15]
Nevertheless craft unionism was by no means a superannuated force
in Russia by 1917.

After the February Revolution workers began by building local and
craft unions. In the metal and allied trades over twenty such unions
appeared in March, but few lasted very long.[16] Many of them were
based on workers in small enterprises, and were quickly absorbed into
the metalworkers' union. Unions of foundryworkers, machinists and
electricians persisted for several months, but amalgamated with the
metalworkers' union before October. Other craft unions resisted
absorption by the metal union.

In April stokers from the Metal, Rozenkrantz and Phoenix works
formed a union, on the grounds that 'we are weaker than other
masterovye, despite doing one of the most severe, strenuous and
responsible jobs'.[17] On 18 September a meeting was held to discuss a
merger with the metalworkers' union, but this proved abortive since
the stokers' union would not accept the metalworkers' collective
contract. It informed the Petrograd Council of Trade Unions that:

'The metalworkers' union mistakenly stands for a narrow production principle, which the Society of Factory and Works Owners exploits in order to weaken the organisational work of Petrograd trade unions.'[18] The stokers argued that theirs was a growing profession, that many of their members were outside manufacturing industry and that to join the metalworkers' union, where there was no independence for each craft, would be 'suicide'. It did not fuse until August 1918.[19]

On 30 April a union of welders was formed, which had a mere 700 members by October, but which proved to be a thorn in the side of the metalworkers' union leadership. Writing in the union journal, A. Shlyapnikov, the Bolshevik chairman of the union, warned of the dangers of craft unionism and cited the example of the Gruntal workshop, where eight welders had joined the welders' union, put forward a wage demand, and then left the factory when it had been refused; thereupon the owner had fired the rest of the workforce, who had never been consulted about the welders' action.[20] The welders' union paid scant regard to the veiled threats of Shlyapnikov, not joining the metalworkers' union until 1918. Other unions, such as those of gold- and silversmiths (1,300 members in October) and watchmakers (360 members) continued in existence until 1918.[21]

In the first phase of its existence, from 1906–8, the metalworkers' union had helped contain pressures towards craft unionism by allowing different trades to set up professional sections within the union, which met separately, but which were represented on and subordinate to the central board of the union.[22] At the first city-wide meeting of factory delegates, which met on 7 May 1917 to elect a central board to the metalworkers' union, the 535 delegates rejected a proposal to set up professional sections within the union.[23] This suggests that it was not merely the leaders of the union who rejected concessions to craft unionism, but that there was at base growing sentiment in favour of industrial unionism.[24]

The Third Trade Union Conference (20–8 June) – the first national conference of trade unions in 1917 – declared in favour of industrial unions. There was pressure from some quarters for 'trade' unions, but Mensheviks and Bolsheviks united to quash this. The resolution accepted by conference declared that unions should be constructed according to branch of industry, and that all workers who worked in the same branch of industry should join the same union, regardless of the job they did.[25]

The only major union to reject the policy of industrial unionism was the woodturners' union – a 'trade union', rather than a strict craft union. By October it had 20,000 members which made it the seventh largest union in the capital.[26] Only a third of its members worked in woodworking factories and joinery enterprises; the rest worked as carpenters and joiners in other industries. In spite of its rampant Bolshevism, the woodturners' union refused to allow woodturners to join the union of the industry in which they worked. On 8 May a delegate council of the union rejected a plea to this effect from the metalworkers' union.[27] At the Okhta powder-works woodturners refused the tariff category into which the chemical workers tried to put them, and at Putilov carpenters and wood machinists objected to being placed in category three of the metalworkers' contract. On 1 August the woodturners' union put a wage contract to the SFWO, which turned it down.[28] Six days later a meeting of 57 factory delegates, having denounced the Kerensky government for imprisoning Bolsheviks, passed the following resolution: 'Every regenerated organisation, if it is to establish its work at the necessary level, must insist, when working out a contract, that one trade is not competent to determine the wages of another.'[29] After two months of abortive negotiation with the employers, the union decided to prepare for a strike. On 12 October it issued a statement saying that a strike would begin four days later, since 'at present the union does not have the wherewithal to restrain desperate workers from protests and excesses.'[30] At the Putilov works woodworkers had already gone on a go-slow in protest at the refusal of management to negotiate with them separately. The Executive of the Petrograd Council of Trade Unions agreed to support the strike on condition that it involve only enterprises where woodworkers comprised a majority of the workforce.[31] A day after the strike had begun, however, an angry meeting of 8,000 woodworkers rejected this stipulation, calling on all woodworkers to join the strike.[32] This call was condemned by Shlyapnikov since it disrupted normal working in hundreds of factories not connected with the wood industry. The strikers rejected charges of causing disorganisation and appear to have won reluctant support from other groups of workers. At the Baltic works and the Okhta explosives works factory committees refused to allow the carrying-out of work normally done by woodturners and called for pressure to be put on the employers to compromise.[33] The strike was still going on when the October Revolution supervened and, on 28 October, it was called off.[34]

Craft unionism was therefore by no means a spent force in 1917, but its strength was not great, if one compares Russia to other countries. By October 1917, Petrograd had one of the highest levels of unionisation in the world, and at least 90% of trade unionists in the city were members of industrial unions. Measured against this achievement, craft unionism must be counted a failure. This failure was partly due to the fact that the guild tradition had never been powerful in Russia, whereas in Western Europe craft unions were heirs to a vital guild 'tradition'.[35] More importantly, however, craft unionism and trade unionism were not suited to an industrial environment where the majority of wage-earners worked in modern factories. Even the skilled craftsmen in these factories were not of the same type as those who had formed the 'new model' unions in Britain after the demise of Chartism. They therefore tended to see their interests as being best defended in alliance with less skilled factory workers, rather than in isolation from them. We shall see that sectional pressures of all kinds existed within the Russian labour movement in 1917 and were a force to be reckoned with, but they did not seriously endanger the project of industrial unionism.

THE POLITICAL COMPOSITION OF THE TRADE UNIONS

Soviet historians are fond of depicting political conflict within the trade unions in 1917 as a straight fight between reformist, economistic Mensheviks and militant, revolutionary Bolsheviks. In reality the political history of the Petrograd trade unions was more complex than this manichaean interpretation allows. Before analysing this history in detail, it is worth pointing out that the political centre of gravity of the Russian labour movement was far to the left of that of most Western labour movements. Prior to 1917 attempts to promote reformism in the labour movement had been made by intellectuals (the 'Economists', led by S.N. Prokopovich and E.D. Kuskova), by the government (the Zubatov and Gapon unions) and by workers themselves (the *Workers of Russia's Manchester* in 1899, the Moscow printers in 1903, the *Workers Voice* group in St Petersburg in 1905 and the *Union of Workers for the Defence of their Rights* in Khar'kov in the same year). These attempts at home-grown reformism never got very far, however, for the simple reason that even the most 'bread and butter' trade union struggles foundered on the rock of the tsarist state; all efforts to separate trade unionism from politics were rendered nugatory by the action of police and troops.[36] In this political climate trade unions grew up fully conscious of the fact that the overthrow of the autocracy was a basic precondition for the improvement of the workers' lot. It is true that there was a powerful moderating tendency in the trade unions, represented by right-wing Mensheviks such as those involved in the Workers' Group of the War Industries Committee, but even this tendency was verbally committed to a brand of socialist trade unionism which would have seemed dangerously radical to the 'business' unionists of the AFL in the USA, or the Liberals of the British TUC. It is thus important to bear in mind, when analysing the conflict between 'left' and 'right' in the Russian unions in 1917, that even the 'right' was fairly radical by Western standards, since it was committed to socialism – albeit at some indefinite time in the future.

The approach to trade unionism of the two major political parties within the unions in 1917 sprang from their respective diagnoses and prognoses of the political situation in Russia. The Mensheviks believed that Russia was in the throes of a bourgeois revolution, and that therefore the unions should raise demands for the maximum democratisation of the social and political system.[37] They did not believe in the political 'neutrality' of the unions (they were on the side of 'democracy' and 'socialism') but nor did they believe that the unions should take up positions on particular questions, such as the demand for all power to the soviets. In contrast, the Bolshevik position was summarised in the resolution on the party and trade unions, passed by the Sixth Bolshevik party Congress in August:

The epoch of world war has inevitably become the epoch of sharpening class struggles. The working class is entering a terrain with vast social horizons, which culminate in world socialist revolution. The trade unions are faced with the completely practical task of leading the proletariat in this mighty battle. Together with the political organisation of the working class, the trade unions must repudiate a neutral stance towards the issues on which the fate of the world labour movement now hangs. In the historic quarrel between 'internationalism' and 'defencism' the trade-union movement must stand decisively and unwaveringly on the side of revolutionary internationalism.[38]

In Petrograd a conflict between these two perspectives took place on the Petrograd Council of Trade Unions. On 15 March the foundations were laid for what became the Central Bureau of the Petrograd Council of Trade Unions, when eighteen representatives from different unions met together. Five days later, an executive committee was elected, which comprised four Bolsheviks (V.V. Schmidt, Razumov, D. Antoshkin, N.I. Lebedev), four Mensheviks (V.D. Rubtsov, I. Volkov, Acheev, G. Gonikberg) and the syndicalist, A. Gastev.[39] The Central Bureau subsequently formalised its structure, changing its name to the Petrograd Council of Trade Unions (PCTU). All unions in Petrograd were invited to send representatives to the Council, according to their size. Until June thirty unions were represented. This later rose to fifty and subsequently to over seventy. Only 'working-class' unions were allowed onto the Council, so unions of workers not considered to be proletarian, such as musicians, writers and theatre employees, were excluded.[40]

According to its constitution, drawn up in May, the powers of the PCTU were coordinative rather than directive. The Council did not have the right to manage or intervene in the affairs of a member union, but in practice it sometimes did this, for example, by encouraging industrial unionism or by helping consolidate union structure. In spite of its self-denying ordinance, the PCTU also intervened in specific economic disputes, by giving advice, publicity or financial help. The range of issues on which the PCTU gave a lead to individual unions is shown by the following statistics. Between March and December the Executive Committee of the PCTU discussed 21 items of a political nature, 101 concerning organisational construction, 26 concerning representation, 10 concerning education, 8 concerning unemployment and 25 miscellaneous items. The 30 plenary sessions of the PCTU discussed 29 matters of a political nature, 26 concerning organisational construction, 14 concerning economic struggles, 4 concerning representation, 3 concerning unemployment, 3 concerning education and 5 miscellaneous items.[41]

The vast bulk of PCTU business was practical and did not incite party conflict. Unlike trade unions in the West, however, the Russian trade unions were vitally interested in political questions. As politics became more polarised in Russian society, so political acrimony between Bolsheviks and Mensheviks on the PCTU increased. The first sign of this came on 1 May, during discussions on the constitution. The Bolsheviks insisted on a sentence about 'coordinating the actions of the unions with the political party of the proletariat'. The Mensheviks demanded that the word 'party' be in the plural. When the matter was put to the vote, they lost by 17 votes to 9.[42] By May the Bolsheviks could command a majority on the PCTU, by getting the support of independents like the *Mezhraionets*, D.B.

Ryazanov, who joined the party in August, and some of the
Menshevik Internationalists.[43] In the May elections to the Executive
Committee, the Bolsheviks won a majority and at the end of the
month the PCTU passed a resolution calling for the transfer of power
to the Soviets. By the beginning of June the Bolsheviks were the
strongest party on the PCTU, but they did not wield supremacy on
this body as they did on the Central Council of Factory Committees,
for the presence of a strong group of Menshevik Internationalists, on
whom the Bolsheviks relied for support, together with disagreement
among the Bolsheviks themselves, meant that the political line of the
PCTU was not always clear-cut. For example, the PCTU supported
the demonstration called by the Soviet EC for 18 June, but it was
taken aback by the Bolshevik success in making this a show of
opposition to the policies of the Soviet EC. Whereas factory
committees busily organised contingents from the factories to march
under Bolshevik banners, only odd unions, such as the needleworkers, strove to mobilise their membership. During the July Days
the PCTU was completely isolated from the abortive insurrection by
workers and soldiers. On 6 July the PCTU met with the Central
Council of Factory Committees (CCFC) and the boards of the major
unions. Trotsky attended this meeting and vigorously castigated the
Soviet leaders for creating the disillusionment in the masses which
had issued forth in the July Days; he called on the meeting to refuse
any kind of support to the Kerensky government. Ryazanov was less
certain: he argued that the new Coalition government could win back
the support of the masses if it undertook bold measures. For two days
no consensus was reached.[44] The final resolution, proposed by three
Bolsheviks (Schmidt, N.A. Skrypnik and N.M. Antselovich),
Ryazanov and two Mensheviks (Astrov and Volkov), was passed
unanimously with four abstentions. It was a milk-and-water affair,
bearing all the hallmarks of compromise and making no mention of a
transfer of power to the Soviets – the main aim of the July
demonstrations.[45]

During the Kornilov crisis at the end of August, when General
Kornilov attempted to overthrow Kerensky and crush the soviets, the
PCTU worked in a more resolute fashion than hitherto. On 26 August
a joint meeting of the PCTU and the CCFC passed a motion on the
defence of Petrograd, introduced by A. Lozovskii, which called for a
workers' militia, an end to the persecution of political leaders,
control of military units, public eating places, an end to queueing and

a programme of public works to minimise unemployment.[46] The next day the joint meeting demanded that the government proclaim a republic, institute workers' control of production and fight the counter-revolution. On 29 August the two organisations threw themselves into the task of arming workers, organising defences around the city centre, and setting up patrols to guard the city centre, as news of Kornilov's advance on the capital filtered through.[47] The PCTU put 50,000 r. at the disposal of the military centres, and the unions of food workers and woodturners also provided help.[48]

This survey of the political history of the PCTU shows that the picture which is sometimes painted of a Menshevik-dominated trade-union movement counterposed to a Bolshevik-dominated factory-committee movement does not correspond to reality, at least in Petrograd. Nationally, and in cities like Moscow, the Mensheviks did enjoy more influence than the Bolsheviks inside the unions, but in Petrograd this was not so. As early as June the Bolsheviks, with the support of Menshevik-Internationalists, could ensure that the political line of the PCTU was considerably to the left of that of the Soviet EC. Yet because of this reliance on Menshevik-Internationalists, political positions were usually arrived at by a process of compromise. On some of the most controversial questions of the day – such as the call for a transfer of power to the soviets – the unions were unable to adopt a firm stance. Thus Bolshevik influence in the unions was far less certain than in the factory committees. The great bulk of trade-union business, however, did not involve politics directly, and so on a day-to-day basis Bolsheviks and Mensheviks worked together quite happily.

On the boards of most major trade unions in Petrograd the Bolsheviks held a majority of places. The political make-up of these central boards was not necessarily a reflection of the political sympathies of the membership, for they were not elected directly by the membership, as were factory committees. Nevertheless the balance of political forces within the union boards does give an indication of the strength of the main political parties within the union movement as a whole.

On the board of the Petrograd metalworkers' union Bolsheviks had a slight majority of places but Mensheviks comprised a large minority, mainly due to the prestige of the individual Mensheviks concerned, rather than because of significant support for their politics amongst the rank-and-file.[49] On the district boards, directly elected by factory delegates, Bolsheviks had more influence than their rivals. They dominated the boards of the Narva, the Petrograd, the I and II City, the Sestroretsk and the Kolpino districts of the capital. In Vyborg and Vasilevskii districts they still shared power with a Menshevik minority. Mensheviks were strong only in the Moscow district (mainly due to their influence at the Dynamo works) and the SRs were significant only in Nevskii district. SRs, generally, were a minor influence in the metal union, most of their industrial members channelling their energies into the factory committees.[50] Menshevik influence in the union began to wane in the autumn of 1917, and at the first national congress of the union in January 1918, 75 delegates were Bolsheviks, 51 belonged to no political party, 20 were Mensheviks, 7 were Left SRs, 5 Right SRs and 3 were anarchists.[51]

In the textile unions Bolsheviks were the dominant influence. The union published a journal, *Tkach*, which took a strongly revolutionary line, and at the first national conference in late September, 48 delegates were Bolsheviks, 10 Mensheviks, 4 SRs and two belonged to no party. The conference called for an energetic struggle to transfer power to the soviets.[52]

Throughout 1917 the woodturners' union was a fortress of Bolshevism, with a Bolshevik chairman, I.F. Zholnerovich, and journal packed with articles critical of the conciliationist majority in the Soviet. In summer the union sent out a questionnaire to woodworking establishments, asking about the political affiliation of their workers. About 80 replies were received, of which 38 declared themselves for the Bolsheviks, 12 for the SRs and one for the Mensheviks. Replies ranged in formulation from 'we belong to the Bolshevik party', 'we sympathise with the Bolsheviks', 'we've secretly joined the Bolshevik party', to 'we have not joined a party, we are members of the workers' party', 'we beg you to explain what is a "party" – we do not yet know; we know we are workers'.[53] The union formed a squad of Red Guards in October, commanded by Zholnerovich, which took part in the storming of the Winter Palace. Yet in spite of its vigorous Bolshevism, the woodturners' union steadfastly rejected official party policy on industrial unionism.

The Bolsheviks were strong in the union of food workers. A group of them on 5 March founded the union of flour workers, which was one of the first unions to publish a journal, *Zerno Pravdy*. As early as 14 May over 700 flour workers passed a resolution proposed by the Bolshevik leader of the union, Boris Ivanov, calling for a transfer of power to the soviets. A motion expressing confidence in the Soviet Executive Committee gained only six votes.[54] In July the union of flour workers amalgamated with the unions of confectionary workers and butchers to form the food workers' union. The flour workers had recalled their Menshevik deputy to the Soviet in May and elected two Bolsheviks and one SR Maximalist instead. The food workers' union came to be represented by a similar mix of deputies. In early November a general meeting of food workers elected seven Bolsheviks, two SR Maximalists and one anarchist to the Soviet.[55]

In the leatherworkers' union a meeting on 12 March elected a board consisting of four Bolsheviks and one sympathiser, five SRs, one anarchist and two non-party workers.[56] In later months the Mensheviks Internationalist, Yuzevich, came to be a leading light in the union. By September there were nine Bolsheviks, six SRs, one Menshevik-Internationalist, one non-party and a handful of unknowns on the board. The political line of the board thus depended upon the way in which non-party members voted, i.e. with the Bolsheviks or with the SRs. The contents of the union journal, *Golos Kozhevnika*, were unequivocally Internationalist, which suggests that the SRs in the union were on the left wing of the party.

In the union of chemical workers, the union of employees of medicine and perfume enterprises and in the union of glass workers, Menshevik-Internationalists and Mensheviks were the major political force. The Bolsheviks were weak in all these unions (though not in Moscow), but in the chemical workers' union, two members did have some influence.[57]

A bastion of Menshevism was the printers' union – the oldest and best-organised union in Petrograd. The peculiarly 'aristocratic' character of many typesetters predisposed them towards moderation in politics and a rejection of extremism. During the war most printers supported the defencist wing of Menshevism, and Mensheviks continued to dominate the union until the civil war period. In Petrograd Bolsheviks were rather more influential in the union than elsewhere, but they had only five places on the city board compared to the Mensheviks' fifteen.[58] The latter tried to steer the union clear of political involvement, though after the Kornilov rebellion – when trade unionists everywhere were flocking to the Bolshevik banners – they adopted the slogan 'Unity in Action by all parties represented in the Soviet'. In the new elections to the union board in October, 9,000 printers elected eleven Internationalists and fourteen defencists.[59] As late as 10 April 1918, when the Petrograd board was again re-elected, 6,145 printers voted for the Menshevik/SR/Unemployed Workers' list, 3,416 voted for the Bolshevik list and 138 ballot papers were invalid.[60]

This survey of the main factory unions reveals that the Bolsheviks, not the Mensheviks, were the most influential political party within the Petrograd trade unions. Nevertheless, as far as the Bolshevik leadership was concerned, the trade unions were less reliable allies than the factory committees, for the presence of significant numbers of non-Bolsheviks in the trade unions meant that their compliance with Bolshevik policy could not be guaranteed.

STRIKES AND INFLATION

Although the cost of living had more than tripled between 1914 and January 1917, the wartime rate of inflation was as nothing compared to the rate for 1917. Strumilin estimates that in the course of that year official fixed prices in Petrograd increased 2.3 times, while market prices rose a staggering 34 times.[61] Stepanov, using budget and price data, reckoned that by October 1917 the cost of living in Petrograd was 14.3 times higher than the prewar level (mixing fixed and market prices).[62] In *Table 13* are reproduced Stepanov's calculations of monthly real-wage levels in six factories between January and October 1917. It is apparent that, despite huge increases in nominal wages, by October real wages were down by between 10% and 60% on the January level which, of course, was already below the prewar level.

Not unexpectedly, spiralling inflation had the effect of pushing more and more workers to strike for higher wages. Nationally, the monthly number of strikers rose from 35,000 in April, to 175,000 in June, to 1.1 million in September, to 1.2 million in October.[63] The geographical area covered by strikes broadened out from the Petrograd and Central Industrial Region in spring, to the whole of European Russia by autumn. All the time, strikes became more organised, more large-scale and more militant. Strikes were a politicising experience for those who took part in them: they saw with their own eyes how employers were going on investment strike, engaging in lockouts, refusing to accept new contracts or to repair plant; how the government was colluding with the employers, curbing the factory committees and sending troops to quell disorder

Table 13: *Real wages: January–October 1917*

Month 1917	Price index (1913=1)	Obukhov works nominal wage in rubles	Obukhov real wage in rubles	Obukhov real wage as % Jan 1917	Parviainen nominal wage in rubles	Parviainen real wage in rubles	Parviainen real wage as % Jan 1917	Baltic works nominal wage in rubles	Baltic real wage in rubles	Baltic real wage as % Jan 1917	Nevskaya cotton nominal wage in rubles	Nevskaya real wage in rubles	Nevskaya real wage as % Jan 1917
January	3.5	160	46	100	144	41	100	86	24	100	63	18	100
April	4.5	192	43	93	212	47.1	115	142	32	133	130	29	151
June	6.0	319	53	115	282	27	114	112	19	79	135	23	128
August	10.5	326	31	67	313	30	73	144	14	58	–	–	–
September	11.4	345	30	65	303	27	66	191	17	70	127	20	111
October	14.3	464	32	69	–	–	–	141	10	42	193	14	78

Month	Kersten mill nominal wage in rubles	Kersten real wage in rubles	Kersten real wage as % Jan 1917	Shaposhnikov tobacco nominal wage in rubles	Shaposhnikov real wage in rubles	Shaposhnikov real wage as % Jan 1917	Chernorabochie (Labour exchange data) as % Jan 1917
January	33	10	100	47	13	100	100
April	100	22	220	–	–	–	86
June	82	14	140	131	22	169	71
August	95	9	90	133	13	100	50
September	93	8	80	180	16	123	43
October	115	9	90	155	11	85	43

Source: Z.V. Stepanov, *Rabochie Petrograda v period podgotovki i provedeniya oktyabr'skogo vooruzhennogo vosstaniya* (Moscow, 1965), pp.54–5.

in the Donbass. The strikes were important, therefore, in making hundreds and thousands of workers aware of political matters and in making the policies of the Bolshevik party attractive to them. Yet from a practical point of view, strikes were less and less effective. Their chief aim was to achieve wage-increases in line with the cost-of-living, but such increases as were achieved merely fuelled inflation still further. As the economic crisis deepened, employers were no longer either willing or able to concede huge increases, and increasingly they preferred the prospect of closure and redundancies to that of bankruptcy caused by a high wages bill. In Petrograd strike activity did not conform to the national pattern. There was a plethora of wage conflicts of a spontaneous, atomised character in the spring, at a time when the working class nationally was relatively calm. The economic crisis set in early in the capital, however, and it quickly became apparent that strikes were no longer an effective weapon for defending jobs and living standards. The labour movement, therefore, from early summer onwards turned its attention to two alternative modes of struggle: first, a fight for collective wage contracts to cover all workers in each branch of industry; secondly, the battle for workers' control of production.

Workers in Petrograd did not stop going on strike after the early summer, but those workers who struck were not, generally, in the major factory industries. They were workers who formerly had been considered 'backward' – workers in non-factory industries, women, etc. Because the focus of this study is on workers in factory industry, these strikes will not be examined, but it is important to mention them, in order to situate the struggle for collective wage contracts (tariffs) in context. In May and June there was a rash of strikes by market-stall tenders and shop assistants, envelope-makers and a threatened strike by railway workers.[64] In June many of the strikes involved extremely low-paid women workers, principally laundry-women, catering workers and women dye-workers – who were on strike for four months.[65] Others who struck over the summer included sausage-makers and building workers. All of these strikes were small, but in spite of the fact that they involved workers with no traditions of struggle, they were militant and fairly well organised – throwing up strike committees and trade unions. In September there were three bigger strikes, led by unions of pharmacy employees, paperworkers and railway workers.[66] Finally, as already mentioned, there was an important strike by woodturners in October. These strikes formed the background to the campaign for collective wage contracts.

The strikes which swept Russia in the summer of 1917 had more than an economic significance. They were a sign of political disillusionment – a reflection of the fact that workers felt cheated of the gains which they had made as a result of the February Revolution. When the Petrograd woodturners' union sent out a questionnaire to its members in the summer, which asked what they had achieved as a result of the February Revolution, only half of the eighty replies bothered to answer the question. Of the rest, many factories replied 'nothing', 'nothing special', 'nothing has changed' or 'nothing, but management is better'. Of those replies which mentioned positive gains, most referred to the eight-hour day: 'we have gone from an eleven-hour to an eight-hour day, but have made no improvement in wages'. Several said that they had achieved increases of 50% in wages. Other factories mentioned the democratisation of the enterprise: 'partially autonomous management has been introduced'; 'hiring and firing is done by the workers'; 'the management has been replaced by a collective of employees in which worker-*starosty* participate'; 'the foremen have been sacked and are now elected'; 'a conciliation chamber and factory committee with *starosty* have been introduced'.[67] It is hard to believe when reading these replies, that only three months previously, workers had been euphoric about the February Revolution. There was thus widespread disappointment among workers at the fact that their economic position had not improved, and this played an important part in radicalising them.

THE CAMPAIGN FOR COLLECTIVE WAGE CONTRACTS

Collective bargaining, or formal negotiation between organised groups of workers and employers, was almost unknown in Russia. It had begun to develop in 1905–6, when some thirty contracts had been signed, most notably in the St Petersburg printing and bakery trades, but it had subsequently faded away.[68] In Western Europe, too, collective bargaining, involving more than a single employer and his workforce, was slow to develop. By 1914 it was probably most advanced in Britain, but even there, bargaining at a regional or national level on questions of pay and hours (as opposed to disputes procedure) was rare.[69] Only after the outbreak of war in 1914 did national agreements on war bonuses and Whitleyism lead to a big expansion of centralised collective bargaining in Britain.[70] The big lead enjoyed by Britain over other countries in this sphere, however, was quickly challenged by Russia in 1917.

The conclusion of collective wage contracts, or 'tariffs' as they were known, was one of the greatest achievements of the trade unions in 1917. Petrograd led the way in this field. Twenty-five contracts were signed in the capital up to October, and a further twenty-four up to July 1918.[71] Moscow, Sormovo, Khar'kov and the Donbass slowly followed the example of the metropolitan unions, though employers' organisations put up stronger resistance to centralised collective bargaining in these regions.[72]

The trade-union leaders of Petrograd were pushed into centralised collective bargaining by the spontaneous, atomised wages struggles of spring 1917, which had meant that the less well-organised, less strategically-placed workers had often been unable to achieve increases in wages on a par with those achieved by workers who were better organised and whose skills were in demand. It was in order to overcome growing unevenness in wage-levels and to help the low-paid, that unions began to draw up contracts. A further consideration which disposed the unions towards collective bargaining was the fact that elemental wages struggles stultified efforts to create an organised, united labour movement. The board of the metalworkers' union issued a strongly-worded statement in early summer which said:

Instead of organisation we, unfortunately, now see chaos [*stikhiya*]; instead of discipline and solidarity – fragmented actions. Today one factory acts, tomorrow another and the day after that the first factory strikes again – in order to catch up with the second. In individual enterprises, alas, we see not even purely mechanical factory actions, but irresponsible actions by individual sections within the factory, such as when one section delivers an ultimatum to another. The raising of demands is often done without any prior preparation, sometimes by-passing the elected factory committee. The metalworkers' union is informed about factory conflicts only after demands have been put to management, and when both sides are already in a state of war. The demands themselves are distinguished by lack of consistency and uniformity.[73]

The contracts, which were drawn up by the unions, were designed to overcome such inconsistency. They sought, first, to specify the wage rates for all jobs in a particular industry and thus to rationalise the pay structure; secondly, to diminish differentials in earnings between skilled and unskilled workers; thirdly, they aimed to standardise working hours, improve working conditions, control hiring and firing and to establish a procedure for the arbitration of disputes.

Collective bargaining, generally, is a double-edged sword. From the point of view of labour, it marks an extension of trade-union power in the sphere of wage bargaining and the recognition by employers of trade-union legitimacy. From the viewpoint of capital, however, collective bargaining can be a means of incorporating unions into an established system of industrial relations and of undercutting the influence of the union rank-and-file in favour of 'responsible' officials. In Petrograd some sections of employers and some circles of government were not unaware of the potential advantages of collective bargaining,[74] but their hopes were quickly dashed, since the balance of power in 1917 was tilted in favour of the unions. The SFWO tended to find the wage-rates proposed by the unions unacceptable and so negotiations proved protracted. Most unions threatened strike action in the course of negotiations, and several unions, including the printers' and paperworkers', actively engaged in strike action. Collective wage contracts were thus not achieved without a fight.

THE METALWORKERS' CONTRACT

The following account of the conflict between the metalworkers' union and the metalworking section of the SFWO over the contract is interesting not just for what it shows about the relationship between organised labour and capital, but also for what it shows about the complex and often tense relationship between the labour leadership and the rank-and-file. It reveals how a section of the working class, considered to be one of the most 'backward', i.e. the *chernorabochie* (unskilled labourers) of the metal industry, organised in pursuit of their economic welfare and developed a revolutionary political consciousness through the experience of this essentially 'economic' struggle. At the same time, the account shows how the militancy of the *chernorabochie* came close to jeopardising the contract being negotiated on their behalf by the union leaders.

In May a special rates commission was set up by the board of the metal union to collect information about wages in the 200 different metal works of Petrograd and to investigate the 166 different claims which had been made by metalworkers in March and April. The task of drawing up a contract was by no means easy, since there were about 300 different jobs in the metal industry.[75] Nevertheless, after nearly two months' work, the union produced a contract which divided metalworkers into four groups – highly skilled, skilled, semi-skilled and unskilled. In calculating wage rates for each job, the union employed three criteria: firstly, the necessary minimum for subsistence; secondly, the skill, training and precision required by each job; thirdly, the difficulty, arduousness or danger of the job. Each of the four skill groups was sub-divided into three categories to take into account differences in length of work experience.[76] The union hoped to persuade the SFWO to accept the wage rates proposed for each of the four categories in return for a promise of no further conflict while the contract was in force.

An explosive conflict had been building up among the low-paid workers of the metal industry which centred on the Putilov works. Accelerating inflation was rendering the situation of the low-paid ever more desperate. Recognising that their weak position on the labour market was aggravated by lack of organisation, *chernorabochie* in a few factories had begun as early as March to band together, and on 9 April they met to form a union.[77] This existed only for a couple of months and then dissolved into the metalworkers' union in June. It was a short-lived but significant development, for it signalled that unskilled workers, having taken little part in the labour movement up to this time, were beginning to move. It was at the Putilov works, where some 10,000 *chernorabochie* were employed, that the unskilled were most active. Wages at Putilov were lower than average and those of the unskilled were barely enough to keep body and soul together. The works committee was in negotiation with management in April and May over a wage rise, which would have given unskilled men a wage of six rubles a day and unskilled women five rubles, but no agreement could be reached on whether the new rates should be backdated.[78] On 21 April the works committee appealed to *chernorabochie* 'to refrain from careless and ill-considered actions at the present time and peacefully await the solution of the problem by the works committee'.[79]

During May prices began to climb and food shortages became acute. By the beginning of June the distress of *chernorabochie* was severe. On 4 June *chernorabochie* from nine metal-works on Vyborg Side met to formulate the demands which they wished the metalworkers' union to include in its forthcoming contract. Although they feared that the skilled leaders of the union might be unresponsive to their plight, they agreed to: 'recognise the necessity of conducting an organised struggle together with all workers in the metalworking industry and to decisively repudiate sectional actions except in exceptional circumstances'. They voted for a daily wage of twelve rubles for heavy labouring and ten rubles for light labouring; equal pay for women doing the same jobs as men; a sliding scale of wage-increases to keep abreast of inflation, and an end to overtime.[80]

At the Putilov works the wage dispute dragged on. At the beginning of June several shops announced that they intended to go on strike. On 8 June the works committee begged them not to, since they were about to refer the wage claim to arbitration by the Ministry of Labour. The committee secretly met Gvozdev, who was now in the Ministry of Labour, to press for his support. This annoyed the leaders of the metal union, who had promised the SFWO to freeze all wage negotiations from 1 June, pending settlement of the contract.[81] On 19 June the Ministry of Labour turned down the rates proposed by the works committee. In a flash, the Putilovtsy came out on strike.[82] The works committee called on the charismatic Bolshevik agitator, V. Volodarskii, to persuade the workers to return to work. The next day he managed to persuade most shops to end their strike, but those with high proportions of unskilled workers embarked on a go-slow.

On 20 June the Petersburg Committee of the Bolshevik party held an emergency meeting to discuss the situation at Putilov. S.M. Gessen described how seething economic discontent at the factory was feeding political radicalism:

The Putilov works has come over decisively to our side. The militant mood of the Putilov works has deep economic roots. The question of wage increases is an acute one. From the very beginning of the revolution, the workers' demands for wage increases were not satisfied. Gvozdev came to the factory and promised to satisfy their demands but did not fulfil his promises. On the 18 June demonstration the Putilovtsy bore a placard saying, 'They have deceived us' ... We will be able to restrain some Putilovtsy, but if there are actions elsewhere, then the Putilov works will not be restrained and will drag other factories behind it.[83]

This proved to be a remarkably prescient analysis, since it correctly forecast the catalytic role which would soon be played by the Putilovtsy in bringing about the July Days.

On 21 June a meeting took place at the Putilov works of repre-

sentatives from 73 metal works committees, from the union and from
the socialist parties, to discuss the contract which the union was to
begin to negotiate with the SFWO the following day. This meeting
agreed unanimously to make preparations for joint action in support
of the contract, including a general strike if necessary; only a Baptist
worker from the Baltic factory demurred to this proposal.[84] The
meeting passed a fiery resolution by 82 votes to 4, with 12 abstentions,
pledging support to the Putilovtsy but warning of the dangers of
trying to go it alone:

Partial economic action under present economic conditions can only lead to a
disorganised political struggle by workers in Petrograd. We therefore propose
that the Putilov workers restrain their justified displeasure at the conduct of
the ministers who have delayed the solution of the conflict by every means.
We believe it is necessary to prepare our forces for a speedy and general
action. Furthermore we propose to the Putilovtsy that they let the metalworkers' union conduct negotiations with the employers and ministers
concerning their demands ... We believe that even if the wage increases are
now granted, the uninterrupted rise in the price of commodities and of
accommodation will render this gain worthless. And so a decisive struggle is
necessary to establish workers' control of production and distribution, which,
in turn, requires the transfer of power into the hands of the soviets.[85]

A Putilov worker, reporting on the conference for *Pravda* explained
how the three-month struggle for better wages had radicalised his
fellow-workers: 'We have seen with our own eyes ... how the present
Provisional Government refuses to take the resolute measures against
the capitalists, without which our demands cannot be satisfied. The
interests of the capitalists are dearer to it than the interests of the
working class.'[86] By the end of June the labour organisations of
Putilov could not contain the militancy of the low-paid, and found
themselves in danger of being sucked into the maelstrom of discontent. On 26 June the works committee and the district soviet set up
a 'revolutionary committee' to keep order at the factory. A Bolshevik
member of the works committee, I.N. Sokolov, reported: 'The mass of
workers in the factory ... are in a state of turmoil because of the low
rates of pay, so that even we, the members of the works committee,
have been seized by the collar, dragged into the shops and told: "Give
us money." '[87] By 3 July the labour organisations could restrain the
workers no longer. Having made contact with revolutionary regiments, they emptied onto the streets.[88]

   The imbroglio of the July Days seems to have had little effect on the
movement of the low-paid. On 1 July the first proper delegate

conference of *chernorabochie* had taken place, with representatives from 29 of the largest factories. This demanded fixed prices on subsistence commodities and voted against action by individual factories.[89] On 7 July the *chernorabochie* at Putilov met together to declare that they could no longer live on 6 r.20 k. a day. They demanded ten rubles and a 'curb on the rapacious appetites of those blood-suckers and pirates who speculate in everyday necessities'.[90] Three days later the second delegate conference of *chernorabochie* met to discuss the deadlock which had overtaken negotiations on the contract.

Negotiations between the metal union and the SFWO had begun on 22 June. They almost immediately reached an impasse, because of what Shlyapnikov described as 'the groundless rejection by our factory delegates of all the SFWO proposals, particularly the point about guaranteed productivity norms'.[91] According to Gastev, only four out of the 200 delegates voted for the productivity clause on 25 June.[92] Only after the board threatened to resign did a further delegate meeting on 2 July agree to accept productivity clauses as a way of 'maintaining production at a proper level' and of 'removing the necessity for trivial personal supervision by members and organs of administration'. The delegates furthermore agreed that the fixing of norms of output 'puts on the agenda the question of workers' control of production as the necessary guarantee of both labour productivity and the productivity of the enterprise as a whole'.[93] Having gained agreement in principle to a productivity clause in the contract, the union went back to the negotiating table on 12 July.

It was only on 8 July that the SFWO was told the rates of pay being proposed by the metal union. The draft contract recommended average hourly earnings of 2 r. to 2 r.20 k. for the highly skilled, 1 r. 90 k. for skilled workers; 1 r.75 k. for semi-skilled workers and rates of between 1 r. and 1 r.50 k. for unskilled male workers, falling to 80 k. for unskilled female workers.[94] The SFWO did not object to the rates proposed for skilled categories, but rejected outright the rates proposed for the unskilled, since the relative cost of conceding the wage-increases to the low-paid would have been much greater than the cost of the increases to the highly-paid. Instead the employers proposed an hourly rate of 70 k. to 1 r. for unskilled men, falling to 60 k. for unskilled women, and between 1 r.30 k. and 1 r.50 k. for semi-skilled workers.[95] Stalemate ensued and it was agreed on 14 July to ask the Ministry of Labour to arbitrate.

Against the advice of the Bolshevik Central Committee, which had not yet recovered from the battering it received at the hands of the Kerensky government after the July Days, the leaders of the metalworkers' union began to prepare for a general strike. The blockage of the contract negotiations had created a further ground-swell of discontent among metalworkers and convinced the union leadership of the need for action. At Putilov around 17 July, mortisemakers, borers, planers and saddlemakers were all on strike – to the annoyance of the shop and works committees – but it was not until 22 July that general unrest blew up, with young workers in the gun-shop wrecking machinery.[96] On that day the government arbitration commission announced its decision: *chernorabochie* were to get around 20% less, and semi-skilled workers around 15% less than had been proposed by the union, but more than was on offer from the SFWO.[97] The latter immediately announced that it would not accept the decision.

On 24 July a city-wide meeting of union delegates agreed, with one vote against and one abstention, to call a general strike. The next day 152 *chernorabochie* from 52 factories backed this decision. They also passed a political resolution which condemned the government for fawning to the capitalists and Kadets and for persecuting the Bolsheviks, and called for the transfer of power to the soviets.[98] No sooner had the commitment to a general strike been made, than the Ministry of Labour announced that the settlement would be made binding on the employers. On 26 July a further meeting of union delegates met to discuss whether or not to go ahead with the strike, in view of the government's decision. The feeling expressed by most factory delegates was that it would be very difficult to sustain a strike in the existing conditions. The union and all the socialist parties recommended acceptance of the arbitration settlement. But whilst the delegates agreed to call off the strike, they voted unanimously, with ten abstentions, not to accept the 20% reduction in the wage rates for *chernorabochie*.[99] In spite of this, the board of the union accepted the reduced offer made by the arbitration commission, and managed to cajole a delegate meeting into accepting that the offer was the best they could hope to achieve. On 7 August the contract was duly signed.[100]

In the state sector there was strong opposition to the metal contract. Workers in enterprises subject to the Artillery Administration insisted that the original rates proposed by the union be accepted, and the Administration reluctantly agreed on 26

September.[101] A conference of workers in Naval Department enterprises accepted the principles of the tariff on 11 September, but again argued for the original union rates. This led to wrangles between the Naval Department, the works committees and the metalworkers' union, and a decision was made to hold a ballot of all workers under the Naval Department. At the Baltic works on 16 October the works committee discussed whether or not to accept the contract. A Bolshevik resolution recommending acceptance was passed by 29 votes to 15, against an anarchist resolution supporting higher rates and smaller differentials.[102] The result of the general ballot, however, was to reject the final contract by 27,000 votes to 23,000.[103] A settlement had still not been reached in the enterprises of the Naval Department at the time of the October uprising.

The compromise reached between the metal union and the SFWO cost the *chernorabochie* dear. Rocketing inflation meant that by the time the contract came into force, the rates for the unskilled barely covered subsistence needs. In general, however, the *chernorabochie* resigned themselves to the contract, feeling that even an inadequate increase was better than none at all. At the Putilov works the *chernorabochie* initially refused to accept the terms worked out by the arbitration commission, but they later changed their minds. A further round of *émeutes* broke out at the factory, however, after management refused to backdate the contract to 9 June – in direct contravention of the contract's terms. Dissatisfaction with the contract, together with political frustration caused by the government's failure to tackle the pressing problems afflicting the Russian people, encouraged *chernorabochie* in the metal industry to continue meeting. During August three conferences took place to discuss redundancies, the growing counter-revolutionary threat and the crisis of the Kerensky government. After the Bolsheviks came to power the *chernorabochie* began to press for a revision of the rates of the tariff, some even arguing for equal pay for all workers.[104] In November the *chernorabochie* refused to accept a new minimum of 10 r. a day, insisting on 12 r. Revised rates were finally implemented on 19 January 1918, and the least skilled were given the biggest percentage increases.[105] The intention of the metalworkers' contract was thus finally realised, but it was a pyrrhic victory, for by this time thousands of workers were being made redundant every day.

To implement the contract, rates commissions were created in the factories. These were to distribute workers into skill-categories and to fix piece-rates. They consisted of equal numbers of worker and management representatives. Any unresolved disputes were to be referred to a Central Rates Commission, consisting of equal numbers from the metal union and the SFWO.[106] With inflation soaring wildly, it was understandable that workers should have attempted to achieve as high a wage classification for themselves as possible. The refusal of the rates commissions to capitulate to such sectional pressure engendered bitter conflict. At the Putilov works a general meeting of planers, borers and mortisemakers called on workers in these three crafts in all factories to come to a conference to discuss their low categorisation in the contract.[107] In the crucible-shop workers walked out in mid-September when they learnt the category to which they had been assigned. A general meeting of workers in the gun-shop called on them to return to work, saying 'your strike only plays into the hands of the employers and disorganises the solid ranks of Putilov workers'.[108] At the New Parviainen works some 200 fitters and turners in the repair department went on strike to protest their contract classification at the beginning of October – an action lauded by anarchists but deplored by the Bolshevik factory committee.[109] Some time later *chernorabochie* at the factory demanded an equal wage for all workers regardless of skill – a demand turned down by a general factory meeting.[110] At the Rosenkrantz works contract disputes had to be referred to the Central Rates Commission, which finally announced its decision in early November. When the decision became known, several groups of workers placed in category three appeared at the director's office armed with rifles to demand reclassification. When the director pointed out that they were flagrantly contravening the decision of the Commission, the workers retorted: 'We spit on the union and on its rates commission.'[111] At the Cable, Anchar and Baranovskii works *chernorabochie* engaged in brief strikes in protest against the low rates of the contract.[112] In a few factories management was coerced into paying more than the going rate, but the metalworkers' union strongly opposed this, suggesting to the SFWO that it fine any of its members who did not abide by the contract.[113]

As early as August, Shlyapnikov wrote a stern article in the union journal condemning sectional opposition to the contract:

We propose to comrades dissatisfied with the rates commissions to send petitions directly to the union and not to try to settle disputes out of court, so as not to bring disorganisation into our ranks ... Our contract does not open the gates to the kingdom of socialism ... it is an agreement between two warring sides and thus has force only in so far as each side is organised.[114]

Three months later Shlyapnikov imputed such sectionalism to exclusive groups of craft workers in the industry:

There cannot be several unions in one enterprise – all trades must unite in one family ... Every attempt by individual trades to use the 'right moment' to raise separate, particularist demands is inadmissible. The conscious layers of skilled metalworkers – fitters, turners, etc. – understand this beautifully, and refrain from any separate demands. The same position is taken by the very unfortunate, badly-paid *chernorabochie*. Despite the severity of their situation, separate demands by *chernorabochie* are rare. Particularism is apparent chiefly among small trades such as welders, who scarcely exceed a thousand people in the whole of Piter, also patternmakers, stokers, draughtsmen, who constitute an extremely limited number, but who are imbued with prejudices to the effect that their own profession is qualitatively different from any other, and that they cannot collaborate with others in the defence of their interests.[115]

Whilst craft consciousness may have played a part in fostering sectional opposition to the metalworkers' contract, it is clear that many of the groups hostile to the contract were those whose earnings had fallen in real terms during the war. This was true, for example, of the importunate planers, borers and mortisemakers in the Putilov works.[116]. One should thus not exaggerate the extent to which craftist sentiment motivated opposition to the contract. The union faced considerable sectional opposition to the contract, but its ultimate success in implementing it in the majority of factories by October was no mean achievement, given the intractability of the industrial crisis. This achievement attests the fact that pressures towards class unity were, in the last analysis, stronger than those towards craft particularism.

THE WAGE CONTRACTS: KEY FEATURES

A central aim of union policy in drawing up contracts was to reduce wage-differentials in each industry. The printers' union was a pioneer in this respect. It was the first union in Petrograd to draw up a collective wage contract in March and it fought hard against sectionalism within the print workforce. Printers had been almost unique among skilled workers in Petrograd in suffering a sharp decline in real wages during the war and in suffering from unemployment.[117] There was thus a considerable head of pressure behind economic demands in March. The union leaders determined to reduce wage-differentials by raising the rates of unskilled printers by 90% to 100%, compared to an increase of 50% for skilled printers. This provoked opposition from a minority of typesetters, mainly those in state print-works. They set up a liaison committee of state print-works which tried to negotiate a separate wage contract, involving vast increases of 75 r. to 87 r. a month for the highly skilled, compared to 20 r. to 30 r. for the unskilled.[118] One angry member of this committee wrote to the union journal lambasting it for 'putting the wretched water-carrier's nag on a par with the drayman's fine mare'.[119] The union rode the storm, but when it came to renegotiating the contract in June, opposition again burst forth. Debate raged in the pages of the union journal as to the virtues of a 'levelling' tariff. K.P. Tik gave a classic defence of wage-differentials, arguing that typesetters were not getting reward for their skills and were scarcely better off than 'bums' (*khamy*) who spent their time playing cards and getting drunk. A union spokesman delivered a vigorous counterblast, asking why typesetters should be different from other skilled workers, and why unskilled workers should not also live decently.[120]

The second contract increased wage-differentials slightly, which suggests that the printers' leaders were forced to make some concession to craft pressure.[121] Negotiation of the contract went less smoothly than in March. When the employers refused to backdate the contract to 1 August, the union brought out twenty print-works, employing 3,000 printers, in a well-organised strike.[122] The employers agreed to backdate the contract, but were criticised by the SFWO for so doing. In return, the union agreed to drop earlier demands for formal recognition of the right to control hiring and firing and for longer holidays. This concession provoked discontent among some radical printers (at the Kan works and elsewhere) and among envelope-makers, which the Bolsheviks did not fail to exploit. Nevertheless the union had the solid backing of the majority of printers – 90% of whom were union members, thus making them the most highly unionised group of industrial workers.[123]

The attempt to reduce differentials was central to the tariff policy of all major unions, as *Table 14* makes clear. Differentials were highest in the glass industry, owing to the very high earnings of an elite of glassblowers, but they diminished dramatically after October. In the metal industry differentials had increased during the war, and the union tried to combat this trend by assigning larger percentage increases to the low-paid than to the higher-paid. The diminution in wage-differentials which came about was not just the result of tariff policy, but of market forces and inflation. The collapse of industry in

Table 14: *Wage-differentials among factory workers in Petrograd 1917–18*
The daily wage of the highest-paid category of workers expressed as a
percentage of the daily wage of the lowest-paid category (= 100)

Collective Wage Contract	% Difference				
	1 June 1917	1 Oct. 1917	1 Jan. 1918	1 April 1918	1 July 1918
Textiles:					
spinning & weaving	–	205.9	140.7	140.7	126.3
cloth-printing & dyeing	–	235.3	150.0	150.0	131.6
sewing	–	116.7	125.0	125.0	138.9
Paper-makers	–	194.4	194.4	157.7	138.9
Envelope-makers	220	216.7	160.0	160.0	138.9
Printers	212.5	250	250.0	250.0	187.5
Woodturners	–	216.7	244.4	173.1	130.6
Metalworkers	–	244.4	173.1	173.1	138.9
Glass-makers	333.3	333.3	192.1	192.3	138.9
Leatherworkers	209.7	173.9	173.9	156.5	138.9
Foodworkers	203.1	203.1	173.1	173.1	141.7
Tobaccoworkers	160.0	200	200	200	184.2
Chemicalworkers	–	–	184.6	184.6	139.8

Source: Materialy po statistike truda, issue 6, 1919 pp.22-3.

early 1918 produced a reduction in differentials, which was especially
marked in the wood, glass, leather, print and chemical industries.
By April 1918 the metal union felt that this 'spontaneous' levelling
had gone too far and, in an effort to create incentives for skilled
workers, increased differentials from 139 to 175 between July and
September.[124]

A second interesting aspect of contracts concerned their policy on
piece-rates. Before 1917 the labour movement had generally opposed
piece-rates, seeing them as the *ne plus ultra* of the capitalist work-ethic
and profoundly inimical to socialism. In 1907, for example, the first
national conference of printers had urged their abolition.[125] After the
February Revolution piece-rates were abolished in many factories in
the private sector, and the first contracts sought to formalise this
abolition. The leather union contract initially demanded an end to
piece-rates, but on 15 August the union dropped this demand in
return for the SFWO's acceptance of the rest of the contract.[126] The
rapid fall in labour-productivity seems to have persuaded other

unions that piece-rates were inevitable. Clause six of the metalworkers' contract declared that: 'work must be done by piece in all
cases where factory management finds such a method of work
possible and technically necessary for the maintenance of production'.[127] The rates commissions were to so determine piece-rates as to
ensure that workers earned the hourly rates proposed by the tariff.[128]
In early October a meeting of 217 members of factory rates-
commissions in the metal industry agreed that piece-rates need not be
a means of 'wringing sweat' from the workers.[129] The woodturners'
contract also specified that piece-rates, determined jointly by the
SFWO and the unions, should be the norm.[130] There is no doubt that
piece-rates were a powerful factor disposing the SFWO to accept
contracts. In early September the employers' newspaper opined:
'The other extremely important point in our collective wage contracts
concerns the introduction of piece-rates ... against which the workers
fought so energetically until recently. This is dictated by the necessity
of raising labour-productivity, which has fallen so low.'[131]

One of the most controversial aspects of the contracts was their
productivity clauses. Employers were implacable in their insistence
that in return for a guaranteed wage there should be guaranteed
output. As we have seen, metal union leaders had to overcome strong
opposition from rank-and-file delegates to get this principle accepted.
The chemical workers' contract included a productivity clause almost
identical in wording to that of the metalworkers' contract.[132] The
paperworkers' contract specified that norms of output should be
agreed jointly by management and workers and that in case of
non-fulfilment of norms, workers should receive only two-thirds the
agreed rate.[133] In September the Provisional Central Committee of
the national metalworkers' union urged local branches to pay greater
heed to productivity:

We must be sure that the organised masses bring into the new world which we
are making a definite level of production, we must be confident that the
working masses will enter the new system with a culture of production
[*proizvodstvennaya kul'tura*] which will guarantee them from chaos under the
new, free forms of economic management.[134]

One can here discern the key elements of a discourse of 'productiv-
ism', which was particularly associated with the metal union in
1917–18. This construed socialism as rooted in production, as
intimately bound up with the creation of a 'labour-culture'; it lauded
the 'producer', 'planning', 'expertise' which derived from large-scale

machine production and welcomed technical innovation.[135] It was propounded, in particular, by a group of metalworkers around A. Gastev, who briefly formed the Platform of Labour Industrialism group in 1918.[136] Although this group rejected the possibility of an immediate advance to socialism in Russia, many of their ideas were taken up by the Bolshevik leadership in the spring of 1918 (see Chapter 10). Increasingly in 1918, however, the stress on maintaining productivity, with its concomitant acceptance of Taylorism and piece-rates, became divorced from a concern with 'new, free forms of economic management'.

One final aspect of the contracts concerns their policy on equal pay for women workers. 'Equal pay for equal work' was a phrase which appeared in most contracts, but it is difficult to assess what it meant in practice. The demand for equal pay did not figure much in the struggles of women workers prior to 1917.[137] The RSDLP, in contrast to the German SPD, did not include a demand for equal pay in the party programme.[138] This may have reflected the fact that very few Russian women did jobs identical to those of men. In 1917 women began to raise the demand. When the metalworkers' union drew up plans for a contract, a meeting of delegates from the Vyborg district warned the leadership not to forget equal pay.[139] The metal contract included a clause on equal pay but, significantly, the rates for unskilled women were lower than those for unskilled men. The same was true of the textileworkers', printers', woodturners' and paperworkers' contracts; it may also have been true of the leatherworkers' and chemicalworkers' contracts, although both included equal-pay clauses.[140] Because the majority of women continued to do jobs different from those of men, it appears that the commitment to equal pay remained an abstract one. The contracts did little to improve the status of women workers, even though they raised their pay.

It is difficult to evaluate the overall success of the contracts. In terms of their overriding objective, they were a depressing failure, for improvements in wages were devoured by ravaging inflation almost before the ink had dried on the contracts. In other respects, particularly in the sphere of working-hours and holidays, gains were more substantial, but the unions made concessions in return for these gains. They agreed to reductions in rates, to 'no-strike' clauses and to the restoration of piece-rates. The contracts thus in no sense represented an unalloyed victory of labour over capital. In other, less tangible respects, however, the contracts represented an important achievement of the labour movement. Firstly, they overcame the situation of spring 1917 in which different groups each fought for themselves; they introduced an element of rationality into wage-determination. Secondly, they succeeded, in spite of considerable sectional opposition, in reducing the gap between the highest- and lowest-paid workers. Thirdly, they helped to strengthen the unity of the working class. This may, at first sight, seem paradoxical, since collective bargaining entails particular groups of workers selling their labour as advantageously as possible on a given job-market, and thus tends to promote sectionalism or 'job' consciousness. In 1917, however, trade-union negotiators were well aware of the danger of institutionalising sectionalism. They consulted with one another and negotiated with the objective of improving the position of the working class as a whole within the capitalist system. Moreover they sought, via the contract-negotiations, to increase union membership and to strengthen members' identification with the union. By consulting with their members, union negotiators managed to create a sense that the union mattered, and that it was responsive to the needs of the members.

RELATIONS BETWEEN WORKERS AND 'SLUZHASHCHIE'

The period between February and October 1917 saw a surge of organisation and militancy among white-collar workers in the factories. The February Revolution was crucial in severing some of the bonds which bound white-collar workers to management, and in encouraging them to form independent organisations of a trade-union type. In the honeymoon period of the revolution, i.e. in the months of March and April, clerical and technical personnel went to great lengths to repair relations with workers on the shop floor, to make a fresh start. This was exemplified in some factories by the desire of white-collar workers to be represented on the factory committees. In early March officeworkers at the Triangle and Rosenkrantz works elected delegates to the works committees. At the Arsenal works a representative of the foremen sat on the committee.[141] At the Admiralty works white-collar workers were allowed four representatives on the committee, but in April it was reported that they were not attending meetings.[142] Generally speaking, white-collar workers set up their own committees independent of the workers' committees. At the Baltic works white-collar workers not only had a works committee but also committees in each shop.[143] At the Nevskii shipyard, *sluzhashchie* refused to sit on the factory committee, challenged its right to dismiss administrative and technical staff, and declared themselves 'depressed' by the director's willingness to attend factory committee meetings.[144]

Both the First and Second Conferences of Factory Committees called for the representation of clerical and technical staff on all workers' committees.[145] At the Tentelevskii chemical works on 1 August workers and salaried employees did agree to dissolve their separate committees.[146] At the Triangle works the three committees of manual, clerical and technical staff formed a joint executive in September.[147] At the beginning of October committees of workers and salaried employees in factories under the Naval Department amalgamated. Yet these were not typical. In most, though by no means all factories in the capital, manual and white-collar workers continued to have separate organisations at enterprise level right up to October.

In the wake of the February Revolution, *sluzhashchie*, like manual workers, began by creating *starosta*-type organisations rather than trade unions. The Central Council of *Starosty* of Factory *Sluzhashchie* (CCSFS) was founded on 24 March and consisted of stewards elected by white-collar workers in each factory. By May white-collar workers in over 200 factories were affiliated to the CCSFS, which aspired to represent *sluzhashchie* both inside and outside industry, but in practice represented mainly *sluzhashchie* in industry, since those in commercial and governmental institutions tended to organise through their trade unions. The leaders of the CCSFS – the Menshevik-defencist, Novakovskii, and the Menshevik (but one-time Bolshevik) Yakovlev – formulated a series of radical demands at the beginning of April, for a six-hour working day, wage-increases, a minimum wage of 150 r. a month, equal pay for women, overtime at time-and-a-half, recognition of the committees of *sluzhashchie* and control of hiring and firing.[148] These demands were put to the SFWO, which took exception to the demands for a six-hour day, equal pay and control of hiring and firing. After abortive negotiation the CCSFS resolved to call a strike on 16 May.[149] In the event, a strike was averted by the intervention of Gvozdev at the Ministry of Labour, who persuaded the SFWO at the end of May to agree to wage rises and the six-hour day, although it would not concede the right to control hiring and firing.[150] Having achieved a partial victory, the CCSFS rapidly went into decline. It had been held together mainly by the duumvirate of Novakovskii and Yakovlev, and when both went to work in the Ministry of Labour, the CCSFS fell apart. By October the rocketing cost of living was causing individual strikes of white-collar workers at the Nevskii shipyard, Tudor, Aivaz and Ippolitov works, but neither the CCSFS nor the clerical workers' union offered much in the way of leadership.[151]

The growth of trade unionism among *sluzhashchie* was remarkable. In the spring and summer of 1917 about thirty unions of *sluzhashchie* sprang to life in Petrograd which, by a process of fusion, decreased in number to around fifteen by October. White-collar workers in factories were organised into a number of different unions. Some were members of the largest union of *sluzhashchie*, the union of commercial and industrial employees (*Soyuz Torgovo-promyshlennykh Sluzhashchikh*), which by October had about 26,000 members. Most of the latter's members were shopworkers, however, which meant that many clerical and technical staff felt unhappy about joining this union ('What has an officeworker in common with a sausagemaker?' being a prevalent attitude).[152] In addition, the union had a strong Bolshevik leadership, which alienated some white-collar workers and encouraged a group of Mensheviks to form a breakaway 'union of factory *sluzhashchie*', which had a limited success in the Petrograd Side and Vasilevskii districts of the capital.[153] The largest of the solely white-collar unions was the union of clerical workers, which by October had a membership of around 20,000, and included many workers in factory offices.[154] The union of factory foremen and technicians had about 6,000 members by October, and the union of draughtsmen about 2,000. A small union of accountants also existed.[155]

It is difficult to generalise about the extent to which workers and *sluzhashchie* supported one another in their struggles. At the Putilov works on 2 June the works committee supported the demands raised by the CCSFS, but warned white-collar workers at the factory from taking any partial action pending the outcome of the Ministry of Labour's arbitration.[156] A couple of weeks later clerical and technical personnel voted not to take joint action with the workers in support of the metalworkers' tariff, arguing that this would be a 'stab in the back to organised revolutionary democracy and to our valiant revolutionary army which has shed its blood for free Russia'. At the Putilov shipyard white-collar workers applauded the June Offensive and expressed admiration for Kerensky.[157] On 19 July a general meeting of clerical workers went on strike because they objected to a bonus system negotiated by the officeworkers' union. Over half of the clerical staff were still earning a paltry 80 r. to 160 r. a month at this time. The works committee condemned the strike as a 'disorganising' move, but the attempt to continue normal working whilst the clerical staff were on strike caused disagreement on the committee. Several members accused the clerical staff of seeking to set up an 'office republic', of flaunting class principles and of philistine, petit-bourgeois attitudes. The sanguinary Bolshevik, Evdokimov, was all for dispersing the strikers at gun-point: 'Let a thousand perish, for 40,000 will be saved', but other Bolsheviks on the committee took a less inflammatory line. A resolution was passed by 14 votes to one, with three abstentions, calling on the clerical staff to end their strike, since it was doomed to failure and would merely encourage similar sectional strikes by other groups of workers.[158]

A couple of weeks later, after the clerical workers' strike had collapsed, the works committee at Putilov felt it incumbent to issue a declaration to the workers, warning amongst other things against: 'the erroneous view that people not engaged in physical labour are not to be tolerated, that they are basically drones and parasites. Comrades who argue thus lose sight of the crucial fact that in industry, in technical production, mental labour is as indispensable as physical labour.'[159] This prejudice against white-collar workers was linked to the prevalent attitude within the working class that only manual labour was authentic work, conferring dignity and moral worth on the worker.

At the Skorokhod shoe factory relations between workers and *sluzhashchie* were better. From the first, junior employees cooperated closely with workers, and after the factory committee supported the CCSFS struggle, senior employees also swung towards the workers. On 18 May they published a declaration which announced: 'We, the *sluzhashchie* of Skorokhod, do not regard ourselves as *sluzhashchie*, but as mental workers, and we will go hand in hand with our worker comrades in other occupations.'[160] The practical support given to the *sluzhashchie* by workers at Skorokhod, Petichev cable works and elsewhere in their wage campaign alarmed the SFWO.[161] In September it called on the government to ban joint committees of workers and *sluzhashchie*, though the government took little notice.

On the whole, despite the fears of the SFWO, it does not seem that the unity of manual and mental workers, which labour leaders sought to forge, was making much headway. There were instances of fruitful cooperation, but these were outnumbered by instances of visceral antagonism. The general situation was probably summed up fairly accurately by a draughtsman in September, who wrote: 'In the majority of factories, the workers have their own organisation and the *sluzhashchie* theirs; each side keeps to itself and decides things for itself ... there is no common understanding, but mutual disregard and animosity.'[162]

6

The theory and practice of workers' control of production

The whole subject of workers' control in the Russian Revolution is awash in confusion. There is not even an agreed theoretical definition of what constitutes 'workers' control of production'. Precisely what kinds of activities should we conceive as 'workers' control'? Can all the activities of the factory committees – which included struggles for higher wages, shorter hours and for the organisation of food supplies – be seen as part of workers' control? Soviet historians, such as V.I. Selitskii and M.L. Itkin, answer in the affirmative.[1] Yet if one sees workers' control as relating to struggles over control of the production process, rather than struggles over the degree of exploitation, as argued in the introduction, then it becomes obvious that not all the activities of the factory committees can be subsumed into the category of 'workers' control'. Z.V. Stepanov is correct to define as workers' control only those measures, 'implemented by proletarian organisations, and linked directly to intervention in the productive and commercial activity of the industrial enterprise, to the organisation of multilateral accounting and to control of the whole of production'.[2] It is difficult to go beyond this rather vague definition. 'Workers' control' is not a concept which can be determined with great theoretical rigour, for in reality it took a plurality of forms, and changed radically in character within a short space of time. Not all the forms of workers' control fit neatly into the category of struggles around capitalist control of the production process: indeed, the slogan raised by workers in 1917 was for workers' control of production *and distribution*, and factory committee activities in the procurement and distribution of food and fuel, for example, related as much to the sphere of consumption as to production. Nevertheless the advantage of this definition is that it excludes from analysis the important struggles around wages and hours which were taking place, and orients us towards examining the various struggles at the point of production, i.e. around the labour-process and the social organisation of production in the enterprise. Theory, however, can take us no further, for under the impact of revolutionary events workers' control soon ceased merely to operate at the point of production and spilt over into a struggle for the abolition of the capitalist system itself.

The second problem of a theoretical nature relates to whether the struggle for workers' control is an 'economic' or 'political' struggle. In *What Is To Be Done?* (1902),[3] Lenin had argued that there is a clear disjunction between the spontaneous 'economic' struggles, which generate 'trade union consciousness', and political struggles, which are based on Social Democratic ideology introduced 'from outside'. Soviet historians have racked their brains trying to decide whether or not the struggle for workers' control is 'economic' or 'political'. In faithfulness to orthodoxy, they conclude that the movement was essentially economic, but politicised by the 'outside' intervention of the Bolshevik party. Western historians appear to be divided on the question. Paul Avrich sees the movement for workers' control as essentially political, but sees its politics as syndicalist rather than Bolshevik.[4] William Rosenberg writes: 'the movement for workers' control throughout the period was primarily a struggle for economic security and material betterment rather than a political movement'.[5] A cursory glance at the factory committees, however, shows that whilst the initial impulse behind workers' control may have been 'economic', it engaged with politics from the first. In fact, the theoretical argument in the introduction shows the inadequacy of Lenin's economics/politics dichotomy. Lenin may have been right to argue that 'economic' struggles in general can only generate 'trade union consciousness', since they do not challenge the status of labour as a commodity and *express* the reality of class society rather than challenge it, but he overlooked an entire realm of 'economic' struggles over control of the production process. Such struggles may have been motivated by 'economic' concerns, but they raised, implicitly or explicitly, questions of power. In a context such as that of 1917, where state power was paralysed, it was possible for such struggles for control to extend into struggles for control of the economy as a whole. The struggle for workers' control of production was thus economic *and* political and can be reduced to neither one nor the other.

Although theoretical confusion abounds in discussions of workers' control, historical interpretation of workers' control in Russia is remarkably consistent. Most Western historians portray the movement as a syndicalist one which sought to oust the bosses and allow the workers to run the factories themselves. Paul Avrich sees the working class as inspired by a kind of chiliastic syndicalism. 'As the workers' committees acquired a greater measure of power in the factories and mines, the vision of a proletarian paradise seemed to grow more distinct and the labouring masses [became] impatient to enter their "golden age".'[6] In practice, according to Avrich, 'the factory committees [contributed] to a form of "productive anarchy" that might have caused Marx to shudder in his grave'.[7] Employers desperately tried to erect a breakwater against 'the syndicalist tide [that] was carrying Russia to the brink of economic collapse',[8] but to no avail. In the same vein, John Keep discusses the meaning of workers' control: 'There is little doubt that the majority of delegates [at the First All-Russian Conference of Factory Committees] took this slogan in its literal sense, as meaning a real transfer of power within the enterprise to the men's chosen representatives, who were to exercise the functions of management in the interests of their electors. Needless to add, they showed no concern whatever for the effects which the full "democratisation" of industrial relations would be bound to have on productivity and the national economy as a whole.'[9] Frederick Kaplan goes even further and asserts categorically that workers actually took over the factories: ' . . . it becomes clear that the workers conceived of control as ownership. Having seized the factories, the workers instituted "a type of cooperative association, a shareholding workers' society", in which all the workers and employees of a particular factory owned a portion of the enterprise and shared in the profits.'[10]

It will be argued that this dominant interpretation fundamentally misreads the reality of workers' control in Petrograd, where the movement was most developed. Whilst it would be idle to deny that there were syndicalist elements within the movement, or that there were instances of workers taking over their factories, or of factory committees exacerbating economic chaos, to put these phenomena at the centre of one's picture is gravely to distort the history of the committees and their efforts to control the economy. We shall begin this critique, firstly, by briefly examining the extent of syndicalist and anarchist influence in the Petrograd labour movement prior to October. We shall then go on to examine the *practice* of workers'

control in its initial stages, before going on finally to survey the
political debates about workers' control of production.

ANARCHISM, SYNDICALISM AND THE PETROGRAD LABOUR MOVEMENT

The slogan of 'workers' control' arose 'spontaneously' among the
workers of Petrograd in the spring of 1917. The Bolsheviks had
nothing to do with it and, in so far as it had any ideological progenitor,
it was an anarcho-syndicalist rather than social-democratic one. The
idea of workers' control had its genesis in the writings of early-
nineteenth-century utopian socialists such as Charles Fourier and
Robert Owen, who saw small producer-cooperatives as the means of
escaping the alienation of large-scale industrial society. The same
theme is echoed later in the nineteenth century by the great Russian
anarchist Peter Kropotkin especially in his *Fields, Factories and
Workshops* of 1898.[11] It was in France, however, in the last decade of
that century that skilled workers, fighting to defend their job-control
against attack by the employers, first formulated 'workers' control' as
a fighting slogan. Out of this experience the revolutionary syndicalists
developed a revolutionary praxis which rejected political parties and
political struggle and emphasised the primacy of the industrial class
struggle, which would be waged through the *syndicats* and *bourses du
travail* to the point where a general strike would bring the state and Big
Business crashing down. The future society would be organised
without a central political state on the basis of local economic units
run by the producers themselves.[12] The De Leonite socialists and
'Wobblies' in America and Guild Socialists in Britain were to develop
the notion of workers' control further.[13] It is difficult to say which of
these influences was crucial in introducing the notion of workers'
control into the Russian labour movement, but small bands of
anarcho-syndicalists emerged during the 1905 Revolution, principally in Odessa and St Petersburg.[14] Prior to 1917, however, there
is no evidence that 'workers' control' featured as a demand of
Russian workers, and when it began to be raised in the spring of
1917, it was not articulated within a discourse of anarchism or
syndicalism.

Anarchists and syndicalists have differed remarkably in their
assessment of the importance of anarchism and syndicalism in the
Russian Revolution. The syndicalist, G. Maksimov, and the anarch-

ist, A. Berkman, argued in their histories of 1917 that anarchists and syndicalists exerted an influence out of all proportion to their numbers. Maksimov, who for a short time was a member of the Petrograd Central Council of Factory Committees, argued that the factory committee movement was under the sway of anarcho-syndicalist ideology.[15] Other anarchists, however, equally involved in the events of 1917, took a very different view. Volin, who became editor of the first anarcho-syndicalist newspaper in Petrograd (*Golos Truda*) on his return from the United States in the summer of 1917, reports that 'the anarchists were only a handful of individuals without influence' and recalls with shocked surprise that 'in the fifth month of a great revolution, no anarchist newspaper, no anarchist voice was making itself heard in the capital of the country. And that in the face of the almost unlimited activity of the Bolsheviks.'[16] As late as November 1917, an anarchist periodical in Petrograd reported that: 'up to now anarchism has had an extremely limited influence on the masses, its forces are weak and insignificant, the idea itself is subject to corruption and distortion'.[17] Whose testimony is one to believe?

True to its philosophy perhaps, anarchism as an organised political force was extremely weak in Russia.[18] By the time of the February Revolution, there were only about 200 active members of anarchist organisations, though by the end of 1917 there were 33 anarchist groups and 21 papers and journals in Russia.[19] In Petrograd anarchist groups were revived in the Vyborg, Narva and Moscow districts during the war, but they were tiny in numbers. In Petrograd in 1917–18 there were two main tendencies within the anarchist movement. The stronger was an anarcho-communist tendency, whose ideology derived from Kropotkin, alongside a somewhat less influential anarcho-syndicalist tendency. Both were small and had few organisational resources. In the course of 1917, the rising tide of economic chaos combined with governmental inertia to strengthen the political and emotional appeal of anarchism to some layers of workers, and especially to sailors and soldiers. There was much admiration of anarchist bravado in organising armed actions, such as the seizure of the print works of the right-wing newspaper, *Russkaya Volya*, on 5 June, and the raid on the Kresty jail two weeks later. Around this time, too, the expulsion of anarchists from the Durnovo villa fostered sympathy for the anarchist cause – and was one of the contributing factors behind the July-Days explosion.[20] In general, crude slogans, such as 'Rob the robbers!' or 'Exterminate the bourgeoisie and its hangers-on!' were the source of anarchism's appeal to desperate and frustrated workers. Only rarely did they try to put across their ideas in a more developed, coherent form.[21] Simple anarchism tended to appeal to some of the same workers who were attracted to the Bolsheviks, but whereas the official policy of the Bolsheviks was to divert the anger and frustration of these workers into organised channels, anarchists were generally content to fuel this anger, with the aim of triggering off a popular explosion which would blow apart the Kerensky Government and the capitalist system.[2] At the end of June, and again in October, the Bolsheviks almost lost the support of these groups of discontented workers, because of their policy of caution and restraint, and it was partly the danger of losing them to the anarchists which convinced Lenin that a seizure of power could no longer be postponed. Nevertheless the appeal of anarchism to Petrograd workers was a minority appeal, and within the organised labour movement the influence of anarchists was very limited.

At the conferences of Petrograd factory committees anarchists always were in a small minority. At the First Conference at the end of May a moderate anarchist resolution, presented by I. Zhuk, the chairman of the Shlissel'burg works committee, gained 45 votes, compared to 290 votes cast for the Bolshevik resolution.[23] At the Second Conference the Bolshevik resolution, presented by V.P. Milyutin, was passed by 213 votes against 26, with 22 abstentions. A resolution put forward by the syndicalist Volin got a paltry eight votes.[24] At the First National Conference in October Milyutin's resolution got 65 votes and Zhuk's resolution 5 votes, but Milyutin found it necessary to refute the anarchist notion of workers taking over their factories, which suggests that at factory level anarchist influence may have been on the increase.[25] This is further suggested by one Menshevik source, which claimed that 18,000 workers voted for anarchist candidates in Petrograd factory committee elections in October although it is not clear what elections are being referred to.[26]

While there is evidence to suggest that anarchist influence was on the increase in the autumn of 1917, there is little to suggest that anarchist conceptions were hegemonic within the factory committee movement at either central or grass-roots level. Volin defines the 'Anarchist idea' as:

to transform the economic and social bases of society, without having recourse to a political state, to a government or to a dictatorship of any sort. That is, to achieve the Revolution and resolve its problems not by political or statist means, but by means of natural and free activity, economic and social, of the associations of the workers themselves, after having overthrown the last capitalist government.[27]

There is no evidence that this was the aspiration of any but a handful in the Petrograd labour movement. Almost nothing in the practice of the factory committees suggests that they rejected the concepts of state power, political struggle or a centrally-planned economy. William Rosenberg is surely correct in his judgment that 'the overwhelming mass of Russian workers lacked this [i.e. syndicalist] outlook, as well as organisations, literature and activists anxious to cultivate it'.[28] In what follows it is hoped to demonstrate that the movement for workers' control, far from aiming at an anarchist utopia based on factory communes, was, in its initial stages at least, concerned with the far more practical aim of limiting economic disruption, maintaining production and preserving jobs.

WORKERS' CONTROL AS A RESPONSE TO ECONOMIC CHAOS

The revolutionary process of 1917 can only be understood in the context of a growing crisis of the economy. Western historians have been so mesmerised by the astonishing political developments of this *annus mirabilis*, that they have failed to see the extent to which a crisis in the economy underpinned the crisis in politics, or the extent to which the struggle to secure basic material needs provided the motive force behind the radicalisation of the workers and peasants. As early as 1916 there were alarming signs that Russia was heading towards economic calamity, but it was not until the summer of 1917 that the economic crisis fully manifested itself. The chief symptoms of the crisis were severe shortages of food, fuel and raw materials. Production of coal, iron and steel had plummeted, and such fuel and raw materials as were being produced were failing to reach the centres of industrial production owing to the breakdown of the transport system. Petrograd was particularly hard hit, since it was isolated on the Western seaboard of the Empire, far away from the sources of fuel and raw materials in the South. By September the output of manufactured goods throughout Russia had fallen by 40% since the beginning of the year.[29] Shortages, spiralling costs, declining labour productivity and the heightened tempo of class conflict made industrialists reluctant to try to maintain output. Increasingly, they faced the stark choice of bankruptcy or closure.

The policy of workers' control of production was first and foremost
an attempt by factory committees to stem the tide of industrial chaos.
Throughout its brief life, the workers'-control movement made a
valiant attempt to maintain production amid mounting economic
chaos. The impulse behind the movement, far from being ideological,
was initially practical. It was the works committee at Putilov which
first took steps to call a conference of factory committees in Petrograd
in May. It discussed the idea with the bureau of factory committees
under the Artillery Administration, and since it could not raise
sufficient funds from the Putilovtsy to finance the conference, secured
the necessary money from the Bolshevik factory committee at the
Parviainen works.[30] The purpose of the conference was outlined in
the opening speech by the SR, V.M. Levin:

All the works and factories of Petrograd are experiencing a crisis, but
management do not display any activism in supplying their factories with a
sufficient quantity of raw materials and fuels. As a result, workers may be
thrown to the mercy of Tsar Hunger, unemployed. Therefore, it is the
workers themselves who must show activism in this sphere, since the
industrialist-employers are not showing any. Only the unified organisation of
factory committees, not only in Petrograd but throughout Russia, can do this.
It is obvious that to do this, there must everywhere exist workers'
organisations which must band together to intervene in industrial life in an
organised manner.[31]

The Conference went on to discuss the state of industry in Petrograd;
control and regulation of production and the flow of production in the
factories; the tasks of the factory committees; unemployment and the
demobilisation of industry; the role of the factory committees in the
trade union movement; their relation to labour exchanges and
cooperatives and, finally, the creation of a unified economic centre,
attached to the Central Bureau of Trade Unions.[32] The Second
Conference of Factory Committees (7–12 August) reflected the same
practical economic concerns although it also discussed politics. On its
agenda were three key questions: firstly, the economic state of the
enterprise (fuel, raw materials, food supplies and the state of
production); secondly, the current situation and the tasks of workers'
control; thirdly, unemployment, the evacuation of the factories and
the demobilisation of industry.[33]

Historians, such as F.I. Kaplan, argue that what was said at
factory committee conferences was one thing, but that what was done
by the committees in the enterprise was quite another. In the majority
of factories, however, the key concern of the committees in the early
stages was to keep production going rather than to establish workers'

self-management. On 8 November the factory committee at the Franco-Russian engineering works sent a letter to the company which began: 'Production and the normal life of the factory are the chief work and concern of the committees.'[34] And the works committee at the Sestroretsk armaments plant claimed: 'Since the first days of our work we have stood by the view that our main aim is the task of maintaining production in the factory come what may ...'[35] In order to establish the fact that for most factory committees workers' control was a question of survival, rather than of utopian aspiration, it is worth looking in detail at the two areas in which factory committees first exercised 'control', viz. the utilisation of fuel and the utilisation of raw materials.

The fuel shortage affected all industrial establishments in Petrograd, but large factories were particularly hard-hit. Both the Second Conference of Factory Committees and the First All-Russian Conference of Factory Committees in October discussed the critical fuel situation, but it was at grass-roots level that the most active work went on. As early as March and April factory committees at the Vulcan and Putilov works began to search out fuel supplies.[36] At the Nevskii shipyard management protested at the officious way in which the factory committee monitored production, but on 10 May told the committee that unless it could find fresh supplies of oil, certain shops would have to close. The committee agreed to try to find fuel in order to avert closure.[37] From early summer onwards, factory committees at the Pipe works, the Arsenal, Rozenkrantz and elsewhere began to send 'pushers' (*tolkachi*) to the Donbass and other parts of Southern Russia in search of fuel.[38] At the Putilov works the fuel shortage was especially acute; the works committee set up a fuel commission which sent 'pushers' to the coal and oil-producing areas, but they came back empty-handed; by autumn output at the factory had slumped to a third of its normal level. The works committee thereupon created a technical commission to effect the conversion of some of the furnaces from mineral fuel to firewood. On 20 October the committee wrote to the Special Commission on Defence, requesting information on fuel supplies in Petrograd and offering to take care of deliveries, but the Commission could offer them little.[39] The Central Council of Factory Committees announced that it would requisition fuel from any factories which had more than three months supply in order to give it to power stations, water-works and flour-mills where it was most needed.[40]

Most factory committees busily monitored stocks of raw materials and incoming and outgoing supplies. In April the Cartridge works committee requested a weigh-scale to check materials coming into the factory.[41] On 7 April a general meeting at the Kebke tarpaulin factory agreed to investigate why management was removing canvas from the factory.[42] At the Paramonov leather works the committee set up control of all goods coming in and out of the factory.[43] At the Petrograd Carriage-Construction company on 8 April the committee forbade management to remove deal boards from the premises.[44] At Rozenkrantz management denied that it had any spare materials when asked by the War Industries Committee, but on 14 July the works committee discovered 4,000 *puds* (65,520 kg) of metal which it offered to factories standing idle.[45]

By summer, factory committees were trying to share what little fuel and raw materials there were. The Central Council of Factory Committees took part in the various supply committees of the government in order to get information on the state of stocks and to ensure equitable distribution.[46] It was thus able to help factory committees share out materials. At the Brenner works the committee was refused a loan by the Ministry of Labour to buy raw materials and turned to the shop stewards' committee at Triangle works, who agreed to loan the committee 15,000 rubles from its strike fund; the Putilov works committee also donated some spare materials.[47] The workers' committee at Rozenkrantz donated some brass to the Baranovskii and Ekval' factories, and at Sestroretsk works the committee received some self-hardening steel from Putilov.[48] Factory committees by the autumn were on guard against covert attempts by management to sabotage production. While factories were being forced to close because of metal-shortages, the administrations at the Duflon works, the Markov box factory and the Nevskii wood- and metal-processing factory were selling off stocks of metal at exorbitant prices, with a view to closing down operations. They were stopped from doing so by their respective factory committees.[49] At the Bezdek sweet-factory the committee on 17 September reported its boss to the authorities for speculative selling of sugar.[50]

The activities of the factory committees in 'controlling' fuel and raw materials in the enterprise were dictated by the practical need to maintain production rather than by any desire to take over the enterprise. As the economic crisis deepened, however, and as class struggle intensified, the forms of workers' control became ever more ambitious, and the movement became more revolutionary and contestatory. Broadly speaking, in the eight months between the February and October, workers' control went from being reactive, defensive and observational to being active, offensive and interventionist. From being concerned essentially to *supervise* production, workers' control developed into an attempt to actively *intervene* in production and drastically limit the authority of capital. It is difficult to periodise this trajectory precisely, for the tempo at which individual factories moved towards a more active, aggressive style of workers' control varied according to the specific conditions of each factory; but crudely speaking, workers' control in Petrograd developed through four phases between February and October, each linked to the different economic and political conjunctures of the revolutionary process. In the first period of March to April, workers' control was confined mainly to state enterprises. Factory committees everywhere attempted to establish some control of hiring and firing, as part of a broader drive to democratise factory relations. Employers were optimistic about the future and prepared to make concessions. In the second phase from May to June, most factory committees began to monitor supplies of raw materials and fuel and to check that their factories were being run efficiently. It was in this period that the Bolsheviks achieved political hegemony within the movement. In the third phase from July to August, economic crisis erupted and class struggle deepened. Employers went onto the offensive and attempted to curb the powers of the factory committees, some of which set up 'control commissions' to monitor all aspects of production, including orders and finances. In the fourth period from September to October, these developments were strengthened. There was a severe economic and political crisis and class conflict polarised. Some employers tried to close their factories and in three cases factory-committees took over the running of their enterprises. Factory committees became actively involved in the battle to transfer power to the Soviets, and workers' control, as a response to economic difficulties, began to mesh with the earlier impulses to democratise factory life, so as to produce a movement groping towards workers' self-management.

THE POLITICS OF WORKERS' CONTROL: FEBRUARY TO OCTOBER 1917

The dominant Western interpretation of workers' control of production posits a dichotomy between the Bolshevik party and the factory-committee movement. The party is seen as committed to a centralised, statist economy, whilst the committees are portrayed as protagonists of a decentralised economy run by the workers themselves. It is argued that the Bolsheviks pursued an opportunist policy towards the movement for workers' control, cynically supporting it until October, not because they agreed with its aims, but because it was creating disorder in industry and undermining the capitalist class. Once they had gained power, however, the Bolsheviks crushed the committees, eradicated workers' control and reorganised the economy on hierarchical lines. Thus Paul Avrich tells us: 'From April to November, Lenin had aligned himself with the Anarcho-Syndicalists, who desired the utter annihilation of the old order ... But after the Bolshevik Revolution was secured, Lenin abandoned the forces of destruction for those of centralisation and order.'[51] In a more conspiratorial vein, F.I. Kaplan writes: 'The factory committees ... were used by the Bolsheviks as a mask for the seizure of economic power. The economy was to be disorganised by means of "workers' control" of industry. Workers' control was to have a dual function; (1) to undermine the economy of the country so that the Provisional Government could not efficiently function; (2) to establish the basis for Bolshevik control over that economy.'[52] O. Anweiler repeats the charge that the Bolsheviks disingenuously exploited workers' control for their own ends: 'The Bolsheviks furthered the syndicalist and anarchist tendencies emerging in factory committees, whose general aim was workers' rule in the plants, without centralised direction from above and without regard to the state of the national economy.'[53] It seems that such a line of interpretation is fundamentally misguided for a number of reasons. Firstly, as argued above, and amplified below, it is inadequate to argue that the aspirations of the factory committees were 'syndicalist'. Secondly, up to October, the Bolsheviks generally were not aware of any incompatibiliy between the workers' control of the factory committees and state organisation of the economy. Thirdly, to counterpose the factory committees to the Bolshevik party is incorrect, since most of the leading cadres of the committees were also members of the Bolshevik party. Finally, such a counter-position suggests that there was a uniformity of views within both the committees and the Bolshevik party which did not in fact exist.

What follows is not an attempt to analyse the political debates about control in detail, but rather to disclose the problematic of such debates and to discuss some of their implications.

Menshevik, SR and anarchist perspectives on control of the economy

The Menshevik and SR demand for state control of the economy was proffered as a solution to the severe crisis racking Russian industry. The left-wing Menshevik economist, F.A. Cherevanin, diagnosed the severity of the crisis at the First Conference of Petrograd Factory Committees in the following terms: 'The economic life of Russia has reached a terrifying state of collapse. The country is already edging towards a catastrophe which threatens destitution and unemployment to the mass of the population and renders futile every struggle of the working masses to improve their position.'[54] He explained this chaos in terms of the structural strain imposed on the economy by the war, rather than in terms of conscious 'sabotage' by the capitalists.[55] The solution which he proposed was:

Planned intervention by the state in economic life via regulation of the distribution of raw materials, fuel and equipment between branches of production; via equal distribution of articles of consumption among the population; via forced trustification of the basic branches of production; via control of the banks, the fixing of prices, profits and wages and increased taxation of capitalist incomes.[56]

The Mensheviks utterly rejected 'workers' control' as a serious strategy for controlling the economy. They believed that the Bolsheviks had popularised the slogan purely as a demagogic device. As a strategy for dealing with economic chaos, they considered it to be a recipe for disaster. Workers' control encouraged decentralised, spontaneous initiatives by atomised groups of workers in individual enterprises and its net effect could only be to exacerbate economic chaos.[57] What was required was planned, centralised, all-embracing control of the economy, and only the state had at its disposal an apparatus adequate to this task. It was only through the state that the whole of democracy – and not just the working class – could participate in a massive public effort at economic control. The Mensheviks, supported by the SRs, favoured the representation of all popular organisations on government organs of economic regulation. They disliked the factory committees for being both parochial and narrowly proletarian, and argued that even at factory level control of management should involve not just the committees but representatives of government and 'revolutionary democracy'.[58]

The official position of the SR party was very similar to that of the Mensheviks. They too believed in state control of the economy rather than in workers' control, but their reasons were somewhat different.

The SRs objected in principle to one class – the working class – controlling the economy in its own interests. All popular forces should be involved in the business of control and this could best be done via the state, 'because only the state is the representative of the interests of both the producers and consumers'.[59] The SRs considered that the factory committees had the job of controlling hiring and firing, but denied them any privileged role in the control of production. They believed that workers' control as practised by the factory committees was leading to the atomisation of the economy and to conflict between the working class and the peasantry.[60] The SRs, however, were a profoundly divided party and opinion within the party was as divided on the question of workers' control as on all other major questions of the day. The left wing of the party rejected out of hand calls for state control of the economy, but was unhappy with the notion of workers' control. Some Left SRs, such as V.M. Levin, the most notable SR in the Petrograd factory committee movement, propounded a notion of workers' control identical to that of the Bolsheviks, but the Left SR newspaper demanded 'public control' of the economy – by producers and consumers – via the factory committees, trade unions, coopera-tives, etc.[61] Other Left SRs called for control by the 'toiling people'. The heterodox SR Maximalists called for the socialisation of the factories, to be run by elected committees, but control of production by the factory committees until this came about.[62]

The attitude of the anarchists and syndicalists to workers' control of production varied. At the First Factory Committee Conference Zhuk presented a mild resolution which called on the 'toiling people' (*truzhenik-narod*) 'to take the organisation of their fate into their hands' and 'quickly to create control commissions which will not only strictly monitor the running of the enterprise, but regulate the activity of the enterprise'.[63] Other anarchists, however, demanded the seizure of factories by workers as a direct act of expropriation of the bourgeoisie. Naturally, they rejected any notion of state organisation of the economy – some going so far as to reject any kind of centralised coordination. The key concept was that of producers' communes linked into federations. Factory committees were seen as the embryos of such communes, whereas trade unions were seen as vestiges of capitalist society at best, or 'living corpses' at worst.[64] Syndicalists, unlike their *confrères* in Western Europe, tended to prefer the factory committees to the trade unions, though some toyed with the idea of federations of autonomous unions rather than of factory committees.

The Bolsheviks and workers' control

The Bolshevik party had no position on the question of workers' control prior to 1917. They began to formulate a position in response to deepening turmoil in the economy. Because the party's ideas were in a process of formation, there is no absolute clarity, still less uniformity, in its attempts to come to terms with the movement for workers' control. Lenin was the outstanding policy-maker in the party and it is largely through his writings that one can chart the development of Bolshevik policy, but it should not be assumed that party members habitually kow-towed to him. For clarity of argument, it will be assumed that Lenin represents official party thinking on workers' control, but later attention will be drawn to differences of thinking within the party.

In the period up to October a bitter debate raged around the question of control of the economy. This is usually presented as a debate between the Menshevik advocates of a statist solution to Russia's economic problems and the Bolshevik supporters of an anti-statist, grass-roots movement for workers' control of production. This is misleading, since it suggests that the key point at issue between the Mensheviks and the Bolsheviks was whether control of the economy should be implemented by the state or by the workers *in situ*. Yet the Bolsheviks never deviated before or after October from a commitment to a statist, centralised solution to economic disorder. The disagreement between the two wings of the socialist movement was not about state control in the abstract, but about what *kind* of state should coordinate control of the economy: a bourgeois state or a workers' state? In May 1917 Lenin wrote: '"State control" – we are for it. But by whom? Who is in control? The bureaucrats [*chinovniki*]? Or the Soviets?'[65] Unlike the Mensheviks, Lenin and the Bolsheviks resolutely refused to support initiatives undertaken by the Provisional Government to control economic chaos, not because they preferred demotic to governmental initiatives, but because they believed that, as a bourgeois government, its initiatives must necessarily be at the expense of working people. Even if the government sincerely tried to restore economic order, its measures would be either totally ineffective or, if more radical, would be sabotaged by capitalist interests. The fond hopes of the Mensheviks and SRs for state control of the economy in the general interest completely overlooked the class dimension of this control. This was the crux of the disagreement between the two wings of the socialist movement. 'In essence', wrote Lenin, 'the whole question of control boils down to who controls whom, i.e. which class is controlling and which is being controlled . . . We must resolutely and irrevocably pass over to control over the landowners and the capitalists by the workers and peasants.'[66] This was the nub of Bolshevik support for workers' control of the economy against the state control advocated by the Mensheviks and SRs.

The Bolsheviks and Mensheviks did not disagree radically in the specific measures which they advocated for control of the economy. In a pamphlet written in September 1917, entitled *The Impending Catastrophe and How to Fight It*, Lenin summarised the major measures which were necessary. By far the most important, in his eyes, was the nationalisation of the banks, since no order could be brought into the economy unless the state had a firm hold on the nation's purse-strings. Second in importance, were measures to nationalise the largest syndicates in industries such as sugar, oil, coal and metallurgy. In addition, industrialists and traders should be forced to join syndicates in order to facilitate government control. Finally, the whole population should be compulsorily organised into consumer societies to facilitate the distribution of subsistence commodities.[67] Lenin stressed in this pamphlet that there was absolutely nothing original in these concrete proposals: his sole point was to emphasise that these very simple measures could only be implemented once the working class wielded state power. If Lenin understood these measures as measures of 'workers' control', it is clear that he is here using the term in a very different sense from that of the factory committees. The proposals which he is advocating are thoroughly statist and centralist in character, whereas the practice of the factory committees was essentially local and autonomous. Should we conclude from this that Lenin never believed in workers' control in any sense other than as a counter-slogan to demands for state control?

The factory committees launched the slogan of workers' control of production quite independently of the Bolshevik party. It was not until May that the party began to take it up. Lenin had cleared an ideological space for the slogan in the April Theses, when he had demanded: 'Such measures as the nationalisation of land, of all banks and capitalist syndicates, or at least, the establishment of immediate control of them by the Soviets of Workers' Deputies, etc. – measures which do not in any way constitute the 'introduction' of socialism.'[68] For a time, the Bolsheviks talked of control by the soviets: a leaflet put out at the beginning of May by the Lesnovskii subdistrict committee of the party, for example, called for the 'establishment of control by soviets of workers' and soldiers' deputies over the production and distribution of products'.[69] As yet little mention was made of the factory committees. Only in May did the Bolshevik party begin to pay attention to the committees.

It was Lenin, no less, who drafted the resolution on the economic crisis and workers' control which was put to the First Conference of Factory Committees by G. Zinov'ev, and passed by 297 votes to 21, with 44 abstentions.[70] This resolution was the first official formulation of policy on workers' control by the factory committees, but it was titled 'resolution on measures to combat disruption in the economy', and in fact had little to say about the factory committees or the practice of workers' control at enterprise level. The resolution attacked attempts at bureaucratic regulation of the economy by the bourgeois state, and called for a national system of workers' control of production and distribution. Workers' control was conceived as operating principally at national level, in the spheres of banking, exchange between town and countryside, labour discipline, labour allocation and workers' defence. Control was to be implemented by assigning to workers' representatives two-thirds (three-quarters, in Lenin's original draft) of the places in all institutions regulating the economy, such as the Factory Conventions and the supply-committees. Although the wording of the resolution was vague, it appears that factory committees and trade unions were to exercise control at factory level by investigating company accounts and order books, but it was not intended that workers should sit on boards of management in the factories.[71] One might sum up the perspective of Lenin's resolution as one of 'state workers' control', i.e. of workers' control operating via worker representation on the official organs of economic regulation.

Although Lenin envisaged workers' control as operating principally at the level of central and local government, this did not preclude its operation at the grass roots. Up to the beginning of 1918, Lenin saw absolutely no contradiction between centralised control and the creative initiatives of workers in the factories; indeed, he never tired of insisting that local initiatives were the bedrock of centralised control. It was precisely the creativity of the masses which qualitatively distinguished workers' control from the reactionary bureaucratic control of the bourgeois state:

Vital creativity of the masses – that is the fundamental factor in the new society. Let the workers take on the creation of workers' control in their works and factories, let them supply the countryside with manufactured goods in exchange for bread. Not one article, not one *funt* [pound] of bread must remain unaccounted for, since socialism is first and foremost accounting. Socialism is not created by orders from on high. Its spirit is alien to state-bureaucratic automatism. Socialism is vital and creative, it is the creation of the popular masses themselves.[72]

'Accounting' and 'control' (*uchet i kontrol'*) were central to Lenin's vision of socialism at this time. Far from regarding working-class self-activity as antipathetic to centralised control of the economy, he viewed it as its absolute precondition. After October he wrote:

Let every factory committee feel concerned not only with the affairs of its factory but let it also feel that it is an organisational cell for the construction of the whole of state life ... There cannot and will not be any concrete plan for the organisation of economic life. No one can offer this. The masses can do this only from below, by their own experience. There will, of course, be instructions given and paths sketched out, but we must begin immediately from above and from below.[73]

Nevertheless it cannot be said that Lenin satisfactorily theorised the relationship between grass-roots workers' control of production and state-wide regulation of the economy. After October the Bolsheviks were to learn through bitter experience how difficult it was to reconcile the two in practice.

THE FACTORY COMMITTEE CONFERENCE DEBATES ON
WORKERS' CONTROL

Five conferences of factory committees took place prior to the Bolshevik seizure of power. The First Conference of Petrograd Factory Committees took place from 30 May to 3 June; the Second from 7 to 12 August; the Third from 5 to 10 September, and the Fourth on 10 October. The First All Russian conference of factory committees took place from 17 to 22 October. When one examines the debates on workers' control at these conferences an immediate problem arises, for it emerges that there is no authentic, spontaneous 'factory committee' discourse which can be counterposed to official Bolshevik discourse. A majority of the delegates were Bolsheviks, and the conferences voted overwhelmingly for Bolshevik-inspired resolutions. It could be argued that the factory committee conferences are not, therefore, a true reflection of opinion within the movement, but rather occasions for the Bolshevik party to win formal ratification of its policies. This is unconvincing on two scores. First, the hundreds of delegates who attended these conferences were *bona fide* representatives sent from individual factories.[74] Secondly, the delegates had to choose between the very different policies on workers' control put forward by the three major factions – Bolshevik, Menshevik and anarcho-syndicalist. If, as Avrich and others argue, factory committees on the ground were 'syndicalist', why did their delegates so decisively reject the perspective projected at these conferences by anarchists and syndicalists such as Zhuk, Volin or Bill Shatov, the former Wobbly? The answer can only be that most factory committee delegates recognised the need for some degree of centralised coordination of control, as the Bolsheviks argued, whereas the anarcho-syndicalists decidedly did not. At every conference they voted overwhelmingly for the formula of 'state workers' control'.

If one examines the debates and resolutions of the factory committee conferences it becomes apparent that the emphasis on centralised, planned control of the economy became ever more pronounced, and that the demand for workers' control of production was increasingly linked to the demand for a transfer of power to the soviets. In other words, the debates of the conferences became more and more politicised. The proclamation which summoned the First All Russian Conference called for: 'the unification of the activities of the working class in the task of regulating the economic life of the country, so that once it has power in its hands, the working class can, finally, with the support of the poor peasantry, fight the self-interest of the counter-revolutionary bourgeoisie and bring planning and organisation into the sphere of production'.[75] At this conference V.P. Milyutin, a member of the Bolshevik Central Committee, introduced his party's resolution on workers' control. It demanded a transfer of state power to the soviets, a break with the policies of the moderate socialist parties, the transfer of land to the peasants and the nationalisation of the major branches of industry. Clause four of the resolution proclaimed: 'The workers' control being implemented in the localities through the factory committees must be organised into a state-wide system, for only then will it achieve real, serious results. A majority (2/3) of the members of the organs of control must be workers, delegated by the factory committees, trade unions and the Soviet of workers' deputies. As well as workers' representatives, there must be scientifically-educated technical personnel (engineers, technicians, etc.).'[76] The resolution was passed in an amended form by 65 votes to 8, with one abstention.[77]

The outstanding support for the perspective of 'state workers' control' suggests that factory committees on the ground recognised that grass-roots activity by itself was not enough and that to be effective, 'control' must be centrally coordinated. There thus never existed a clear-cut antinomy between the Bolshevik party, the proponent of state-wide, centralised control, and the factory committees, proponents of local initiative. All the major statements from factory committee organisations both before and after October bear ample testimony to their belief that order could be restored to the economy only by the action of a proletarian government. Yet one should not infer that there was consonance on the question of workers' control between the party leadership and the factory committees. Differences did exist, but they were ones of emphasis rather than principle. They were not differences between 'syndicalists' and Bolsheviks, but differences *within* the Bolshevik party. These differences centred, firstly, on the efficacy of grass-roots workers' control as a cure for Russia's economic ills; secondly, on the importance of the factory committees as agencies of workers' control.

Two broad currents of opinion emerged at the factory committee conferences with respect to the capacity of workers' control to resolve the economic crisis. The chief exponents of 'state workers' control', V.P. Milyutin and Yu. Larin, put the main emphasis on central planning rather than grass-roots control. In so doing, they were close ideologically to important Bolshevik trade-union leaders such as Ryazanov, Lozovskii, Shlyapnikov and Schmidt. In contrast, the Bolsheviks on the Central Council of Factory Committees, such as N.A. Skrypnik, V.Ya. Chubar', N.K. Antipov and P.N. Amosov, whilst supporting 'state workers' control', placed heavy emphasis on the importance of local initiatives. They were more optimistic than leading Bolshevik economists and trade unionists about the potential of workers' control for alleviating economic disorder. This was not because they were principled believers in decentralisation, but because they shared with many rank-and-file workers a belief that the crisis in the economy was caused essentially by the conscious sabotage of industrialists, and could thus be halted by determined action on the part of factory committees. They tended to ignore the complex structural character of the crisis, seeing the economic disruption as the direct product of sabotage. Until autumn, at least, many factory committees rather naively assumed that by combating disorganisation in their particular enterprise they would bring order into the economy as a whole, and create the conditions for its transformation along socialist lines.

The second area in which there was a difference of emphasis related to the first, and concerned the precise responsibilities of the factory committees. Bolsheviks connected with the factory committees assigned responsibility for workers' control of production chiefly to the committees. This never became official Bolshevik party policy. Party statements suggested that workers' control was the responsibility not only of factory committees, but of all labour organisations. Milyutin's resolution to the Third All-Russian Conference of Trade Unions on workers' control did not mention factory committees and spoke of control being the joint responsibility of soviets and trade unions.[78] Again the Sixth Bolshevik Party Congress spent much time discussing the trade unions and the economic crisis, but barely mentioned the factory committees.[79] To those who believe that the Bolsheviks connived to jump on the factory committee bandwagon, it must come as a shock to realise how little attention leading Bolsheviks paid to the committees. They were, after all, probably the most important organisations in the Russian Revolution – more important even than the soviets, from the point of view of their closeness to the masses and their function of mediating between the mass of workers and the Bolshevik party. Yet when Lenin came to revise the party programme in the autumn, he did not mention the committees or the need for democratic organisation in the factories.[80] This, it seems, was largely because of his total absorption in the political question. Whilst he spent the whole summer trying to understand the soviets as embryonic forms of the proletarian state, he paid scant attention to the factory committees, for he considered that the struggle for state power took precedence over the struggle for power in production. He believed that there could be no proletarian power in the factory before the achievement of proletarian power in the state.[81] It is true that both Ordzhonikidze and Trotsky claim that Lenin toyed with the idea of making state organs of factory committees, instead of the soviets, but this was a purely tactical turn, reflecting Lenin's anxieties about the political reliability of the soviets.[82] It did not represent a worked-out integration of the committees into a strategy for the achievement of socialism. This neglect of the theoretical and political problems of articulating the

movement for workers' control with the drive for soviet power was to
have grave consequences after October, leading to a foreclosure of the
movement for workers' self-management.

THE POLITICS OF WORKERS' CONTROL AT FACTORY LEVEL

In view of the deeply political cast of the discussions of the factory
committee conferences, it comes as a surprise to see how rarely factory
committees on the ground discussed political matters. The committees concerned themselves overwhelmingly with the practical affairs
of the workplace, and rarely referred to matters outside. Yet it would
be false to deduce from this that the committees were apolitical. If
they did not discuss politics, it was because they felt that general
meetings of the whole workforce were the proper forum for political
discussion. General meetings were the sovereign bodies in the
factories and it was there, rather than in the committees, that the
general will of the workforce was expressed. Nevertheless, whilst
abstaining from direct discussion of politics, the committees took a
deeply political approach to their day-to-day work. The majority of
members of factory committees were members of socialist parties and
they were elected on party slates. It was widely felt that the political
make-up of a factory committee should reflect the political opinion of
the majority of the workforce. The committees thus changed their
political complexion in response to the changing political sentiments
of those whom they represented.

Initially, many factory committee members were self-selected.
Others were elected because of their personal standing in the factory,
rather than because of their political affiliation. Party differentiation
within the factory committees was only weakly developed in the
spring of 1917. In the textile industry a majority of members of
factory committees belonged to no political party. At the Pal',
Leont'ev and Northern weaving-mills almost all factory committee
members were non-party.[83] At the First spinning-mill the chairman
of the committee was a right-wing SR, but apart from one Menshevik
woman and a Menshevik joiner, the rest were non-party.[84] At
Kozhevnikov weaving-mill the chairman of the committee was a
Bolshevik, but the five women and two male scutchers who made up
the rest of the committee belonged to no political party.[85] In other
industries the political make-up of factory committees in the spring of
1917 was similar. At the Skorokhod shoe factory most of the 40

committee members belonged to no political party; only one woman was a Bolshevik.[86] At the Triangle rubber works SRs comprised a majority of the 16 members of the committee in March and April; the Bolsheviks had two members on the committee.[87]

In the metalworking industries political parties were more entrenched. Here Mensheviks and SRs tended to dominate the committees, just as they dominated the soviets in the spring of 1917. At the Pipe works almost all the forty shop stewards were members of the SR party, although there were two or three Bolsheviks.[88] At the Obukhov works only five of the 32 members of the committee were Bolsheviks, the rest being SRs or Mensheviks.[89] At the Nevskii shipyard, elections in early April put three Mensheviks, three SRs and one Bolshevik on the factory soviet. Even in factories where Bolsheviks were soon to become extremely powerful, the moderate socialists tended at first to dominate the committees. Thus at the radical Aivaz, Nobel, New Lessner and Langenzippen works the first committees comprised mainly Mensheviks and SRs.[90] At the New Parviainen works Bolsheviks were somewhat better represented, comprising three members of the committee, against three non-party members and one Menshevik. Factories where Bolsheviks had a majority from the first were few. At the Phoenix works the Bolsheviks were the largest political grouping; and at the 1886 Electrical Light Company on 17 April Bolsheviks won 673 votes and 7 places on the committee, whilst Mensheviks and SRs in a joint slate won 506 votes and 4 places.[91]

In the spring of 1917 the election of members of a particular political party to a factory committee was not necessarily evidence of support for that party within the workforce. Individual reputation counted for as much as political affiliation. The fact that Bolsheviks such as V.Ya. Chubar', I.I. Lepse, A.K. Skorokhodov, N.I. Derbyshev, A.E. Vasil'ev, Ya. A. Kalinin, V.N. Kozitskii were chairmen of their factory committees is more a reflection of their individual prestige than of support for Bolshevik policies within the workforce.[92] The Putilov works is a good example in this connection, for the giant plant did not swing decisively to the Bolshevik party until after the July Days, yet from April the works committee consisted of 12 Bolsheviks, 7 non-party, 2 SRs and one anarchist.[93] Similarly, the fact that there were more Mensheviks and SRs than Bolsheviks on the first committees may partly be due to the fact that there were more of them around in March, since they had lost fewer members than the

Bolsheviks as a result of wartime repression. Nevertheless the moderate socialists so decisively outnumbered Bolsheviks on the factory committees, especially in the metal industry, that one is justified in assuming that they represented prevailing sentiment in the working class after the February Revolution. The political complexion of the first factory committees, like the political complexion of the city and city-district soviets, reflected a mood within the working class which Lenin termed 'revolutionary defencism'. This was an enthusiasm for the February Revolution and a willingness to defend the gains of the revolution against the foreign foe. The moderate socialists, rather then Bolsheviks, best responded to this mood.

Being the institutions closest to the mass of workers, the factory committees were the first to respond to the shift to the left which occurred in popular political attitudes. Those moderate socialists on the factory committees who refused to swing into line with their constituents were soon removed. From the early summer the number of Bolsheviks on the factory committees began to increase. In June at the Langenzippen works Bolsheviks won a majority of places on the committee after new elections.[94] After the failure of the June offensive and the July Days, the process of 'Bolshevisation' accelerated. At the Skorokhod works Bolsheviks swept the board in new factory committee elections at the end of July, winning 64 places, against ten to the SRs and five to the anarchists.[95] At the Sestroretsk works on 1 August Bolsheviks won eight places on the committee, the SRs five and the Mensheviks two.[96] At the Parviainen works Bolsheviks got 1,800 votes and the SRs 300 in new elections.[97] In the wake of the Kornilov rebellion the tempo of Bolshevik success quickened. At the Lessner works the Bolsheviks gained 471 votes, non-party candidates 186, SRs 155 and the Mensheviks a mere 23 votes.[98] At the Dynamo works the Bolsheviks received one-and-a-half times as many votes as the SRs in new factory committee elections.[99] At the Mint five Bolsheviks, three non-party candidates and one SR were elected to the committee.[100]

Nowhere was the collapse of moderate socialism in the face of a rising tide of popular Bolshevism more evident than at the Pipe works, which for long had been a bastion of the SRs. At the beginning of June new elections to the factory committee and district soviet were held, in which the SRs gained 8,852 votes (56% of the vote), the Bolsheviks and Internationalists 5,823 (36%) and the Menshevik defencists 1,061 (7%). As a result, the SRs got 21 places on the committee, the Internationalists 14 places and the defencists two places.[101] The committee came into increasing conflict with the workers after it refused to pay workers who had struck during the July Days. On 13 October workers succeeded in getting new elections. Of the 15,117 votes cast the Bolsheviks gained 9,388 (62% of the vote), the SRs 3,822 (25%), anarchists 640 (4%) and the Mensheviks 552 votes (3.7%). As a result, the Bolsheviks gained 23 places on the committee, the SRs 16, the anarchists two and the Mensheviks one.[102]

Very few medium or large factories failed to register 'Bolshevisation' to some degree. Typical exceptions were two textile-mills in the bourgeois Aleksandro-Nevskii ward of central Petrograd. At the Pal' factory the committee consisted of twelve non-party members, four SRs, one Bolshevik and one Menshevik in October. At the Maxwell cotton mill the committee comprised five non-party, four SRs and three Bolsheviks.[103] In many smaller factories political radicalisation was not yet apparent among the workers, but only a minority of the city workforce were in such factories. In some huge state factories, such as the Pipe, Obukhov and Izhora works, the Bolsheviks won paramountcy only late, and did not always enjoy an absolute majority over all other parties. Nevertheless, even taking into account these exceptions, it is apparent that the Bolsheviks had the support of a majority of factory workers by October and were much the largest political party in the factory committees.

Before going on to analyse how the struggle for workers' control of production was at the heart of 'Bolshevisation', it is crucial to note that there was no direct correlation between the political radicalism of a factory and the scope of workers' control at the plant. Factories which were Bolshevik strongholds were not necessarily under strong workers' control. Bolshevik-dominated factory committees at Rozenkrantz, the 1886 Electric Light company, the Sestroretsk arms works and the Skorokhod shoe-company did implement organised and far-reaching control, but the similarly constituted committees at the Baranovskii, Renault and Nobel works operated in a very moderate fashion. If one turns to the state sector, a glaring paradox emerges, for it becomes clear that it was the SR- and Menshevik-dominated factory committees at the Izhora, Baltic, New Admiralty, Radio-Telegraph, the Cartridge, the Gun, the Arsenal and the Okhta explosive-works which implemented the most systematic and radical forms of workers' control. The

Gun works, for example, was situated in a wealthy area of the city centre and employed 3,500 workers. It was a bulwark of moderate socialism: in early May the workforce voted overwhelmingly in favour of the Coalition government; on 11 July all parties at the factory, including the Bolsheviks, condemned the July Days and expressed support for Kerensky.[104] Only on 5 September did new elections to the Soviet return two Bolsheviks and two SRs.[105] The factory committee consisted overwhelmingly of Mensheviks and SRs, although its chairman was the Bolshevik and leading light of the factory committee movement, V.Ya. Chubar'. Yet from spring onwards, the works and shop committees asserted their right of control over all aspects of production and factory life. The management took administrative and technical decisions, but communicated them via the control commission of the factory committee. All foremen and lower administrative personnel were elected by the workers; senior administrative and technical personnel were appointed, but the workers had the right to contest an appointment. If administrators had complaints against any worker, they had to refer them to the committee, and workers, similarly, were required to refer their grievances to the shop committees.[106] The Mensheviks and SRs thus operated in complete violation of the official policy of their respective parties in executing such radical forms of workers' control. It seems, however, that they found their parties' policy – of simple rejection of workers' control – to be of no practical use to them in the work situation. Chubar' admitted that 'they [the moderate socialists] quite often deviated from the line of their leaders and went hand in hand with us on practical questions'.[107] Present-day Soviet historians find this fact embarrassing. Stepanov, for example, states that the Gun-works committee restricted workers' control to 'making requests' of management.[108] Nevertheless, the evidence is considerable that many moderate socialists, particularly in the state sector, followed the Bolshevik policy in the sphere of workers' control: they were simply responding to a situation which seemed to call for radical measures. At factory level Bolshevik talk of workers' control made more sense to them than their own parties' talk of state control of the economy. It is more than likely that many of those who voted for the Bolshevik resolution at the First Conference of Factory Committees still identified with the moderate socialist parties. Nevertheless, the failure of the moderate socialist parties to respond to what rank-and-file workers felt was the pressing need for workers' control lost them a great deal of support. There is no doubt that the notion of workers' control of production was very popular at the grass roots, and it was the willingness of the Bolsheviks to support this demand which was a central reason for their growing appeal.

A sense of the popularity of the idea of workers' control can be gained by examining the resolutions passed by general meetings of workers in individual factories. One cannot assume that such resolutions were the spontaneous utterances of rank-and-file workers, for they were sometimes drafted by local party organisations and put to general meetings for endorsement. Nevertheless, even where workers did not themselves draft their resolutions, several different resolutions would usually be put to a meeting for discussion, so the choice of a Bolshevik rather than a Menshevik resolution is some indication of opinion within the factory.

An analysis of the resolutions passed in the months of August and September, which mention control of the economy, reveals an overwhelming preference for the Bolshevik formula of 'workers' control of production and distribution'. Resolutions using this formula were passed by workers at the Baltic, Triangle, Putilov, Kuznetsov and Westinghouse works, at several textile mills and by the Vasilevskii district council of factory committees.[109] In September many resolutions use the rather more orthodox Bolshevik formula of 'workers' control of production at a state-wide level' to distinguish workers' control from any anarchist project of individual factory seizures. Resolutions at Aivaz, Langenzippen, the Pipe works and one by Lithuanian workers on Vyborg Side use this formula.[110] Occasionally, resolutions were passed which appear to be attempts to bridge differences between Bolshevik and Menshevik conceptions of control. Resolutions passed at the Stein company, the Baranovskii works and elsewhere in July, called for 'state control with a majority of workers',[111] as did a resolution by Obukhov workers in October.[112] A resolution passed by metalworkers' union delegates on 26 July called for 'the implementation of real control of production and distribution of products and state regulation of industry'.[113] In September the first national textileworkers' conference, which had a big Bolshevik majority, passed a resolution calling for 'state regulation of industry on a national scale under workers' control'.[114] In contrast to Moscow, however, the Menshevik call for 'state control of the economy' had little resonance within the Petrograd labour movement.[115]

More common in Petrograd were workers' resolutions which called
for control of production by the 'toiling people', suggesting Left SR or
anarchist influence. It is interesting to note, however, that the
Marxist notion of the 'working class' often underwent a populist
inflection in working-class discourse – apparently spontaneously – to
become the 'toiling people' (*trudovoi narod*). Resolutions incorporating
this formula, therefore, may not necessarily have been drafted by Left
SRs or anarchists. At the beginning of August workers in the
iron-rolling shop at Putilov passed an earthy resolution which
demanded:

... total control of the branches of industry by the toiling people ...
From you capitalists, weeping crocodile tears, we demand you stop weeping
about chaos which you yourselves have created. Your cards are on the table,
the game is up, your persecution can no longer be successful. Go off and hide.
Think your own thoughts and don't dare show your noses, or else you'll find
yourselves without a nose, and without a head to boot.[116]

On 14 September workers at the Cable works agreed that 'the normal
course of life can go on only if there is strict control of enterprises and
of all products and also a transfer of power into the hands of the toiling
people'.[117] Resolutions which show clear Left-SR influence sometimes used the 'workers' control' formula, and, in spite of their
populism, clearly conceived of this control as operating in a
centralised fashion. One such resolution passed by workers at the
New Admiralty shipyard on 30 September and published in the Left
SR newspaper, condemned the Democratic Conference for not
expressing the 'people's will' (*narodnaya volya*) and went on to demand:

the establishment of a genuinely revolutionary government [*vlast'*], a
government of the soviet of workers', soldiers' and peasants' deputies. This
must strengthen and deepen the gains of the revolution by immediately
summoning a Constituent Assembly to resolve economic disorder; by
instituting workers' control of production and distribution, taking no account
of the interests of the handful of pirates; by bringing an end to the war, having
declared democratic conditions for peace and having torn up the tsarist
treaties; and by giving land to the peasants and bread to the urban
democracy.[118]

It is difficult to find obviously anarchist or syndicalist resolutions
on economic questions passed by workers in Petrograd. One clear
example is the resolution passed by workers in one of the shops at
Langenzippen in July, which stated that 'the country can be brought
out of the chaos in its finances and food supplies only by the

proletariat, in union with the peasantry, organised into pure class-autonomous organisations, united on the basis of federalism, which will implement full control in all branches of industry without exception'.[119] A symptom of anarchist influence may have been the use of a formula about workers taking the factories 'into their own hands'. Zhuk, the syndicalist Piotrovskii, and the SR Maximalist, Vas'ko, all employed this formula at the factory committee conferences. Other evidence shows that left Bolsheviks also used the phrase, as a way of talking about workers' self-management, though Milyutin expressly ruled out this phrase at the national conference.[120] The resolution which calls most directly for the transfer of factories into the hands of the workers was passed by two branches of the metalworkers' union rather than by a factory committee. The Kolpino district delegates of the metal union on 10 August and the Nevskii district delegates on 25 August, recommended: 'as the only radical method of struggle ... that the metalworkers' union take all factories and works into its own hands ... and liaise closely with the CCFC ... so that when the time comes for the factories to be transferred into the hands of the workers, there will be cells in the localities ready not just to take over but to continue running the factories'.[121]

This impressionistic survey of workers' resolutions on control of the economy can hardly claim to be a scientific analysis of working-class attitudes to the question, but it does show that the Bolshevik formula of 'workers' control of production and distribution' was the one most widely supported by workers in Petrograd. Populist formulations about control by the 'toiling people' figure fairly prominently, but Menshevik, anarchist or syndicalist formulations are rare. Despite a limited degree of variety in the formulations used, suggesting some variation in conceptualisations of control of the economy, the vast majority of resolutions share one thing in common. This is a belief that economic disruption is primarily the result of wilful 'sabotage' by the employers. 'Sabotage' and 'saboteur' were key words in popular discourse during the revolution and Bolsheviks in the factory committees harped constantly on this theme. It was the willingness of the Bolsheviks to fight 'sabotage', in order to protect jobs and the democratic gains of the February Revolution, which was the secret of their rapidly growing popularity in the summer and autumn of 1917.

7

Deepening economic chaos and the intensification of workers' control

ECONOMIC CRISIS AND INDUSTRIAL RELATIONS

By midsummer 1917 the crisis in Russian industry was leading to factory closures and rising unemployment. Between March and July, 568 factories – mainly textile and flour mills – employing some 104,000 workers, shut down operations. The *Torgovo-Promyshlennaya Gazeta* analysed the chief causes of closure as being: first, shortages of cotton, grain and other raw materials; secondly, the 'excessive' demands of the workers; thirdly, too few orders; fourthly, lack of fuel; fifthly, declining profitability. The regions worst affected were the Moscow Industrial Region and Southern Russia.[1] After July the scale of unemployment increased, as supplies of fuel and raw materials began to dry up. It was mainly small firms which closed down, but larger firms contributed their share to the pool of unemployment.

Up to October Petrograd was not as badly affected by unemployment as other regions, although there are no reliable data on the number of unemployed in the capital. The number of metalworkers who registered with the union as unemployed rose from 37.4 per day in July to 71.3 in October. Skilled metalworkers could still manage to find jobs, however, so that only about 3% of members of the metal union were unemployed in October.[2] Other industries were worse hit: the shortage of sugar meant that the Petrograd confectionary industry was on the verge of extinction, thus imperilling the livelihood of 4,000 workers.[3] Grain shortages meant that many bakery workers were out of work.[4] In the print industry unemployment was growing rapidly owing to the paper shortage, and by October about 1,000 printers in the capital were out of work.[5] Other industries, such as textiles, tailoring and woodworking, were not yet suffering closures and redundancies, though their prospects were bleak. In all, there were probably about 8,000 registered unemployed in the middle of October, and although the real figure was almost certainly much higher, the rate of unemployment in the capital was still lower than elsewhere in the country. This was due to the success of factory committees and trade unions and, to some extent of the Factory Convention, in blocking attempts by employers to cut the size of their workforces and to begin the transfer to civilian production.

As the economic crisis deepened, so the tempo of class conflict accelerated. As the workers became more combative and as profits disappeared, so industrialists became less willing to invest in their enterprises or to take on new orders. At the beginning of June the Minister of Trade and Industry declared that 'entrepreneurs, not feeling themselves on firm ground, have lost the appropriate energy. They desire a halt to production or seek to transfer the rocketing costs of production onto the broad circles of consumers and onto the exchequer by exorbitant increases in commodity prices.'[6] In Southern and Central Russia from early summer industrialists began to wage war on the working class, seeking to crush its militancy with the cudgel of unemployment. In the Urals and the Donbass, and to some extent in the industrial region round Moscow, organisations of employers launched a coordinated strategy of lockouts, designed to demoralise workers and to prove to the public that interference in production, excessive wage-increases and the eight-hour day were bringing industry to its knees.[7]

In Petrograd the policy of cutbacks, closures and lockouts was less aggressive. The large factories had not yet been pushed into a corner, and working-class resistance was too well-organised to be easily quashed. By June Petrograd employers were alarmed that they had made a terrible miscalculation in plumping for a policy of concession rather than repression after the February Revolution. The workers, instead of succumbing to the blandishments of a liberal industrial-relations policy, were growing ever more 'immoderate' in their demands. The SFWO complained: 'Industrialists have made very significant concessions, they have made a big sacrifice in the hope of restarting work in the factories and mills, but the demands of workers and employees have gone beyond what is possible.'[8] From June onwards, Petrograd employers tried to pursue a much tougher labour policy, resisting wage-increases and cutting back production in the hope that growing unemployment would make the workers 'see sense'.

The shift in the attitude of employers was paralleled by a shift in the attitude of the government towards the labour problem. Under the first Coalition Government, formed at the beginning of May, a proper Ministry of Labour had come into being. This was headed by the Menshevik, M.I. Skobelev, assisted by P.N. Kolokol'nikov, an experienced trade unionist of right-wing Menshevik persuasion, and K.A. Gvozdev, *bête noire* of the labour left because of his pivotal role in the Workers' Group of the War Industries Committee. These Mensheviks came into the new Ministry committed to a programme of 'broad social reforms'.[9] Skobelev promised to meet the just demands of the masses, to intervene in the economy and to confiscate the profits of the captains of industry,[10] but these promises stuck in the throats of the majority of staunchly conservative government ministers. They despatched Skobelev's reform proposals into the labyrinth of government committees from whence few saw the light of day. On 11 July labour inspectors were established, as a first step towards revamping the system of factory inspection.[11] In the same month the 1912 insurance legislation was extended to all workers.[12] On 8 August night work was banned for women and minors under 17 – except in defence enterprises. And on 8 October maternity pay was introduced. All other proposals for comprehensive social insurance failed to reach the statute book, owing to opposition from within the government and from the employers, who accused the Ministry of Labour of 'defending the exclusive interests of the working class ... completely ignoring the interests ... of the other side'.[13]

By June the reforming zeal of the Menshevik ministers was being overtaken by a concern to defuse explosive class antagonisms. The Ministry of Labour tried to encourage a partnership between capital and labour, but although Skobelev still paid lip-service to the plight of the working class, he tended increasingly to see low labour-productivity as the root of Russia's economic ills. When visited by a deputation of mineowners from Southern Russia on 13 June, Skobelev reportedly promised them help in curtailing working-class demands, which he concurred where 'immoderate' and 'in conflict with the general well-being'. In an address to workers on 28 June Skobelev condemned 'arbitrary' actions by workers which 'disorganise industry and exhaust the exchequer'.[14] The need for 'sacrifice' became the leit-motif of Skobelev's speeches, one which modulated into appeals for an end to industrial conflict 'in the name of strengthening the revolution and honouring our ultimate ideals'.[15] In spite of extravagant displays of impartiality, however, Skobelev could not win the trust of the Minister of Trade and Industry, A.I. Konovalov, who led an onslaught against further wage-increases, at a time when the Ministry of Labour was enmeshed in painful negotiations over union wage contracts.[16] Efforts to establish cooperation between the two sides of industry were thus rendered void not only by bitter class conflict in industry, but by resistance from bourgeois ministers within the government.

After the July Days the Kerensky government shifted sharply to the right, under sustained pressure from industrialists, financiers and the General Staff. Demands from employers for the militarisation of labour in defence industries and in transport, and for a declaration of a state of emergency in the Donbass evoked a favourable response from the Ministry of Trade and Industry and from the Special Commission on Defence. The position of the Ministry of Labour became more and more untenable, as it was torn between the irreconcilable forces of capital and labour. It oscillated between minor concessions and promises of reform and puny displays of strength, such as the Skobelev circulars (see below).

WORKERS RESIST ATTEMPTS TO EVACUATE INDUSTRY

As early as 1916 the tsarist government had discussed the possibility of the 'off-loading' (*razgruzka*) from Petrograd of some of its factories, in order to ease the fuel shortage.[17] On 6 July 1917 a special committee was set up to plan the 'off-loading' of industry. In August it recommended that plant and equipment be evacuated from 47 large factories in Petrograd, including all state enterprises and the largest private engineering and chemical works.[18] Only some of the workers at these factories were to be evacuated; the rest were to be dismissed with two weeks' pay. The German occupation of Riga on 21 August caused the government to expand the scope of its evacuation plans. These plans were motivated by a desire to rationalise war production and by a fear that the Germans would occupy Petrograd. In working-class circles, however, they were seen as a thinly-disguised attempt to break the power of the revolutionary movement by the simple device of destroying its physical base.

When news first broke in May of plans for the 'off-loading' of industry, workers lost no time in letting the government know their views. On 20 May workers in the Putilov gun shop, which was dominated politically by Mensheviks, unanimously resolved:

If the 'off-loading' of Petrograd is necessary in the interests of rational distribution of food products and rational allocation of fuel, for the benefit of all toilers, then Petrograd must be 'off-loaded' in the first place of:
(1) idlers, drones, men and women in monasteries, those who live off their incomes, those who do not work or serve;
(2) those hired workers brought by force or deception from Asia, who should be sent back;
(3) The transfer of all luxury items along the rail- and water-ways should be halted and these means of transport should be used to convey fuel, fodder and foodstuffs to wherever they are required. We protest against the slanders that accuse workers of disrupting transport, and point out that it is those who defend the monks and the opponents of the democratic republic who are causing and aggravating chaos in the state, and who should be replaced immediately by elected representatives of the peasants and workers.
... We demand control of production, industry and capital, since the capitalists and industrialists are deliberately leading the country to ruin.[19]

Another resolution passed at Putilov by 700 workers in the boiler and steam-boiler shops denounced evacuation plans as a 'counter-revolutionary trick of the bourgeoisie to rid Petersburg of organised revolutionary workers and to scatter them to the backwoods [*glush'*] of Russia'. They called for the city to be 'off-loaded' of 'the bourgeois idlers who stroll along Nevskii and Morskaya streets stopping off at restaurants'.[20] Workers in the Putilov forge also denounced the evacuation plans as a counter-revolutionary plot and continued:

We, workers and peasants, will stay put, since we believe that once the right balance of conflicting forces is struck, the people will have the opportunity to take power into their own hands and then no crisis need occur. We suggest that Petrograd be unloaded of its monasteries, infirmaries, asylums, almshouses and many thousands of idle bourgeois. We also propose to find out why where is such a great concentration of Chinese in the city.[21]

These three resolutions all display a fierce hostility to the parasitic bourgeoisie, a strong sense of the workers as a productive class, a deep anti-religious feeling, not to say a certain lack of sympathy for immigrant workers and the unfortunates of the alms-houses and asylums.

The themes encapsulated in the Putilov resolutions were echoed in many other protests. Somewhat unusually, workers at Sestroretsk blamed the industrial chaos not on deliberate sabotage, but on 'the disorganisation and anarchy of the capitalist system'. To the standard list of proposed evacuees, they added 'courtesans, those who play the stock-exchange, speculators and other social parasites'.[22] Bolshevik workers at New Lessner added to the list, 'yellow labour' and 'peasants to be sent back to the fields'; while workers at the Pella engineering works had the bright idea of 'ridding Petrograd ... of the gentlemen who can only cry "War to Victory!"'[23] Resolutions, condemning the evacuation plans as a move to disperse the revolutionary proletariat, were passed by workers at the Russo-Baltic works, the Arsenal, the Kebke factory and the Petichev engineering works.[24] Only occasionally did workers admit that some degree of evacuation might be inevitable in view of the fuel, raw-materials and transport crisis, but even then, they stated that it was up to workers to decide if and how evacuation should be carried out.[25]

In the autumn some factory owners began surreptitiously to move equipment out of their factories. Factory committees actively thwarted these manoeuvres. In September the Putilov administration attempted to send machinery by canal to Saratov, but the works committee held up the barge for a month until the administration had proved to their satisfaction that the machinery was not needed in Petrograd.[26] At the Pipe works management planned to remove operations to Penza, Voronezh and Ekaterinoslav, transferring 4,000 machines, 20,000 workers and about 40,000 members of their families. When the works committee visited these places, however, they discovered that none of them was ready to receive the evacuees, and that in reality management intended to transfer only 1,281 workers and fire the rest. Without hesitation, the works committee blocked the proposed plans.[27] Similar discoveries were made by factory committees at the Okhta explosives works and the Optics factory when they visited the sites to which their factories were to be evacuated.[28] At the Arsenal works and the Okhta powder works the committees obstructed evacuation plans since they had been inadequately prepared.[29]

Not all factory committees opposed evacuation in principle. At the Parviainen works the Bolshevik-controlled committee on 22 August drew up an agreement with management which specified in detail the terms of the transfer of operations out of the capital.[30] At the Baltic works the committee drew up emergency evacuation plans in case of German invasion.[31] At the Nevskii shipyard the committee was fully involved in arrangements to evacuate the plant.[32] At

Sestroretsk the committee searched for a place to which the arms factory could be evacuated.[33]

Officially, the factory committees opposed plans for evacuation. The Third Conference passed a resolution which argued that the practical difficulties of setting up factories in new areas without a proper social and industrial infrastructure were enormous; that the transport system could not bear the strain of evacuation; that it would be too costly, and that it was a counter-revolutionary plot. The resolution argued that the way out of the crisis lay in a revolutionary popular government bringing the war to a close. The resolution, however, did allow for partial evacuation of single enterprises, so long as this were done under strict workers' control, with the full consent of the workforce, and so long as three months' redundancy pay were given to those who did not wish to move.[34]

The attitude of the trade unions was more or less in line with that of the factory committees, though there was greater willingness to recognise that evacuation might not always be against the interest of the working class. In May the Petrograd Council of Trade Unions strongly attacked the evacuation plans and persuaded the workers' section of the Petrograd Soviet to do likewise.[35] Interestingly, however, the metalworkers' union did not share the general antipathy to evacuation. At a meeting in May of the union board it was unanimously agreed that: 'we should broaden the partial question (of 'off-loading') to include the general regulation of the whole of our national industry. We thus insist on the immediate creation of a national centre of regulation, on which the representatives of organised labour will have a big say in deciding questions about the organisation of the economy'.[36] Later the Bolshevik V. Schmidt persuaded the union to take a more critical position, but the union shifted back to its original position in July, justifying evacuation by the argument that 'the ruin of the national economy would lead to the destruction of the revolution'.[37] At the beginning of September the union managed to persuade the PCTU of the necessity of limited evacuation under workers' control.[38] Thus by October the unions had a less intransigent position on evacuation than the CCFC.

THE FACTORY COMMITTEES AGAINST REDUNDANCIES

In the autumn of 1917 the factory committees of Petrograd became very active in fighting attempts at closure and redundancy. At the

Baranovskii, Parviainen, Vulcan, Pulemet, Metal, Erikson, Siemens-Schukert and Dynamo works, management plans for closure were blocked by the works committees.[39] At the Baranovskii works management on 1 August announced 1,500 redundancies owing to fuel shortages. The committee responded by cutting working hours and transferring workers from one shop to another.[40] On 16 August management at the Vulcan works fired 633 workers and announced the closure of the factory on 7 September. When the factory committee discovered that there were stocks of fuel and raw materials to last six months, it accused the director of 'sabotage' and tried to have him removed from his post.[41] At the end of August management at Parviainen announced that 1,630 redundancies were in the pipeline, but the committee managed to defer them by ensuring a more economical use of remaining fuel-supplies.[42]

At the Putilov works the administration had tried to lay off 1,200 workers as early as May, but it was not until the end of August that it tried in earnest to implement redundancies. It announced that 10,000 workers would lose their jobs as a consequence of fuel shortages.[43] The works committee declared this unacceptable and began a desperate search for fuel. It managed to find some, but the administration could not afford to buy it. Workers and managers set up a commission to investigate production at the factory and concluded that 3,200, not 10,000 workers would have to lose their jobs. On 25 September members of the works committee met with the vice-president of the Commission on Defence, Pal'chinskii, to discuss the fuel crisis and redundancies, He proposed a 'participation' scheme whereby workers would be given places on the new company board in return for implementing redundancies. The committee rejected this out of hand since 'workers cannot dismiss workers', but they conceded that some redundancies were necessary, since 'we cannot allow the factory to become an alms-house'.[44] On 10 October the works committee met with representatives from the Peterhof district soviet and from the CCFC to discuss further the question of redundancies. Committee members were criticised for agreeing to one month's redundancy pay instead of two. The meeting agreed that workers should only leave voluntarily, though some felt that shop committees should pressurise the better-off workers into leaving.[45]

Some factory committees tried to shift the burden of redundancies on to women workers, on the grounds that their sojourn in industry was a temporary one brought about by the war, and that the wives of men in work could live off their husbands' wages. At the Franco-Russian, Arsenal, Nevskii, Lessner and Russian-Baltic works, the committees took steps to phase out female employment.[46] At the Baltic works the committee said that every effort would be made to find alternative work for women but if this were not available they would be dismissed.[47] At the Putilov works the shrapnel and other shop committees tried to fire married women, but they were prevented from doing so by the works committee.[48] The Bolshevik party, the CCFC and the metalworkers' union condemned attempts by factory committees to make women workers bear the brunt of redundancies, arguing that this would fatally divide the ranks of the working class.

On the whole, the attempt by factory committees and trade unions to prevent redundancies was successful up to October. Only two factories, employing more than 500 workers, closed down in Petrograd – the Semenov engineering works and the Precision Engineering company.[49] The majority that managed to stave off redundancies, however, proved after October to have been merely postponing the inevitable.

WORKERS' CONTROL BECOMES MORE RADICAL

As more and more jobs became threatened, the scope of workers' control expanded. Factory committees strengthened their control of fuel and raw materials and new forms of control began to appear. One of the most important of these was the effort to extend workers' control into the sphere of company sales and finances. Until June such control was rare.[50] Finance sub-committees had been set up in March in some factories, such as the Pipe and the Okhta explosives works, but they did little but organise the finances of the committees themselves. As early as May, however, Major-General Belaev, the director of the Izhora works, permitted the works committee to monitor financial operations and pricing policy.[51] At the Russo-Belgian metallurgical company 400 workers, threatened with loss of their jobs owing to the financial difficulties of the company, opened the company books in June to discover that orders were in a healthy state. They offered to guarantee the profitability of the company for the rest of 1917 if they were given the right to check company accounts, but management refused.[52] At the Langenzippen works the committee in June attempted to stop the payment of dividends to shareholders, pending an enquiry.[53] The First Conference of Petrograd Factory Committees called for the abolition of commercial secrecy, and the Central Council of Factory Committees claimed wide powers of checking company accounts, calculating debts and credits, costs of production and rates of profit.[54] Yet in spite of increased activity in this sphere, control of company finances remained an aspiration rather than a reality. Much of the crucial information which the committees needed, in order to evaluate the true financial position of the companies, was in the hands of the banks, and the banks were not prepared to part with such information. Even in cases where factory committees gained access to company accounts, they were unable to make sense of them without the help of a trained accountant, and often the accountants would not cooperate with the committees.

In order to forestall closure, the factory committees in a handful of enterprises attempted to remove the official board of management and to run the factories themselves. At the small Brenner copper-smelting and engineering works the owner informed the factory committee on 19 May that he had no funds left. He begged it to help him expedite outstanding orders as quickly as possible, which the committee agreed to do; five days later Brenner announced that he was going to shut the factory for two weeks. The committee objected to this, since the factory had received advances of 420,000 rubles from the War Industries Committee for orders which had not yet been completed. The committee therefore decided to dispense with Brenner and run the factory themselves. On 6 June they issued an appeal to the Ministry of Labour and to the Petrograd Soviet:

In view of the fact that the owner of the factory has not appeared since 24 May, and that the factory has been working under the supervision of the factory committee, we are seeking your permission to run production, to receive and fulfil orders both state and private, and to continue production when those state orders begun under Brenner have been finished and despatched to the institutions from which they were received. Without your permission, the committee will be deprived of the possibility of continuing production at the factory and this will make it difficult for the workers to receive their wages.[55]

On 16 June the Peterhof district soviet agreed to check the accounts of the Brenner works and to make an inventory of stock. It later agreed to oversee an experiment in self-management, by putting the deputy to the soviet in charge of operations at the factory.[56] The factory was desperately short of capital, so the committee turned to other factory committees for help. The Triangle works lent the factory 15,000 rubles and the Putilov works sent some raw material, but this did not really help. At one stage the committee began negotiations with Brenner about his possible return, but his terms proved unacceptable. By August productivity was sliding fast, workers were not receiving their wages and drunkenness was on the increase. On 24 August the commissar of the local militia reported to the Peterhof soviet that he had received an order from the government to eject the workers from the factory.[57] The committee then turned to the government to demand sequestration. After pressure from the CCFC, the government agreed in September to place the factory in charge of the Factory Convention.[58]

At the V.A. Lebedev airplane factory the thousand workers in late May demanded a large increase, which management refused to countenance. The SRs at the factory called for the wage claim to be referred to the conciliation chamber, but they suggested that if management persisted in its recalcitrance, the workers should demand the removal of the director. Another group of workers, however, demanded the immediate expulsion of the director 'for disseminating false rumours aimed at disorganising the workers and employees of the factory'. They won the toss and the workers forced the removal of the director from the board of the company. On 2 June another general meeting was summoned at which a call was made for workers to take over the running of the factory themselves. Some pointed out that this was impractical, since they did not have any capital to continue operations. A worker by the name of Tamsin proposed the following resolution: 'We empower the factory committee to take over the running of the factory by itself, to inform the board of this step and to invite a government commissar to the factory and to inform the metalworkers' union.' The SR chairman of the factory committee resigned at this point, and the next day the SR factory cell called a meeting which the Bolsheviks refused to attend. This meeting agreed that 'the question of transferring the factory into the workers' hands cannot be decided by an open vote, but only by a secret ballot of all comrade-workers, so that each worker considers himself responsible for the decision'. A member of the City Soviet was called to the factory and he eventually dissuaded the workers from taking over the factory, leaving it in charge of the board of directors.[59]

In a few instances workers tried to force the government to

'sequestrate' their factories, by nominating a new board of management to run the enterprise, or by appointing a government official to
oversee the running of the enterprise. In general, the government was
not keen to do this and it resisted demands from workers at the
Slyusarenko airplane, the Langenzippen works and elsewhere for it to
take responsibility for management of their factories.[60] In a couple of
cases, however, the government did agree to sequestration. At the
Rykatkin engineering works, where twenty-four workers were employed, the government provided loans during the war of nearly a
million rubles for defence orders, but the value of completed orders
was less than 100,000 rubles. Suspecting peculation, the War
Industries Committee mounted an investigation. After a conflict with
the workforce in May, the owner, V.I. Rykatkin, resolved to close his
factory and began secretly to remove tools and equipment. After he
was caught one night, the Menshevik-dominated factory committee
refused him entry to the factory and petitioned the government to
sequester the enterprise. At first, the Ministry of Labour refused, but
at the end of July it acceded to the request.[61]

At the Respirator factory, where 7,000 workers were employed in
making gas-masks, the administration quit the factory at the end of
August. The factory committee couched its demand for sequestration
in unambiguously defencist terms:

We have made clear our position regarding the sabotage of our factory by the
administration, which has gone away at this most pressing and critical
moment. We consider this to be an act of desertion of the home front. In order
not to disrupt or harm production of gas-masks for the front, and in order that
the factory can work normally – in spite of the eight-day absence of the
administration – we unanimously resolve: As circumstances will not permit of
any delay, to demand the immediate appointment of a commissar to take care
of the legal side of things and that he be someone neutral. The works
committee and shop stewards' committee take responsibility for production
and maintaining output ...
In no circumstances must our factory be subject to the War Industries
Committee, but to the state. We demand that the administration, which is
guilty of desertion, be handed over to a democratic court ...[62]

The government seems to have resisted the demand for sequestration,
for the factory soon closed down.[63]

The examples of the Brenner, Lebedev, Rykatkin and Respirator
works show clearly that efforts by workers to remove the administration were not inspired by syndicalist utopianism: they were designed
to save jobs. The committees behaved in an organised fashion and
liaised with the soviets and the government. They sought to force the

government into taking responsibility for the factory, and the sheer practical difficulties of running a factory seem to have discouraged them from attempting to run the factories by themselves. Factory seizures, or 'socialisations' were almost non-existent in Petrograd, although they were beginning to take place in the Ukraine by the autumn of 1917.

As workers' control became more aggressive and expansionist, opposition to it from factory owners hardened. Everywhere employers began to resist 'interference' by factory committees and to reassert their 'right to manage'. Attempts by the Society of Factory and Works Owners to confine the activities of the committees to the area demarcated by the law of 23 April failed dismally. Employers therefore tried to constrain the committees in other ways. They attempted to stop them meeting during working hours. They threatened to stop paying wages to committee members. They deprived committees of premises in which to meet and threatened individual members with dismissal or conscription into the army.[64] More significantly, the SFWO put pressure on the Ministry of Labour to use its legal powers to curb the ambitions of the committees. Anxious to meet objections from employers and to be seen to be doing something, the Ministry of Labour took steps to limit workers' control. On 23 August it issued a circular affirming that the right of hiring and firing workers belonged exclusively to the employers. On 28 August it issued a second circular which forbade factory committees from meeting during working hours. The circulars provoked uproar in the labour movement, not least because they appeared at precisely the time when General Kornilov was organising to drown the revolutionary movement in blood. Meetings of workers at Putilov, the Admiralty works, the Cable works, Nobel and Lebedev works heaped obloquy on the Ministry of Labour for capitulating to the counter-revolutionary demands of the employers.[65] At Langenzippen, the workers passed a resolution which said:

We reject with indignation the malicious slanders of the Ministry of Labour that the work of the factory committee lowers labour-productivity. The factory committee declares that ...
(1) Skobelev's circular has a purely political character and is counter-revolutionary. It prevents the labour movement from following an organised course and supports the organised march of the counter-revolution, which aims to sabotage industry and reduce the country to famine.
(2) We are forced to conclude that in the present context [of Kornilov] the Ministry for the 'protection of labour' has been converted into the Ministry

for the protection of capitalist interests and acts hand in hand with Ryabushinskii to reduce the country to famine, so that the 'bony hand' may strangle the revolution.[66]

At the Obukhov works a general meeting declared: 'We consider the existence of the factory committees to be a matter of life and death for the working class. We believe that the implementation of Skobelev's circular would mean the destruction of all the gains of the working class. We will fight with all our might and by all means, including the general strike, for the existence of our factory committees.'[67] The Third Conference of Petrograd Factory Committees (5–10 September) was hastily summoned to discuss the circulars. It roundly condemned them, jeering at Kolokol'nikov's pathetic attempts to explain away the circulars on behalf of an embarrassed Ministry of Labour.[68]

Some employers saw the circulars as a green light to go ahead and bring the factory committees to heel. At the Skorokhod shoe factory and the Aivaz engineering works management announced that they were going to stop paying members of the factory committee and stop their interference in hiring-policy.[69] On 1 September the administration at Vulcan announced that it intended to halve the wages bill of the factory committee. The committee resisted and was fully supported by the workers, who, going further in their resistance than the committee wished, clamoured for the removal of the director. After several weeks' bitter conflict, the wages of committee members were restored to their former level.[70] At the Nevskii footwear factory management persisted for a week in trying to stop meetings during working hours and in refusing to pay workers to guard the factory, but it then gave in.[71] In general, labour organisations in Petrograd were strong enough to thwart efforts by employers to constrain them, and in most factories employers do not seem to have thought it worth even trying.

After the failure of attempts to curb workers' control by legal means, employers were thrown onto the defensive. By September workers' control had been transmogrified from an essentially defensive tactic of maintaining production into an offensive means of forcing employers to keep open their factories come what may. The dominant feeling amongst employers was aptly summed up in the *Torgovo-Promyshlennaya Gazeta*: 'The sole dream of the industrialist has become to give up business and to close his enterprise, if only for a short time. If cases of closure are not so numerous, it is only because the threat of mob law, sequestration and unrest hangs over him.'[72]

Although the main impulse behind the workers' control movement was a practical concern to save jobs, the movement also reflected the continuing concern of workers to realise the democratic gains of the February Revolution. The expanding scope of workers' control was seen as further limiting the arbitrary authority of management and fortifying the power of workers in production. Indeed the concern with maintaining output and the concern with democracy were mutually reinforcing: the effort to combat potential sabotage by the employer necessitated a curtailment of his authority. This is made clear by the preamble to the resolution on workers' control, passed by the First All-Russian National Conference of Factory Committees, which stated: 'Having overthrown autocracy in the political sphere, the working class will aspire to achieve the triumph of the democratic system in the sphere of production. The idea of workers' control, which arose naturally in the circumstances of economic ruin created by the criminal policy of the ruling classes, is the expression of this aspiration.'[73]

The concern with workplace-democracy continued to be more vital in the state sector than in the private sector up to October. At the beginning of July the first national congress of factory and port committees subject to the Naval Ministry discussed the possibility of workers' self-management. Kaffeman, a delegate from the Izhora works, and probably an SR, introduced a resolution which called for naval enterprises to be run solely by the factory committees.[74] It was envisaged that the latter would elect a director and administrative staff, and that the Naval Ministry would send representatives to the factories for purposes of 'control'. An opposing resolution introduced by a Menshevik, Nabokov, from the Okhta shell shop, said that factory committees should not run the naval enterprises, for this was the job of the official administration, but that they should have rights of information and inspection. Nabokov's resolution was passed by 48 votes to ten, with seven abstentions.[75] It is ironic that the Mensheviks Nabokov and Solomon Schwarz should have proposed workers' control instead of workers' self-management at the conference, for their party officially rejected even workers' control, but clearly it was seen as a lesser evil to full-blown self-management. The same conference, however, initially overrode attempts by the

Mensheviks to stop workers electing the administration, as they already did at the Baltic and Izhora works. A resolution was passed proposing that a list of candidates for the posts of director and chief technician be drawn up by the Naval Ministry, factory committees and technicians' union, from which the workers would then make a choice. The chosen director would then draw up a list of candidates for administrative jobs at departmental and shop level, from which the workers again would choose. They would, however, still retain the right to raise objections (*otvod*) to particular administrators or technicians. Engineers, who generally sat on the naval factory committees in Petrograd, strongly condemned this resolution, arguing that modern production required planning and expertise, and that an elected administration would mean that popularity with the workers would count for more than scientific training. In view of this condemnation, the conference, two weeks later, overturned the resolution by 37 votes to 29, though it upheld the right of workers to object to administrative and technical personnel.[76] The conference also reaffirmed that the factory committees should only exercise 'informational' or 'preliminary' control, not 'responsible' control.

In the autumn of 1917, as workers intervened more deeply into the sphere of management, the distinction between the two types of control seemed to grow more specious, for it was difficult for workers to 'control' production on a broad scale, without taking some responsibility for it. This problem greatly exercised the committee at the Putilov works. As early as June the committee had gone to the Ministry of Labour to demand a new administration, and discussions had taken place within the committee as to the number of workers' representatives that should sit on the new company board. Most of the committee held that workers should demand a two-thirds majority of the eighteen places on the board but the Bolshevik chairman, Vasil'ev, believed that this would vest workers with responsibility for production willy-nilly.[77] On 25 September members of the works committee met with the vice-chairman of the Defence Commission, Pal'chinskii, to discuss the state of production at Putilov. He proposed that a joint commission of workers and management be established to supervise the running of the factory and to take charge of cutting the workforce and raising productivity. The majority of Bolsheviks and Menshevik-Internationalists on the works committee rejected this proposal, since they were unwilling to take responsibility for sackings and redundancies; instead they called for strict 'control' of the administration.[78] As Vasil'ev pointed out, however, it was becoming difficult to prevent 'control' from entailing 'responsibility': 'Assuming the functions of control, we will be drawn unwillingly, but quite naturally, into the sphere of operations and of factory productivity, into a sphere which is very ticklish from the point of view of preserving the principles of revolutionary democracy and observing the principles of class struggle.'[79]

A conference of metalworkers on 15 October pondered further the contradictions of workers' control. The syndicalist, A.K. Gastev, opened the discussion, arguing forcefully that the factory committees were fooling themselves if they thought that 'control' could avoid entailing responsibility. Speakers debated the relative merits of 'informational' versus 'responsible' control and a clear majority spoke up for the latter. Although the conference took place only a week before the October uprising, the expectation of the delegates was that capitalism would continue for an indefinite time, but that the state would regulate production on an increasing scale.[80] The next day, however, a conference of works committees under the Artillery Administration reaffirmed the orthodox position: 'responsibility for production lies exclusively with the administration ... but the works committees have the right of control, which means that the works committee, in the shape of its control commission, has the right to attend all board meetings and to demand exhaustive information'.[81]

Three days later, the First National Conference of Factory Committees continued the debate. The Bolshevik Larin proposed that the factory committees send one member to sit on each organ of administration, though only with an advisory voice. Chubar' rejected this, arguing that the committee representatives would be cast in the role of 'adjutants to the generals', that they would become embroiled in paper work, that they would be used by management as 'pushers', and that they would become targets of rank-and-file hostility. He proposed that the factory committees control commission should oversee the work of the administrative organs, but refuse to sit on them.[82] The resolution of the conference insisted that management keep the committees fully informed of its decisions and of the state of production, and allow it full access to correspondence and accounts.[83]

The debates about workers' control in the autumn of 1917 arose from the fact that the movement for workers' control had a relentlessly forward-moving dynamic. The demand for workers' control was, in Trotsky's parlance, a 'transitional' demand, which stemmed from the immediate practical needs of workers, but which pushed them ever forward into battle with the capitalism itself. Workers' control implied a kind of 'dual power' in the factory which, like 'dual power' at state level, was intrinsically unstable and necessitated resolution at the expense of one class or another.

By October the movement for workers' control had become a mass movement. The Soviet historian, M.L. Itkin, estimates that 289,000 workers, or 74% of the city's industrial workforce, worked in enterprises under some form of workers' control.[84] Yet this should be kept in perspective, for Itkin calculates that workers' control operated in only 96 enterprises. Since there were 1,011 enterprises of all sizes in the city and its suburbs[85], this means that 90% of enterprises, predominantly small or medium-sized factories, were not touched by workers' control, Moreover only a minority of factory committees practised workers' control. It has been calculated that there were 244 factory committees in Petrograd province by October[86], so if Itkin is correct, only 39% operated workers' control. Workers' control thus affected only large factories and left the majority of smaller enterprises untouched.

THE RELATIONSHIP OF THE FACTORY COMMITTEES TO THE TRADE UNIONS

The coexistence of factory committees and trade unions raised problems about their respective spheres of competence. The factory committees in the private sector had initially pursued activities of a conventional trade-union type. After the re-establishment of trade unions, the factory committees withdrew from the sphere of collective bargaining and began to concentrate on workers' control of production. It was not clear, however, whether the committees should operate independently of the trade unions, or whether they should merge into them. At the First Conference of Factory Committees a majority of delegates spoke in favour of the committees being separate from the trade unions, on the grounds that their job – that of controlling production – was different from that of the trade unions, as conventionally understood. The minority of trade-union spokesmen at the conference, principally the *Mezhraionets*, D. Ryazanov, and the Menshevik, V.D. Rubtsov, argued that there was not room for two labour organisations, and that the factory committees should become the primary cells of the trade unions.[87] The trade-union leaders seem to have been particularly worried by the proposal to set up a Central Council of Factory Committees. Initially, the proponents of a CCFC had envisaged that it would be attached to the Petrograd Council of Trade Unions,[88] but in the course of the conference, they seem to have decided in favour of an autonomous body. Replying, on behalf of the majority, to trade-union objections, the Bolshevik delegate from the New Parviainen works said: 'At present to turn the factory committees into departments of the trade unions in the factories, as Comrade Ryazanov proposes, seems impossible, in view of the fact that the factory committees have the special task of bringing order to the economic life of the factories and of implementing control – tasks with which the unions are not and cannot be concerned.'[89] An anodyne resolution was carried which bypassed the issues at stake and called merely for close liaison between the new CCFC and the PCTU.[90]

A week later, on 11 June, the central board of the Petrograd metalworkers' union issued a statement on the relationship of the factory committees to the trade unions. It called unequivocally for the strict subordination of the factory committees to the unions:

The union is the highest and only organisation responsible for the conduct of workers in a particular branch of production. It alone has the right to put demands on the organisations of capitalists and on the state on behalf of the whole profession. It alone has the right to conduct either general or partial disputes. It alone may put demands on the state concerning social security. It alone can express the will of the whole profession on questions concerning the forms of regulation and control of production ... Local factory committees occupy a position of subordination to the trade union, within the general framework of organisation of the branch of production ... but the overall structure of the union must be made more complex by involving the factory committees, so that the union combines within itself the organisation of its members by branch of production and ... by enterprise. However, the central organisation of the whole trade union must be constituted so that the preponderance of union representatives over individual factory representatives is guaranteed. The strength of factory committee representation must be broadest where the union is acting as regulator and controller of production, and narrowest where the union is pursuing purely militant aims.[91]

This was a scarcely-veiled attack on the newly-created CCFC, opposing the factory committees' setting-up a centralised structure alongside that of the unions. It is interesting to note that the metal-union proposals concerning the relationship of the two organisations, prefigured with uncanny accuracy the relationship which was to be established after October.

The unwillingess of the metal-union leadership to accept a division of labour between the factory committees and trade unions sprang from their 'productivist' ideology. A significant group on the central board believed that the trade unions should no longer concern themselves merely with the defence of workers' interests, but should prepare to take up the tasks of regulating the economy as a whole. They were sceptical of the efforts of the factory committees to organise production at a local level. On 21 July the Provisional Central Committee of the union passed a resolution, influenced by the thinking of the Austro-Marxist, Rudolf Hilferding, which argued that a new phase of state capitalism was coming into being which would entail far-reaching trustification of production and distribution by the state. It demanded the active participation of unions in the Economic Council which was to be set up by the government.[92] The aspiration of the metal union that trade unions should be involved in state regulation of the economy became a reality after October but, at this stage, was not widely shared within the trade-union movement.

On 20 June the Third All-Russian Conference of Trade Unions opened in Petrograd – the first national conference of trade unions since the February Revolution. The 211 delegates comprised 73 Bolsheviks, 36 Mensheviks, 6 Menshevik-Internationalists, 11 Bundists, 31 non-fractional Social Democrats, 25 SRs, 7 members of no political party (others unknown).[93] The moderate socialists commanded a majority. The Menshevik, V.P. Grinevich, introduced the discussion on the tasks of the trade unions. He argued that the basic task of the unions was to conduct the economic struggle of the working class, whose chief weapon within the framework of capitalism was the strike. He insisted that unions should not involve themselves in the regulation of production, as this was the job of the government.[94] The Internationalists excoriated the Mensheviks for their support of state control of the economy rather than workers' control. The Bolshevik spokesman, N. Glebov-Avilov, in effect, argued that the job of workers' control was too important to be left to the factory committees, that it should be taken over by the trade unions and that the factory committees should be subordinated to the trade unions: 'The factory committees must be the primary cells of the unions. Their activities in the localities must be made dependent on the economic-control commissions of the unions.'[95] This adumbrates the position adopted by the Bolsheviks after October, but is at variance with the line taken by the First Conference of Factory Committees. The position adopted by the Mensheviks, which was accepted by Conference by 76 votes to 63 votes, was also inconsistent. The Mensheviks disliked workers' control, but so opposed were they to the trade unions becoming involved in the work of controlling production, that they insisted that the factory committees take sole responsibility for this. At the same time, they called on the unions to turn the factory committees into their supports (*opornye punkty*) in the localities and to execute their policies through them.[96]

A full discussion of the relationship of the factory committees to the trade unions took place at the Second Conference of Petrograd Factory Committees (7–12 August). Lozovskii, later a key advocate of the organisational subordination of the factory committees to the unions, put forward a position which was designed to bridge the divide between the two organisations. He argued that they both had different spheres of interest: trade unions had to defend the wages and conditions of labour and oversee the implementation of labour-protection legislation; factory committees had the task of regulating production. He argued that the committees should be subordinate to the unions, insofar as they should be obliged to implement union decisions at factory level, and should not strike without union permission.[97] This position was fiercely denounced by the anarcho-syndicalist, Volin, who lauded the factory committees as the only revolutionary organisations capable of pursuing the struggle of labour against capital, and dismissed the trade unions as being eternally condemned to mediate between capital and labour.[98] He, in turn, was attacked by Voskov, the Bolshevik delegate from the Sestroretsk arms works, who argued that the factory committees:

cannot unite workers in the same way as the unions do. The whole fragmented mass of workers in a particular factory is included in the factory organisation and if the factory closes, this organisation dissolves. The factory committee hangs by a thread, it can be replaced on the slightest pretext. The union unites the truly conscious, organised workers; it remains constant; the closure of individual factories does not undermine it.[99]

Lozovskii's resolution, proposing a division of labour between the unions and the factory committees, won the day. Volin's resolution gained a mere eight votes.[100]

On 20 October the All Russian Conference of Factory Committees discussed once more the relationship of the factory committees to the trade unions. The Bolshevik, Ryazanov, and the Menshevik, Lin'kov, on behalf of the trade unions, accused the factory committees of separatism and called for their organisational subordination. They were particularly unhappy about the existence of the CCFC alongside the All-Russian Central Council of Trade Unions, and called for the disbandment of the former. They were bitterly opposed by the anarcho-syndicalist Piotrovskii, from Odessa, and by the Left SR Levin, from the CCFC, both of whom contrasted the vitality of the committees to the lassitude of the unions.[101] The Bolshevik V. Schmidt, from the metalworkers' union, conceded that the factory committees had a particular role to play in the sphere of control of production but wished to see them working under the auspices of the unions.[102] The Bolshevik Skrypnik, from the CCFC, emphasised that there could at this stage be no question of making the committees the executive organs of the unions, but went some way towards placating the trade unionists by agreeing that the CCFC should collaborate with the city organisations of trade unions in the realm of control of production.[103]

There is some evidence that by October opinion within the labour movement was beginning to shift towards acceptance of the idea of a merger of the trade unions and factory committees. A commission of the All-Russian Conference of Factory Committees went some way towards recognising trade-union primacy. Whilst stressing the independence of the two organisations and the right of the factory committees to organise into a national structure, the commission called for the CCFC to include trade-union representatives and for it to be given the status of a department of workers' control of the All-Russian Central Council of Trade Unions. In addition, it called for councils of factory committees to be established in each branch of industry, which would become the sections for workers' control of the respective industrial unions.[104] Nevertheless the issue remained unresolved on the eve of October. It was to take several months for the Bolsheviks to resolve, since the party was divided by the institutional loyalties of its members.

8

The social structure of the labour movement

In Chapter 1 it was argued that two broad groups can be discerned within the Petrograd working class in 1917: the proletarianised, skilled, mainly male workers, and the new, younger peasant and women workers. It was the former group of 'cadre' workers who built the factory committees and trade unions after the February Revolution. Quantitative data to bear out this contention are lacking, although a survey of fitters at the Putilov works in 1918, conducted by Strumilin, showed that skilled workers dominated all labour organisations and had been the first to join the metal union in 1917.[1] This is borne out by a complaint in the industrialists' newspaper in the spring of 1917 that 'it is usually the most skilled workers, they being the most conscious, who participate in the different committees – the factory committees, soviets etc.'.[2] The same sentiment was voiced by A. Gastev at the first national congress of metalworkers: 'in the unions we operate by basing ourselves on the skilled element of the workforce, for example, the turners and fitters ... this is the most active section of the working class. The unskilled workers are, of course, less active.'[3] Skilled, experienced workers had a greater capacity than new workers to initiate a social movement and to carry out consciously-willed social change.[4] They had more 'resources' for organisation: they were better-paid and had more money and time at their disposal; they were at home in the factory and understood how production worked; they had experience of organising strikes and trade unions, of informal shop-floor organisation and of job-control; they were more literate and thus better-placed to participate in political discourse. The shift in the balance of class forces which resulted from the February Revolution created opportunities for 'cadre' workers to mobilise these 'resources' in order to create an organised labour movement.[5]

The 'cadre' workers who built the labour movement, of whatever political persuasion, tended to see the new, inexperienced workers as the 'dark' or 'backward' masses, who had brought 'disorder' and 'anarchy' into the labour movement. As early as 1916 the Workers' Group of the War Industries Committee noted that:

During the war the composition of the working class has changed; many alien, undisciplined elements have come into the workforce. In addition, the intensification of work, the broad application of female and child labour, uninterrupted overtime and holiday work ... have increased the number of grounds for conflict of all kinds and these often arise spontaneously. Instead of organised defence of their interests, workers engage in elemental outbursts and anarchic methods.[6]

A Latvian Bolshevik on the CCFC, A. Kaktyn', made a similar point in 1917, blaming 'anarchic disorders' on the 'not yet fully proletarianised mass of workers consisting of refugees, people from the countryside and others temporarily swept into industry by the war'.[7] Employers too ascribed disorders to what they called the 'alien element' (*prishlyi element*). At the Franco-Russian works management complained that those who had come to the factory during the war had had a bad effect on the discipline of the workforce as a whole.[8] One must treat the accounts of 'disorders' by workers new to industry with a certain caution, for the sources reflect the perceptions and values of the 'organisation builders', not those of the new workers themselves. We shall see that while the former were by no means unsympathetic to their less experienced comrades, they often underestimated the capacity of new workers for self-activity and political understanding, because the forms of their activity did not fit the leaders' own model of appropriate action.

The 'backward masses' (*otstalye massy*) were counterposed to the more 'conscious' (*soznatel'nye*) workers. The new workers were perceived as 'backward', either because they were apathetic and indifferent to the labour movement and to politics, or because they indulged in uncontrolled militancy (*stikhiinost'*). These characteristics, which at first sight appear mutually exclusive, typified the traditional pattern of behaviour of the Russian peasants: long periods of quiescence punctuated by bouts of rebelliousness (*buntarstvo*). The major task facing 'cadre' workers was to convince the new workers of the need for organisation: to break them from their apathy or persuade them of the advantages of planned, sustained pursuit of their goals over sudden bursts of militancy, born of anger and emotion, rather than of calculation. This was not so easy in the spring of 1917, for direct action proved fairly effective in removing hated administrators ('carting out') or in extracting concessions from the employers. As the economic crisis worsened, however, the limitations of sectional, spontaneous actions became more and more apparent. The promotion of the interests of labour as a whole against capital required durable organisation and clearly-formulated goals and strategies. Volatile militancy tended to get in the way of this, and was thus disliked by labour leaders. They sought to channel the militancy of the new workers into organisation or, alternatively, to rouse interest in organisation if workers were bogged down in apathy.

Women workers

In its first issue, the Menshevik party newspaper did not fail to note that whilst women had courageously faced the bullets of the police during the revolution, not one woman had as yet been elected to the Petrograd Soviet.[9] Observations that working women were not participating in the nascent labour movement were commonplace. A report on the Svetlana factory at the end of March noted that 'it is almost exclusively women who work there. They but dimly perceive the importance of the current situation and the significance of labour organisation and proletarian discipline. For this reason, and because of low pay, a certain disorder in production is noticeable.'[10] On 22 April fifty women from state factories, including twenty-two from the Pipe works, met to discuss how to organise women. They agreed that 'women workers everywhere are yearning to take part in existing labour organisations, but up to now have joined them only in small numbers, on nothing like the same scale as men'.[11] As late as June, a woman from the Pipe works described the situation in shop number four, where 2,000 women were employed on automatic machines which cut out and processed fuses:

Sometimes you see how the women will read something, and from their conversation it emerges that a desire to step forward has been kindled in their hearts. But to our great regret, there is at present very little organisation among the women of the Pipe works. There are no women comrades among us to fan the spark of consciousness or point out to us the path to truth. We really need a comrade who can speak on the tribune in front of a sea of faces and tell us where to go, whom to listen to and what to read.[12]

If women workers did act to defend their interests, it was often by means of elemental bouts of direct action. This is apparent from the example of two notoriously 'backward' textile-mills on Vyborg Side, where at the end of June two spectacular examples of 'carting out' took place. After the textile union began contract negotiations with the textile section of the SFWO, the latter called a halt to further wage-increases in the industry, pending the settlement of the contract.[13] When the director of the Vyborg spinning-mill tried to explain to a general meeting of workers that he was unable to consider their demand for a wage-increase, the women seized him, shoved him in a wheelbarrow and carted him to the canal where, poised perilously on the edge of the bank, he shakily signed a piece of paper agreeing to an increase.[14] When L.G. Miller, the redoubtable chairman of the textile section of the SFWO, heard of this he demanded that the textile union send an official to the mill to sort out the women, but the women refused to listen to the official. The director, therefore, agreed to pay the increase and was fined 30,000 r. by the SFWO for so doing.[15] Only days later, women at the neighbouring Sampsionevs-kaya mill, where Miller himself was director, demanded a similar increase. When Miller rejected their demand at a general meeting, women workers – who comprised 91% of the workforce – seized him and called for a wheelbarrow ('*V meshok i na tachku!*' ['Tie him in a sack and shove him on a barrow!']). Male apprentices tried to dissuade them, but Miller climbed quietly into the barrow, asking only that the women should not put a sack over his head. Instead they tied it to his feet and, with raucous shouts, wheeled him around Vyborg Side, urging him to agree to a wage-rise. Miller might have been thrown off the Grenadier bridge had not a group of off-duty soldiers intervened. Thoroughly shaken by his ordeal, Miller had to be carried back to the factory, but he remained obdurate, and the women did not receive a wage-rise.[16]

One should not assume from this that women remained outside the orbit of the labour movement. Thanks to the efforts of small numbers of socialist women, working women rapidly began to join the trade unions and to engage in more organised forms of struggle. There are no data on the number of women in the trade unions, but it does not appear that the industries with the highest proportions of women workers were necessarily those with low densities of trade-union membership. In the food and textile industries women comprised 66% and 69% of the workforce, respectively, but trade-union membership stood at about 80% and 70%.[17] Trade-union membership was lowest in the chemical industry – at about 48% – which does seem to have been linked to the fact that the skilled men joined the metal and woodturners' unions, leaving the peasant women machine-operators, who comprised 47% of the workforce, to fend for themselves.[18] In the metal industry, however, men encouraged women workers to join the union, and it is probable that a majority of working women joined trade unions in the course of 1917, although the evidence does not suggest that they participated actively in union life. Women were poorly represented in leadership positions in the unions, even in industries where they comprised a majority of the workforce. Eleven out of twenty members of the first board of the textile union were women, but only two remained after its reorganisation – alongside thirteen men.[19] The Petrograd boards of the metal, leather and needleworkers' unions were equally unrepresentative – each having a solitary woman member.[20]

In the factory committees a similar situation existed. Women comprised a third of the factory workforce, but only 4% of the delegates to the First Conference of Factory Committees.[21] At the Triangle rubber works 68% of the workforce was female, but only two of the twenty-five members of the factory 'soviet' were women.[22] At the Nevskaya footwear factory 45% of the workforce was female, but none of the *starosty* was a woman.[23] At the Pechatkin paper-mill 45% of the workforce was female, but only two out of thirteen *starosty* were women. At the Sampsionevskaya cotton-mill, where 85% of the workforce were women, representation was rather better, for four out of seven members of the committee were women.[25] This suggests that in industries where women were in the majority, they may have tended to be less dependent on men – and more self-reliant.

Those socialist women who devoted so much effort to organising working women accused the labour leaders of not paying enough attention to the special needs of women. In June A. Kollontai reproached the delegates to the Third Trade-Union Conference for not taking up questions of maternity provision and equal pay.[26] In September she wrote an article for the journal of the Petrograd Council of Trade Unions, which urged union leaders to treat women 'not as appendages to men, but as independent, responsible members of the working class, having the same rights and also the same responsibilities to the collective'.[27] In October she spoke to the First All-Russian Conference of Factory Committees warning of the political danger of their remaining indifferent to the plight of women workers.[28] At none of the conferences of the labour movement in 1917, however, was there a full discussion of the problems of working women and of their relationship to the organised labour movement.

At factory level women workers often met with active discrimination from men in their attempts to organise. At the Pipe works a woman complained. 'It happens, not infrequently even now, that the backward workers, who lack consciousness, cannot imagine that a woman can be as capable as a man of organising the broad masses, and so they make fun of the elected representatives of the women workers, pointing their fingers as though at a savage, and saying with a sneer: "there go our elected representatives".'[29] M. Tsvetkova wrote to the leatherworkers' journal, complaining about the behaviour of her male colleagues:

Instead of supporting, organising and going hand-in-hand with the women, they behave as though we are not equal members of the working family and sometimes do not bother with us at all. When the question of unemployment and redundancies arises, they try to ensure that the men stay and that the women go, hoping that the women will be unable to resist because of their poor organisation and feebleness. When women attempt to speak, in order to point out that the men are behaving wrongly and that we must jointly find a solution, the men will not allow us to speak and will not listen. It is difficult even for the more conscious women to fight against this, the more so since often the mass of women do not understand and do not wish to listen to us.[30]

Labour leaders, generally, opposed active discrimination against working women (for example, over redundancies). They encouraged them to organise, and the struggles of working women began to assume a more disciplined character, although 'spontaneous' militancy by no means disappeared. Labour leaders were genuinely solicitous of the needs of working women as low-paid workers, but less solicitous of their needs as women. They spurned any idea of specific policies for working women, believing that this would be a deviation towards bourgeois feminism. The result was that women joined the labour movement, but played a passive role within it. After October this was to result once more in women becoming apathetic and indifferent.

Peasant and unskilled workers

Like women workers, peasant and unskilled workers displayed a preference for direct action over formal organisation, and a certain distrust of labour leaders. At the Metal works a carpenter described the attitude of new workers to the trade unions as follows:

A majority of workers ... in essence do not belong to the category of true proletarians. These people have come to the factory from the countryside in order to avoid military service and the war, or to assist the rural household with a good factory wage. This element ... will move only when it feels that it is directly defending its own interests, but it has not grasped the principle of organising the working masses into unions for permanent, day-to-day struggle. They reduce this principle merely to paying subscriptions, and argue that they do not need this extra expense, or frankly admit that they are going to leave the factory as soon as the war is over and return to the countryside.[31]

He also blamed the 'cadre' workers for 'neglecting the organisation of their less conscious comrades'. When the union tried to implement the metalworkers' contract in autumn, over half the workers in the Metal works refused the wage category into which they were placed by the rates commission, inundating the factory committee with demands to be upgraded. In November unskilled painters beat up a representative of the metalworkers' union and refused to release him until he agreed to sign an order granting all workers a wage of twelve rubles a day, backdated to 5 June.[32]

At the Pipe works the Bolsheviks, whose fortunes were in the ascendant, agitated for new elections to the Vasilevskii district soviet, which were fixed for 17 May. The Petrograd Soviet Executive, however, arranged a meeting at the factory for that day, so the shop stewards agreed to postpone elections. The peasant workers in the foundry were outraged and resolved to press ahead with the elections. Kapanitskii, a shop steward and an SR deputy to the Soviet, was sent to persuade the foundryworkers to change their minds. The official protocol of a general factory meeting describes what happened: 'The foundryworkers sat comrade Kapanitskii in a wheelbarrow, beat him and threatened to throw him in the furnace, but then decided to save the furnace for other people. They confined themselves to wheeling him out into the factory yard and then to the river. It was only thanks to the intervention of comrades in shops numbers eight and four that he was released.'[33] A few Bolsheviks seem to have provoked or connived in this action. The shop steward of the foundry blamed the violence on a handful of workers, when he made a public apology to the general meeting.[34]

Like women workers, unskilled and peasant workers did begin to organise in 1917. *Chernorabochie* set up a trade union in April, which later merged with the metal union, and Chapter 5 described how they became organised and politicised during the course of the protracted contract negotiations of the metal union. Similarly, peasant workers and soldiers formed some seventy *zemlyachestva* in the capitals to bring together migrants from the same area and to undertake political agitation among the peasantry. The total membership of the *zemlyachestva* may have been as high as 30,000, and by September the major ones had swung from the SRs to the Bolsheviks.[35]

Young Workers

Workers under the age of eighteen showed a far greater capacity for self-organisation than women or peasant workers, though girls were far less active than boys. They built a youth movement – which acquired a strongly Bolshevik character – in the shape of the Socialist Union of Working Youth (SUWY).[36] Through this, they played a leading role in the political events of 1917 (the July Days and the October seizure of power). Many young workers joined the Bolshevik party and the Red Guards: it has been estimated that 19% of those joining the Petrograd Bolshevik party were under twenty-one, and no fewer than 28% of Red Guards were of this age.[37] Working youth played a less prominent part in the organised labour movement, however, which seems to have been connected to the fact that workers under eighteen were in a relationship of dependence on adult workers in the workplace.[38]

In the wake of the February Revolution, young workers began to set up committees in the factories, first in the metal works of Vyborg, Narva and Vasilevskii districts, and then spreading to other industries and areas.[39] Out of these factory youth groups there developed district youth organisations and, subsequently, the city-wide youth movement. From the first, these factory youth groups demanded representation on the factory committees. At some of the more politically radical enterprises this demand was conceded. At the Phoenix, Aivaz and Renault works the factory committees allowed young workers two representatives.[40] At the Cable works the committee supported the young workers' demand for the vote at

eighteen and called on the Provisional Government to withdraw
eighteen-year-olds from the Front if it would not enfranchise them.[41]
A majority of factory committees, however, were more reluctant to
allow young workers special representation and to take up their
demands.[42] Under pressure, committees at the Baltic, Putilov and
Gun works allowed youth representatives to sit on the committees but
not to vote.[43] Young workers at the Gun works condemned the
committee's refusal to allow their representatives voting rights: 'We
protest because the father-proletariat, in spurning his children,
makes it harder for us to become, in the future, experienced, hardened
fighters for right, honour and the triumph of the world proletariat
and, of course, in the first place, of our own proletariat.'[44] At the
Kersten knitting mill the factory committee – which was the first in
the textile industry to implement workers' control – also refused
voting rights to the two representatives of the 660 girls at the mill. The
youth committee condemned this policy, but argued that 'your
representative on our committee may only have an advisory voice
since no organisation may interfere in the affairs of youth'.[45] In May a
conference of factory committees on Vyborg Side agreed that young
workers should have voting rights on the committees, but only on
matters affecting their economic position.[46]

The trade unions supported the demands for improved wages for
young workers and came out in support of a six-hour day for young
workers.[47] They were slower to take up demands for the overhauling
of the system of apprenticeship and for the vote at eighteen, although
Bolshevik-dominated unions supported them. There are no statistics
on the age structure of union membership. Young workers seem to
have joined the unions, but many officially debarred workers under
the age of sixteen from membership.[48] For obvious reasons of age and
inexperience, workers under 18 were not represented at leadership
level in the unions, but union leaders were by no means old. At the
first national congress of metalworkers in January 1918 the average
age of delegates was twenty-nine, and at the first congress of
leatherworkers, at around the same time, 54% of delegates were
under thirty, although only 15% were under twenty-five.[49]

It is clear that the forms of collective action engaged in by most
women, peasant and unskilled workers were different from those of
'cadre' workers. In general, the former lacked 'resources' for sustained, institutionalised pursuit of goals, and turned most easily to

forms of 'direct action', such as 'carting out', wildcat strikes, go-slows. These forms of action were often violent and always sectional, but they were not as irrational as they may seem. 'Carting out', for example, entailed a level of communication and coordination, and a conception of appropriate action, though not necessarily a specific plan of action.[50] It was a symbolic action, born of anger and emotion rather than calculation, but it had a certain rationality as a type of 'collective bargaining by riot'.[51] The evidence suggests that as the economic crisis grew worse, such forms of 'direct action' became increasingly less effective – a sign of desperation and weakness, rather than of confidence and strength.

To the leaders of the factory committees and trade unions, spontaneous forms of militancy on the part of the new workers were a threat to the project of building an organised labour movement, and were thus condemned as 'backward'. The labour leaders sought to direct 'spontaneity' into organised channels, for they believed that the pursuit of the interests of workers as a class, and the achievement of far-reaching social and political changes on their behalf required effective organisation and clearly-formulated goals. Whilst spontaneous militancy might be effective in securing the aims of a section of workers in the short term, it could not secure the ends of the working class as a whole. They recognised, moreover, that only formal organisation and planned action could achieve maximum gains at minimum cost. They thus sought to 'tame' the volatile, explosive militancy of the new workers, and aspired to bring them within the orbit of the organised labour movement: to teach them habits of negotiation, formulation of demands, the practices of committees and meetings. They seem to have had some success, nothwithstanding the unpropitious economic circumstances, in subordinating *buntarstvo* to bargaining.

The labour leaders were sincerely anxious to promote the welfare of those workers less fortunate than themselves. They believed that both new and experienced workers shared the same class interests and could best pursue these through united organisation and struggle. They were, however, unwilling to recognise that there might be contradictions of interest between women and men, youths and adults, or unskilled and skilled. They thus would not give special treatment to any of these groups, for example, by setting up organisations within the unions for women workers or by allowing young workers special representation on the factory committees.

Although they justified their position in political terms – the working class is a unity in which there are no diversities of interest – this attitude reflected the social position of the leaders themselves. For within the craft tradition of the 'organisation-builders', skill was closely bound up with masculinity and a degree of condescension towards women and youth. Thus in spite of their very best intentions – their determination to involve all workers in the labour movement – the efforts of the labour leaders were stymied by an unconscious paternalism towards those whom they were trying to organise.

DEMOCRACY AND BUREAUCRACY IN THE TRADE UNIONS AND FACTORY COMMITTEES

Democracy in the trade unions

One usually thinks of 'democratic centralism' as the organisational principle espoused by the Bolshevik party, but the principle was accepted by the labour movement as a whole. The Third Trade-Union Conference resolved that 'democratic centralism' should underpin the organisational construction of the trade-union movement, in order to ensure 'the participation of every member in the affairs of the union and, at the same time, unity in the leadership of the struggle'.[52] 'Democratic centralism' did not represent a coherent set of organisational rules; it was rather a vague principle of democratic decision-making, combined with centralised execution of decisions taken. The balance between 'democracy' and 'centralism' was thus not fixed with any precision, and within the trade unions, in the course of 1917, the balance tended to shift away from democracy towards centralism.

The great majority of Petrograd factory workers joined trade unions in 1917, but the data on membership are unreliable, and so one cannot determine the percentage of members in each branch of industry. Rough calculations suggest that the percentage was highest in printing (over 90%); that in the leather, wood and metal industries it was 80% or more; that in the textiles it was around 70%, but that in chemicals it was as low as 48% (compare *Tables 1* and *12*). In many metal-works general meetings of workers voted to join the union *en bloc*, though in a minority of factories, such as the Metal works, the factory committees resisted this 'closed shop' policy.[53] In other industries, too, with the exception of chemicals, workers tended to make the decision to join the union collectively rather than individually. On 8 May delegates of the woodturners' union threatened to expel from the factories any worker who refused to join the union.[54]

Union subscriptions were designed to attract all workers, including the low-paid, into the union. Initial membership of the metal union cost one ruble, and monthly dues were graduated according to earnings. Workers earning more than ten rubles a day paid two rubles a month; those earning between six and ten rubles a day paid 1 r. 40 k.; those earning less than six rubles, paid 80 k. a month, and apprentices paid 50 k.[55] Union delegates would stand outside the finance-office on pay day to ensure that all workers paid their dues. Initially, most union members seem to have paid their dues: in the metal union the monthly sum of subscriptions rose from 94,335 r. in June to 133,540 r. in July;[56] in the textile union it rose from 4,800 r. in May to 10,000 r. in July.[57] As the economic crisis set in, however, non-payment of union dues became a major problem. In the leather union the monthly sum of dues fell from 18,093 r. in May to 15,167 r. in July.[58] The glass union reported in September that 'subscriptions are being paid promptly', but in December reported that only 326 out of 807 members in Petrograd had paid their dues that month.[59]

The collection of monthly dues, the distribution of union publications, the convening of union meetings and the liaison between the individual enterprise and the union hierarchy devolved on factory delegates. These delegates were elected by all the union members in a particular enterprise: in the textile industry delegates were elected on the basis of one delegate for every twenty union members; in the metal industry on the basis of one delegate for every hundred union members.[60] In some of the larger factories union delegates formed councils within the factory, but the main job of delegates was to liaise with other factories in the same industry and district of Petrograd. In the print industry the delegates (*upolnomochennye*) had a similar job to factory delegates in other industries, except that they also formed the workshop committee. The division between the trade union and the factory committee thus did not exist in the print industry. Union delegates from each enterprise met at city-district level at least once a month to discuss union business, to oversee the activities of the union board and to discuss problems in individual enterprises. In many unions, including the metal, print and leather unions, the delegates elected district boards of the union, which were responsible for liaising between the city board of the union and the individual enterprise and for organising recruitment and the collection of subscriptions. In the metal and print unions some delegates defended the autonomy of the district boards from the city board, fearing that too much centralisation at city level would lead to bureaucratisation of the union.

In principle, if not always in practice, power was vested in the city boards, not the district boards, of the unions. The city boards were elected by city-wide meetings of union delegates (comprising either representatives of city-district delegate meetings or all district delegates *en masse*). On 7 May 535 delegates elected the Petrograd board of the metal union.[61] On 4 June 300 delegates from twenty-six textile mills elected sixteen members to the city board of the textile union.[62] The city board was responsible for coordinating economic struggles, dispensing strike funds, publishing the union journal and for negotiation with the SFWO and the government.[63] In those unions, such as the print, leather and food unions, where professional sections representing individual crafts existed, these were subordinate to the city board. Where district boards existed, these too were subordinate to the city board, though resistance to central control by the district boards was by no means unknown – particularly in the sphere of finance. The members of the city boards – and often the secretaries and treasurers of the district boards – were usually employed full-time by the union.

By the summer of 1917, the Petrograd metal union had almost a hundred full-time officials.[64] Clearly, 'bureaucratisation' was under way, although it would be wrong to exaggerate the extent of this. The powers of the city boards were strictly circumscribed, and in all unions the boards in theory were strictly subordinate to the city-wide meetings of union delegates. It was these meetings, rather than the boards themselves, which decided all major policy issues. The boards reported to city delegate meetings at least once a month and members of the boards could be recalled by the delegates. Conflicts arose between the boards and the delegates, as the discussion of the metalworkers' contract in Chapter 5 showed, which reflected the ambitions of the boards to extend their power, and the determination of the delegates to resist this process. The extent of democracy in the unions thus depended on the activism and enthusiasm of the delegates. Where they were remiss in their duties, then not only did the union board develop into an oligarchy but the ordinary members of the union tended to lapse into apathy. This seems to have been an increasing problem in the metal union by the later months of 1917. A worker wrote to the union journal complaining of the behaviour of many factory delegates:

If the central and district boards [of the union] are responsible to the meetings of [factory] delegates, then the delegates themselves are responsible to nobody. The majority of delegates, once elected, do not fulfil their duties, they do not recruit members, they do not collect subscriptions and do not even appear at delegate meetings ... All the time we observe a host of instances where the majority of our members are not aware of the policies and decisions of the central organs ... Naturally such ignorance at times causes apathy in the membership. Often one feels that the central organs of the union are totally cut off from the mass of the members. This threatens to turn the central organisation into a bureaucracy.'[65]

By the end of 1917 there is growing evidence that power within the union was passing away from the rank-and-file to the full-time officials of the unions. This should not, however, blind us to the fact that before October a significant degree of membership participation in the affairs of the union existed.

DEMOCRACY IN THE FACTORY COMMITTEES

Factory committees were much closer to ordinary workers than trade unions. They embraced all the workers in a single enterprise, whereas the trade unions embraced workers in a branch of industry. The committees represented all workers in a factory regardless of their job, whereas workers in the same factory might be members of different trade unions, despite the principle of industrial unionism. The factory committee represented everyone *gratis*, whereas one had to pay to be a member of a trade union. The committee usually met in working hours on the factory premises, whereas trade unions usually did not. For all these reasons, therefore, factory committees tended to be the more popular organisation. The SR, I. Prizhelaev, wrote: 'The factory committees have the crucial merit of being close to the worker, accessible, comprehensible to everybody – even the least conscious. They are involved in all the minutiae of factory life and so are a wonderful form of mass organisation ... The trade unions are less accessible because they appear to stand further away from the rank-and-file worker.'[66] 7,000 workers at the Respirator factory on 3 September described the factory committees as 'the best mouthpieces of the working class and the only real and true reflection of the moods of the toiling people'.[67]

Every worker could vote in the election of a factory committee, regardless of job, sex or age. Any worker might stand for election, so long as he or she did not perform any managerial function.[68] Some factories, such as the Putilov works, stipulated that workers under the age of twenty might not stand for election.[69] Elections were supposed to be by secret ballot, according to the constitution drawn up by the conference of representatives of state enterprises (15 April), the statutes published by the labour department of the Petrograd Soviet and the model constitution passed by the Second Conference of Factory Committees.[70] Initially, factory committees were elected for one year, but the Second Conference specified that they should be elected for six months only. Factory committees could be recalled at any time by general meetings,[71] and they were required to report on their activities to general meetings at least once a month.[72]

The extent to which the working-class movement was permeated by a commitment to direct democracy is reflected in the fact that it was not the factory committee *per se* which was the sovereign organ in the factory, but the general meeting of all workers in the factory or section. It was this general assembly which passed resolutions on the pressing political questions of the day or decided important matters affecting the individual enterprise. This Rousseauesque concept of sovereignty was established in practice from the first. At the conference of representatives from state enterprises on 15 April it was decided that general meetings of the factory workforce should take place at least once a month and should be called by either the factory committee or by one-third of the workforce.[73] The Second Conference lowered this requirement, by stipulating that one-fifth of the workforce might summon a general meeting, which should be attended by at least one-third of the workers in order to be quorate. The Conference laid down that authority was vested in the workforce as a whole rather than in the committee.[74]

Marc Ferro has argued recently that we should not allow ourselves to be bewitched by the far-reaching democracy of the paper constitutions of the popular organisations of the Russian Revolution: reality was a very different matter. He argues that long before October the popular organisations were undergoing a process of bureaucratisation 'from above' and 'from below'. In the case of the factory committees, Ferro argues that the leadership of the movement became more entrenched and less accountable to the membership. Bureaucratisation 'from above' was manifest in a decline in the proportion of delegates at factory-committee conferences elected from the factories and in an increase in the proportion of 'bureaucratically appointed' delegates.[75] Bureaucratisation 'from below' was evident in the refusal of factory committee members on the ground to submit to re-election, and in the growing practice of inquorate meetings taking decisions.[76] It is not the present purpose to criticise Ferro's work in detail,[77] although scrutiny of his evidence suggests neither that the proportion of 'bureaucratically appointed' delegates at the factory committee conferences was on the increase in 1917, nor that they were in a position to influence conference decisions, since many of them did not have voting rights. What is pertinent to the concerns of this chapter is the extent to which factory committees on the ground were subject to re-election prior to October.

Re-elections took place at the Putilov, Electric Light, Pipe, Dinamo, Langenzippen, Skorokhod, Parviainen, Lessner, the Mint, Promet and Okhta shell-works. In other factories individual members of the committees were replaced. At the Baltic works the first committee was self-selected, but it was properly elected in the second half of April.[78] At the end of July a general meeting expressed no confidence in the committee, but the committee did not immediately resign.[79] Only when a further general meeting on 15 September voted for its immediate recall, did it step down.[80] Any party or non-party group was allowed to put up a slate of candidates in the new election, providing it could muster fifty signatures. The slates were then published and voting took place on 18 September by secret ballot. The Bolsheviks won a majority of the forty places.[81] Even if the committees in a majority of factories did not submit for re-election (and it is not clear that this was the case), it was not necessarily a sign of their bureaucratisation, for many had not completed their six-month term of office by October.

Data on the proportion of workers who took part in factory committee elections are exiguous, but they suggest that in most factories a majority of workers took part. At the Pechatkin paper mill in March 57% of workers voted in elections.[82] At the Sestroretsk arms works the committee declared soviet elections void when only half the electorate bothered to vote. It urged workers that: 'In view of the seriousness of the present moment, general factory meetings must be well-attended. It is the duty of every worker, as an honest citizen, to attend discussions of all questions concerning both the factory itself and the government in general.'[83] On 1 August, when the Sestroretsk works committee was re-elected, 72% of the workers voted.[84] In the same month 88% of workers at Parviainen voted in factory committee elections.[85] In September 69% of workers at New Lessner took part in elections, and in October 74% of workers at the Pipe works.[86]

Surveying the available evidence, it becomes clear that the degree of democracy in operation varied between factories, and that undemocratic practices were by no means unknown. Yet what strikes one about the period prior to October is not the growing bureaucratisation of the factory committees in Petrograd, but the extent to which they managed to realise an astonishing combination of direct and representational democracy.

This is not to dispose of the problem of 'bureaucracy', however, for 'bureaucracy' and 'democracy' need not be polar opposites. It depends in part how one understands 'bureaucracy'. Max Weber emphasised the inter-relationship of bureaucracy, rationality and legitimate authority (*Herrschaft*), and the factory committees were, to an extent, 'bureaucratic' in the Weberian sense. Far from being anarchic, protozoan bodies, the committees were solid, structurally-ramified organisations which functioned in a regular routinised manner.[87] The duties of the committees and their sub-commissions were fixed by rules and administrative dispositions; their activities were spelt out in written records; to a point, the committees followed 'general rules which are more or less stable, more or less exhaustive and which can be learned'.[88] In other respects, the committees operated in marked contrast to the Weberian model. There was no strict hierarchical system of authority, such that the lower levels of the factory committee movement were subordinate to the higher levels, though this was, arguably, the aspiration of the CCFC. The members of the committees in no way saw themselves as functionaries operating according to fixed rules. They were policy-makers in their own right who viewed their 'office' as a means of effecting economic and social change. They were not trained for office and enjoyed no stability of tenure. Finally, they were not appointed by some impersonal organisation, but elected by and accountable to the workers. Nevertheless, in order to implement the goals of workers' control, the committees had begun to develop a degree of bureaucracy and autonomy from the rank-and-file to ensure that spheres of day-to-day, practical activity were left to their discretion.[89] Herein lay a potential for the factory-committee leaders to become a bureaucratic stratum separate from, rather than organically linked to their worker constituency. Moreover, within labour organisations this potential for bureaucratisation existed in a different form, which has been succinctly analysed by Richard Hyman in relationship to trade unionism:

> There is an important sense in which the problem of 'bureaucracy' denotes not so much a distinct *stratum of personnel* as a *relationship* which permeates the whole practice of trade unionism. 'Bureaucracy' is in large measure a question of the differential distribution of expertise and activism: of the *dependence* of the mass of union membership on the initiative and strategic experience of a relatively small cadre of leadership – both 'official' and 'unofficial' ... the 'bad side of leadership' still constitutes a problem even in the case of a cadre of militant lay activists sensitive to the need to encourage the autonomy and initiative of the membership.[90]

In the Russian labour movement the dependence of the rank-and-file on the initiative and experience of the leadership was particularly acute, in view of the fact that the rank-and-file comprised unskilled or semi-skilled women and peasant workers unused to organisation. The skilled, proletarianised male leaders of the labour movement sought to bind these inexperienced workers into a disciplined unity, so that they might realise their democratic potential and exercise power on their own behalf. In so doing, they ran the constant danger of *dominating* the rank-and-file. As early as autumn, a woman from the Nevka cotton-spinning mill, where 92% of the workforce were women, complained of the behaviour of the overwhelmingly male factory committee: 'They have done a lot to organise the dark mass, but now reveal a desire to concentrate all power in their hands. They are beginning to boss their backward comrades, to act without accountability ... They deal with the workers roughly, haughtily, using expressions like "To the devil's mother with you!" '[91] Later a leatherworker from the Osipov saddle factory wrote to the leatherworkers' newspaper:

> ... Often members of the committees gradually become cut off from the masses, they become alienated from them and lose their confidence. Quite often the masses blame them for becoming autocrats, for taking no account of the mood of the majority of workers, for being too conciliatory. This, it is true, is explained by the peculiar conditions of the present time, by the acerbity of the masses, by their low level of culture; but sometimes the factory committee members themselves provoke such a reaction by their behaviour. They get on their high horse and pay scant attention to the voice of the workers. Sometimes they show little enthusiasm or do very little and this causes discontent among the masses.[92]

The balance between democracy and bureaucracy in the labour movement depended on the economic and political conditions in society at large. So long as these conditions were favourable to the revolutionary goals which the labour leaders had set themselves, then democratic elements overrode bureaucratic elements, i.e. the conditions were such that the popular forces could check the effectivity of bureaucratic forces. Once these conditions changed radically, as they did after October, bureaucratic elements came to the fore, which fostered the emergence of a bureaucratic stratum dominating the whole of society. After October the Bolshevik leaders of the factory committees, sincerely committed to workers' democracy, but losing their working-class base, began to concentrate power in their hands, excluded the masses from information and decision-making and set up a hierarchy of functions. The trade unions, too, became less accountable to their members, since they were now accountable to the government, and soon turned primarily into economic apparatuses of the state. This may all suggest that bureaucratisation was inscribed in the revolutionary process in 1917, but if so, it was inscribed as a *possibility* only: one cannot pessimistically invoke some 'iron law of oligarchy'. Democratic and bureaucratic elements existed in a determinate relationship in all popular organisations – a relationship which was basically determined by the goals of the organisations and the degree to which those goals were facilitated by political and economic circumstances. These circumstances were to change dramatically in the autumn of 1917, and it was this change which shifted the balance between the forces of democracy and bureaucracy in favour of the latter.

9

The October revolution and the organisation of industry

THE DECREE ON WORKERS' CONTROL

The Bolshevik seizure of power on 24–5 October was welcomed by a big majority of workers in Petrograd, who had tired of Kerensky's 'government of swindlers'. The Bolshevik action was seen as inaugurating a revolutionary government by the people, though the precise shape which this government should take was a matter of dispute. For industrial workers, one of the most important of the initial measures passed by the new government was the Decree on Workers' Control, published on 14 November.[1] This Decree legalised the *de facto* control which had been established in the factories of Petrograd since the February Revolution.

The All-Russian Council of Factory Committees (ARCFC), set up after the First All-Russian Conference, drafted a decree on workers' control, which they discussed with Lenin and representatives from the All-Russian Council of Trade Unions as early as 26 October. Astonishingly, their decree was entirely about the creation of a central apparatus to regulate the economy, i.e. what subsequently was to be established as the Supreme Council of National Economy (VSNKh). It said nothing about workers' control, i.e. about the activities of workers at the grass roots, and for this reason it was criticised by Lenin. He therefore proceeded to draft an alternative decree.[2] This decree breathes a spirit of libertarianism which reflects Lenin's profound faith at this time in the creativity of the masses. It recognised the right of workers in all industrial enterprises of whatever size to control all aspects of production, to have complete access to all spheres of administration, including the financial, and, finally, the right of the lower organs of workers' control to bind

employers by their decisions.[3] It was Lenin's draft which was taken as
the basis for the decree on workers' control. This awkward fact makes
nonsense of the claim in Western historiography that, once power was
in his grasp, Lenin, the stop-at-nothing centraliser, proceeded to
crush the 'syndicalist' factory committees. In fact, the reverse is true.
At this stage the ARCFC was more concerned with centralised
regulation of the economy, whilst Lenin was more concerned with
legalising grass-roots control.

On 8 November the All-Russian Central Executive Committee of
the Soviets (VTsIK) set up a five-person commission, which included
Milyutin, Lozovskii and two left SRs, Kamkov and Zaks, to scrutinise
Lenin's draft and to amend it in accordance with proposals from the
factory committees and trade unions.[4] On 14 November Milyutin
introduced the Decree to VTsIK for discussion. He explained that
three broad objections to the Decree had been made whilst it was
being amended by the commission. First, critics had objected that
workers' control could only be discussed in the context of a planned
economy but, Milyutin countered, 'we have been overtaken by events
... we have had to coordinate the [work of] control [organs] set up in
the localities, and to draw them into a single, streamlined state
apparatus, even at the cost of proceeding in an unsystematic fashion'.
Secondly, critics had objected that 'the commission was extending
powers of control too far [downwards] and that these powers should
be limited'. Milyutin countered: 'we proceeded from the principle of
control from below. We based the control apparatus on the local
factory committees, so that the higher instances of control will consist
of their central bodies, filled out by representatives of trade unions
and soviets.' The third point that gave rise to objections was the
question of whether or not employers should be bound by the
decisions of the control organs. Critics felt that to make decisions
mandatory would endanger the interest of the general economic plan;
but the commission, whilst agreeing that employers should have three
days in which to object to decisions, felt that workers' control would
be unworkable if the decisions of the control organs were not
binding.[5] VTsIK proceeded to ratify the Decree, which gave workers
full rights of control over production, distribution, finance and sales.
The chief difference between Lenin's draft and the final Decree lay in
the fact that a hierarchy of central organs was established by the
latter, so that organs of control in the enterprise were subject to
regional councils of control which, in turn, were subject to an
All-Russian Council of Workers' Control.[6]

On 16 November the Fifth Conference of Petrograd Factory Committees met to discuss the Decree. It was attended by 96 Bolsheviks, 24 SRs, 13 anarchists, 7 Mensheviks, 6 miscellaneous and 21 whose party affiliation was unknown or non-existent.[7] The Decree was opposed by Kotlov, chairman of the technical commission of the Ministry of Labour, who felt that it unduly restricted workers' self-activity. Taking their cue from him, the anarcho-syndicalists called for factories to pass into the hands of the workers. Bolsheviks on the CCFC urged active, wide-ranging control in the localities, but stressed that this was but one aspect of regulating production, directed mainly against sabotage by factory owners. Skrypnik put the Decree to the vote and it was passed with only one vote against and twenty abstentions.[8] The conference resolution, however, suggests that the delegates ascribed a more far-reaching significance to workers' control than did the drafters of the Decree. Whereas the Decree spoke of workers' control being 'in the interests of planned regulation of the economy', the conference resolution said that 'the decree lays a firm foundation for the further regulation of production and distribution, for the compulsory amalgamation of banks and enterprises and for other measures aimed at the organisation of the country's economy *in the direction of a socialist system*'.[9]

The importance of the Decree was more symbolic than real. As it existed, it was unworkable, for it envisaged a hierarchy of control organs at enterprise, district, city and national level, which would have proved too cumbersome. Further problems arose from the fact that the Decree did not spell out in concrete detail how workers' control was to be implemented. A number of local soviets, trade unions and provincial conferences of factory committees worked out sets of instructions on the execution of the Decree, by far the most important of which were the Instructions issued by the CCFC in Petrograd, and those issued by the All-Russian Council of Workers' Control. It is worth examining these Instructions in detail, since they reveal clearly what was at issue in the debate about workers' control which soon erupted.

The Instructions of the CCFC, first published in *Izvestiya* on 7 December, are remarkable for the radicalism with which they tackle the question of workers' control. They represent a bold advance on the positions taken by factory committee conferences before October, no longer seeing control as 'inspection' but as active intervention in production:

Workers' control of industry, as an integral part of control over the whole of economic life, must be understood not in the narrow sense of simple inspection [*revizii*], but, on the contrary, in the broad sense of intervening in the employer's disposal of capital, stocks, raw materials and finished goods in the factory; in the sense of actively supervising the proper and expedient fulfilment of orders and utilisation of energy and labour power; in the sense of participating in the organisation of production on rational lines, etc. Control will only achieve its end and justify the hopes pinned on it, if it is, firstly, implemented by workers' organisations at both central and local level in the most energetic and vigorous manner, not stopping short of active measures to restrain employers who are clearly approaching the fulfilment of their duties in a negligent or harmful fashion; and secondly, if it is closely coordinated with and firmly tied to the general regulation and organisation of production, both in the individual enterprise and in the branch of industry as a whole. Control must be seen precisely as a transitional stage towards organising the whole economic life of the country on social lines, as the first step in this direction taken from below, parallel with work at the top in the central organs of the economy.[10]

The Instructions then proceed to specify the tasks of workers' control in a very broad fashion. They envisage active interference in management, without clarifying precisely what powers and responsibilities remain with management. The decisions of the control organs are made binding on management. The factory committees, organised into a national hierarchy, are vested with sole responsibility for workers' control; trade union activity is confined to the area of wages. Didier L. Limon argues that these Instructions, in effect, are about workers' self-management rather than workers' control.[11] This is undoubtedly true, insofar as the Instructions were drawn up against a background assumption that there was to be a rapid transition to socialism, in which workers' control would be transmogrified into workers' self-management. Yet these Instructions in no sense represent a syndicalist effort to decentralise the running of the economy. At the Sixth Conference of Factory Committees, 22–7 January 1918, the anarchist, Bleikhman, criticised the CCFC Instructions for their 'centralism', though he conceded that this was a 'democratic' type of centralism.[12] Control was envisaged as taking place at both state level and factory level and local initiatives were to be organised into a hierarchy of local and regional Councils of National Economy (*sovnarkhozy*), topped by the Supreme Council of National Economy (VSNKh). This was not an anarcho-syndicalist schema but a plan for the democratic socialisation of production, which had the support of perhaps a majority of Bolsheviks at this stage, including, for a short period, Lenin himself. It is for this reason that the Secretariat of the Bolshevik Central Committee sent these Instructions, rather than those of the All-Russian Council of Workers' Control, to provincial bodies who requested information on how to implement the Decree on Workers' Control.[13]

The All-Russian Council of Workers' Control (ARCWC) was brought into being by the Decree on Workers' Control, but it was virtually stillborn. It met but twice before it was absorbed into VSNKh (established on 1 December).[14] The ARCWC included only five representatives from the factory committees, out of more than forty members. The rest comprised representatives from the soviets, the Petrograd Council of Trade Unions, the cooperatives, and included some Mensheviks and SRs. It was chaired by the Bolshevik leader of the metal union, V.V. Schmidt. The Council's one act of significance was to produce an alternative set of Instructions on workers' control, more moderate than those of the CCFC. The ARCWC Instructions emphasised the necessity of a centralised system of control in which individual factory control commissions would be subordinated to the control-distribution commission of the trade union of the particular branch of industry. This has led some Soviet historians to argue that these Instructions were an attempt by Menshevik trade-union leaders to subordinate the control organs to the trade unions rather than to the state. That they represent an attempt to assert trade-union suzerainty over the factory committees is beyond dispute, but this was an aspiration shared as much by Bolshevik trade-union leaders as by Menshevik. The Instructions cannot be interpreted as an effort to diminish the role of the government, since the trade-union control commissions were to be subject to regional councils of workers' control which, in turn, were to be subject to VSNKh. The second significant feature of the ARCWC Instructions is that they laid down that management functions should remain in the hands of the employer: 'Administrative (*rasporyaditel'nye*) rights to manage the enterprise and its operations and activities remain with the owner. The control commission does not take part in the management of the enterprise and does not bear any responsibility for its operations and activity.'[15] This was merely a restatement of the position of successive factory committee conferences prior to the October Revolution. It offered no solution to the problem, outlined in Chapter 7, of how factory committees were to avoid responsibility for the enterprise if they had more *de facto* power than the official administration in the areas of supplies, output, equipment, labour discipline, purchasing or demobilisation.

The two sets of Instructions on the implementation of the Decree on Workers' Control were at the centre of the debate between the factory committees and trade-union leaders at the end of 1917. The Instructions of the CCFC were seen by both trade-union leaders and factory committee militants as giving *carte blanche* to individual factory committees to implement the most far-reaching schemes of grass-roots 'control'. It was at these Instructions, therefore, that much of the fire of the trade-union opposition was directed. The most devastating critique of the Instructions was undoubtedly that mounted by the Bolshevik trade-union leader, A. Lozovskii, in a pamphlet published on 8 January 1918.[16]

According to Lozovskii, 'the basic defect of the projected law is that it makes no connection with the planned regulation of the economy and disperses control of production instead of centralising it'.[17] Lozovskii and the other trade-union leaders believed that: 'the lower control organ must act within limits which are strictly defined by the higher organs of control and regulation, whereas the comrades who stand for decentralisation and workers' control uphold the independ-ence and autonomy of the lower organs, suggesting that the masses themselves will imbue the proclaimed principle of workers' control with concrete content'.[18] Lozovskii argued that the Instructions of the CCFC were completely illogical, for whilst they talked of the employer and of profit, they effectively abolished the old management by totally subordinating it to the factory control organ. In reality the Instructions did not aspire to workers' control at all, but to the complete reorganisation of the economy along socialist lines and to workers' self-management: 'The notion of workers' control thus no longer represents a transitional measure but rather the immediate realisation of a new mode of production.'[19]

There is much truth in Lozovskii's strictures. The Bolshevik seizure of power, together with ever-deeper economic chaos, had caused the leaders of the CCFC to develop a more ambitious concept of workers' control than they had entertained prior to October. The Bolshevik, Kaktyn', explained in the CCFC journal, *Novyi Put'*, how the nature of workers' control was changing now that socialism was on the agenda: no longer was it merely a question of controlling the activities of capital in order to maintain production – workers' self-management was now a possibility. 'We are living through the greatest socialist revolution, not only in the political, but more fundamentally, in the economic sphere ... A most cruel war ... has unavoidably brought the toilers of all countries, firstly, to an ideological revolution – to the overthrow of the prejudices of bourgeois society ingrained by the centuries – and, secondly, to a social revolution, which has begun in Russia, the country most exhausted by the war – a revolution which is rolling in a mighty wave through all countries of the world, breaking out in mass uprisings, first here, then there.'[20] For Kaktyn', as for the other CCFC leaders, the actuality of permanent revolution completely transformed the nature of workers' control, as he went on to explain in the same article:

It is clear that in our situation there can no longer be any talk of the old method of passive control of production and distribution so cherished by our spineless intelligentsia. Even if individual comrades in the Bolshevik party, along with *Novaya Zhizn'*, defend the idea, and try to extend it through the higher economic organs and cast it in a form which totally distorts the original Decree on Workers' Control, and even if all those seize on it, who fear the dictatorship of the proletariat and socialism more than death (the trade-union elite, the union of engineers and technicians and others, not to mention the employers), then it only serves to emphasise their feebleness.[21]

Lozovskii correctly linked the debate on workers' control to the fundamental question of the Russian Revolution: was socialism on the immediate agenda?:

It is absolutely essential to counterpose the *organisation* of production to the *regulation* of production. For in these two terms are encapsulated two systems and two views on the next tasks of the proletariat in the Russian Revolution. If one thinks that Russia can pass to the immediate realisation of a socialist system, if one thinks that socialism in Russia is a practical task of the day, then one must speak of the organisation of production, and not only speak of it, but execute it in practice. One must socialise all enterprises and hand the whole apparatus into the hands of the workers.[22]

Lozovskii himself took up what was in essence a Menshevik-Internationalist, rather than a Bolshevik, position:

There can be no doubt that the immediate socialisation of the means of production and exchange is not on the agenda of the Russian Revolution. We are faced, and not only we but the whole of Western Europe, with living through a rather lengthy transitional period of state capitalism or state socialism, under which the working class will act against the state-employer in selling its labour power ... Workers' control is a transitional revolutionary measure ... [it] does not affect the foundations of the capitalist system. It leaves intact the private property in the means of production and the whole private trading apparatus – not because this is better from the point of view of proletarian interests, but because at the present historical moment the proletariat does not have the power to do more, given its lack of organisational experience, and in the absence of a socialist revolution in the economically advanced countries of Western Europe. The proletariat can lay hands on the whole productive apparatus, can move close to the whole process of production, can take an active part in carrying out the state-wide plan of regulation, can reduce the appetites of the ruling classes with a rough hand and force them to submit to its control – but more than this it cannot do.[23]

The majority of Bolsheviks were not impressed by the cogency of Lozovskii's economic views, merely shocked at what seemed to be his political pusillanimity. To men like Kaktyn' or Skrypnik, the prospect of resigning themselves to a whole historic epoch of state capitalism was anathema. Nor were they prepared to sit back and await a revolution in Western Europe. They were determined rather to push the revolution in Russia as far in a socialist direction as it would go, in the hope of stimulating international revolution. To such men nothing looked easier than the abolition of capitalism in a country in the throes of revolution, war and economic crisis. Capitalism was tearing itself apart and it was the duty of revolutionaries to ensure that socialism was established in its place.

Although in Petrograd a majority of metalworkers seem to have supported the radical interpretation of workers' control,[24] in other regions and industries there was considerable support for the moderate interpretation of Lozovskii. The unions of textileworkers and needleworkers, *sovnarkhozy* in Kostroma, Moscow etc. followed the ARCWC Instructions in implementing workers' control.[25]

THE ROLE OF THE TRADE UNIONS

The Third Conference of Trade Unions in June had defined the main function of the trade unions as the conduct of the economic struggle in defence of workers' living standards, and had rejected the notion of unions controlling or intervening in production. As early as the summer, however, the Petrograd metal union had begun to argue that a historically new task now faced the union movement – that of participating in the regulation of the economy. The installation of a workers' and peasants' government caused Bolshevik trade-union leaders to dramatically reassess the role of unions. G. Veinberg argued in *Metallist* that the job of the trade unions was no longer to promote workers' economic interests, since the government could be relied upon to do this, but the far more important one of 'participating in the organs regulating and controlling production and the economy'.[26] The resolution on the role of the trade unions passed by the First All-Russian Congress of Trade Unions, 7–14 January 1918, declared that 'the centre of gravity of trade-union work must now shift to the organisational-economic sphere. The unions, as class organisations of the proletariat ... must take on the major work of organising production and reviving the disrupted productive forces of the country.'[27]

This redefinition of the tasks of the trade unions threw into relief the problem of their relation to the state. If the task of defending workers' economic interests were to pass from the unions to the state, and if the unions were to become organs of economic regulation directed by the state, could they any longer be said to have functions separate from those of the state? Should they not logically cease their independent organisational existence, and merge into the state apparatus? This was one of the questions which were to dominate the proceedings of the First All-Russian Congress of Trade Unions.

Some 500 delegates attended the congress, of whom 428 had voting rights. Nineteen national unions were represented with a total membership of 2.5 million, including 600,000 from the metal union, 500,000 from the textile union, 200,000 from the leather union.[28] Of the voting delegates 281 were Bolsheviks, 67 Mensheviks, 21 Left SRs, 10 Right SRs, 6 SR Maximalists, 6 anarcho-syndicalists and 37 belonged to no political party.[29] Interestingly, the right-wing minority consisted of proportionately more national executive members than rank-and-file delegates. 43% of national executive members were Mensheviks and Right SRs, compared to 13% of local delegates. Only 37% of national executive members were Bolsheviks, Left SRs, SR Maximalists or anarcho-syndicalists, compared to 79% of local delegates.[30]

The debate about the role of the unions and their relationship to the state took place in a highly charged political atmosphere. Zinoviev argued on behalf of the Bolsheviks that: 'The political victory of workers and poor peasants over the imperialists and their petit-bourgeois agents in Russia is bringing us to the threshold of international socialist revolution and to victory over the capitalist mode of production. The Soviets of workers', soldiers' and peasants' deputies have become the organs of government and the policy of the

workers' and peasants' government is a policy of socialist reconstruction of society.'[31] In an early draft of his resolution, Zinoviev did not
hesitate to draw the conclusion that the congress should 'proclaim the
trade unions state organisations', but the Moscow party organisation
objected to this.[32] The final resolution stated that 'the trade unions
will inevitably become transformed into organs of the socialist state,
membership of which will be a civic duty for all those employed in a
particular branch of industry'.[33] This compromise formula merely
said that 'statisation' of the unions would not come about at once; it
was not a recognition of qualified trade-union independence. The
right to strike, for example, was explicitly rejected by Zinoviev ('the
strike would be directed against the workers themselves') and the
Bolshevik resolution on workers' control in its final version deleted a
clause recognising the right to strike.

Martov led the Menshevik opposition which, in spite of profound
internal schisms, operated on a common platform of 'unity and
independence of the trade-union movement'.[34] He began by remind-
ing the congress that in 1906 Lenin had stated that it was impossible
to jump from autocracy to socialism, since the preconditions for
socialism were lacking. The proletariat was neither sufficiently
homogeneous to see in socialism the sole solution to its problems,
nor sufficiently experienced to manage the economy. Concentration
of production had not yet reached a level where it governed the
dynamic of the whole economy since small-scale production was still
preponderant. The present revolution was thus still objectively a
bourgeois one. Replying to Zinoviev, Martov cried: 'To say that the
very fact of existence of soviets is proof of a new era in the life of
mankind – the era of socialism – is vacuous rubbish.' If the
Bolsheviks continued their socialist experiments, he maintained, not
only would they destroy the economy, they would disenchant the
workers and pave the way for a capitalist restoration. So long as
workers continued to sell their labour power, he concluded, free and
independent unions were necessary to defend workers' interests.
This did not mean, however, that unions should not take part in the
business of economic regulation; rather they should inject into it
'realism, Marxism and scientific socialism'. Martov's resolution
received 84 votes against 182 cast for Zinoviev's.[35]

As it turned out, the trade unions continued to enjoy considerable
independence from the government during the next couple of years,
owing to the fact that energies were channelled into winning the civil

war. In 1920–1, however, the issue of the relationship of the trade unions to the state flared up once again.[36]

THE SUBORDINATION OF THE FACTORY COMMITTEES TO THE TRADE UNIONS

We saw in Chapter 9 that there had been growing acceptance within the factory committees of the idea of a merger with the trade unions. The redefinition of the tasks of the unions after October meant that the division of labour between the two organisations, which had been established in the summer of 1917, broke down. Trade unions now sought to enter the sphere of activity formerly reserved to the factory committees. Two different organisations were thus seeking to do the same job of regulating production – yet another example of the *mnogovlastie* ('multiplicity of powers') which was so much a feature of the revolution at this time. Writing in *Metallist*, G. Veinberg complained that: 'as soon as the Petrograd union of metalworkers took steps in this direction [that of regulating industry], it unfortunately clashed with another organisation – the CCFC. Questionnaires on the state of the metal industry, sent out by the union to each factory, were matched by questionnaires sent out by the CCFC. Two labour organisations were doing the same work, completely separately, wasting limited energies and expending double the resources.'[37]

Trade-union leaders harshly criticised the factory committees for being unsuitable vehicles for regulating the economy. The charge of 'parochialism' was one that had long been made against the committees, and it was one which they themselves in part accepted. At the Second Conference of Factory Committees Skrypnik had condemned the 'patriotism of one's parish [*kolokol'nya*]'.[38] Increasingly, the charge of parochialism was a stick used by trade unionists to beat the committees. At the metal union contract conference on 15 October, A. Gastev argued:

The committees are frequently buried in the narrow shell of local factory problems ... Such a narrow 'local' politics goes hand in hand with a 'broad' understanding of immediate tasks ... In general one must say that it's completely inadequate to control a single industrial enterprise; one must also control the highest organs of finance and management. One must remember that large-scale speculation and the major levers of production are found outside the factory, and under the present system of 'control', the factory committees sanction speculative operations suggested by financial dealers who are unknown to them.[39]

In one of the most rancorous polemics against the committees, Ya.
Boyarkov, a Bolshevik from the Khar'kov metal union, asserted that:
'workers' control by itself is an anarchist attempt to establish
socialism in one enterprise and leads in practice to clashes between
groups of workers'.[40] On 29 December at a conference of factory
committee and union representatives from the Petrograd metal
industry, G. Veinberg again attacked the committees for their
localism and selfishness, and called for a centralised system of
workers' control. He argued that only the trade unions – organisations which embraced whole industries – could tackle the problems of
the economy. Committee representatives, led by the S.R. Voronkov,
sharply rebutted Veinberg's charges and upheld the CCFC Instructions on the Decree on Workers' Control. The Bolshevik Commissar
of Labour, A. Shlyapnikov, repeated the charge of parochialism,
accusing the committees of collaborating with the employers in order
to squeeze financial aid from the government.[41]

We shall see that there was a reluctance on the part of the CCFC to
merge with the trade unions – not so much on principle, but because
the terms were unacceptable. In the localities, however, the harsh
facts of economic life were forcing the factory committees and trade
unions together. On Vasilevskii Island shortages of fuel and raw
materials, unemployment and the threat of closures forced the unions
and committees to form an Economic Council of Workers of
Vasilevskii District on 9 December.[42] On 15 January the Vyborg
district council of factory committees called for an immediate
amalgamation of the committees and trade unions.[43] At the end of
November a conference of committee and union representatives in the
textile industry set up a central control commission.[44] In the leather,
paper and chemical industries cooperation between the two organisations was well advanced by the end of 1917. Only in the metal
industry was conflict as to the terms of amalgamation rife.

The conflict was settled in brusque fashion at the First All-
RussianCongress of Trade Unions. Introducing the Bolshevik resolution, Ryazanov called on the factory committees 'to choose that form
of suicide which would be most useful to the labour movement as a
whole'.[45] His resolution argued that 'the parallel existence of two
forms of economic organisation in the working class with overlapping
functions can only complicate the process of concentrating the forces
of the proletariat', and he called for the committees to become the
basic cells of the unions in the workplace.[46] The anarcho-syndicalists

were furious. Bill Shatov fulminated against the trade unions, calling them 'living corpses', whilst Maksimov hailed the factory committees as 'children of the revolution, the direct offspring of the workers themselves ... manifesting all the intelligence, power and energy of the working class in the localities'.[47] But they were fighting a rearguard action: the anarcho-syndicalist resolution gained a mere six votes. Mensheviks for once voted with Bolsheviks in support of Ryazanov's resolution.

It is probable that the CCFC would have accepted the subordination of the committees to the unions more enthusiastically, had the congress not passed another resolution which considerably narrowed the scope of workers' control, and shifted responsibility for control from local organs to central ones. It was, ironically, Lozovskii, the fiercest critic of the CCFC Instructions, who introduced the official resolution on workers' control to the trade-union congress – even though he had recently been expelled from the Bolshevik party. His resolution defined workers' control as involving stock-taking of fuel and raw materials, investigation of finances, the determination of output and productivity, inspection of accounts and supervision of the general running of the factory. The resolution emphasised, however, that such control was part of a general system of planned economic regulation, and that 'it is necessary to repudiate in the most unequivocal fashion all notions of dispersing workers' control, by giving workers in each enterprise the right to take final decisions on matters affecting the very existence of the enterprise'. The resolution vested responsibility for control in the trade unions and exhorted them to preach the virtues of centralised control. It specified that factory control-commissions should be subject to the control-commissions of the unions and should include union representatives not working at the factory. In turn, the union control-commissions should include factory committee representatives, as well as technicians, accountants and statisticians. The resolution, finally, endorsed the much-maligned Instructions on workers' control which had been worked out by the All-Russian Council of Workers' Control.[48]

The CCFC attacked what it termed the 'discrepancy between the verbal revolutionism of the (trade-union) congress and its actual conservatism'.[49] It criticised the unions for their 'unrelenting tactic of subordinating the factory committees to themselves and of absorbing all their functions, without examining whether the immense and unorganised apparatus of the unions can execute even one of these functions'; instead of planning a smooth merger, the unions were content merely to attack the alleged parochialism of the committees: 'one detects a total unwillingness to deal with this new revolutionary organisation as a worthy collaborator in common work. Instead there is a stubborn striving to put the committees at a lower level – to equate them with anarchic, unconscious, mass elementalism'.[50]

The sixth and final conference of Petrograd factory committees was held from 22 to 27 January. It recognised that the time had come for the committees to become the workplace cells of the unions, but it called for the boards of the unions to be elected by conferences of factory committees within the branch of industry.[51] It would thus be wrong to interpret the resolution as a gracious admission of defeat by the committees. As Zhivotov is reported to have said: 'if they [the unions] want to refashion us, they won't succeed. By going into the unions, we are going to refashion them.'[52] As if to underline the seriousness of this intent, the conference reaffirmed its support for the CCFC Instructions on Workers' Control, in spite of the fact that the trade union congress had ratified the ARCWC Instruction only days previously. The Sixth Conference thus genuflected to the notion of trade-union supremacy, but at root the will of the factory committees to be independent remained unbowed.

The central board of the metal union agreed to the replacement of the delegate councils of metalworkers at district and city level by conferences of factory committees, but on 1 February this concession met with considerable opposition from the city delegate-council of the metal union. Eventually, the delegates approved it by 159 votes to 59.[53] On 1 April trade unions and factory committees in the Petrograd metal industry finally fused. At the fusion conference Zhivotov emphasised the necessity of strong factory committees in each enterprise as the foundation stones of the union, but wisely avoided saying too much about the precise functions of the committees. Subsequent events were to prove that these were as much in dispute as ever.

Had the six months since the October seizure of power witnessed the triumph of the unions over the committees? In one sense it clearly had, for the factory committees, which had been far more influential than the unions in 1917, were now absorbed into the union apparatus. At a deeper level, however, the 'victory' of the unions was far more ambiguous. As G. Binshtok wrote in the journal set up by the Mensheviks to defend trade-union autonomy against the Bolshevik state: 'with complete justice the trade unions can say to the factory committees "Thou hast conquered, O Galilean!", since the trade unions, having taken on the organisation of production, have in fact been transformed into unified factory committees'.[54] In other words, even if the factory committees, as an institutional form, were now subordinate to the unions, it was the committees' definition of tasks – the regulation of production – which had prevailed.

In practice, the institutional subordination of the committees to the trade unions proved to be more aspiration than reality, just as did the 'statisation' of the trade unions. Civil-war developments, including the nationalisation of industrial enterprises and the attempted restoration of one-man management, merely raised again – in a new form – the old problems about the scope of workers' control and the relationship of the factory committees to the trade unions. As late as April 1920 – two years after he had helped promote the fusion of the factory committees and the trade unions – Lozovskii could report to the Third All-Russian Congress of Trade Unions: 'We must subordinate the work of the factory committees and collectives to complete control and to the complete influence of the trade unions. You know from the experience of the last two years, particularly of the last year, that very often the factory committees or collegial boards consider themselves absolutely independent of the unions.'[55] It is clear from this that long after the formal integration of the committees into the union apparatus, factory committees still displayed that spirited independence and concern for self-management which had been a hallmark of their activity in 1917. They refused, in other words, to 'commit suicide', as Ryazanov had urged at the First Congress of Trade Unions.

TOWARDS A SOCIALIST ECONOMY

On coming to power the Bolsheviks had little sense of the form or tempo of the transition to socialism. The party was agreed on the need to nationalise the banks and a number of syndicates in the oil, coal, sugar, metallurgy and transport sectors,[56] but beyond this, there was little agreement about the extent of the socialist measures which could be undertaken. Lenin seems to have envisaged an economic system combining state ownership of key sectors with extensive private ownership of industry under government direction and workers' control – what he termed 'state capitalism'. On the left of the party, however, Bukharin dubbed the notion of 'state capitalism' a 'nonsense, a half-baked idea'; he and his co-thinkers argued that 'a proletarian-peasant dictatorship which does not entail the expropriation of the expropriators, which does not eliminate the power of capital in the mines and factories can only be a temporary phenomenon'.[57] On the right of the party, meanwhile, many felt that nationalisation was inopportune and that only private capital could rebuild the battered productive forces of the country.[58] In the event, the government's policy developed rapidly in a socialist direction, but this was due less to political calculation than to the exigencies of class conflict and economic chaos.

The CCFC was a strong force actively pushing the government in the direction of a planned socialist economy during the first months of soviet power. As early as 26–7 October, the CCFC had proposed the setting-up of a Supreme Council of National Economy (VSNKh), which was duly established on 1 December. The task of VSNKh was defined as 'the organisation of the economy and state finances by means of a plan for the regulation of the economic life of the country and the coordination and unification of the activity of the central and local organs of regulation'.[59] On 23 December a decree provided for the creation of regional councils of national economy (*sovnarkhozy*),[60] and in February the *Sovnarkhoz* of the Northern Region (SNKh S.R.) began to function in the Petrograd area. Until that time, the CCFC effectively ran the economy of the capital.[61] It was then absorbed into SNKh S.R. The latter had the comprehensive task of planning and regulating all aspects of the regional economy, including industry, transport, agriculture, supplies, finance and labour power.[62] The SNKh S.R. was headed by a presidium, and divided into industrial sections. By April there were eleven branch-of-industry sections, plus two for transport and one for trade.[63] Each section was divided into departments of organisation, supply and distribution, labour, and statistics.[64] The department of organisation had the job of running nationalised enterprises, of directing the organs of workers' control in private enterprises and of settling conflicts between workers and management.[65] Each industrial section was headed by a collegium which consisted of workers, elected at industrial-branch conferences of factory committees and trade unions, delegates from the soviets and cooperatives, and technical and commercial experts.[66]

VSNKh was vested with the power to 'confiscate, requisition, sequester or compulsorily syndicate different branches of trade and industry', but it was not envisaged in December that it should embark on whole-scale nationalisation. Pressure for nationalisation began to well up from the localities (see next chapter), and local *sovnarkhozy* were increasingly compelled to take enterprises into state ownership. The factory committees spearheaded a campaign to press the government into adopting a more vigorous policy of nationalisation. The Sixth Conference of Petrograd Factory Committees, for example, passed a resolution which demanded the transfer of all factories and mines into the hands of the state.[67] At first the government resisted this pressure, but it increasingly succumbed during the spring of 1918, by endeavouring to centrally coordinate the wave of local 'nationalisations'. Finally, on 28 June it announced the whole-scale nationalisation of all major branches of industry.[68]

As active proponents of nationalisation, this decision marked a 'victory' for the factory committees: yet it was a qualified one. For the committees had linked the demand for nationalisation to the demand for workers' management of the enterprises which passed into state ownership. The Sixth Conference of Factory Committees, in its resolution calling for nationalisation, argued that 'the political power [*vlast'*] of the proletariat can only be real power under conditions of its economic rule [*gospodstvo*]'. It went on to demand that:

In view of the fact that the supreme government organs have no special organisations capable of running the enterprises transferred into ownership of the republic, and in view of the fact that the government of workers, soldiers and peasants is strong only so long as it enjoys the confidence of the toilers and their organisations, in all cases of nationalisation, the workers' committees should be put in charge of the enterprises in the localities and should work under the direction of VSNKh.[69]

As we shall see in the next chapter, nationalisation issued not in workers' self-management, but in a more centralised structure of industrial management, which undercut the power of the factory committees.

LENIN, THE BOLSHEVIKS AND WORKERS' CONTROL AFTER OCTOBER

We have seen that Lenin's draft decree on workers' control emphasised the activity of workers *in situ* rather than 'state workers' control'. This reflected his faith in the creativity of the masses – so much a feature of his thinking during the first three months of soviet power.

He was intoxicated by the spectacle of workers, soldiers and peasants taking power into their own hands, and profoundly optimistic about the potential inherent in such self-activity. In an article of late December entitled 'How to Organise Competition', Lenin wrote:

One of the most crucial tasks at present, if not the most crucial, is to develop the independent initiatives of the workers and toilers and exploited generally in the sphere of creative, organisational work. At all costs, we must destroy that old, absurd, savage, vile and loathsome prejudice that only the so-called 'upper classes' can run the state.[70]

Nevertheless even when Lenin's thinking was its most libertarian, he did not abandon his belief in the necessity of complementing the independent initiatives of the masses with action at state level. In early October he had reminded his Menshevik critics that: 'We are for centralism and for a plan by the *proletarian* state: proletarian regulation of production and distribution in the interests of the poor, the toilers and the exploited – *against* the exploiters.'[71] As winter set in, the honeymoon period of the revolution began to draw to a close, and the Bolsheviks became more and more aware of the appalling economic and social difficulties facing them. To Lenin the existence of proletarian state power seemed to be the one beacon in the enveloping gloom. Increasingly, the theme of state initiative assumed precedence in his discourse over the theme of mass initiative. With regard to workers' control, Lenin qualified his initial optimism about the capacity of workers and peasants to resolve the economic crisis through their own efforts. More and more, he insisted that only centralised, planned intervention by the state on a national scale could begin to tackle the anarchy induced in the economy by three years of war. At first, Lenin does not appear to have had any definite position on whether the trade unions should supersede the factory committees as organs of economic regulation. The increasingly radical practice of workers' control in the winter of 1917, however, seems to have persuaded him and other leading Bolsheviks of the correctness of the arguments of those trade-union leaders who castigated the factory committees for their parochial, tunnel-visioned approach to economic problems. As Lenin's commitment to central-ised state regulation of the economy increased, he appears to have come round to the idea that the trade unions were better suited than the committees to the task of economic regulation, since they had their base not in the individual enterprise but in the branch of industry as a whole.

The leaders of the factory committees were not at all ill-disposed to centralised state regulation of the economy: indeed they were a major force pressing the government in this direction. Having successfully campaigned for the establishment of VSNKh, the committees in the early months of 1918 began to pressure the government to nationalise the whole of industry, to end private ownership of the means of production. Lenin was less keen than the committee leaders to undertake rapid nationalisation, but this was not the main point at issue between them. It was rather that the committees linked the question of state ownership of industry to that of workers' management of the enterprise, and on this matter Lenin had increasingly authoritarian views.

Throughout 1917 workers' control of industry had aimed, principally, to minimise capitalist disruption of industry, but it had never been concerned exclusively with that: it had also aimed to democratise relations of authority within the enterprise and to create new relations of production in which workers could display maximum initiative, responsibility and creativity. Out of this, there emerged a concern for workers' self-management, which became particularly apparent after October. Although explicit references to 'self-management' (*samoupravlenie*) are fairly rare in the discourse of the factory committees, the concept was at the very heart of their practice. When workers talked of the 'democratic' factory, or of taking the factory 'into their own hands', they were talking about self-management. After October, although the factory committees pressed for a planned, state-owned economy, this did not mean that they believed that the transfer of legal ownership of the factories to the proletarian state would by itself bring an end to the subordination and oppression of workers. In a vague, incoherent way the committee leaders recognised that unless the transfer of power to workers at the level of the state were accompanied by a transfer of power at the level of production, then the emancipation of labour would remain a chimera. During the winter of 1917–18 the committees emphasised in their discourse, and above all in their practice, the initiative of the direct producers in transforming the process of production. What appears to be accelerating 'anarchism' in the movement for workers' control after October is, in large part, a recognition that the hierarchical relations of domination and authority within the enterprise would have to be contested, if capitalist relations of production as a whole were to be overcome. This recognition, however, remained confused and was never articulated into a perspective for socialist transition alternative to that of Lenin and the majority of the Bolshevik leadership.

Lenin never developed a conception of workers' self-management. Even after October, workers' control remained for him fundamentally a matter of 'inspection' and 'accounting'. Although he constantly drove home the importance of grass-roots initiatives by workers, he regarded these as having the function of limiting chaos in the economy and countering tendencies to bureaucratisation, rather than as being necessary to the transformation of the process of production by the direct producers. For Lenin, the transformation of capitalist relations of production was achieved at central-state level, rather than at enterprise level. Progress to socialism was guaranteed by the character of the state and achieved through policies by the central state – not by the degree of power exercised by workers on the shop floor. As galloping chaos overtook the economy, workers' autonomy faded as a theme in Lenin's discourse, and increasingly he came to stress the need for strict discipline and centralism. From March 1918 he began to call for the restoration of one-man management in the factories. In 'The Current Tasks of Soviet Power', he wrote:

Any large-scale machine industry, and this is precisely the material productive source and foundation of socialism – calls for unconditional and strict unity of will, in order to coordinate the simultaneous work of hundreds, thousands and tens of thousands of people ... Unqualified submission to a single will is unconditionally necessary in the success of the labour processes, organised on the lines of large-scale machine industry.[72]

The slow and uneven restoration of one-man management during the Civil War had no bearing for Lenin on the question of the socialist character of the soviet state, for this was guaranteed by its ostensibly proletarian character, rather than by the degree of dissolution of capitalist relations at the point of production. Because a state representing the interests of workers and poor peasants now presided over Russia, it was possible to organise production in any manner which would ensure maximum productivity: 'there is ... absolutely *no* contradiction in principle between Soviet (that is, socialist) democracy and the existence of dictatorial powers by individuals'.[73]

The factory committee leaders had an inchoate awareness that socialism would remain a mere formality unless the direct producers – and not just the state on their behalf – took over and radically reconstructed relations of production within the enterprise, but they never really formulated this awareness in theoretical terms. Only the

Left Communist faction of the Bolshevik party came near to registering at a theoretical level the importance of overcoming the separation of workers from the means of production during the transition to socialism. V.V. Osinskii (V.V. Obolenskii) was chairman of VSNKh until March 1918, when he resigned because of his opposition to the Treaty of Brest Litovsk. In a brilliant article in the first number of the Left Communist journal in April 1918, entitled 'On Socialist Construction', he loosed a far-reaching critique of the official Bolshevik policy of socialist transition, central to which was the following insight:

> ... Although the transition to socialism is signalled by the nationalisation of enterprises, nationalisation of itself – i.e. the transfer of enterprises and state-ownership – is not, in any sense, equivalent to socialism. In order for nationalisation to have that significance, i.e. for it to become socialisation, it is necessary (a) that the system of management of enterprises be constructed along socialist lines, so that capital's power of command is destroyed and so that in the arrangement of the enterprise there are no longer bases on which this command might be restored; (b) it is necessary that the public authority into whose hands property in the means of production is transferred, is a proletarian authority ... Is it possible for the proletarian elite [*verkhushka*], which will sit with the capitalists on the boards of the trusts, to guarantee that real proletarian power is in command in production? I very much doubt it, since the proletariat as a class will become a passive element, the object, rather than the subject of the organisation of labour in production.[74]

He argued that unless the proletariat were actively involved in reorganising the process of production, then state capitalism, not socialism, would be the end-product of the government's policies. Although the practical proposals for workers' self-management which Osinskii outlined in the second part of this article were disappointingly sketchy, the article is noteworthy for marking the limit-point to which any Bolshevik went in formally recognising the crucial importance of workers' self-management in a strategy of socialist transition. One should not, however, exaggerate the significance of Osinskii's article. The Left Communists never really posed self-management as a central aim, their Theses of April 1918 merely mentioning the need for 'the complete removal of capitalist and feudal survivals in the relations of production'.[75] The factory committees strove in practice to transform relations of authority at enterprise level, but their failure to theorise this practice into an alternative strategy of transition helped to bring about their own ultimate demise and that of workers' self-management.

10

The economic crisis and the fate of workers' control: October 1917 to June 1918

FROM WORKERS' CONTROL TO WORKERS' SELF-MANAGEMENT

The October seizure of power was a workers' revolution in the simple sense that it transferred state power to a government which enjoyed the support of a majority of the working class. As an essentially political act, it had little immediate effect on the daily lives of workers. The economic crisis, rapidly getting worse, was a far more important influence on their position than the change in political regime. Nevertheless at a subjective level, the coming to power of a soviet government had a profound effect on the way that workers perceived the deteriorating situation in the factories. The ease with which the Bolsheviks had toppled the Kerensky government persuaded many workers that the time was ripe to follow up the political dispossession of the capitalist class with their economic dispossession. The inauguration of a government of workers and peasants, coupled with the breakup of the economy, seemed to many to toll the death-knell of capitalism. The Decree on Workers' Control, in particular, was seen as a signal to advance to socialist society without delay. Speaking to the national congress of trade unions in January 1918, the Menshevik, Maiskii, remarked: 'According to my observations, the majority of the proletariat, particularly in Petrograd, looks on workers' control as an entry into the kingdom of socialism. It's precisely this psychology which creates huge dangers for the whole socialist movement in Russia in the future, because ... if workers' control suffers defeat, then the masses will become disillusioned with the very idea of socialism.'[1] Most militant workers despised such jeremiads: they had won state power, what else was left to do except go forward to socialism?

In many provincial areas the Decree on Workers' Control initiated workers' control of production for the first time, but in Petrograd it legitimated the already-existing forms of workers' control and extended their scope. The factory committees now set up special control-commissions charged with overseeing and intervening in the running of the factories. Such commissions already existed in the largest factories of the capital, but they now sprang up elsewhere. By the autumn of 1918, 212 factories in Petrograd province had control-commissions: 24% of these had been established before November 1917; 51% had been established between November and March 1918, and 25% after March 1918.[2] These commissions not only monitored stocks of fuel and raw materials, they also checked orders and company finances and intervened in the technical side of production. They left employers in no doubt that they were now in charge. Not surprisingly, the employers hit back.

On 22 November the Petrograd SFWO announced: 'We categorically reject non-state, class control by workers over the country's industrial life (as decreed by the government) since it does not, in practice, pursue national ends and is not recognised by the majority of the Russian population.'[3] Three days later an unofficial meeting of the biggest commercial and industrial organisations in Petrograd decided on a tough line: 'In the event of demands for workers' control being put forward ... the enterprise must be closed.' It claimed that 'the government, by completely handing over management of the factories into the hands of the working class is erecting a barrier to the further participation of capital in industrial life'.[4] Opposition to workers' control was fiercest amongst the owners of metal-plants, who were already in a perilous situation owing to the critical shortages of fuel and raw materials. In the leather and textile industries, where things were less tight, the employers proved more conciliatory. In January 1918 the Petrograd leather manufacturers agreed to a supervisory mode of workers' control, such as had been elaborated in the Instructions of the ARCWC.[5]

In some factories sharp conflicts between management and the factory committees were provoked by attempts to implement the Decree on Workers' Control. At the Triangle rubber-works the director, Pasternak, told the control commission: 'If you establish control, then I'll close the factory. I cannot work under control.'[6] At the Langenzippen works the owner stormed out of the factory when the control commission imposed far-reaching control. The factory committee refused to allow him back, and in June was criticised by the metal section of SNKh S.R. for misinterpreting control over production as meaning control over the individual capitalist.[7] At the Nevskii footwear factory, management politely informed the control-commission: 'In answer to your memorandum of 9 December, we consider it our duty to inform you that nowhere in the regulations on workers' control is anything said about the commission having the right to "direct" management to do something, and we consider that such a form of "direction" – without any appeal – is utterly inadmissible under a democratic system.'[8]

A good insight into the industrial disputes which arose over attempts to institute far-reaching control can be gained by examining one enterprise in detail. At the Nevskii shipyard fuel shortages had, by October, drastically cut back production. After the Bolsheviks seized power, management waited, believing that the government could not hold power for long. The financial position in the enterprise was grave, and management decided that as soon as war orders stopped, they would have to dismiss 2,476 workers.[9] On 16 November, in response to the Decree on Workers' Control, the factory committee set about extending its sphere of influence, but met with strong resistance from management. A week later, it demanded to have two representatives with voting rights on the board of the company, but management refused. The factory committee then demanded that no payments be made without its approval. Management pointed out that 'to recognise your demand for actual control over the finances of the factory would not be in accordance with the Decree on Workers' Control, which does not envisage the right of workers to interfere in the management functions of the factory administration'.[10] On 27 November the factory committee tried to occupy the finance office. On 3 December they requested the Military-Revolutionary Committee of the Petrograd Soviet to send a commission of experienced people to look into the affairs of the company. The next day the government declared the factory under workers' control. On 8 December the factory committee insisted that all papers from management be countersigned by the factory committee. A few days later it announced that the present director of the shipyard would be replaced by the engineer, A.A. Ustitskii. The control commission was effectively in charge from then on. On 23 December the board of this state enterprise announced: 'The company board of the Nevskii works is not the representative of capital, but the representative of the government, appointed by it not to exploit the enterprise in order to make shareholders rich, but to see that the enterprise functions properly from the government's point of view.'[11] But the workers were in no mood to compromise. The old board of management was ousted on 17 January when the shipyard was nationalised.[12]

The newer, radical style of workers' control tended to create conflict not only between workers and management, but between workers and technical and clerical staff. The Decree on Workers' Control made provision for the latter to sit on the control commissions, but the professional organisations of technical and clerical personnel objected to the terms of the Decree. At the beginning of November the union of engineers, which represented senior industrial engineers, warned: 'we will firmly protect the personal and professional dignity of our members and will give a firm rebuff to any attempt by any commissar or agent of the usurping government to give directions to the engineers, to interfere in their affairs or force them to do anything by threat'.[13] More junior technical personnel, represented by the union of foremen and technicians, were also hostile to the government but to a lesser extent. On 17 November a delegate meeting of the Petrograd branch of the union declared:

We have always regarded ourselves as an integral part of the proletariat, and have always been interested in strengthening the gains of labour over capital ... And so we call on our members in the union to join with the workers and support them in their creative work by every means, without yielding to their political views, and to be respectful towards those organisations in the factory which receive the sanction of the proletariat. In cases of insult, abuse or infringement of your rights, the union will powerfully defend you, but our best defence will be tact and sincere love for the proletariat ... Concerning the question of workers' control, we support the idea of workers' control on a broad state basis, but consider the Decree of the People's Commissars completely incompatible with present productive and economic relations, and, not wishing to take responsibility for the ruinous consequence of putting it into practice, we as an organisation will fight in the central organs of control to change that part of the draft which concerns the powers of the local control organs, so as to coordinate the operations of all enterprises.[14]

The All-Russian Congress of Clerical workers, which met from 3–8 December, took a similar position towards workers' control:

Congress considers the immediate and urgent task of the moment to be the rapid organisation of central, regional and local organs of control and regulation of industrial life. Such organisations, invested with authority, power and stability, can be created only by a central, democratic state power

enjoying the popular recognition of a Constituent Assembly ... Employees
are recommended to take active part in the control of production ... only in
those circumstances where a purely defensive control is being instituted for
protection against possible sabotage.[15]

In general, the factory committees were anxious to win the
cooperation of technical and clerical staff in the implementation of
control, since they needed their expertise if the control were to be
effective. The political opposition of such staff towards the Bolshevik
regime, however, led to bitter clashes between blue-collar and
white-collar workers. At the Robert Krug engineering works the
committee asked technical personnel to sign a pledge to abide by the
decisions of the workers' organisations and to recognise the government of People's Commissars. The technicians refused to sign it and
the committee threatened to hand them over to a military-revolutionary tribunal for counter-revolutionary activity.[16] At the Aivaz works
engineers went on strike in November and were arrested by the
factory committee and Red Guards. On 19 February the CCFC
warned the committee to take a 'cautious approach' to the
engineers.[17] At the Putilov works on 31 October, office staff voted by
315 votes to 18, with 14 abstentions, against the Bolshevik seizure of
power and called for a socialist coalition government.[18] They agreed
not to strike, however, as the staff of government ministries were
doing. A couple of days later, draughtsmen at the factory passed an
almost identical resolution, by 97 votes to 11, with 12 abstentions.[19]
The works committee took a dim view of these resolutions. It elected
N. Grigor'ev – a worker in the turret shop – commissar of the Putilov
works, and his appointment was confirmed by the Military-
Revolutionary Committee. On 9 November Grigor'ev sent a worker
to supervise the work of clerical staff in their offices; they were
enraged, and demanded a meeting with the works committee. On
arriving for the meeting at the works theatre, they found it sur-
rounded by armed Red Guards. The 429 *sluzhashchie* refused to take
part in a meeting under these conditions, pointing out that the
Military-Revolutionary Committee had forbidden armed persons to
attend public meetings. They then proceded to break off relations
with the works committee.[20] A meeting of all the shop committees
reprimanded the *sluzhashchie* for having 'abandoned the toiling family
of workers' and insisted that a 'refusal to submit to the commissar is a
refusal to submit to the government'.[21]

As the economy collapsed around them, and as the factory

committees became more obstreperous, employers often lost the will to carry on. Some began to run down their operations, refusing new orders and selling off stock, fuel and raw materials. Some began to squander their capital, others to transfer their assets abroad. Some stopped paying wages, claiming that this was now the responsibility of the government. Others simply abandoned the sinking ship: 'the owner has vanished' was the plaintive cry of a few factory committees in December. At the Bromley Mill, for instance, almost all the members of the board fled to England. At the First Yarn Mill, when the factory committee announced that it would henceforth pay management their salaries, the English directors, who had been at the factory for twenty-five years, decided that it was time to pack their bags and go abroad.[22]

It is often suggested that the intense class conflict of the post-October period engendered widespread anarchist sentiment within the working class. It is certainly the case that anarchists began to step up their campaign for factory seizures. *Golos Truda*, the anarcho-syndicalist journal, ran an article on 3 November which said: 'We affirm that it is not state power which needs to be seized, but production, because with the seizure of production we destroy both capitalism and the state at one blow and we will replace both of them with a genuinely socialist society, resting on real freedom, equality and brotherhood.'[23] At the Fifth Factory Committee Conference on 15–16 November, at which about 8% of the delegates were anarchists, the anarchist Terent'ev declared: 'We must take over both works and factories ... control is possible only when everything is ours and this is impossible so long as there are factory owners. The first thing we must do is requisition the factories.'[24] Renev, an anarchist from the Baltic shipyard, continued in the same vein: 'The Decree on Workers' Control is slowing down the movement. To go forward we must remember that the Decree is not our idol.'[25]

These notions proved attractive to some groups of workers. In the textile factories of Petrograd, for instance, several attempts were made by workers to take over the running of their factories. Popular anarchist militants like Troshin, a worker at the Kozhevnikov textile mill, Kotov and Kolovich went about calling on workers to seize the factories for themselves.[26] At the Kersten knitwear factory, where women comprised three-quarters of the workforce, the factory committee arrested the manager because of his refusal to recognise their spokesman, the mechanic Tseitlin. The clerical workers went on strike in protest at this. On 22 November an anarchist proposed to a general meeting that the workers divide up the factory property among themselves. Alexandra Kollontai, who had been sent to speak on behalf of the Bolsheviks, managed to dissuade the women from this, but she was unable to dissuade the committee from trying to run the factory by itself. It had no money, and though it tried to raise capital out of wage deductions and received a small loan from the Vulcan works, it was soon forced to abandon its experiment because of financial difficulties. The committee called on the Ministry of Labour to sequester the factory, but at that point the textileworkers' union intervened to bring about a reconciliation between the committee and management, who agreed to recognise Tseitlin.[27]

Despite such incidents, what is remarkable about Petrograd is the very limited influence which anarchists had on the factory committees. Factory seizures were extremely rare in the capital, though they were now more common in provincial areas, such as the Middle and Lower Volga, Vyatka, the Western provinces, and the Central black-earth region, where workers took over many small light-industrial enterprises, especially food-processing plants.[28] According to the judicious calculations of V.Z. Drobizhev, only twenty-seven factories in Petrograd province were taken from their owners between November 1917 and March 1918, and none of these takeovers turns out to have been inspired by an anarchist desire to get rid of the boss on principle.[29]

At the Metal works in mid-November the works committee set up a workers' directorate, consisting of nine workers elected by the workforce, to achieve 'direct, active participation in the management of production and of the factory, and liaison with government and private institutions and personnel on an equal basis with the company directors'.[30] These directors were to sit on all boards in order to 'supervise and direct' their work. Management lost no time in informing the directorate that it would not tolerate such 'interference in management by outsiders, not responsible for their actions'. On 1 December it closed the factory, whereupon the directorate took over the running of the Metal works until the government agreed to its nationalisation on 16 January. By March, however, there were only 276 workers left at the factory.[31] At the Franco-Russian works on 8 November the works committee wrote to the company as follows: 'the factory is financed by money from the state treasury . . . so the workers and the factory committee must have a full assurance that this money is not going to enrich a handful of exploiters at the expense of labour, but is going to meet the needs of all who work in the factory. Productive work and a conscientious attitude to our duties will only come about once the board is headed by an elected group who enjoy the confidence of all who toil in the factory. Such a supreme organ should consist of workers, *sluzhashchie* and toilers.'[32] Pending a decision to nationalise the Franco-Russian works, VSNKh agreed on 20 February to the establishment of a temporary board along the lines suggested by the committee, which comprised one representative from VSNKh, one from the metal union, an engineer, a white-collar worker and three elected workers.[33]

At the Aivaz works in December a control commission, consisting of seven workers and four *sluzhashchie*, was set up to counterpose to 'the uncontrolled, unorganised conduct of the economy by the capitalists ... the idea of public control, organisation and regulation of economic life in the interests of the exploited class'.[34] It declared that 'the directors have no right to enter any commitments or to conclude contracts without the sanction of the control-commission; the latter shall examine all aspects of management and shall ratify all management decisions; moreover it shall ensure that health and safety aspects of the enterprise are at the proper level'.[35] Management refused to work under the control-commission, and on 23 December it announced the closure of the factory. The control commission then endeavoured to keep production going by itself, until the factory was nationalised in August 1918.[36] At the Robert Krug engineering works, where 190 workers were employed, a general meeting issued the following statement on 12 December:

Having heard a report from the control-commission about the conflict which took place between the commission and management at a meeting on 11 December, when management stated clearly and unambiguously that it did not recognise the works committee, the control commission or the Instructions on Workers' Control, and when a management representative, [citizen] Lerkhe, clearly hinted at stopping production at the factory ... the general meeting of workers and *sluzhashchie* has decided:
(1) not to allow such sabotage
(2) to avert the final closure of the factory, and the unemployment which would ensue from this
(3) to take the factory into its own hands.[37]

This was no wild seizure, for the workers requested that the Factory Convention supervise the running of the factory. Self-management could not negate economic realities, however, and on 9 March 1918 the factory closed.[38]

These examples show that even in the small number of cases where

workers took over the running of their factories, they were not in the
grip of some anarchist delirium. They were determined to exercise
far-reaching control over management, in order to prevent 'sabotage'
or closure, and it was the attempt by management to close down the
enterprise which prompted a workers' takeover. In only a tiny
number of small factories, such as Kan paper mill and Berthold print
works, did a workers' takeover prove viable.[39] In all larger enterprises, workers' management proved incapable of dealing with the
immense problems affecting production. In these instances, however,
it seems clear that the workers took over their enterprises without any
intention of taking sole charge of production. The takeovers were
temporary measures, designed not merely to forestall closure, but to
force the government to take responsibility for the factory by taking it
into state ownership or control. At the Nobel works, for example, a
meeting of the workforce on 19 January heard a report which showed
that the factory was bankrupt and that management could not afford
to pay their wages. The meeting resolved 'to declare the factory the
property of the Russian Republic and to entrust the factory committee to organise and regulate production in liaison with the Commissariat of Labour'. A delegation of four was sent to VSNKh to ask for
money to pay wages and to request nationalisation of the factory, but
VSNKh seems to have refused.[40] At the Northern Iron-Construction
Company the factory committee had been inactive up to October.[41]
Having been re-elected, it began to resist management more actively.
On 6 March 1918 it reported to the metal section of SNKh S.R. that:
'The factory committee regards itself as an organ of state control, and
as such cannot allow management to spend the people's money as it
likes ... In view of the fact that the board has no money to carry out
demobilisation or to transfer the factory to civilian production, and
that it is greatly in debt to the state, the committee requests SNKh
S.R. to confiscate the factory along with all its property and
remaining money ... for the benefit of the All-Russian republic.'[42] A
few days later the committee wrote again to SNKh S.R., informing it
that the workers had elected a directorate to take charge of the
factory, but it was at pains to explain that 'we do not wish to engage in
a separatist action such as the seizure of the factory, and so we are
transferring the factory to the charge of VSNKh'.[43] At the Soikin
print works the autonomous commission justified its takeover as
follows: 'the only way of preserving the enterprise from ruin and
disaster ... lies in temporarily taking matters into our own

hands, until such time as the government will take over from us'.[44] At the Vulcan works on 23 March the committee called on SNKh S.R. to nationalise the factory: 'the whole policy of management is to close down the factory. If it has not already closed down, this is solely because the energies of the factory committee have sustained the life of the factory ... The kind of control which management will accept is purely token, for it will remain boss of the factory, whilst responsibility for running the factory will rest entirely with the control-commission. Thus dual power will not be eliminated.'[45] It requested that SNKh S.R. sequestrate the Vulcan works, which was duly effected on 30 March.

Pressure to nationalise individual enterprises came from the factory committees, who saw in state ownership or state control the sole alternative to closure. V.P. Milyutin wrote that: 'the process of nationalisation went on from below, and the soviet leaders could not keep up with it, could not take things in hand, in spite of the fact that many orders were issued which forbade local organisations to enact nationalisations by themselves'.[46] He remarked that many of these local 'nationalisations' had a punitive character. This sentiment was echoed by A.I. Rykov at the first congress of *sovnarkhozy* in May: 'Nationalisation was carried out for not implementing the rules of workers' control, and because the owner or the administration had fled, or simply for not fulfilling the decrees of soviet power, etc. ... The nationalisation of enterprises had a straightforwardly punitive rather than economic character.'[47] Data collated by V.Z. Drobizhev seem to bear out this interpretation.[48] Of 836 warrants issued to dispossess factory owners between November and December, 77% were issued by local bodies – a sure sign that pressure to nationalise came from below. On 19 January the Council of People's Commissars forbade 'nationalisations' without the permission of VSNKh, and the ban was repeated on 16 February. On 27 April VSNKh again informed local soviets and local *sovnarkhozy* that they would receive no funds for any enterprise which they had confiscated without permission.[49] Nevertheless, between November and March, only 5.8% of nationalisations, sequestrations, confiscations or socialisations in the country as a whole were carried out by the Council of People's Commissars or the central organs of VSNKh.[50]

In Petrograd 'nationalisations from below' were not as common as elsewhere. All state-owned factories were, of course, nationalised as a matter of course, and a further sixteen private factories (beginning

with the Putilov works on 27 December) were formally nationalised
up to 1 April. These included a few large factories, but were mainly
small or medium-sized enterprises such as the Military-Horseshoe
works.[51] By April about forty enterprises in the city were officially
nationalised, including former state enterprises, and a further 61 were
being run temporarily by factory committees.[52] The latter factories
had been 'sequestrated' or 'confiscated' with the permission of SNKh
S.R. or the local soviet, but no clear distinction existed between
'sequestration' and 'nationalisation'.[53] Between April and June a
further score of enterprises in what was by now the former capital
passed into formal state ownership.

   To what extent had workers' control developed into workers'
self-management by the time that the government nationalised the
whole of industry at the end of June? It is difficult to answer this, since
it is impossible to draw neat distinctions between workers' control
and workers' management. Workers' management seems to have
been confined to a minority of enterprises in Petrograd. The Soviet
historian, M.N. Potekhin, calculates that, on 1 April, 40 enterprises
were nationalised; 61 were being temporarily run by factory committees; 270 were under workers' control and 402 were still being run by
their owners, although these were overwhelmingly small workshops.[54]
In the major factories, therefore, workers' control was still the norm.
In practice this meant that the official management existed alongside
the factory committee, but that its orders could not be effective
without the ratification of the factory committee or its control
commission. Most organs of control saw to the execution of various
jobs to be done, investigated the state of equipment, finances, order
books, accounts, fuel and raw material, and, in addition, the factory
committee was responsible for laying off workers, for internal order,
productivity and working conditions.[55] In those enterprises where the
factory committees were in complete charge, this was not, generally,
considered to be a permanent arrangement, but a makeshift arrangement until such time as the government formally nationalised the
enterprise and appointed a new board of management. Finally, the
management of factories which had been officially nationalised varied
a great deal. At former state enterprises the boards of management
were gradually reorganised. Thus a new board was appointed at the
Obukhov works on 20 January, which consisted of eight workers, two
technical personnel, the chief engineer and a representative of the
sluzhashchie.[56] In some nationalised private factories the boards of

management consisted of workers and technicians, trade-union and *sovnarkhoz* representatives. Often, however, the control-commission remained in charge, the only change being that a commissar, responsible to VSNKh, was appointed to keep a strict eye on production at the factory. In some instances, the old board of management remained in charge of a nationalised factory, but now worked under a VSNKh commissar. Overall, therefore, there was considerable variation in the structure of management of Petrograd's factories, although since October there had been a significant move in the direction of worker participation in management.

In Chapter 9 we saw that at their final conference in January 1918, the Petrograd factory committees had demanded that nationalised enterprises be run by workers' committees. In March, however, Lenin made the first of a series of appeals for a return to one-man management. The controversy about workers' collegial management came to a head at the First Congress of *sovnarkhozy* from 25 May to 4 June 1918. The commission of the congress which drew up the resolution on enterprise management, strictly circumscribed the right of VSNKh to influence the make-up of the boards of nationalised enterprises, by proposing that two-thirds of the board be elected by workers at the enterprise. When Lenin heard of this he was outraged, and he, together with Rykov and Veinberg, drafted an alternative resolution.[57] This was, eventually, passed by the conference. It specified that nationalised enterprises should be run by a collegial board of management, one-third of whose members should be nominated by the *oblast' sovnarkhoz*; one-third nominated by either VSNKh or the *oblast'* or national trade union; and the other third by the workers of the enterprise. The board was then to elect a director responsible to VSNKh. N.K. Antipov, formerly of the CCFC, Andronnikov, from the Urals *oblast' sovnarkhoz*, and Kostelovskaya, from the textile union, argued for full workers' management and were opposed by Veinberg, Lozovskii and others, who called for virtually complete control of the enterprise by VSNKh.[58] The resolution passed was a compromise between these two positions, but it marked a strengthening of centralism, since it subordinated management boards to the *sovnarkhoz*. This form of collegial management thus considerably modified the concept of workers' management which had been advocated by the factory committees a few months earlier. Later during the Civil War, the committees were to strenuously defend this compromise against the advocates of one-man management. In 1919 only 10.8% of enterprises in Russia were under one-man management, though this percentage rose dramatically during 1919–20.[59] In Petrograd the resistance to one-man management was especially strong, particularly in large factories. In March 1920 69% of factories employing more than 200 workers were still run by a collegial board.[60] Petrograd workers, therefore, the most enthusiastic exponents of the 'democratic' factory in 1917, proved most resistant to recentralisation of management authority during the Civil War.

ECONOMIC CATASTROPHE AND THE DISSOLUTION OF THE WORKING CLASS

The expansion of workers' control is usually considered to be a major cause of the accelerating chaos in the economy. In fact it was less a cause and more a response to that chaos, which had its roots in the whole system of war capitalism. During the war the output of Petrograd's industry had doubled, and by 1917 it was meeting two-thirds of the nation's defence requirements. The crisis in the war industries, which began to build up during the summer of 1917, came to a head in the winter of that year. As soon as the Bolsheviks sued for peace, the bottom fell out of the capital's economy.

The People's Commissariat of Labour (*Narkomtrud*) began in December to draw up plans for the orderly demobilisation of the war industries and for the evacuation of both factories and workers. On 20 December it ordered the closure of factories for up to a month, so that the transfer to civilian production could be carried out.[61] It was envisaged that the experienced, skilled workers would remain in the demobilised factories, and that the majority of less experienced workers would be encouraged to leave Petrograd, the Labour Exchange paying their travelling expenses. Factory committees began to draw up detailed plans for redundancies within their enterprises. At the Okhta explosive works the factory committee agreed that workers should be made redundant in the following order: first to go would be volunteers; second, merchants, traders, yard-keepers, caretakers and others who had entered the factory in order to avoid conscription; third, those who had refused to join a trade union; fourth, members of families in which more than one member worked at the factory; fifth, youths under the age of eighteen, unless they had dependants or were without families; sixth, those with some property or element of fixed income; seventh, those from families in which other members were still employed, though not at the factory; eighth, single people with no dependants; ninth, and last to go, would be workers with dependants, according to the number of dependants they had.[62] Similar redundancy plans were drawn up at the Old Parviainen works and at Putilov.[63]

In the event, little came of the plans for an organised demobilisation of Petrograd industry. In the New Year, the plight of thousands of workers, facing the loss of their jobs, was suddenly compounded by the prospect of a German occupation of the city and a cut in the bread ration. On 27 January the bread ration was reduced to 150 grams per day; on 14 February to 100 grams (one-quarter of a *funt*), and on 28 February it reached its lowest level of 50 grams.[64] Mass starvation loomed ahead, and this, together with the imagined horrors of a German occupation, induced panic in the population and an exodus from the capital. Four months after 'demobilisation', the metal section of SNKh S.R. reported: 'there was not even any discussion of a full, detailed survey of enterprises, there was neither the technical means nor the time for this, since any delay in dismissing workers threatened to cost colossal sums. The workers, too, hurried to leave in order to get out of Petrograd as quickly as possible, to escape starvation and the threat of invasion.'[65] Those who had ties with the countryside hurried back to their native villages, in the hope of qualifying for some of the land that was being distributed. Others, dismissed from their jobs, set out from the capital in the hope of finding food. In the first six months of 1918 over a million people left Petrograd.[66]

Within a matter of months, the proletariat of Red Petrograd, renowned throughout Russia for its outstanding role in the revolution, had been decimated (see *Table 15*). By April 1918 the factory workforce of the capital had plummeted to about 40% of its January 1917 level, and it shrank still further thereafter. The branches of industry worst affected were those producing directly for the war effort – metalworking and engineering, shipbuilding, chemicals and woodworking. In the metal factories of Petrograd province, employing more than a hundred workers, the total workforce slumped from 197,686 on 1 January to 57,995 on 1 May.[67] Less severely affected were light industries such as textiles, food, paper and printing. Big factories suffered more than small factories; private factories more than state-owned ones. Those factories which had expanded most dramatically during the war, contracted most dramatically when the war ended.[68] On 28 February 1918 the huge Triangle rubber works closed down: within a matter of months only 756 of its 15,000 staff remained.[69] Despite the flight of workers from the city, there were still 60,000 registered unemployed at the beginning of May.[70]

The Soviet historians, Drobizhev and Vdovin, argue that it was the less experienced wartime recruits to industry who left Petrograd, leaving a nucleus of 'cadre' workers more or less intact.[71] This picture, however, is in need of qualification. It was to be expected that workers with close ties to the countryside should have left the capital, given the availability of food and land in their native villages. Similarly, it was to be expected that the shutdown of war production should have made large numbers of unskilled and semi-skilled war recruits jobless. This is borne out by data from the Central Commission for the Evacuation of Petrograd (and later from the city Labour Exchange) which show that no less than 53% of those who applied for travelling expenses were *chernorabochie*.[72] However, since only a minority of those who left the city claimed travelling expenses, those who did so, were more likely to have been the worst-off workers, i.e. the unskilled. Other evidence suggests that the process of demobilisation was so cataclysmic that it made skilled, as well as unskilled workers, redundant.[73] Even if experienced workers were not as badly affected as their less experienced comrades, it was among the former group that the Bolsheviks had their most committed supporters, and so many of them decided to leave the factories in order to serve the new soviet government. They enlisted in the Red Army, assumed posts of responsibility within the government and party apparatuses, or joined the food detachments. O.I. Shkaratan estimates that about 6,000 workers left Petrograd to join the Red Army prior to April.[74] Young workers, fired by revolutionary élan and without family commitments, were especially eager to quit the factories in order to defend soviet power. Over half of those who claimed evacuation expenses were single men, and by April the proportion of youths in the factory workforce was only half that of the previous year.[75] In October 1917 there had been about 43,000 Bolsheviks in the capital – of whom two-thirds were workers.[76] By June 1918 only 13,472 were left.[77] It would seem, therefore, that at least the keener Bolsheviks among the 'cadre' workers left the factories of Petrograd in the early months of 1918.

Table 15: *The decline in the number of factory workers in Petrograd, 1917–18*

Branch of Industry	Number of enterprises	Number of enterprises which had closed by 1 April 1918	Number of workers at 1 January 1917	Number of workers at 1 April 1918
Textiles	45	10	37,478	31,855
Cloth	26	8	5,238	1,781
Paper	30	7	4,829	3,784
Printing	147	6	14,508	20,432
Woodworking	52	21	4,956	2,293
Metals	213	109	167,192	43,129
Minerals	18	8	2,323	645
Leather	35	8	11,181	7,680
Food	47	12	13,000	10,075
Chemicals	55	17	22,535	5,691
Electrotechnical	28	6	13,371	5,095
Power Stations	11	–	1,831	1,778
Ships, carriages, automobiles and aeroplanes	39	11	29,850	8,024
Optical and surgical instruments	25	6	5,490	3,807
Rubber goods	2	2	17,228	2,641
TOTAL	773	231	351,010	148,710

Source: M. N. Potekhin, *Pervyi Sovet proletarskoi diktatury*, (Leningrad, 1966), p.253.

245

THE LABOUR ORGANISATIONS AND THE CRISIS OF
LABOUR DISCIPLINE

The exalted hopes unleashed by the October insurrection lasted until the beginning of 1918. Then signs of working-class disillusionment with the regime began to grow. This was not so much a response to the political policies of the new government, as to its failure to stem the chaos in the economy. Bolshevik actions such as the dissolution of the Constituent Assembly and the conclusion of the Treaty of Brest Litovsk caused murmurs of disquiet, but rocketing unemployment and the chronic dearth of food caused open disaffection in some quarters. The moderate socialists sought to give political shape to these grievances. It is not the purpose of the present work, however, to examine the character and scope of this anti-Bolshevik reaction in the Petrograd working class, but rather to examine how the chaos in the economy affected the situation in the workplace.

The chaos which engulfed industry gave rise to violent, destructive moods among a minority of workers. Calls from anarchists to 'smash', 'bring down' or 'occupy' evoked a definite response. In February the government warned factory committees to be ready to dismantle machinery in the event of a German advance. In one or two factories this led to an orgy of machine-breaking, even though the Germans got no nearer the capital than Pskov.[78] Negative feelings were manifest in conflicts between unemployed and employed workers. At the Siemens-Schukert works 7,000 workers were made redundant, and some of them threatened violence to those whose jobs had been spared. In April groups of the unemployed picketed the Obukhov works as the morning shift went into work.[79] The unemployed began to organise, but in a manner which socialists could not condone. A meeting of the unemployed in Vyborg, Lesnyi and Novoderevenskii districts issued a statement, under the signature of the 'Party of the Unemployed', which declaimed: 'The people have come to understand the dirty deeds of the Yids. Jews have settled on all the committees. We suggest that they leave Petrograd within the next three days.'[80] The proto-fascist Union of the Russian People seems to have come out of hiding at this time and may bear some responsibility for this revival of antisemitism. Such ugly moods, however, were characteristic of only a minority.

The Mensheviks sought to channel the discontent of the unemployed in an anti-Bolshevik direction. A Committee for Struggle

Against Unemployment was set up, which organised a demonstration of the unemployed on 24 March. This voiced harsh criticism of the government and, in particular, of the redundancy terms fixed by the trade unions.[81] Fearing the political mileage which the Mensheviks might make out of unemployment, the Bolsheviks convened an official conference of the unemployed on 2 April. A wide range of issues was discussed, and demands were raised for state unemployment benefit. The Bolshevik, Medvedev, said that the government could simply not afford this at present. Some scepticism was expressed at the idea of setting up a union of the unemployed, but the general feeling was that this would be a good idea. The conference called for an end to compulsory work on public projects (which led to one losing one's place in the queue at the Labour Exchange), and for the creation of *artels* and cooperative workshops. The government was asked to 'tax the propertied classes unmercifully', to deduct contributions to a fund for the unemployed from the wages of those in work, and to issue extra rations cards to the unemployed.[82] In spite of the initiatives of both Mensheviks and Bolsheviks, however, the success of organisations of the unemployed appears to have been linited.

Among those workers who remained in work, the problem of labour-discipline grew ever worse. From their inception, the factory committees and trade unions had taken an active interest in labour-discipline, and the problem now became of acute concern to them, as discipline broke down under the impact of unemployment and starvation. At Putilov the works committee issued a warning to the workforce immediately after the seizure of power: 'Regrettably, there are some comrades (not many, it is true) who understand freedom as licence for their desires, as unruliness, and this always harms the general affairs of the working class. So it is the duty of every comrade to curb and prevent the emergence of licentiousness and unruliness.'[83] Some 12,000 Putilovtsy stayed away from work during November because there was nothing for them to do. When the works committee managed to procure sixty wagonloads of coal through a 'pusher', it called on the absentee workers to return to the factory to unload the coal. Only two workers turned up for work. The rest did not bother, since they were receiving two-thirds their normal pay whilst they were laid off. The committee decided to take drastic measures by sacking persistent absentees and by cutting off the pay of skilled workers who refused to do unskilled jobs.[84] In spite of these harsh measures, labour discipline at Putilov continued to be poor throughout 1918. On 10 May the Petrograd Soviet called on Putilovtsy to improve productivity, and the works committee promised to do so.[85] On 17 May SNKh S.R. informed the factory that: 'whoever wastes even one *pud* of coal, whoever causes the factory chimney to smoke in vain for even five minutes is a criminal'.[86] Three days later the works committee promised: 'we shall strain every nerve; we shall drive the lazy and those with little consciousness; working hours shall be devoted solely to work'. It ended its resolution with the twin slogans 'Long live labour-discipline!' and 'Long live the world revolution!'[87]

Pressure for tough measures to counter labour indiscipline arose as much from the grass roots as from government authorities. On 24 January the workers at the Nevka cotton mill met to discuss how to combat deteriorating labour-discipline at the factory. Their resolution said: 'Having discussed the anarchy which holds sway in production, which is beneficial only to our enemies, the capitalists, who seek to profit from falling labour-productivity by increasing the price of goods, we now realise the seriousness of the situation in the country and will not allow our enemies to gloat at us. We must show that we are not the old, browbeaten workers of tsarism, and that the capitalist stick is now totally unnecessary. Their interests are alien to us, it is our own interests which matter, and the best defence of our power is to uphold the country's industry. We shall start along the path of creative, constructive work and none of us has the right to leave a machine five minutes before finishing time. Whoever finishes before time and leaves the workshop, will be sacked immediately or brought before a court and then dismissed.'[88]

Some labour leaders were opposed to the use of punitive sanctions, such as dismissal, to restore productivity. Larin, for example, argued that even the most draconian measures could not halt the decline in labour-productivity, since this was due to starvation rather than indiscipline. He called for higher wages, greater workers' control and moral suasion.[89] A survey by Strumilin of twenty-seven factories in Petrograd lent support to Larin's diagnosis. He calculated that nearly half the fall in labour-productivity was due to sheer physical exhaustion of workers, and only 21% to the decay of discipline and motivation.[90] Most trade-union leaders, however, felt that the breakdown of labour-discipline reflected a change for the worse in workers' attitudes.

In a speech to VTsIK (the All-Russian Central Executive

Committee) on 20 March 1918, A. Shlyapnikov, the Commissar of Labour, painted a gloomy picture of the Moscow railways and Petrograd factories where, he claimed, efforts by factory committees, to improve productivity had led to their members being recalled and replaced by representatives more compliant with the wishes of the rank-and-file. He argued that the only solution to the crisis of labour-discipline was the abolition of the guaranteed wage and the revival of piece-rates. This speech marked a turning-point, for it announced a decree which centralised management on the railways, restored the power of individual administrators and granted 'dictatorial' powers to the Commissariat of Communications.[91]

On 2 April the All-Russian Council of Trade Unions declared that 'one of the major causes of the fall in labour-productivity is . . . the lack of any kind of production discipline'. It proposed the reintroduction of piece-rates, guaranteed norms of output, bonuses and work books, in which workers would record their individual productivity. Workers who did not fulfil output norms for three days in a row would be transferred to a lower category, and if they continued to work below par would be dismissed. The ARCTU also proposed sanctions against lateness for work and opposed workers meeting during working hours; it called on factory committees to enforce these decisions.[92]

The most contentious of the proposals designed to improve productivity proved to be the revival of piece-rates.

Although the unions had agreed to piece-rates in their contracts of 1917, little progress had been made in restoring them in practice. In January 1918 the Petrograd board of the metal union reaffirmed its support for piece-rates,[93] but the Petrograd Council of Trade Unions appears to have been less happy with the idea. This seems to have been due to the influence of D. Ryazanov on the PCTU, who saw piece-rates as incompatible with socialism.[94] On 25 May the metal union persuaded a conference of Petrograd metalworkers to accept piece-rates, but only as a temporary measure, and only on condition that a worker did not earn more than 25% or 50% above the basic rate of the contract. The conference declared: 'The working class, which fought against piece-rates during the years when it had no rights, because they were a means of deepening exploitation in the hands of the employers, must now agree to their reintroduction under strict and effective control, so that, having stripped this method of its other features, we can use that which is valuable in it to help restore industry.'[95] In fact, the attempt to revive piece-rates did not meet with widespread success.[96] On 11 October 1918 a second conference of Petrograd metalworkers voted to abolish piece-rates except in exceptional circumstances. The metal section of SNKh S.R. pressed for the reversal of this decision, but many factories continued to reject piece-rates during the next two years.[97]

Other measures designed to restore productivity were more successfully implemented. The summer of 1918 saw the widespread introduction of guaranteed norms of output, bonus incentives and the forty-eight-hour week. More controversially, the guaranteed wage was abolished and wage-differentials were widened. In a few factories, production was reorganised along Taylorist lines.

Finally, the months of May and June 1918 saw the labour organisations of Petrograd begin to take a tough line against strikes. A strike by the 'aristocratic' electricians of the Putilov works was roundly condemned by a plenary session of the Petrograd Soviet on 29 May.[98] At the Nevskii shipyard a threatened strike was denounced by the Petrograd Council of Trade Unions, which accused the workers of demanding lay-off terms which would 'turn factories into simple tools for extracting money from the national exchequer, to the detriment of the whole people'.[99] In June a go-slow at the Obukhov works caused the Petrograd board of the metal union to take the unprecedented step of locking out the workers and declaring the factory closed. The decision was taken with five votes against and three abstentions, and was confirmed by SNKh S.R.[100] Two months later, after the old factory committee had been dissolved, the Obukhov works was reopened.[101] In spite of the strict measures which were being adopted towards strikes, however, stoppages, like poor labour-productivity, continued to occur throughout the Civil War.

Although the trade unions led the drive to increase labour-discipline and productivity, the factory committees also played a part in the battle to increase output. This had always been a concern of the committees, but it now took precedence over their other concerns. During 1918 the desire to transform relations of authority within the enterprise gave way to the drive for greater productivity. Workers' control was no longer seen in terms of the transformation of the relations of workers to production, but in terms of the passive supervision of production and, above all, in terms of upholding labour-discipline.[102] Yet one cannot see in this a triumph of the Bolshevik party over the factory committees. From the first, the committees had been committed both to maintaining production and to democratising factory life, but the condition of industry was such that these two objectives now conflicted with one another. The factory committees, in general, consented to the prioritisation of productivity: they acquiesced in, and even initiated, impulses towards stricter labour-discipline. Nevertheless, they and the organised rank-and-file resisted impulses towards authoritarianism which they disliked. In spite of the great respect and affection in which Lenin was held, for example, his views on one-man management were quietly ignored. Similarly, while most organised workers agreed to the priority of restoring productivity, they were not prepared to countenance the unconditional reintroduction of piece-rates. Party leaders and trade-union officials were thus not able to 'impose' their policies on the factory committees. In any case, there was no need to do so, for they could count on the support of the factory committees, who could see no alternative to the unpleasant policies being advocated.

After October labour organisations were no longer accountable only to their members: they were also accountable to the Bolshevik government. There thus began the process whereby these organisations lost their independent character and became incorporated into the new state apparatus. Already by early 1918 the relationship of labour organisations to their members was distinctly less democratic than in the preceding year. Most factory committee activists believed that the policies of the government were in the interests of the working class, but it was not always easy to persuade the workers that this was so. Efforts by the committees to strengthen labour-discipline at a time when redundancies and starvation were ravaging working-class life proved particularly unpopular. 'Bureaucratic' tendencies, which had existed within the committees from the start, now began to come to the fore. There were complaints that factory committees at the Pipe, Nobel, Old Lessner, Langenzippen and the Cartridge works had ignored demands from general meetings that they submit for re-election.[103] The Mensheviks saw in this, a 'system of terror, violence and tyranny in which one section of the workers has become a tool at the service of the government, bringing discord and demoralisation into the ranks of the working class and ultimately disorganising and weakening it'.[104] One need not concur with this judgement, to recognise that the committees were beginning to exploit the degree of autonomy which they enjoyed as representative organs, in order to resist what they regarded as dangerous demands from the shop floor, threatening the security of the revolution. From the beginning of 1918, they began to bypass democratic practices when these seemed to conflict with higher goals. The triumph of bureaucratic tendencies over democratic ones was by no means a foregone conclusion at the point at which we break off our story, but since 1917 the balance between the two had shifted decisively in favour of the former.

Conclusion

The labour movements of Western Europe were dominated by skilled artisans for most of the nineteenth century. Trades, such as tailors, shoemakers, cabinet-makers, carpenters and the building trades, spearheaded the radical and labour movements.[1] In contrast, the factory proletariat, which consisted to a large extent of women and children, was, with certain exceptions, badly organised and politically quiescent.[2] Only in the last quarter of the nineteenth century did trade unionism begin to expand beyond the ranks of an elite of artisans and skilled factory craftsmen. The evolution of the Petrograd labour movement was far more telescoped that its counterparts in the countries of Western Europe. Although the number of strikes and informal labour organisations grew rapidly during the last quarter of the nineteenth century, it was not until the 1905 Revolution that a formal labour movement was inaugurated. Although artisans played an important part in creating trade unions and socialist organisations,[3] by 1917 the labour movement of the Russian capital was based predominantly on workers in factory industry, workers employed in huge enterprises which were among the most modern in the world. Whilst this working class corresponded in some respects to the Marxian model of the modern working class, since it was employed in large-scale machine industry, in other respects, it was not yet a fully-developed proletariat. Within its ranks, urbanised, hereditary proletarians were still outnumbered by newcomers to industry, who retained strong ties to the countryside. The labour movement which was re-established in Petrograd after the February Revolution, therefore, had a hybrid character. Based on the modern factory rather than the artisanal workshop, it embraced a gamut of types of workers from the traditional artisan, to the skilled worker of the modern assembly plant, to the peasant migrant worker, so familiar in the Third World today.

The factory workforce of Petrograd was highly differentiated by degree of proletarianisation, by skill and wage-level, by gender, age and education. Each of these variables had its own effectivity within the struggles of the working class in 1917, and, in particular circumstances, could become 'overdetermined', as for instance, in the conflict between male and female workers over redundancies, or the conflict between skilled and unskilled workers during the metal-union contract negotiations. Nevertheless, one can crudely generalise, and say that within the workforce in 1917 there were two broad groups of workers: the first, consisting of proletarianised, skilled, literate, male workers, who comprised around 40% of the total factory workforce; the second, consisting of workers new to industry – mainly rural migrants, women and youth. The first group – sometimes called by contemporaries 'cadre' workers – should not, as a whole, be considered a 'labour aristocracy', for although there were aristocratic strata within it – the best-paid type-setters in the print trade, the *starshie* in the armaments factories or the glass-blowers of the glass industry – the majority of skilled men, whilst earning higher wages and being culturally distinct from the new workers, lacked the strong craft traditions on which the power of the 'labour aristocracy' in nineteenth-century Britain had been based. Moreover, their skills were not the all-round skills of the artisanal workshop, but the more specialised skills of the modern factory. The widespread introduction of the new technology of mass production during the First World War facilitated the big increase in numbers of the second group of new workers. The expansion of mass production in the metal and chemical industries allowed the rapid absorption of new workers into semi-skilled and unskilled jobs. The working-class women, the peasant youths and the urban petit-bourgeois who poured into the factories of the capital had little prior experience of wage-work in modern industry, but it did not take long to train them to operate automatic machinery or tend assembly lines. They quickly adapted to the fevered tempo of work in the war industries and to the discipline of the piece-rate system. The young, in particular, were soon at home in the factory and the city. Nevertheless, in 1917 the new workers were still culturally distinct from the 'cadre' workers, who tended to regard them as the 'backward masses'.

The existence of two broad social groups within the workforce was by no means a new phenomenon brought about by the war. As far back as the 1880s, contemporaries had noted the phenomenon and had speculated on the revolutionary propensities of each group. Kropotkin, one of the fathers of Russian anarchism, predicted that it would be the spontaneous militancy of the *fabrichnie*, the down-trodden peasants and women of the textile mills, which would spark off the social revolution.[4] In contrast, Plekhanov, the father of Russian Marxism, envisaged that the *zavodskie*, or skilled workers of the metal plants, would provide the basis of the revolutionary movement, because of their greater proletarianisation, literacy and leisure time.[5] The experience of 1917 suggests that the two groups played different, but largely complementary roles in the revolutionary process. Those who built the labour movement were the 'cadre' workers, especially metalworkers, for they had more time and money at their disposal, were at home in the factory, were more literate, had experience of informal shop-floor organisation and a degree of job-control, and were thus better placed to participate in labour and political activities. The new workers, on the other hand, were often more turbulent than the 'cadre' workers because they combined the manifold discontents of the low-paid worker with the grievances of the poor peasants and the specific oppressions of women and youth. Their militancy, however, was often of an explosive, sectional and volatile kind, and tended to threaten the attempts of the factory committee and trade-union leaders to build sustained, formal organisations. The labour leaders were not unsympathetic to the plight of the new workers, but they sought to direct their militancy into organised channels. They had some success in this, for women and peasant workers began in 1917 to engage in organised pursuit of their goals and to join trade unions. Young workers in particular, displayed a remarkable propensity for self-organisation. In this sense, working-class unity became a reality after February, in spite of profound divisions within the factory workforce. Yet contradictions of interest – between skilled and unskilled, men and women, young and old – remained: contradictions which labour leaders were reluctant to recognise. For while they aspired to bring the inexperienced and badly-off groups of workers into the orbit of the labour movement, they were unwilling to make special provision for the particular needs of the unskilled, the peasant migrants, working women or of youths. As a result, the participation of the latter in labour organisations and in revolutionary politics more generally, remained fairly tenuous. As the economy collapsed in early 1918, contradictions of interest between different groups of workers came to the fore, with the result that the unity of the previous year began to fall apart.

The tsarist factory was, in certain respects, a microcosm of the wider society. The structure of authority, the conditions of work, the low wages placed workers in a semi-servile position, and they welcomed the February Revolution as emancipation from this 'serfdom'. Workers saw the overthrow of the Romanov dynasty as the signal to create a democratic, or 'constitutional' factory order: firstly, by expelling the most unpopular administrators and, secondly, by establishing representative institutions to promote their interests as wage-earners within both the factory and society at large. In a very short time, workers won the eight-hour day and big wage-increases to compensate for wartime inflation. The Petrograd employers' association, having long resisted a more liberal industrial-relations policy, quickly reconciled itself to the 'constitutional' order in the factories, and conceded the greater part of the workers' demands.

The factory committees were the greatest gain made by workers as a result of the February Revolution. They had their roots in the tradition of the *starosty*, and perhaps, too, in the informal job control of skilled workers, which was increasingly threatened by rationalisation and de-skilling. The committees were strongest in the state sector, where skilled workers of a defencist persuasion temporarily took over the running of their enterprises, in order to ensure that production for the war effort was not put in jeopardy. It was out of this experience that the ideas of workers' control of production and collegial management were born. In the private sector the factory committees at first had largely trade-union functions, for it took some time for the unions to re-establish themselves, but everywhere the committees took on a wide range of tasks within and without the workplace. They asserted their right to monitor hiring and firing, to supervise the general running of the factory, and they intervened in areas as diverse as food-supply, education and law and order. Because state power was relatively ineffective, the committees became a central part of that 'counter-state' which was built up by workers between February and October, and in whose name the Bolsheviks seized power.[6]

The trade unions took some time to get off the ground, especially in the metal industry, where the factory committees were strongest. Throughout 1917 the unions were less influential than the committees, for the latter were more popular, more democratic and more powerful than the unions. It would be wrong, however, to minimise the importance of the unions, for they grew at a remarkable rate, becoming genuine mass organisations, and playing a crucial part in the revolutionary process. Craft unionism proved relatively weak in Petrograd, guild traditions never having been as strongly rooted in Russia as in Western Europe. The 'modern' character of the factory workforce seemed to call for industrial unionism, and the socialists who led the union movement found this more politically appealing than craft unionism. Although the reformist socialists were a powerful influence in the unions at a national level, in Petrograd the Bolsheviks and Mensheviks were fairly evenly balanced, with the influence of the former growing rapidly. Given their large size and the inhospitable conditions in which they began to operate, the unions proved themselves surprisingly effective as organisations representing the interests of workers as a whole. It was only after October, when the unions became subject to the Bolshevik government, that bureaucratisation developed on a significant scale.

Accelerating inflation rapidly undermined the wage-gains which workers had made in the spring, largely by means of small-scale, localised struggles. The unions sought to restore the real wages of workers by negotiating city-wide contracts covering all workers in each branch of industry. The contracts aimed to improve the position of the low-paid, in part by diminishing wage-differentials, and so many low-paid workers joined the unions in the summer of 1917. Negotiations of the contracts were often protracted, however, and as the position of the low-paid grew progressively worse, they turned increasingly to unofficial direct action in an effort to defend themselves against rocketing inflation. This brought some sections of the rank-and-file into conflict with union leaders – conflict which was exacerbated when the compromises made between union negotiators and the employers became known. There was considerable opposition to the final terms of the metal contract, for example, because ferocious inflation had eaten away the value of the wage increases by the time the contract was signed. Given the intractability of the economic crisis, it was probably an achievement for the unions to have succeeded in implementing the contracts at all. The contracts, by rationalising the pay structure, by setting-up rates commissions and, above all, by linking wages to productivity, prefigured aspects of Bolshevik labour-policy after 1917. And within the metal union a 'productivist' current, which celebrated efficiency, planning and the 'culture of production', adumbrated the movement for the 'scientific organisation of labour' which was to develop in the 1920s.

The deepening crisis of the economy provides the backdrop to the political radicalisation of Petrograd workers. The inability, or perceived unwillingness, of the Kerensky government to protect the gains made by workers after the February Revolution, led to growing disillusionment with the moderate socialists who supported the government. Workers now began to look to their own organisations for protection. It was the movement for workers' control of production which translated growing economic discontent into sympathy for the Bolshevik party. Workers' control had its roots in the democratisation of factory life, but the main impulse behind the movement sprang from the efforts of the factory committees to maintain production and to defend jobs – at a time when massive redundancies and the collapse of the war industries loomed on the horizon. Initially, the scope of workers' control was fairly modest: it aimed to supervise the activities of management in order to ensure that it did not 'sabotage' production or endanger workers' jobs. As economic disorder and class conflict grew, however, the factory committees broadened the scope of control. No longer did they confine themselves to procuring fuel and raw materials and to inspecting the process of production, they increasingly intervened in every sphere of management decision-making, demanding the right to attend board meetings and access to financial accounts and order-books. Although the movement aimed to limit the power of management, it cannot be considered a 'syndicalist' movement, for the determination of the committees to combat 'sabotage' was motivated more by practical than ideological considerations. Within Petrograd, anarchist and syndicalist influence was limited, and conceptions of workers' control were not articulated in syndicalist terms at either factory level or on the CCFC.[7] Whilst the committees rejected Menshevik and SR calls for state control of the economy, they endorsed Bolshevik perspectives for centralised coordination of the economy by a proletarian state power. There were, however, differences of emphasis between the leaders of the factory committees, the majority of whom were Bolsheviks, and the official party spokesmen. Committee activists appear to have had more faith in the capacity of grass-roots control to restore order in the economy than did some party leaders. Moreover they linked the battle to combat economic disorder to the struggle to limit the prerogatives of the employers and, consequently, placed much greater emphasis than did most party leaders on the necessity of transforming authority-relations at enterprise level, as part of the transition to socialism.

It would be wrong, however, to conclude that the Bolsheviks cynically manipulated the factory committees for their own ends. The radicalisation of the movement for workers' control gave the party enormous opportunity to win wide support for its policies, but it did not control the movement: it responded to it, trying to steer it in the direction it believed was proper. It was the organised working class, not the Bolshevik party, which was the great power in society – more powerful than even the capitalist class, as its success in resisting redundancies suggests. The collapse of the system of war capitalism, however, in early 1918 destroyed the strength of the working class, and it was only at that point that the Bolsheviks were in a position to achieve a monopoly of power.

The advent to power of the Bolsheviks in October raised the hopes and aspirations of workers in a similar way to the February Revolution, yet it made little difference to their working lives, for the economic situation continued to get worse. Initially, Lenin supported a radical interpretation of the Decree on Workers' Control, although he did not envisage a rapid transition to a socialist economy. Gradually, however, he became convinced that workers' control could not cope with the deep structural crisis of the economy, and he came to side with the trade-union critics of the factory committees. The Bolsheviks on the CCFC favoured a speedy transition to socialism, and they were the most vocal section of the party pressing for a system of central economic planning and state ownership of industry. Under such a system, the factory-committee Bolsheviks envisaged that workers' control would be transmuted into workers' management of individual enterprises. At factory level, many committee activists saw the Decree on Workers' Control as opening the way to workers' self-management, but in practice most of the control-commissions set up by the Decree confined themselves to circumscribing drastically the power of management, whilst not displacing it altogether. In the circumstances, this policy did not prove workable. Most employers resisted the more ambitious style of workers' control, and preferred to close down their factories rather than to submit to it. As a result, in a few instances, the control-commissions were forced to take over the actual running of the factories in a vain effort to save jobs. Such takeovers – although occurring in only a minority of Petrograd factories – were crucial in pushing the government in the direction of full-scale nationalisation. 'Nationalisations from below', together with escalating chaos in industry, persuaded the government finally to nationalise the whole of industry in June 1918. This proved, however, not to be the realisation of self-management, as the factory-committee activists had expected, but the first step in a process which culminated in the full restoration of one-man management.

There is some indication that prior to October the factory committees were beginning to accept the idea of a merger with the trade unions, but after October conflict between the two organisations flared up, as both tried to compete in the business of regulating the economy. The factory committees were accused by the unions of being selfish, parochial organisations, unsuited to the broad tasks of restoring order to the economy. Instances of such parochialism were in fact few in Petrograd, but there were just enough examples of committees refusing to share precious stocks of fuel and raw materials (at the Metal, Triangle and Copper-Rolling works)[8] to make the trade-union charges stick. There is no real evidence that the committees were exacerbating the chaos in the economy, as the unions claimed, but nor were they managing to cope with it, as they claimed they could. As the factories closed down, and as hundreds of thousands of workers fled from Petrograd, centralism and firm discipline became the order of the day. Only the unions seemed capable of achieving these things. Consequently, the government decided that the factory committees must be absorbed into the apparatus of the trade unions.

By the spring of 1918, Lenin was haunted by the fact that the economic infrastructure of socialism did not exist in Russia. The political superstructure was there, in the shape of a soviet government, but not the material base. This existed only in the West – above all, in Germany. This led him to observe that: 'History has taken such a peculiar course that it has given birth to two unconnected halves of socialism, existing side by side like two future chickens in a single shell of international imperialism. In 1918 Germany has become the most striking embodiment of the material realisation of the economic, productive and socio-economic conditions for socialism on the one hand, and Russia, the embodiment of the political conditions on the other.'[9] The Treaty of Brest Litovsk signalled the fact that revolution would not break out immediately in Germany. Every effort, therefore, had to be made to build up the productive forces in Russia. As Lenin argued:

The task of the day is to restore the productive forces destroyed by the war and by bourgeois rule; to heal the wounds inflicted by the war and by the defeat in the war, by profiteering and the attempts of the bourgeoisie to restore the overthrown rule of the exploiters; to achieve economic revival; to provide reliable protection of elementary order. It may sound paradoxical, but, in fact, considering the objective conditions mentioned, it is absolutely certain that at the present moment the Soviet system can secure Russia's transition to socialism only if these very elementary, extremely elementary problems of maintaining public life are practically solved.[10]

This meant, first and foremost, raising the productivity of labour: 'the Russian worker is a bad worker in comparison with the advanced nations ... To learn to work is the task that the Soviet government must set the people in all its scope.'[11] In turn, this meant the restoration of 'iron discipline' in the workplace, the revival of piece-rates, productivity deals and, above all, one-man management.

Implicit within the movement for workers' control was a belief that capitalist methods cannot be used for socialist ends. In their battle to democratise the factory, in their emphasis on the importance of collective initiatives by the direct producers in transforming the work-situation, the factory committees had become aware – in a partial and groping way, to be sure – that factories are not merely sites of production, but also of reproduction – the reproduction of a certain structure of social relations based on the division between those who give orders and those who take them, between those who direct and those who execute. The leaders of the factory committees never developed these insights into a systematic strategy for socialism, alternative to that of Lenin and the majority of the Bolshevik leadership; yet inscribed within their practice was a distinctive vision of socialism, central to which was workplace democracy.

Lenin believed that socialism could be built only on the basis of large-scale industry as developed by capitalism, with its specific types of productivity and social organisation of labour. Thus for him, capitalist methods of labour-discipline or one-man management were not necessarily incompatible with socialism. Indeed, he went so far as to consider them to be inherently progressive, failing to recognise that such methods undermined workers' initiatives at the point of production. This was because Lenin believed that the transition to socialism was guaranteed, ultimately, not by the self-activity of workers, but by the 'proletarian' character of the state power.

Maurice Brinton, the libertarian critic of Bolshevism, has exposed the inadequacy of his conception:

None of them [i.e. the Bolshevik leaders] saw the proletarian nature of the Russian regime as primarily and crucially dependent on the exercise of workers' power at the point of production (i.e. on workers' management of production). It should have been obvious to them as Marxists that if the working class did not hold economic power, its 'political' power would at best be insecure and would in fact soon degenerate. The Bolshevik leaders saw the capitalist organisation of production as something which, in itself, was socially neutral. It could be used indifferently for *bad* purposes (as when the bourgeoisie used it with the aim of promoting private accumulation) or *good* ones (as when the 'workers'' state used it 'for the benefit of many').[12]

This critique is absolutely on target. There is no doubt that Lenin did conceive proletarian power in terms of the central state and lacked a conception of localising such power at the point of production.[13]

A more far-reaching critique of Bolshevik strategy at this time has been developed by writers of Maoist persuasion – principally, the French economist Charles Bettelheim. He argues that the Bolsheviks were wrong to believe that the possibility of socialist advance is, in any sense, determined by the level of productive forces. He follows Mao Zedong in arguing that the transformation of relations of production clears the way for the development of productive forces rather than vice versa.[14] He contends that because the Bolsheviks – with the heroic exception of Lenin, whom he unwarrantedly excludes from his strictures – erroneously believed that the level of productive forces dictates the possibilities of socialist advance, they therefore subordinated the transformation of capitalist social relations to the drive to increase industrial output. The consequent absence of a strategy for transforming work-relations meant that output increased within a framework of capitalist rather than socialist relations of production. The capitalist division of labour and the ideological and political relations which are an effect of this division, were thus constantly reproduced, paving the way, Bettelheim avers, for the ultimate restoration of a 'state bourgeoisie'.

There is much in Bettelheim's stimulating critique with which one can agree. The Bolshevik strategy of transition did indeed centre on building the 'economic base' ('socialism equals electrification plus soviet power'), with little attention being paid to transforming social relations. But in denying that the level of productive forces exercises any constraint on the possibilities of socialist advance, Bettelheim is guilty of the grossest voluntarism. The implication of his argument is that the subsequent development of the Soviet state was the consequence of a simple theoretical error ('economism'). Whilst he mentions the intractable economic and social circumstances in which the Bolsheviks found themselves, these objective constraints do not really function as part of his explanation of the degeneration of the revolution.

A satisfactory examination of the theoretical relationship of forces of production to relations of production, would take us into rarefied spheres well outside the scope of this work. Marx centrally assumed that the creation of socialist relations of production was possible only on the basis of a certain level of productive forces, but his treatment of this question is problematical, because his concept of the 'productive forces' at times smacks of technological determinism. This led the Second International to interpret the question in a way that was unambiguously technological-determinist. Theoreticians such as K. Kautsky conceived the 'productive forces' as technology and the ever-growing scale of production. They argued that these, being social in character, would come into ever-increasing conflict with the constricting mode of appropriation based on private ownership. Finally, the productive forces would burst the fetters of private ownership, but would provide the material base for a socialist reorganisation of society, once a socialist government came to power. It is possible, however, to find in Marx's writings, a broader conception of 'productive forces', which does not reduce them to technology or productive capacity. This conceives productive forces as all those capacities and resources which are harnessed to producing use-values. These forces, which can never be divorced from the social forms in which they are embodied, include not merely types of industrial and agricultural production, but modes of social cooperation, the application of knowledge and cultural forms.[15] Above all, Marx sees the principal 'productive force' as being the working class itself.[16] In the light of this broader conception, it becomes clearer why Marx considered that a developed level of productive forces was necessary to the construction of socialism; for only a high level of productive forces could make possible the big reduction in necessary labour time which would enable the whole people to participate in self-government and civilisation. Without an adequate level of productive forces, 'want is merely made general and, with destitution, the struggle for necessities and all the old filthy business is necessarily reproduced'.[17] Socialism, in other words, would cease to be the entry into freedom, and become a struggle for survival instead.

With this in mind, it is possible to understand the cruel dilemma in which the Bolsheviks found themselves in 1918. They were intent on creating democratic socialism, but their priority had to be the reconstruction of the productive forces, especially, the revival of labour-discipline. In the short term, the limited use of forms of compulsion, in particular, the application of capitalist methods of labour-discipline and labour-intensification, was probably unavoidable. Yet most of the Bolshevik leadership seemed unaware of the dangers posed to the goal of democratic socialism by the long-term use of methods which undermined workers' self-activity in production. This was largely a consequence of the ideological problematic within which they thought through the problems of socialist construction. This problematic – still, in large part, that which had been inherited from the Second International – construed the productive forces in a narrow, technicist fashion and conceived the types of productivity and social organisation of labour engendered by capitalist society as being inherently progressive. Moreover within this problematic the absence of a notion of workers' self-activity in the realm of production as being a constituent element of socialist transition was especially glaring. If the Bolsheviks had been more critical of this Second International problematic, it is possible that they would have been more alive to the dangers of using coercive methods to restore the battered productive forces, except as an emergency measure. Whether such an awareness could have prevented the degeneration of the democratic socialist revolution in the long term, however, as Bettelheim suggests – given the persistence of war, economic isolation and cultural backwardness – seems doubtful. The depressing experience of socialist societies to date suggests that the imperatives of economic and social development in underdeveloped societies necessitate types of compulsion which ultimately conflict with the creation of free social relations. In other words, even if the Bolshevik government *had* been more percipient concerning the dangers to democratic socialism posed by the methods which it was forced to adopt, it seems probable that objective circumstances would ultimately have conspired to drain socialism of its democratic content. As it was, blind to the risks that it was running, the government was very quickly forced along a path which in October 1917 it had never dreamed of traversing. Already by 1921, the Bolsheviks no longer represented a socialism of liberty, but one of scarcity, in which the needs of individual and human liberation were firmly subordinate to the exigencies of economic development.

Notes

INTRODUCTION

1 T. Skocpol, *States and Social Revolutions* (Cambridge University Press, 1979); *Revolutions in Modern European History*, ed. H. Lubasz (New York, Macmillan, 1976).

2 Excellent accounts of the general developments of the Russian Revolution are available in the following works: J.L.H. Keep, *The Russian Revolution: a study in mass mobilisation* (London, Weidenfeld and Nicolson, 1976); M. Ferro, *The Russian Revolution of February 1917* (London, Routledge, 1972); M. Ferro, *October 1917* (London, Routledge, 1980). The July Days are examined in A. Rabinowitch, *Prelude to Revolution* (Bloomington, Indiana University Press, 1968). The October insurrection has two fine histories in R.V. Daniels, *Red October: the Bolshevik Revolution of 1917* (New York, Scribners, 1967) and A. Rabinowitch, *The Bolsheviks Come to Power* (New York, Norton, 1976). Although the present study discusses briefly the policies of the major political parties on 'economic' affairs, an attempt has been made to avoid duplicating the comprehensive accounts already available in P. Avrich, *The Russian Revolution and the Factory Committees* (Columbia University, Ph.D., 1962); R.J. Devlin, *Petrograd Workers and Workers' Factory Committees* (State University of New York at Binghampton, Ph.D., 1976).

3 N. Poulantzas, *Classes in Contemporary Capitalism* (London, New Left Books, 1975); N. Poulantzas, *State, Power and Socialism* (London, New Left Books, 1978); R. Hyman, *Industrial Relations: a Marxist Introduction* (London, Macmillan, 1975), p.26; S. Lukes, *Power: a Radical View* (London, Macmillan, 1974), pp.34–5.

4 V.I. Lenin, 'What is to be done?', *Selected Works* (in two volumes), vol.1 (London, Lawrence and Wishart, 1946).

5 C. Goodrich, *The Frontier of Control* (London, Pluto Press, 1975).

6 *Spisok fabrichno-zavodskikh predpriyatii Petrograda* (Petrograd, 1918), pp.7–16.

NOTES TO CHAPTER I

1 *Materialy po statistike Petrograda*, issue 1 (Petrograd, 1920), p.10. Estimates vary from 2.3 million to 2.7 million. A.G. Rashin, *Formirovanie rabochego klassa Rossii* (Moscow, 1958), p.354; S.G. Strumilin, 'Obshchii obzor severnoi oblasti', *Materialy po statistike truda severnoi oblasti*, issue 1 (Petrograd, 1918), p.17.

2 A.G. Rashin, *Naselenie Rossii za sto let* (Moscow, 1956), pp.25, 97.

3 *Mat. po stat. Pet.*, issue 1, p.10.

4 E.E. Kruze and D.G. Kutsentov, 'Naselenie Peterburga' in *Ocherki istorii Leningrada*, vol.3 (Moscow, 1956), p.106.

5 A more detailed statistical discussion of the demographic structure of St Petersburg can be found in: S.A. Smith, *The Russian Revolution and the Factories of Petrograd, February 1917 to June 1918*, Ph.D. (Birmingham University, 1980), pp.2–5. These generalisations are based on Rashin, *Naselenie*; and *Mat. po. stat. Pet.*, issue 1.

6 *Statisticheskie dannye Petrograda* (Petrograd, 1916), p.8.

7 Kruze and Kutsentov, 'Naselenie', pp.104–46.

8 P.V. Volobuev, *Proletariat i burzhuaziya Rossii v 1917g.* (Moscow, 1964), p.47.

9 *Oktyabr'skoe vooruzhennoe vosstanie*, ed. S.N. Valk, vol.1 (Leningrad, 1967), p.47.

10 *ibid.*, pp.419–21.

11 P.I. Lyashchenko, *History of the National Economy of Russia* (New York, Macmillan, 1949), p.714.

12 *Oktyabr'skoe vooruzhennoe vosstanie*, vol.1, p.423.

13 M.E. Falkus, *The Industrialisation of Russia, 1700–1914* (London, Macmillan, 1972), pp.77–8.

14 *Oktyabr'skoe vooruzhennoe vosstanie*, vol.1, pp.403–5.

15 *Spisok fabrichno-zavodskikh predpriyatii Petrograda* (Petrograd, 1918); *Istoricheskii arkhiv*, 5, 1961, 158–65.

16 *Oktyabr'skoe vooruzhennoe vosstanie*, vol.1, pp.408–9.

17 O. Crisp, 'Labour and Industrialisation in Russia', *Cambridge Economic History of Europe*, vol. VII, part 2 (Cambridge, 1978), p.404.

18 A. Gerschenkron, *Economic Backwardness in Historical Perspective* (Cambridge, Mass., Harvard, 1962), pp.135–8.

19 E.E. Kruze, *Polozhenie rabochego klassa Rossii v 1900–14gg. (Leningrad, 1976)*, p.127.

20 Ya. S. Rozenfeld and K.I. Klimenko, *Istoriya mashinostroeniya SSSR* (Moscow, 1961), pp.102, 105, 109.

21 V.I. Grinevetskii, *Poslevoennye perspektivy russkoi promyshlennosti* (Moscow, 1918), p.46.

22 Rozenfeld and Klimenko, *Istoriya*, pp.116, 123.

23 *Istoriya rabochikh Leningrada*, ed. S.N. Valk, vol.1 (Leningrad, 1972), p.463.

24 Lyashchenko, *National Economy*, p.762.

25 Rashin, *Formirovanie*, p.196.

26 Z.V. Stepanov, *Rabochie Petrograda v period podgotovki i provedeniya oktyabr'skogo vooruzhennogo vosstaniya* (Moscow, 1965), pp.25–6.

27 *Spisok fabrichno-zavodskikh predpriyatii, passim.*
28 *Rabochii klass i rabochee dvizhenie v Rossii v 1917g.* (Moscow, 1964), p.75.
29 Rashin, *Formirovanie*, p.83.
30 *Rab. klass i rab. dvizhenie*, p.76.
31 E.E. Kruze, *Peterburgskie rabochie v 1912–14gg.* (Moscow, 1954), p.69.
32 A.I. Davidenko, 'K voprosu o chislennosti i sostave proletariata Peterburga v nachale XX veka', *Istoriya rabochego Klassa Leningrada*, issue 2 (Leningrad, 1963), p.97; Kruze, *Peterburgskie rabochie*, p.69.
33 L.S. Gaponenko, *Rabochii Klass Rossii v 1917g.* (Moscow, 1970), p.88.
34 Stepanov, *Rabochie Petrograda*, p.32.
35 *ibid.*
36 *ibid.*, p.33.
37 *ibid.*
38 J.H. Bater, *St. Petersburg: Industrialisation and Change* (Montreal, McGill, 1976).
39 Stepanov, *Rabochie Petrograda*, p.30.
40 *Statisticheskie dannye Petrograda*, p.11.
41 *Materialy po statistike Petrograda*, issue 1, p.33.
42 Bater, *St. Petersburg*, p.352.
43 Stepanov, *Rabochie Petrograda*, p.59.
44 *Vyborgskaya storona* (Leningrad, 1957), p.11.
45 S.N. Semanov, *Peterburgskie rabochie nakanune pervoi russkoi revolyutsii* (Moscow, 1966), p.152.
46 *Ist. rab. klassa Len.*, vol.1, p.409.
47 S.N. Prokopovich, *Byudzhety peterburgskikh rabochikh* (St Petersburg, 1909), p.10.
48 Stepanov, *Rabochie Petrograda*, p.58.
49 *ibid.*, p. 59.
50 Kruze and Kutsentov, 'Naselenie', p.108.
51 *ibid.*, p.109.
52 R.E. Johnson, *Peasant and Proletarian* (Leicester University Press, 1979); R. Munting, 'Outside Earnings in the Russian Peasant Farm: the case of Tula province, 1900–17', *Journal of Peasant Studies*, 3 (1976), 444.
53 Kruze and Kutsentov, 'Naselenie', p.106.
54 N.A. Shuster, *Peterburgskie rabochie v 1905–7gg.* (Leningrad, 1976), p.18; Stepanov, *Rabochie Petrograda*, p.40.
55 Shuster, *Peterburgskie rabochie*, p.21.
56 A.S. Smirnov, 'Zemlyacheskie organizatsii rabochikh i soldat v 1917g.', *Istoricheskie zapiski*, 60 (1957) 86–123; T. Trenogova, *Bor'ba petrogradskikh bol'shevikov za krest'yanstvo v 1917g.* (Leningrad, 1949), p.78.
57 Prokopovich, *Byudzhety*, p.7.
58 M. Davidovich, *Peterburgskii tekstil'nyi rabochii v ego byudzhetakh* (St Petersburg, 1912), p.8.
59 Shuster, *Peterburgskie rabochie*, p.30.
60 P. Timofeev, *Chem zhivet zavodskii rabochii* (St Petersburg, 1906), pp.12–13, 18.
61 Tsentral'noe Statisticheskoe Upravlenie (Ts.S.U.), *Trudy*, vol.xxvi, issue 2, pp.25, 35.

62 A.G. Rashin, *Sostav fabrichno-zavodskogo proletariaia* (Moscow, 1930), pp.25, 35.

63 V.Z. Drobizhev, A.K. Sokolov and V.A. Ustinov, *Rabochii klass Sovetskoi Rossii v pervyi god proletarskoi diktatury* (Moscow, 1975), p.93.

64 One should not interpret these figures, as does L.M. Ivanov, to mean that by 1914 the working class itself had become the main source of recruits to industry rather than the peasantry. It is likely that many peasants who came to industry in the pre-1917 period left during the upheavals of the Civil War and were no longer working in industry by the time of the 1929 census. L.M. Ivanov, 'Preemstvennost' Fabrichno-zavodskogo truda i formirovanie proletariata v Rossii', *Rabochii klass i rabochee dvizhenie v Rossii, 1861–1917gg.* (Moscow, 1966).

65 E.P. Thompson, 'Time, work-discipline and industrial capitalism', *Past and Present*, 38 (1967), 56–97.

66 Rashin, *Formirovanie*, p.504.

67 Kruze, *Peterburgskie*, p.75.

68 Volobuev, *Proletariat i burzhuaziya*, p.20.

69 I.P. Leiberov and O.I. Shkaratan, 'K voprosu o sostave petrogradskikh promyshlennykh rabochikh v 1917g.', *Voprosy istorii*, 1 (1961), 52.

70 *ibid.*, 53–4.

71 Stepanov, *Rabochie Petrograda*, p.36.

72 I.P. Leiberov, *Na shturm samoderzhaviya* (Moscow, 1979), p.17. This contradicts the claim of Ivanov, 'Preemstvennost'', p.76, and Rashin, *Sostav*, p.30, that more wartime recruits came from the working class than from the peasantry.

73 Leiberov and Shkaratan, 'K voprosu o sostave', p.51.

74 *Krasnaya Letopis'*, 3 (1939), 169.

75 M.D. Rozanov, *Obukhovtsy* (Leningrad, 1965), p.278.

76 Leiberov and Shkaratan, 'K voprosu o sostave', p.47.

77 *Rab. klass i rab. dvizhenie v 1917g.*, p.82.

78 M.I. Gilbert, 'K voprosu o sostave promyshlennykh rabochikh SSSR v gody grazhdanskoi voiny', *Istoriya proletariata SSSR*, 3 (1934) 214–15; N.P. Payalin, *Zavod imeni Lenina, 1857–1918* (Moscow, 1933), p.313.

79 Stepanov, *Rabochie Petrograda*, p.42.

80 Stepanov, *Rabochie Petrograda*, pp.43–4, concludes that 'the figure of 50% for new recruits to the working class of Petrograd during the war years can scarcely be considered an underestimate'. L.M. Kleinbort, *Istoriya bezrabotitsy v Rossii, 1857–1919gg.* (Moscow, 1925), p.272, says, without citing a source, that at the beginning of 1918 the Commissariat of Labour (Narkomtrud) reckoned that half the workers of Petrograd were either tied to the land or inexperienced wartime recruits.

81 N.D. Karpetskaya, *Rabotnitsy i velikii oktyabr'* (Leningrad, 1974), p.19.

82 *Golos rabotnitsy*, 5–6, 17 June 1917, p.14. A perusal of the job-vacancies column of *Petrogradskaya Gazeta* shows that the type most sought after as a domestic servant was a rural girl with no male acquaintances and prepared to work hard.

83 S.G. Strumilin; 'Sostav proletariata sovetskoi Rossii v 1917–19gg.', *Dva goda diktatury proletariata* (Moscow, 1919), p.15.

84 A. Shlyapnikov, *Semnadtsatyi god*, vol.1 (Moscow, 1923), pp.8–11.
85 Cited by Rashin, *Formirovanie*, pp.235–6.
86 *Vestnik professional'nykh soyuzov*, 2, 15 July 1918, p.7.
87 *ibid.*, p.9.
88 J.W. Scott and L.A. Tilly, *Women, work and the family* (New York, 1978).
89 Kruze, *Peterburgskie rabochie*, p.80.
90 *ibid.* p.80.
91 Ts.S.U., *Trudy*, vol.XXVI, issue 2 (Moscow, 1921), pp.18–23.
92 *ibid.*
93 *Metallist*, 6, 18 June 1918, p.10.
94 *ibid.*
95 *Materialy ob ekonomicheskom polozhenii i professional'noi organizatsii peterburg-skikh rabochikh po metallu* (St Petersburg, 1909), p.85.
96 S.G. Strumilin, *Problemy ekonomiki truda* (Moscow, 1964), pp.69–71.
97 *ibid.*; S. Bernshtein-Kogan, *Chislennost', sostav i polozhenie peterburgskikh rabochikh* (St Petersburg, 1910), pp.51, 54.
98 V. Yu. Krupyanskaya, 'Evolyutsiya semeino-bytovogo uklada rabochikh', *Rossiiskii proletariat-oblik, bor'ba, gegemoniya* (Moscow, 1970), p.277.
99 *Tkach*, 2 (1917), 7.
100 Compare I. Pinchbeck, *Women Workers and The Industrial Revolution* (London, Frank Cass, 1969), p.313; S. Rowbotham, *Hidden from History* (London, Pluto, 1973), p.57; T. Dublin, 'Women, Work and Protest in the Early Lowell Mills', *Labor History*, 16, no.1 (1975).
101 M. Freysinnet, *Le processus de déqualification – surqualification de la force de travail* (Paris, 1974), pp.121–2.
102 A. Gorz, 'Technology, technicians and class struggle', in A. Gorz, ed., *The Division of Labour*, (Brighton, Harvester, 1976). D. Lee, 'Skill, craft and class: a theoretical critique and a critical case', *Sociology*, 1 (1981); H.A. Turner went so far as to argue that workers are skilled or unskilled 'according to whether or not entry to their occupations is deliberately restricted and not, in the first place, according to the nature of the occupation itself.' H.A. Turner, *Trade Union Structure and Growth* (London, George, Allen & Unwin, 1962), p.182.
103 A. Touraine, *L'évolution du travail ouvrier aux usines Renault* (Paris, 1955); see too H. Braverman, *Labor and Monopoly Capital* (New York, Monthly Review Press, 1974).
104 *Rukovodyashchie materialy i postanovleniya tsentral'nogo komiteta vserossiiskogo soyuza rabochikh metallistov*, issue 3 (Moscow, 1924), pp.80–193.
105 E.J. Hobsbawm, *Labouring Men* (London, 1968); K. Burgess, *The Origins of British Industrial Relations* (London, Croom Helm, 1975), Ch. 1.
106 Strumilin, *Problemy*, p.63.
107 A.M. Buiko, *Put' rabochego: zapiski starogo bol'shevika* (Moscow, 1934), p.30.
108 A. Buzinov, *Za Nevskoi zastavoi* (Moscow, 1930), pp.20–1.
109 The Bolshevik, M.I. Kalinin, recalled in 1940: 'I remember how in the underground a dispute arose among us: was a worker-revolutionary obliged to work as well as he was able ... Some said: "We cannot, we are

organically incapable of letting a bad piece of work out of our hands – it would sicken us and demean our dignity." Others argued against them that it was not for us to worry about the quality of our work. It was the job of the capitalist. We only worked for them.' Cited by O.I. Shkaratan and A.Z. Vakzer, 'Razvitie sotsialisticheskogo otnosheniya k trudu: rabochie Leningrada v 1917–24gg.', *Uchenye zapiski Len. gos. ped. in-ta.*, 165 (1958), p.108. See also Timofeev, *Chem zhivet*, p.8, for another example.

110 Timofeev, *Chem zhivet*, pp.10–11.
111 M. Mitel'man, B. Glebov, A. Ul'yanskii, *Istoriya putilovskogo zavoda, 1901–17*, 3rd edn. (Moscow, 1961), p.357.
112 S. Haber, *Efficiency and Uplift: Scientific Management in the Progressive Era, 1890–1920* (Chicago, 1964), p.120.
113 *Materialy po istorii professional'nogo dvizheniya v Rossii*, 1 (Moscow, 1925), pp.16–17.
114 J. Hinton, *The First Shop Stewards Movement* (London, Allen and Unwin, 1973); C. Goodey, 'Factory Committees and the Dictatorship of the Proletariat, 1918', *Critique*, 3 (1974), 31.
115 I. Gordienko, *Iz boevogo proshlogo, 1914–18gg.* (Moscow, 1957), p.34. My emphasis. To say that the mood of skilled workers was 'indifferent', is not to say that there was not a certain latent hostility to the new wartime recruits. The syndicalist leader of the metalworkers' union, A. Gastev, wrote: 'Even in Russia, where craft consciousness [*tsekhovshchina*] has not built as strong a nest for itself as in the West, in the factories among both management and workers there is a suspicion of all newcomers who are not connected with factory professions. Among turners and fitters one still finds a scornful attitude towards the "shoemakers" and "bakers" who are joining the ranks of the factory *chernorabochie* [unskilled workers] in their hundreds.' *Vestnik metallista*, 2 (1918), p.10.
116 S.G. Strumilin, *Zarabotnaya plata*, p.15. His method was to examine wage-levels in different industries between June 1914 and June 1916, and to translate the wages of all categories of worker into ratios of the wages of an adult male *chernorabochii* – letting the latter's wage equal 100. By determining the changes in these ratios during the war, Strumilin obtained an indirect index of de-skilling. It seems to me, however, that there are problems with this method. Firstly, it assumes that the 'skill' of a *chernorabochii* is constant across industry and across time. Secondly, wages are not a good indicator of skill, both because of inflation and of inter-factory variation.
117 S.G. Strumilin, *Problemy*, p.57. Although international comparisons are treacherous because of the different classifications used, for what it is worth, it was estimated that in Germany the proportion of skilled workers in electrical, machine-construction, car, wire and cable industries was 30% in 1914 and 29% in 1925. In England in the mechanical-engineering industry, 37% of the workforce were skilled in 1913 and 35% in 1925. G. Friedmann, *Industrial Society* (Glencoe, Illinois, Free Press, 1955), p.200.
118 Drobizhev et al., *Rabochii klass sovetskoi Rossii*, p.84.

119 Rashin, *Formirovanie*, p.83.
120 *Materialy k uchetu rabochego sostava i rabochego rynka* (Petrograd, 1916), p.128.
121 *Istoriya leningradskogo soyuza rabochego poligraficheskogo proizvodstva*, vol.1 (Leningrad, 1925), pp.11–13.
122 A. Tikhanov, 'Rabochie-pechatniki v gody voiny', *Materialy po istorii professional'nogo dvizheniya v Rossii*, vol.3 (Moscow, 1925), p.117.
123 *Ist len. soyuza rab. polig.*, p.15.
124 A.G. Rashin, 'Gramotnost' i narodnoe obrazovanie v Rossii v XIXv. i nachale XXv., *Istoricheskie zapiski*, 37 (1951), 37.
125 Rashin, *Formirovanie*, p.595.
126 *Materialy po statistike Petrograda*, issue 4 (1921), p.23.
127 Stepanov, *Rabochie Petrograda*, p.44.
128 *Vestnik professional'nykh soyuzov*, 2 (1918), p.9.
129 *Metallist*, 6 (1918), p.8.
130 Strumilin, *Problemy*, p.61.
131 Leningradskii gos. ist. arkhiv (LGIA), f.416, op.5, d.24, 1.21.
132 Rashin, *Formirovanie*, p.583.
133 *Statisticheskie dannye Petrograda* (1916), p.24.
134 *ibid.*
135 Strumilin, *Problemy*, p.63.
136 *ibid.*, 63–9.
137 L. Haimson, 'The Problem of Social Stability in Urban Russia, 1905–17', *Slavic Review*, 23, no.4 (1964); vol.24, no.1 (1965); Johnson, *Peasant and Proletarian*.
138 R. Zelnik, 'Russian Workers and the Revolutionary Movement', *Journal of Social History*, 16, no.2 (1972–3); V.E. Bonnell, 'Trade Unions, Parties and the State in Tsarist Russia', *Politics and Society*, 9, no.3 (1980); S.A. Smith, 'Craft Consciousness, Class Consciousness: Petrograd 1917', *History Workshop*, 11 (1981).
139 At the Putilov works in 1913 the daily earnings of an unskilled woman worker were 36% of those of the highest-paid man. In Germany in the same year the hourly earnings of an unskilled metalworker were 26% of those of a skilled one. A.P. Serebrovskii, *Revolyutsiya i zarabotnaya plata rabochikh metallicheskoi promyshlennosti* (Petrograd, 1917), p.8; G. Bry, *Wages in Germany, 1871–1945* (Princeton, N.J., 1960), p.71.
140 L. Althusser, *For Marx* (London, Penguin, 1969), Ch.3.

NOTES TO CHAPTER 2

1 V.Ya. Laverychev, *Tsarizm i rabochii vopros, 1861–1917gg.* (Moscow, 1972); G. von Rimlinger, 'Autocracy and factory order in early Russian industrialisation', *Journal of Economic History*, 20 (1960), 67–92.
2 Laverychev, *Tsarizm i rabochii vopros* (Moscow, 1972).
3 J. Schneiderman, *Sergei Zubatov and revolutionary Marxism* (New York, Ithaca, 1976); D. Pospielovsky, *Russian Police Trade Unionism* (London, Weidenfeld, 1971).

4 P.A. Berlin, *Russkaya burzhuaziya v staroe i novoe vremya* (Moscow, 1922), p.204.

5 V.E. Bonnell, 'Trade Unions, Parties and the State in Tsarist Russia', *Politics and Society*, 9, no.3 (1980).

6 S. Pollard, *The Genesis of Modern Management* (London, 1965).

7 S.N. Semanov, *Peterburgskie rabochie nakanune pervoi russkoi revolyutsii* (Moscow, 1966), p.110.

8 *ibid.*

9 On 1905 see S.M. Schwarz, *The Russian Revolution of 1905* (Chicago, 1967); W. Sablinsky, *The Road to Bloody Sunday* (Princeton, N.J., 1976).

10 S. Gvozdev, *Zapiski fabrichnogo inspektora* (Moscow, 1911), pp.117, 119.

11 O. Crisp, 'Labour and industrialisation in Russia', *Cambridge Economic History of Europe*, vol. VII, part 2 (Cambridge, 1978), p.382.

12 *Istoriya rabochikh Leningrada*, ed. S.N. Valk, vol.1 (Leningrad, 1972), p.347; N.P. Payalin, *Zavod imeni Lenina, 1857–1918* (Moscow 1933), p.258; K. Marx, *Capital*, vol.1 (London, Penguin, 1976 edn.), p.549.

13 A. Stinchcombe, 'Bureaucratic and Craft Administration of Production', *Administrative Science Quarterly*, 4 (1959–60).

14 P. Timofeev, *Chem zhivet zavodskii rabochii* (St Petersburg, 1906), pp.5, 48.

15 *ibid.*, p.92; F. Bulkin, *Na zare profdvizheniya, Istoriya peterburgskogo soyuza metallistov, 1906–14* (Moscow, 1924), p.297.

16 Timofeev, *Chem zhivet*, pp.57, 97; compare J. Foster, *Class Struggle in the Industrial Revolution* (London, Methuen, 1974), pp.227–8.

17 Stinchcombe, 'Bureaucratic and Craft Administration'; C.R. Littler, 'Understanding Taylorism', *British Journal of Sociology*, 29, no.2 (1978).

18 A. Gastev, 'Novaya industriya', *Vestnik metallista*, 2 (1918), 22; V.I. Grinevetskii, *Poslevoennye perspektivy russkoi promyshlennosti* (Moscow, 1918), p.151.

19 A.G. Rashin, *Formirovanie rabochego klassa Rossii* (Moscow, 1958), p.63.

20 S.G. Strumilin, 'Sostav proletariata sovetskoi Rossii v 1917–19gg.', *Dva goda diktatury proletariata* (Moscow, 1919), p.15; *Narodnoe khozyaistvo*, 5 (1921), 143–6. My calculation.

21 *Materialy po statistike Petrograda*, issue 2 (Petrograd, 1920), p.44.

22 For the concept of 'contradictory class location', see E.O. Wright, 'Class Boundaries in Advanced Capitalist Societies', *New Left Review*, 98 (1976).

23 In 1917 the Socialist Revolutionary, M. Kapitsa, wrote: 'Along with their immediate clerical, technical and accounting duties, *sluzhashchie* took on duties of a police-administrative character, which placed them squarely on the side of management, and which encouraged a benighted class consciousness.' *Delo Naroda*, 124, 11 August 1917, p.1.

24 Bulkin, *Na zare profdvizheniya*, pp.60–1.

25 Timofeev, *Chem zhivet*, p.110.

26 A.E. Badaev, *The Bolsheviks in the Tsarist Duma* (London, 1932).

27 *Ist. rab. Len.*, p.473; *Krasnaya letopis'*, 3 (1926), 8.

28 *Rabotnitsa*, 1–2, 10 May 1917, p.12.

29 *Pravda*, 32, 14 April 1917, p.4.

30 Stepanov, *Rabochie Petrograda*, p.63.

31 *ibid.*

32 *Ist. rab. Len.*, pp.348, 407.

33 M.G. Fleer, *Rabochee dvizhenie v Rossii v gody imperialisticheskoi voiny* (Leningrad, 1926), pp.65–6.

34 *Ist. rab. Len.*, p.472.

35 Stepanov, *Rabochie Petrograda*, p.62.

36 A.F. Vovchik, *Politika tsarzisma po rabochemu voprosu v predrevolyutsionnyi period, 1895–1904* (L'vov, 1964); S.V. Murzyntseva, 'Iz istorii ekonomicheskogo polozheniya rabochikh na predpriyatiyakh voennogo i morskogo vedomstv v 1907–14gg. v Peterburge', *Uchenye zapiski Len. gos. universiteta, seriya ist. nauk,* issue 32, 270 (1959).

37 *Trudy pervogo vserossiiskogo s"ezda delegatov rabochikh zavodov, portov i uchrezhdenii Morskogo vedomstva* (Petrograd, 1917), protocol 2, p.2.

38 Stepanov, *Rabochie Petrograda,* p.62.

39 I.P. Leiberov, *Na shturm samoderzhaviya* (Moscow, 1979), pp.52–60.

40 *Rabochee dvizhenie v Petrograde v 1912–17gg.* (Leningrad, 1958), pp.425–6.

41 Leiberov, *Na shturm,* p.58. In 1917 there were 17 hospitals run by the Petrograd City Duma and about 40 free doctors. In addition, there were seven factory hospitals. I.A. Baklanova, *Rabochie Petrograda v period mirnogo razvitiya revolyutsii (mart–iyun' 1917g.)* (Leningrad, 1978), p.53.

42 S. Milligan, 'The Petrograd Bolsheviks and Social Insurance, 1914–17', *Soviet Studies,* 20, no.3 (1969), 372.

43 S.G. Strumilin, *Problemy ekonomiki truda* (Moscow, 1964), p.479.

44 *ibid.; Materialy po statistike truda Severnoi oblasti,* issue 2 (Petrograd, 1919), p.14.

45 M. Balabanov, *Ot 1905g. k 1917g.* (Moscow, 1927), p.14.

46 *Materialy ob ekonomicheskom polozhenii i professional'noi organizatsii peterburgskikh rabochikh po metallu* (St Petersburg, 1909), p.119; Timofeev, *Chem zhivet,* pp.38–9.

47 S.G. Strumilin, *Zarabotnaya plata i proizvoditel'nost' truda v promyshlennosti* (Moscow, 1923), p.44.

48 *ibid.,* p.49, *Materialy po statistike truda,* issue 2 (1919), pp.14–15.

49 *ibid.*

50 A.P. Serebrovskii, *Revolyutsiya i zarabotnaya plata rabochikh metallicheskoi promyshlennosti* (Petrograd, 1917) p.8.

51 M. Gordon, *Workers before and after Lenin* (New York, 1941), p.71 cites a study by the British Board of Trade which reckoned that in 1905–8 the family income of Russian workers was half that of German workers, 37% that of English workers and 27% that of American workers.

52 Strumilin, *Problemy,* pp.453, 474.

53 *Materialy po statistike truda,* issue 6 (Petrograd, 1919), p.54. Payment in kind was far less widespread in St Petersburg than in Russia as a whole; far less was spent on accommodation by employers, and the truck system was less prevalent. S. Bernshtein-Kogan, *Chislennost', sostav i polozhenie peterburgskikh rabochikh* (St Petersburg, 1910), pp.120–2.

54 S.N. Prokopovich, *Byudzhety peterburgskikh rabochikh* (St Petersburg, 1909), p.9.

55 *ibid.;* M. Davidovich, *Peterburgskii tekstil'nyi rabochii v ego byudzhetakh* (St Petersburg, 1912), p.14.

56 Prokopovich, *Byudzhety*, p.9.
57 Davidovich, *Peterburgskii tekstil'nyi rabochii*, p.10.
58 *Rabochaya gazeta*, 59, 18 May 1917, p.3.
59 Gordon, *Workers before and after Lenin*, pp.217–18.
60 Prokopovich, *Byudzhety*, p.9.
61 Davidovich, *Peterburgskii tekstil'nyi rabochii*, pp.11, 13.
62 *Rabochaya gazeta* 59, 18 May 1917, p.3.
63 M.P. Kokhn, *Russkie indeksy tsen* (Moscow, 1926), p.18.
64 *Statisticheskie dannye Petrograda* (Petrograd, 1916), p.38; K. Sidorov, 'Rabochee dvizhenie v Rossii v gody imperialisticheskoi voiny, 1914–17gg.' in *Ocherki po istorii oktyabr'skoi revolyutsii*, ed. M.N. Pokrovskii, vol.1 (Moscow, 1927), p.233.
65 *ibid.*
66 Strumilin, *Problemy*, p.334.
67 *Ist. rab. Len.*, p.477.
68 *ibid.*, p.471.
69 *ibid.*, p.470.
70 Strumilin, *Zarabotnaya plata*, p.7.
71 For a fuller discussion of wages during the war, see my Ph.D. thesis pp.84–91.
72 *Professional'noe dvizhenie v Petrograde v 1917g.* ed. A. Anskii (Leningrad, 1928), p.13.
73 Stepanov, *Rabochie Petrograda*, p.52.
74 Payalin, *Zavod imeni Lenina*, p.322.
75 Serebrovskii, *Revolyutsiya i zarabotnaya plata*, pp.24–5.
76 Strumilin, *Problemy*, pp.337, 340; Strumilin, *Zarabotnaya plata*, pp.11–12.
77 *Vestnik metallista*, 1 (1917), 13; Strumilin, *Problemy*, pp.337, 340.
78 Strumilin, *Problemy*, pp.337, 340.
79 Baklanova, *Rabochie Petrograda*, p.23.
80 *ibid.*
81 *Materialy po statistike truda*, issue 3 (Petrograd, 1919), p.28.
82 Baklanova, *Rabochie Petrograda*, p.23.
83 Laverychev, *Tsarizm i rabochii vopros*, Ch.6.
84 I.P. Leiberov, 'Stachechnaya bor'ba petrogradskogo proletariata v period mirovoi voiny', *Istoriya rabochego klassa Leningrada*, issue 2 (Leningrad, 1963), pp.166, 177, 183. This supersedes M.G. Fleer, *Peterburgskii komitet bol'shevikov v gody imperialisticheskoi voiny, 1914–17gg.* (Leningrad, 1927) and I.I. Krylova, 'K voprosu o statistike stachek petrogradskikh rabochikh v gody pervoi mirovoi voiny', in *Iz istorii imperializma v Rossii* (Moscow, 1959).
85 *Ist. rab. Len.*, p.476.
86 *ibid.*, pp.483–5.
87 *ibid.*, pp.502–4.
88 'Go-slows', working-to-rule and other forms of restricting output became very common in Petrograd after 1905. Such practices originated in Britain in 1889, when Glasgow dockers systematically practised ca' canny. They were popularised by the French anarcho-syndicalist, Emile Pouget, in the 1890s and widely applied by the French C.G.T. In Russia these practices

were known as 'Italian strikes' (*ital'yanskie zabastovki*), probably after the dramatic work-to-rule by Italian railworkers in February 1905. See G. Brown, *Sabotage: a study in industrial conflict* (Nottingham, Spokesman, 1977), Ch.1 and C. Seton-Watson, *Italy: from Liberalism to Fascism, 1870–1925* (London, Methuen, 1967), p.256.

89 *Ist. rab. Len.*, p.511.

90 It was decided to leave out tables showing the participation of different factories in the wartime strike movement, since similar tables have recently been published in T. Hasegawa, *The February Revolution – Petrograd 1917* (Seattle, Washington University Press, 1981), appendix 2. My analysis of these data differs significantly from that of Hasegawa, *ibid.*, pp.101–2. Sources for the generalisations on the size and composition of the workforces of different factories and on their political complexion in 1917 are not cited, in order to avoid burdening the text with footnotes. The data came from my personal factory file which is based on Soviet secondary works, contemporary newspapers and Soviet archival sources.

91 D. Koenker, 'Urban Families, Working-Class Youth Groups and the 1917 Revolution in Moscow', in *The Family in Imperial Russia*, ed. D.L. Ransel (Urbana, University of Illinois Press, 1978).

NOTES TO CHAPTER 3

1 T. Hasegawa, *The February Revolution: Petrograd, 1917* (Seattle, University of Washington Press, 1981; G. Katkov, *Russia 1917: The February Revolution* (New York, Harper and Row, 1967); M. Ferro, *The Russian Revolution of February 1917* (London, Routledge, 1972).

2 Lists of police agents were published in early March in the working-class press, after police stations had been ransacked. See, for example, *Pravda*, 7, 12 March 1917, p.4. As late as May, police spies were still being uncovered, cf. the exposure of Roman Berthold, editor of the anarchist newspaper, *Kommuna. Rabochaya Gazeta*, 49, 6 May 1917, p.2.

3 *Krasnaya Letopis'*, 3 (1932), 172.

4 M.O. Mitel'man, *1917 god na Putilovskom zavode* (Leningrad, 1939), p.33; *Rabochii kontrol' v promyshlennykh predpriyatiyakh Petrograda, 1917–18gg.*, vol.1 (Leningrad, 1947) p.45.

5 Leningrad State Historical Archive, (LGIA), f.416, op.5, d.30, 1.24.

6 *Professional'noe dvizhenie v Petrograde v 1917g.*, ed. A. Anskii (Leningrad, 1928), p.82.

7 *ibid.* p.81.

8 *Rab. Kontrol'*, p.50.

9 V. Perazich, *Tekstili Leningrada v 1917g.* (Leningrad, 1927), p.19.

10 *Krasnaya Letopis'*, 5–6 (1932), 189–90.

11 *Prof. dvizh.*, p.93.

12 V.M. Freidlin, *Ocherki istorii rabochego dvizheniya v Rossii v 1917g.*, (Moscow, 1967), p.129.

13 N.P. Payalin, *Zavod imeni Lenina, 1857–1918* (Moscow, 1933), pp.363, 366.

14 LGIA, f.1278, op.1, d.84, 1.6–21.

15 *Torgovo-Promyshlennaya Gazeta*, 124, 14 June 1917, p.1.
16 P. Timofeev, *Chem zhivet zavodskii rabochii* (St Petersburg, 1906), pp.80–1. This tradition was still very much alive. After the death of Ya. Sverdlov in March 1919, M.I. Kalinin was made Chairman of the Central Executive Committee of the Soviets and was projected in the press as 'All-Russian Starosta' in an effort to win the confidence of the peasantry. T.H. Rigby, *Lenin's Government: Sovnarkom, 1917–22* (Cambridge University Press, 1979), p.174.
17 For the text of the law on *starosty*, see A.M. Pankratova, *Fabzavkomy Rossii v bor'be za sotsialisticheskuyu fabriku* (Moscow, 1925), pp.343–5.
18 P.A. Berlin, *Russkaya burzhuaziya v staroe i novoe vremya* (Moscow, 1922), p.207.
19 *Istoriya Leningradskogo soyuza rabochego poligraficheskogo proizvodstva*, vol.1 (Leningrad, 1925), pp.255, 273.
20 G. Borisov, S. Vasil'ev, *Stankostroitel'nyi zavod im. Sverdlova* (Leningrad, 1962), p.98; *Sestroretskii instrumental'nyi zavod im. Voskova, 1721–1967* (Leningrad, 1968), p.124.
21 *Fabrichno-zavodskie komitety Petrograda v 1917g.*, ed. I.I. Mints (Moscow, 1979), pp.112–13.
22 B. Shabalin, *Krasnyi Treugol'nik, 1860–1935* (Leningrad, 1938), pp.158, 160; *Trudorezina*, 1, 22 April 1917, p.4.
23 J. Hinton, *The First Shop Stewards' Movement* (London, Allen and Unwin, 1973); B. Pribicevic, *The Shop Stewards' Movement and Workers' Control* (Oxford, Blackwell, 1959).
24 D. Geary, 'Radicalism and the Worker: metalworkers and revolution, 1914–23', *Society and Politics in Wilhelmine Germany*, ed. R. Evans (London, 1978); D.W. Morgan, *The Socialist Left and the German Revolution* (Ithaca, Cornell University Press, 1975); R. Comfort, *Revolutionary Hamburg* (Stanford, 1966).
25 G.A. Williams, *Proletarian Order* (London, Pluto, 1975); P. Spriano, *The Occupation of the Factories* (London, Pluto, 1975); M. Clark, *Antonio Gramsci and the Revolution that Failed* (New Haven, Yale University Press, 1977).
26 See the insightful article by C. Goodey, 'Factory Committees and the Dictatorship of the Proletariat', *Critique*, 3 (1974), p.32.
27 D.A. Kovalenko, 'Bor'ba fabrichno-zavodskikh komitetov Petrograda za rabochii kontrol' nad proizvodstvom', *Istoricheskie Zapiski*, 61 (1957), p.73.
28 *Sestroretskii zavod*, pp.150–1.
29 *Rab. Kontrol'*, p.44.
30 *ibid.*, pp.178–9.
31 In Russian, the word 'kontrol'' has the sense of 'supervision' or 'inspection'. See Chapter 6.
32 *Oktyabr'skaya revolyutsiya i fabzavkomy*, ed. P.N. Amosov, vol.1 (Moscow, 1927), p.29.
33 *ibid.*, p.42.
34 *ibid.*
35 LGIA, f.1304, op.1, d.3669, 11.51–2.

36 *ibid.*
37 *Rab. kontrol'*, p.48.
38 *Okt. rev. i fabzavkomy*, vol.1, pp.30–1.
39 *ibid.*, p.32.
40 *ibid.*, p.40.
41 *Trudy pervogo vserossiiskogo s"ezda delegatov rabochikh zavodov, portov i uchrezhdenii Morskogo vedomstva* (Petrograd, 1917), protocol 1, p.3.
42 *ibid.*, protocol 10, p.4.
43 *Okt. rev. i fabzavkomy*, vol.1, p.34.
44 *Rab. kontrol'*, pp.58–9.
45 *ibid.*, p.180.
46 *Revolyutsionnoe dvizhenie v iyule: iyul'skii krizis* (Moscow, 1959), p.383.
47 *Fab. zav. kom. passim.*
48 L.S. Gaponenko, *Rabochii klass Rossii v 1917g.* (Moscow, 1970), p.345.
49 V.P. Volobuev, *Proletariat i burzhuaziya Rossii v 1917g.* (Moscow, 1964), p.153.
50 *Rabochaya Gazeta*, 2, 8 March 1917, p.4.
51 Payalin, *Zavod imeni Lenina*, p.349.
52 Volobuev, *Proletariat i burzhuaziya*, pp.105–8.
53 LGIA, f.1278, op.1, d.183, 1.29.
54 S.G. Strumilin, *Problemy ekonomiki truda* (Moscow, 1964), p.365.
55 *Materialy po statistike truda Severnoi oblasti*, issue 1 (Petrograd, 1918), 56.
56 Z.V. Stepanov, *Rabochie Petrograda v period podgotovki i provedeniya oktyabr'skogo vooruzhennogo vosstaniya* (Moscow, 1965), p.75. *Znamya truda*, 1, 23 August 1917, p.3; *ibid.*, 8, 31 August 1917, p.2.
57 *Rab. Kontrol'*, pp.52–3; LGIA f.1477, op.3, d.1, 1.4.
58 LGIA, f.1182, op.1, d.96, 1.1.
59 *Pravda*, 11, 17 March 1917, p.4; *Rabochaya Gazeta*, 10, 17 March 1917, p.2.
60 *Revolyutsionnoe dvizhenie posle sverzheniya samoderzhaviya* (Moscow, 1957), p.470; *Pravda*, 17, 25 March 1917, p.4.
61 *Materialy po statistike truda Severnoi oblasti*, issue 3 (Petrograd, 1919), p.20.
62 *Delo Naroda*, 82, 23 June 1917, p.4.
63 *Ekho derevoobdelochnika*, 3, 12 December 1917, p.14.
64 A. Tikhanov, 'Rabochie-pechatniki v 1917g.', *Materialy po istorii professional'nogo dvizheniya v Rossii*, 4 (1925), p.180.
65 G.L. Sobolev, *Revolyutsionnoe soznanie rabochikh i soldat Petrograda v 1917g.* (Leningrad, 1973), p.58.
66 *Prof. dvizh.*, p.136.
67 *Rab. Kontrol'*, pp.73–4.
68 *Istoriya leningradskogo obuvnoi fabriki, Skorokhod, im. Ya. Kalinina* (Leningrad, 1969), pp.136–7. The size of these concessions caused great consternation among members of the SFWO, who felt that a dangerous precedent had been set.
69 *Pravda*, 66, 26 May 1917, p.4.
70 G. Linko, 'Rabochee dvizhenie na fabrike Kenig v 1917g.', *Krasnyi Arkhiv*, 58 (1933), 136–7.
71 I.A. Baklanova, *Rabochie Petrograda v period mirnogo razvitiya v Petrograde* (Leningrad, 1978), p.21.
72 *ibid.*, p.20.

73 S.G. Strumilin, *Zarabotnaya plata i proizvoditel'nost' truda v promyshlennosti* (Moscow, 1923), pp.13–14.
74 A.P. Serebrovskii, *Revolyutsiya i zarabotnaya plata rabochikh metallicheskoi promyshlennosti* (Petrograd, 1917), p.6.
75 Strumilin, *Zarabotnaya plata*, pp.13–14.
76 *Pischebumazhnik*, 1, 16 September 1917, p.12.
77 *Materialy po statistike truda*, issue 3 (Petrograd, 1919) pp.7, 14.
78 Sobolev, *Revolyutsionnoe soznanie*, p.67.
79 *Pravda*, 15, 22 March 1917, p.4.
80 *Rabochaya Gazeta*, 13, 21 March 1917, p.2; Sobolev, *Revolyutsionnoe soznanie*, p.68.
81 A. Pankratova, *Fabzavkomy i profsoyuzy v 1917g.* (Moscow, 1927), p.39; Baklanova, *Rabochie Petrograda*, p.25.
82 Baklanova, *Rabochie Petrograda*, p.25.
83 *Rabochaya Gazeta*, 39, 25 April 1917, p.3. It compared badly with the minimum rates achieved by militant action at Skorokhod (10 r.) and the Triangle works (7 r. for men and 5 r. for women). Baklanova, *Rabochie Petrograda*, p.22.
84 *Ist. len. soyuza rab. polig. proizvodstva*, p.345; F. Bulkin, *Na zare profdvizheniya* (Leningrad, 1924), p.127.
85 Serebrovskii, *Zarabotnaya plata*, pp.10, 16.
86 *Trudy s"ezda rabochikh Morskogo ved.*, protocol 1, p.6.
87 *Pechatnoe Delo*, 4, 10 July 1917, p.14.
88 I.F. Gindin, 'Russkaya burzhuaziya v period kapitalizm – ee razvitiye i osobennosti', *Istoriya SSSR*, 2 (1963) 60–5 and 3 (1963), 57; J.D. White, 'Moscow, Petersburg and the Russian Industrialists: a reply to Ruth Amende Roosa', *Soviet Studies* 24, no.3 (1973), 414–20.
89 G. Hosking, *The Russian Constitutional Experiment, 1907–14* (Cambridge, 1973).
90 Volobuev, *Proletariat i burzhuaziya*, pp.45–6.
91 R.Sh. Ganelin and L.E. Shepelev, 'Predprinimatel'skie organizatsii v Petrograde v 1917g.' in *Oktyabr'skoe vooruzhennoe vosstanie v Petrograde* (Moscow, 1965), p.265.
92 *Vestnik obshchestva zavodchikov i fabrikantov*, 1, 1 June 1917.
93 *Prof. dvizh.*, p.102.
94 Volobuev, *Proletariat i burzhuaziya*, pp.83–4.
95 *ibid.*, p.175.
96 *The Russian Provisional Government*, eds. R.P. Browder and A.F. Kerensky, vol.1 (Stanford, 1971), p.710.
97 A. Kats, 'K istorii primiritel'nykh kamer v Rossii', *Vestnik truda*, 10 (1923), 186–7.
98 This distinguished 'conciliation chambers' (*primiritel'nye kamery*) from 'arbitration courts' (*treteiskie sudy*), in which an independent chairman had a casting vote.
99 *Izvestiya*, 33, 6 April 1917, p.2.
100 By the summer of 1917 conciliation chambers existed in most state enterprises and in ninety private factories of Petrograd. Baklanova, *Rabochie Petrograda*, p.74.
101 The success rate of the conciliation chambers can be judged by the

following figures on the number of cases successfully resolved between April and August: at the Baltic works, 12 out of 160 cases heard; at the Izhora works, 7 out of 50; at New Admiralty, 3 out of 29; at Obukhov, 3 out of 20. Baklanova, *Rabochie Petrograda*, pp.80–1.

102 Freidlin, *Ocherki istorii*, p.138.

103 *Ekonomicheskoe polozhenie Rossii nakanune velikoi oktyabr' skoi sotsialisticheskoi revolyutsii*, vol.1 (Moscow, 1957), p.512.

104 V.I. Selitskii, *Massy v bor'be za rabochii kontrol': mart–iyun', 1917g.* (Moscow, 1971), p.161.

105 *Okt. rev. i fabzavkomy*, vol.1, pp.25–6.

106 *The Russian Provisional Government*, vol.1, pp.718–20; *Edinstvo*, 10, 11 April 1917, p.4.

107 Volobuev, *Proletariat i burzhuaziya*, pp.326–8.

108 *Torgovo-Promyshlennaya Gazeta*, 86, 27 April 1917, p.3; and *ibid.*, 98, 13 May 1917, p.2.

NOTES TO CHAPTER 4

1 This contrasts with the situation in 1908, when levels of trade-union membership in the metal industry were highest in enterprises of 50 to 500 workers, and lowest in enterprises of a thousand plus. F. Bulkin, *Na zare profdvizheniya* (Leningrad, 1924), p.306.

2 These generalisations are based on calculations using *Oktyabr'skaya revolyutsiya i fabzavkomy*, ed. P.N. Amosov, vol.2 (Moscow, 1927), pp.217–31 and *Spisok fabrichno-zavodskikh predpriyatii Petrograda* (Petrograd, 1918).

3 *Ibid.* and *Materialy po statistike truda Severnoi oblasti*, 1 (Petrograd, 1918), p.10.

4 *Golos Kozhevnika*, 6–7, 25 January 1918, p.18.

5 *Pechatnoe Delo*, 7, 19 August 1917, p.15; *Delo Naroda*, 168, 30 September 1917, p.14.

6 V.Z. Drobizhev, *Glavnyi shtab sotsialisticheskoi promyshlennosti* (Moscow, 1966), p.56.

7 *Oktyabr'skaya revolyutsiya i fabzavkomy*, ed. P.N. Amosov, vol.1 (Moscow, 1927), p.33.

8 *Ibid.*, p.242.

9 *Novyi Put'*, 1–2, 15 October 1917, p.15.

10 M.I. Mitel'man, *1917 god na Putilovskom zavode* (Leningrad, 1939), p.33.

11 *Raionnye sovety Petrograda v 1917g.*, vol.2 (Moscow, 1965), pp.91, 122.

12 D.A. Kovalenko, 'Bor'ba fabrichno-zavodskikh komitetov Petrograda za rabochii kontrol' nad proizvodstvom (mart-oktyabr' 1917g.)', *Istoricheskie Zapiski*, 61 (1957), 75.

13 *Putilovets v trekh revolyutsiyakh*, ed. I.I. Gaza (Leningrad, 1933, p.333.

14 'Every decision of the shop committee must be minuted and sent to the committee for ratification', *ibid.*, p.335; W. Rosenberg, 'Workers and Workers' Control in the Russian Revolution', *History Workshop*, 5 (1978), 94.

15 *Ibid.*, pp.333–5.

16 Leningrad State Historical Archive (LGIA), f.1304, op.1, d.3669, 1.23.
17 I.A. Baklanova, *Rabochie Petrograda v period mirnogo razvitiya revolyutsii* (Leningrad, 1978), pp.96, 99.
18 *Okt. rev. i fabzavkomy*, vol.1, p.35.
19 M.L. Itkin, 'Tsentry fabrichno-zavodskikh komitetov Rossii v 1917g.', *Voprosy Istorii*, 2 (1974), 27.
20 Z.V. Stepanov, *Rabochie Petrograda v period podgotovki i provedeniya oktyabr'skogo vooruzhennogo vosstaniya* (Moscow, 1965), p.108.
21 *Okt. rev. i fabzavkomy*, vol.2, pp.36–7.
22 *Rabochii kontrol' v promyshlennykh predpriyatiyakh Petrograda 1917–18gg.* vol.1 (Leningrad, 1947), pp.211–12; 218–19.
23 Stepanov, *Rabochie Petrograda*, p.108.
24 B.M. Freidlin, *Ocherki istorii rabochego dvizheniya v Rossii v 1917g.* (Moscow, 1967), p.146.
25 *Okt. rev. i fabzavkomy*, vol.2, p.37.
26 *Ibid.*, pp.175–6; 259–60; *Novyi Put'*, 1–2, 14 January 1918, p.7. The Factory Convention was created at the end of 1915 to coordinate war production in the state and private factories of Petrograd region. After February 1917 it was democratised by the addition of representatives from labour organisations.
27 M.L. Itkin, 'Tsentral'nyi Sovet fabrichno-zavodskikh komitetov', *Oktyabr'skoe vooruzhennoe vosstanie v Petrograde* (Moscow, 1980), p.179–80.
28 S. Schwarz, 'Fabrichno-zavodskie komitety i profsoyuzy v pervye gody revolyutsii' in *The Russian Provisional Government*, eds. R.P. Browder and A.F. Kerensky, vol.2 (Stanford, 1961).
29 *Okt. rev. i fabzavkomy*, vol.1, pp.170, 190.
30 *Ibid.*, pp.47–8.
31 A.A. Sviridov, 'Fabrichno-zavodskie komitety kak forma organizatsii piterskikh rabochikh v 1917g.', *Uchenye zapiski Leningradskogo gos. ped. inst.*, 298 (1971), 78.
32 D.A. Tseitlin, 'Fabrichno-zavodskie komitety Petrograda v fevrale–oktyabre 1917g.', *Voprosy Istorii*, 11 (1956), 86.
33 Freidlin, *Ocherki istorii*, p.129.
34 M. Fleer, 'Putilovskii zavod v 1917–18gg.', *Bor'ba Klassov*, 1–2 (1924), 288–9.
35 *Fabrichno-zavodskie komitety Petrograda v 1917g.*, ed. I.I. Mints (Moscow, 1979), pp.307, 317.
36 *Ibid.*, p.595.
37 J.L.H. Keep, *The Russian Revolution: a study in mass mobilisation* (London, Weidenfeld, 1976), Ch.3.
38 P.I. Lyashchenko, *History of the National Economy of Russia* (New York, Macmillan, 1949), p.767.
39 *Torgovo-Promyshlennaya Gazeta*, 140, 4 July 1917, p.3; E.A. Adibek-Melikyan, *Revolyutsionnaya situatsiya v Rossii nakanune Oktyabrya* (Erevan, 1967), p.156; Stepanov, *Rabochie Petrograda*, pp.66–7.
40 *Professional'noe dvizhenie v Petrograde v 1917g.* (Leningrad, 1928), p.15.
41 S.G. Strumilin, *Problemy ekonomiki truda* (Moscow, 1964), p.350.
42 Stepanov, *Rabochie Petrograda*, p.67.

43 V.I. Binshtok and L.S. Kaminskii, *Narodnoe pitanie i narodnoe zdorov'e* (Moscow, 1929), pp.31, 54; *Uslovye byta rabochikh v dorevolyutsionnoi Rossii* (Moscow, 1958), p.14; E. Kabo, *Pitanie russkogo rabochego do i posle voiny* (Moscow, 1926), p.69.

44 *Trud*, 2–3 Sept. 1917, pp.25–6; *Rabochii kooperator*, 1, 12 Dec. 1917, p.3; L.V. Ol'khovaya, 'Rabochaya kooperatsiya kak forma organizatsii proletariata', *Rossiiskii proletariat: oblik, bor'ba gegemoniya* (Moscow, 1970).

45 *Rab. Kontrol'*, p.106.

46 Stepanov, *Rabochie Petrograda*, p.68.

47 S.E. Loginova, 'Partiya bol'shevikov-organizator revolyutsionnogo tvorchestva mass v reshenii prodovol'stvennoi problemy v period podgotovki oktyabrya', *Uchenye zapiski Leningradskogo universiteta*, seriya ist. nauk, 31 (1959), 77.

48 Stepanov, *Rabochie Petrograda*, p.68.

49 *Raionnye Sovety Petrograda v 1917g.*, vol.3 (Moscow, 1965), p.264; A. Pankratova, *Fabzavkomy i profsoyuzy v revolyutsii 1917g.* (Moscow, 1927), p.38.

50 *Kommuna*, 1, 17 March 1917, p.7.

51 *Ibid.*

52 *Vestnik obshchestva zavodchikov i fabrikantov*, 5, 10 June 1917, p.3.

53 *Torgovo-Promyshlennaya Gazeta*, 64, 25 April 1917, p.2.

54 *Rabochaya Gazeta*, 154, 7 Sept. 1917, p.4; *Putilovets v trekh rev.*, p.415.

55 *Rabochaya Gazeta*, 114, 23 July 1917, p.3; Stepanov, *Rabochie Petrograda*, pp.129–30.

56 *Rabochaya Gazeta*, 174, 30 Sept. 1917, p.3.

57 *Ibid.*

58 *Rabochaya Gazeta*, 17, 26 March 1917, p.4; *Rabochaya Gazeta*, 18, 28 March 1917, p.1.

59 *Okt. rev. i. fabzavkomy*, vol.1, p.53.

60 Leningrad State Historical Archive (LGIA), f.1477, op.3, d.1, 1.90.

61 V.F. Shishkin, *Velikii oktyabr' i proletarskii moral'* (Moscow, 1976), pp.74–5.

62 *Ibid.*, p.75–6.

63 *Rab. Kontrol'*, pp.195–6.

64 Stepanov, *Rabochie Petrograda*, p.130.

65 J. Saville, 'The Ideology of Labourism', in *Knowledge and Belief in Politics*, ed. R. Benewick (London, Allen and Unwin, 1973).

66 See, for example, M.K. Eroshkin, *The Soviets in Russia* (New York, 1919), p.44.

67 *Rabochii Put'*, 39, 18 Oct. 1917, p.2.

68 *Rossiiskii proletariat: oblik, bor'ba, gegomoniya* (Moscow, 1970), p.278.

69 S.N. Prokopovich, *Byudzhety peterburgskikh rabochikh* (St Petersburg, 1909), p.7; M. Davidovich, *Peterburgskii tekstil'nyi rabochii* (St Petersburg, 1912), p.20.

70 A. Buzinov, *Za Nevskoi zastavoi* (Moscow, 1930), pp.25–6; A.M. Buiko, *Put' rabochego: zapiski starogo bol'shevika* (Moscow, 1934), p.11.

71 Buzinov, *Za Nevskoi zastavoi*, p.73.

72 Binshtok and Kaminskii, *Narodnoe pitanie*, pp.45–6.
73 *Ibid.*
74 *Ibid.*
75 *Novaya Zhizn'*, 24, 16 May 1917, p.2.
76 *Pravda*, 59, 17 May 1917, p.4.
77 *Rabochaya Gazeta*, 78, 11 June 1917, p.4.
78 *Fab. zav. kom.* p.241.
79 *Ibid.*, pp.532, 578.
80 *Ibid*, pp.144, 151, 293–4, 401.
81 Stepanov, *Rabochie Petrograda*, p.131.
82 *Ibid.*
83 *Ibid.*
84 Shishkin, *Velikii oktyabr'*, p.182.
85 P. Timofeev, *Chem zhivet zavodskii rabochii* (St Petersburg, 1906), p.8.
86 Fleer, 'Putilovskii zavod v 1917–18gg.', p.297.
87 Baklanova, *Rabochie Petrograda*, p.75.
88 I. Gordienko, *Iz boevogo proshlogo, 1914–18gg.* (Moscow, 1957), p.100.
89 V.I. Lenin, *Polnoe sobranie sochinenii*, 5th ed., vol.45 (Moscow, 1964), p.381.
90 Lenin, *ibid.*, p.454. Note Trotsky's comment: 'The Russian worker – except the very top of the class – usually lacks the most elementary habits and notions of culture (in regard to dress, education, punctuality, etc.). The West European worker possesses these habits. He has acquired them by a long, slow process under the bourgeois order. This explains why in Western Europe the working class – at any rate its superior elements – is so strongly attached to the bourgeois regime, with its democracy, free capitalist press, etc. The belated bourgeois regime in Russia had no time to do any good for the working class and the Russian proletariat broke with the bourgeoisie all the more easily and overthrew the bourgeois regime without regret ... History gives us nothing free of cost. Having made a reduction on one point – in politics – it makes us pay the more on another – in culture.' L. Trotsky, *Problems of Everyday Life* (New York, Pathfinder, 1973), p.20.
91 Fleer, 'Putilovskii zavod v 1917–18gg.', p.295.
92 Mitel'man, *1917 god na Putilovskom zavode*, p.213.
93 *Fab. zav. kom.* pp.93, 149.
94 *Ibid.*, pp.203, 213, 382–3, 397.
95 *Ibid.*, pp.566, 587, 596.
96 *V ogne revolyutsionnykh boev*, vol.2 (Moscow, 1971), p.45.
97 N.S. Sergeev, *Metallisty: istoriya Leningradskogo Metallicheskogo zavoda im. XXII s"ezda KPSS*, vol.1 (Leningrad, 1967), p.338.
98 *V ogne revolyutsionnykh boev*, vol.1 (Moscow, 1967), p.151; see the description by N. Krupskaya, Lenin's wife, of teaching a literacy class in Vyborg district in 1917. N. Krupskaya, *Memories of Lenin* (London, Panther, 1970), p.307.
99 I.D. Levin, 'Rabochie kluby v Peterburge, 1907–14', *Materialy po istorii professional'nogo dvizheniya*, 3 (1925), 4.
100 *Rabochaya Gazeta*, 10, 17 March 1917, p.2.

101 *Novaya Zhizn'*, 70, 9 July 1917, p.5.
102 *Novaya Zhizn'*, 76, 16 July 1917, p.5.
103 *Novaya Zhizn'*, 124, 10 Sept. 1917, p.4.
104 *Novaya Zhizn'*, 106, 20 Aug. 1917, p.5.
105 See the survey of working-class taste in L.M. Kleinbort, *Ocherki rabochego intelligentsii: teatr, zhivopis', muzika*, vol.2 (Petrograd, 1923), pp.14, 42.
106 *Novaya Zhizn'*, 70, 9 July 1917, p.5.
107 *Novaya Zhizn'*, 76, 17 July 1917, p.5; *ibid.*, 106, 20 Aug. 1917, p.5.
108 *Novaya Zhizn'*, 82, 23 July 1917, p.5.
109 *Novaya Zhizn'*, 31, 25 May 1917, p.5.
110 *Novaya Zhizn'*, 94, 6 Aug. 1917, p.2; *Yunyi Proletarii*, 2, 25 Jan. 1918, p.3; *Rabochii*, 6, 29 Aug. 1917, p.4.
111 *Novaya Zhizn'*, 70, 9 July 1917, p.5.
112 *Novaya Zhizn'*, 128, 15 Sept. 1917, p.7.
113 The proceedings of this conference make fascinating reading, foreshadowing, as they do, the later debates within Proletkult. Lunacharsky, Gorky, Osip Brik and many others took part in discussions about art, education and proletarian culture. The fullest account of the conference proceedings is in P. Gorsen and E. Knödler-Bunte, *Proletkult: System einer Proletarischen Kultur*, Band 1, Dokumentation (Stuttgart, 1974).
114 *Profsoyuzy SSSR*, ed. I. Borshchenko, vol.1 (Moscow, 1963), p.425.
115 V.I. Lenin, *Collected Works*, 4th ed., vol.29 (London, Lawrence and Wishart, 1965), p.70.
116 See the excellent discussion of this question by C. Claudin-Urondo, *Lenin and the Cultural Revolution* (Sussex, Harvester, 1977), Ch.3; S. Fitzpatrick, *The Commissariat of Enlightenment: Soviet Organisation of Education and the Arts under Lunacharsky* (Cambridge, 1970), Ch.5.
117 N. Ya. Ivanov, *Velikii oktyabr' v Petrograde* (Leningrad, 1957), p.42.
118 V.I. Startsev, *Ocherki po istorii Petrogradskoi krasnoi gvardii i rabochei militsii* (Moscow, 1965), pp.44–5.
119 *Revolyutsionnoe dvizhenie posle sverzheniye samoderzhaviya* (Moscow, 1957), p.448.
120 Startsev, *Ocherki*, p.59.
121 *Ibid.*, p.57.
122 Tseitlin, 'Fabrichno-zavodskie komitety', pp.89–90.
123 Startsev, *Ocherki*, p.48.
124 *Rev. dvizh. posle sverzheniya*, pp.56–8; *Pervyi legal'nyi komitet: sbornik materialov i protokolov zasedanii Peterburgskogo komiteta RSDRP (b.)* (Moscow, 1927), p.36.
125 'Iz istorii krasnoi gvardii', *Istoricheskii Arkhiv* 5, (1957), 122–3.
126 Startsev, *Ocherki*, p.52.
127 *Ibid.* pp.66–9; V. Vinogradov, 'Krasnaya gvardiya Petrogradskogo metallicheskogo zavoda', *Krasnaya Letopis'*, 2 (23) (1927), 166.
128 Startsev, *Ocherki*, p.74.
129 *Ibid.*, p.64.
130 *Fab. zav. kom.*, pp.71, 451.
131 Startsev, *Ocherki*, pp.104–7.

132 'Iz istorii krasnoi gvardii', p.124.
133 *Leningradskie rabochie v bor'be za vlast' sovetov* (Leningrad, 1924), p.24.
134 *Ibid.*, p.23.
135 'Iz istorii krasnoi gvardii', p.125.
136 *Pravda*, 44, 29 April 1917, p.4.
137 *Novaya Zhizn'*, 10, 29 April, p.4.
138 *Rabochaya Gazeta*, 43, 29 April, p.1; *Izvestiya*, 29 April, p.1.
139 Startsev estimates that by the end of June as many as 52 factories had contingents of Red Guards, numbering more than 5,000 members (Startsev, *Ocherki*, p.129). Many of these, however, must have been units of workers' militia rather than the more politicised Red Guards. An earlier Soviet historian is surely correct to say that 'down to the Kornilov rebellion, the Red Guard was not a broad mass organisation'. E. Pinezhskii, *Krasnaya gvardiya*, 2nd ed. (Moscow, 1933), p.33.
140 Startsev, *Ocherki*, pp.82–3.
141 *Ibid.*, p.86.
142 *Fab. zav. kom.*, pp.144, 284, 458–9.

NOTES TO CHAPTER 5

1 R. Michels, *Political Parties* (New York, Macmillan, Free Press, 1968).
2 V.E. Bonnell, 'Trade Unions, Parties and the State in Tsarist Russia', *Politics and Society*, 9, no.3 (1980).
3 *Revolutionary Situations in Europe, 1917–22: Germany, Italy, Austria-Hungary*, ed. C. Bertrand (Montreal, Inter-University Centre for European Studies, 1977); C. Maier, *Recasting Bourgeois Europe* (Princeton University Press, 1975).
4 I.P. Leiberov, *Na shturm samoderzhaviya* (Moscow, 1979), p.61.
5 *Pravda*, 12, 18 March 1917, p.4; *Tkach*, 1, Nov.1917, p.28.
6 *Pravda*, 9, 15 March 1917, p.4; *Metallist*, 12 (1922), 63.
7 A. Shlyapnikov, *Semnadtsatyi God*, vol.2 (Moscow, 1925), p.133.
8 *Professional'noe dvizhenie v Petrograde v 1917g.*, ed. A. Anskii (Leningrad, 1929), p.119; *Rabochaya Gazeta*, 42, 28 April 1917, p.4.
9 F.A. Bulkin, *Na zare profdvizheniya. Istoriya peterburgskogo soyuza metallistov, 1906–14gg.* (Leningrad, 1924), pp.290–1.
10 The membership figures for the paper, print, tobacco, leather and wood unions exceed the total number of workers in the respective industries in Petrograd. This may partly be due to the fact that these unions included workers in the province of Petrograd, and not just the city, but it seems more likely to be due to the fact that the figures represent not current membership in October and July, but the number of enrollments since March, i.e. they make no allowance for dropouts. Compare V. Ya. Grunt's analysis of the figures for trade-union membership in Moscow in *Istoriya SSSR*, 1 (1965), 232.
11 Such a level of unionisation – achieved in less than six months – did not compare badly with the levels in the West. In 1912 about 20% of the total occupied labour force in Britain were members of trade unions; in Germany about 25%; in the USA and Italy about 11% and in France

only 8%. Yu. I. Kir'yanov, 'Ob oblike rabochego klassa Rossii', *Rossiiskii proletariat — oblik, bor'ba, gegemoniya* (Moscow, 1970), p.130.

12 The term 'craft union' is used to denote a narrow, exclusive union of workers of one specific trade; the term 'trade union' is used to denote a union of workers in several related trades; the term 'industrial union' is used to denote a union which embraces all workers in a branch of industry, regardless of their job.

13 E. Schneider, *Industrial Sociology* (New York, McGraw Hill, 1957), Ch. 10. *The American Labor Movement*, ed. D. Brody (New York, Harper and Row, 1971). H. Clegg, A. Fox, A.F. Thompson, *A History of British Trade Unionism* (Oxford, Clarendon Press, 1964) Chs.1,4.

14 M. Hanagan, *The Logic of Solidarity* (Urbana, University of Illinois Press, 1980); B.H. Moss, *The Origins of the French Labor Movement* (Berkeley, University of California Press, 1976); D. Geary, 'The German Labour Movement, 1848–1919', *European Studies Review*, 6 (1976) 297–330.

15 Bulkin, *Na zare profdvizheniya*, p.309.

16 *Metallist*, 12 (1922), p.66.

17 *Pravda*, 41, 26 April 1917, p.4.

18 *Professional'nyi Vestnik*, 7, 16 Dec. 1917, p.7.

19 *Prof. dvizh. v 1917g.*, p.125; *Petrogradskaya Pravda*, 167, 6 Aug. 1918, p.4.

20 *Metallist*, 1–2, 17 Aug. 1917, p.14.

21 *Prof. dvizh. v 1917g.*, p.341.

22 Bulkin, *Na zare profdvizheniya*, p.226.

23 *Pravda*, 51, 7 May 1917, p.3; *Pravda*, 57, 14 May 1917, p.3.

24 Professional sections existed within the printers', leatherworkers', woodworkers' and other unions in 1917.

25 *Tret'ya vserossiiskaya konferentsiya professional'nykh soyuzov 1917g.* (Moscow, 1927). Pankratova is quite wrong to claim that the Bolsheviks believed in revolutionary industrial unions, whereas the Mensheviks believed in neutral trade unions. A. Pankratova, *Fabzavkomy i profsoyuzy v revolyutsii 1917g.* (Moscow, 1927), p.56.

26 Z.V. Stepanov, *Rabochie Petrograda v period podgotovki i provedeniya oktyabr'skogo vooruzhennogo vosstaniya* (Moscow, 1965), p.89.

27 *Ekho derevoobdelochnika*, 2, 19 Oct. 1917, p.12.

28 *Ibid.*, p.14.

29 *Ekho derevoobdelochnika*, 3, 12 Dec. 1917, p.15.

30 *Revolyutsionnoe dvizhenie v Rossii nakanune oktyabr'skogo vooruzhennogo vosstaniya* (Moscow, 1962), p.277.

31 *Rabochii Put'*, 36, 14 Oct. 1917, p.4.

32 *Oktyabr'skoe vooruzhennoe vosstanie v Petrograde* (Moscow, 1957), p.277.

33 Stepanov, *Rabochie Petrograda*, p.90.

34 *Professional'nyi Vestnik*, 7, 10 Dec. 1917, p.6.

35 Gilds (*tsekhi*) had been legalised by Peter the Great in 1722 but had never become deeply entrenched. In the 1850s and 1860s there was a campaign to abolish them. On the latter, see R. Zelnik, *Labor and Society in Tsarist Russia* (Stanford University Press, 1971) pp.120–33. For an interesting account of the *tsekh* system in the bakery trade at the beginning of this century see B. Ivanov, *Po stupen'yam bor'by: zapiski starogo bol'shevika* (Moscow, 1934), pp.167–9.

36 R. Zelnik, 'Russian Workers and the Revolutionary Movement', *Journal of Social History*, 16, no.2 (1972–3); A. Wildman, *The Making of a Workers' Revolution* (Chicago University Press, 1967), pp.123–6, 137–49.

37 See, for example, the article by D. Kol'tsov, *Professional'nyi Vestnik*, 3–4, 15 Oct. 1917, p.6.

38 *Shestoi s"ezd RSDRP (6): Protokoly* (Moscow, 1958), p.264.

39 *Prof. dvizh. v 1917g.*, p.45.

40 *Ibid.*, pp.57, 63.

41 *Ibid.*, pp.58–9.

42 *Ibid.*, p.48. At the Third Conference of Trade Unions a row broke out over the same phrase. Conference voted to substitute the word 'movement' for 'party'. See John Keep's excellent discussion, J.L.H. Keep, *The Russian Revolution: a study in mass mobilisation* (London, Weidenfeld and Nicolson, 1976), p.89.

43 The so-called Interdistrict Group of Social Democrats, of which Trotsky became leader after his return from the USA in 1917.

44 *Prof. dvizh. v 1917g.*, p.50.

45 *Revolyutsionnoe dvizhenie v iyule: iyul'skii krizis* (Moscow, 1959), p.337.

46 *Prof. dvizh. v 1917g.*, p.53.

47 Stepanov, *Rabochie Petrograda*, p.172.

48 *Bor'ba*, 3, Sept. 1917, p.1; *Rabochii Put'*, 10 Sept.1917, p.4.

49 *Prof. dvizh. v 1917g.*, p.123.

50 *Ibid.*, p.119. The SRs were a significant influence in the leatherworkers' union, the transport union and the union of postal employees.

51 *Metallist*, 2, 19 Feb. 1918, p.9.

52 S. Volin, *Deyatel'nost' men'shevikov v profsoyuzakh pri sovetskoi vlasti* (New York, 1962), p.32.

53 *Ekho derevoobdelochnika*, 2, 19 Oct. 1917, p.6.

54 *Zerno Pravdy*, 1–2, 10 July 1917, pp.11–12.

55 *Nabat*, 5, 18 Nov. 1917, p.10. There was conflict between Bolsheviks and SR Maximalists in the union, with the latter accusing the former of trying to monopolise control of the union, and the former accusing the latter of sabotaging union work in certain bread-factories. *Ibid.*, p.12 and *Rabota soyuza muchnykh izdelii i osnovanie soyuza pishchevikov 1917g.* (Leningrad, 1927), p.6.

56 *Prof. dvizh. v 1917g.*, p.135.

57 T. Shatilova, *Ocherk istorii leningradskogo soyuza khimikov, 1905–18gg.* (Leningrad, 1927), p.64; Volin, *Deyatel'nost' men'shevikov*, p.29.

58 Volin, *Deyatel'nost' men'shevikov*, p.23.

59 *Pechatnoe Delo*, 13, 8 Dec. 1917, pp.10–11.

60 *Novyi Den'*, 26, 11 April 1918, p.4.

61 S.G. Strumilin, *Zarabotnaya plata i proizvoditel'nost' truda v promyshlennosti* (Moscow, 1923), p.25.

62 Stepanov, *Rabochie Petrograda*, p.53.

63 L.S. Gaponenko, *Rabochii klass Rossii v 1917g.* (Moscow, 1970), pp.378, 384, 436.

64 *Bor'ba*, 1, Sept. 1917, pp.9–12; *Bor'ba*, 3, Sept.1917, pp.13–14; *Bor'ba*, 4, Sept. 1917, pp.14–15.

65 *Nashe Slovo*, 1, 12 Oct. 1917, p.13; *Rabotnitsa*, 3, 20 May 1917, pp.5–6; *Professional' noe dvizhenie rabochikh khimikov i stekol'shchikov, 1905–18gg.*, ed. Yu. K. Milonov (Moscow, 1928), p.48.

66 Stepanov, *Rabochie Petrograda*, pp.87–9; *Vestnik aptechnogo truda*, 14–15, 15 Nov. 1917, pp.8–9; *Pischebumazhnik*, 2–3, 21 Oct. 1917, pp.19–21.

67 *Ekho derevoobdelochnika*, 2, 19 Oct. 1917, pp. 7–8.

68 L.I. Leskova, 'Kollektivnye dogovory rabochikh s predprinimatelyami v 1905–7gg.', *Rabochii klass i rabochee dvizhenie v Rossii* (Moscow, 1966).

69 P. Stearns, *Lives of Labor: Work in a Maturing Industrial Society* (New York, Holmes and Meier, 1975)

70 H.A. Clegg, *The System of Industrial Relations in Great Britain* (Oxford, Blackwell, 1970); K. Burgess, *The Challenge of Labour: Shaping British Society, 1850–1930* (London, Croom Helm, 1980), pp.119–21.

71 *Materialy po statistike truda*, issue 6 (Petrograd, 1919), 10.

72 *Vestnik Metallista*, 1 (1917), 18.

73 *Za dvadtsat' let*, ed. V. Rabinovich (Leningrad, 1926), pp.98–9.

74 *The Russian Provisional Government*, ed. R.P. Browder and A.F. Kerensky, vol.2 (Stanford University Press, 1961), p.170; *Len. gos. ist. arkhiv* (LGIA), f.1278, op.1, d.113, 1.86.

75 A.P. Serebrovskii, *Revolyutsiya i zarabotnaya plata rabochikh metallicheskoi promyshlennosti* (Petrograd, 1917), p.22.

76 *Metallist*, 1–2, 17 Aug. 1917, p.7.

77 *Rabochaya Gazeta*, 33, 16 April 1917, p.4; *Len. Gos. ist. arkhiv* (LGIA), f.1296, d.1, op.17, 11.12–13.

78 *Putilovets v trekh revolyutsiyakh*, ed. I.I. Gaza (Moscow, 1933), pp.327–8.

79 *Ibid.*, p.329.

80 *Pravda*, 77, 9 June 1917, p.4; *Zemlya i Volya*, 63, 9 June 1917, p.3.

81 *Rab. Gazeta*, 89, 24 June 1917, p.4.

82 *Putilovets v trekh rev.*, p.334.

83 *Ibid.*, pp.346–7.

84 I.I. Gaza, *Putilovets na putyakh k oktyabr'yu* (Moscow, 1933) p.106.

85 *Rab. Gazeta*, 89, 24 June 1917, p.4.

86 *Putilovets na trekh rev.*, pp.349–50.

87 Gaza, *Putilovets na putyakh*, p.109.

88 For an excellent account of the July Days see A. Rabinowitch, *Prelude to Revolution* (Bloomington, Indiana University Press, 1968).

89 Gaza, *Putilovets na putyakh*, p.110.

90 *Ibid.*, p.112.

91 *Metallist*, 1–2, 17 Aug. 1917, p.4.

92 *Trudy pervogo vserossiiskogo s"ezda sovetov narodnogo khozyaistva* (Moscow, 1918), p.380.

93 *Metallist*, 1–2, p.20.

94 *Vestnik Metallista*, 1, 1917, p.16.

95 *Pravda*, 93, 28 June 1917, p.4; *Za dvadtsat' let*, pp.105, 112.

96 *Fabrichno-zavodskie komitety Petrograda v 1917g.* (Moscow, 1979), p.459; *Rab. Gazeta*, 14, 23 July 1917, p.4.

97 *Rab. Gazeta*, 117, 27 July 1917, p.3.

98 Gaza, *Putilovets na putyakh*, p.129.

99 *Za dvadtsat' let*, pp.117–18; *Len. gos. ist. arkhiv*, f.1477, op.3, d.1, 1.66.
100 *Vestnik Metallista*, 1, pp.1–6. The SFWO signed reluctantly. At a meeting of the Petrograd district section of the city SFWO on 3 August A.G. Berger urged colleagues to accept the contract, since, although its wage-rates were high, it would bring uniformity and, made provision for piece-rates and productivity deals. *Len. gos. ist. arkhiv* (LGIA), f.1278, op.1, d.183, 1.127.
101 *Rab. Gazeta*, 171, 27 Sept. 1917, p.4.
102 *Fab. zav. kom.*, pp.395–6.
103 *Ibid.*, p.404.
104 See the speech by Konovalenko at the first national metalworkers' tariff-conference on 17 October. *Vserossiiskaya tarifnaya konferentsiya soyuzov metallistov* (Petrograd, 1918), p.58.
105 *Natsionalizatsiya promyshlennosti v SSSR, 1917–20gg.*, ed. I.A. Gladkov (Moscow, 1954), pp.250–6.
106 *Metallist*, 12 (1922) 43; *Vestnik Metallista*, 1, p.47.
107 Gaza, *Putilovets na putyakh*, p.128.
108 Stepanov, *Rabochie Petrograda*, p.82.
109 *Novaya Zhizn'*, 148, 6 Oct. 1917, p.4; *Rab. Put'*, 35, 13 Oct. 1917, p.4.
110 *V ogne revolyutsionnykh boev*, vol.2 (Moscow, 1971), p.43.
111 *Tarifnaya konferentsiya*, p.136.
112 *Rab. Put'*, 46, 30 Oct. 1917, p.4; *Novyi Put'*, 1–2, 15 Oct. 1917, p.15; *Tarifnaya konferentsiya*, p.137.
113 *Vestnik Metallista*, 1, p.48.
114 *Metallist*, 1–2, p.6.
115 *Metallist*, 5, 9 Nov. 1917, p.2.
116 Serebrovskii, *Rev. i zar. plata*, pp.24–5.
117 A. Tikhanov, 'Rabochie-pechatniki v gody voiny', *Materialy po istorii professional'nogo dvizheniya v Rossii*, vol.3 (Moscow, 1925), 114.
118 *Pechatnoe Delo*, 4, 10 July 1917, pp.7, 13.
119 A. Tikhanov, 'Rabochie-pechatniki v 1917g.', *Mat. po ist. prof. dvizh.*, vol.4 (1925), p.166.
120 *Pechatnoe Delo*, 5, 22 July 1917, pp.9–10.
121 *Materialy po statistike truda*, issue 6 (Petrograd, 1919), 52–3.
122 *Pechatnoe Delo*, 8, 1 Sept. 1917, p.3; *Delo Naroda*, 118, 4 Aug. 1917, p.4; *ibid.*, 126, 13 Aug., p.4.
123 Tikhanov, 'Rabochie-pechatniki v 1917g.', p.162.
124 Strumilin, *Zarabotnaya plata*, pp.35–6.
125 *Istoriya leningradskogo soyuza rabochego poligraficheskogo proizvodstva*, vol.1 (Leningrad, 1923), p.345.
126 *Rev. dvizh. v iyule*, 341; *Golos Kozhevnika*, 4–5, 1 Dec. 1917, p.21.
127 Serebrovskii, *Rev. i zar. plata*, p.28.
128 *Ibid.*
129 *Metallist*, 4, 18 Oct. 1917, pp.8–9.
130 *Ekho derev.*, 2, p.14.
131 *Torgovo-promyshlennaya Gazeta*, 195, 8 Sept. 1917, p.2.
132 *Prof. dvizh. v 1917g.*, pp.164–5.
133 *Pischebumazhnik*, 2–3, p.19.

134 *Metallist,* 12 (1922), 22.
135 M. Clark, *Antonio Gramsci and the Revolution that Failed* (New Haven, Conn. Yale University Press, 1977), pp.17–18.
136 *Professional'nyi Soyuz,* 2, 1 May 1918, p.10; 'Alexei Gastev and the Soviet Controversy over Taylorism', *Soviet Studies,* XXIX, no.3 (1977), 373–94.
137 R.L. Glickman, 'The Russian Factory Woman, 1880–1914', *Women in Russia,* ed. D. Atkinson and G. Lapidus (Stanford University Press, 1977).
138 *Vtoroi s"ezd RSDRP (1903): Protokoly* (Moscow, 1959), pp.198–207; W. Thonnessen, *The Emancipation of Women* (London, Pluto, 1976), p.54.
139 *Pravda,* 77, 9 June 1917, p.4.
140 *Vestnik professional'nykh soyuzov,* 1, 20 May 1917, p.13; *Tkach,* 1, pp.21–2; *Delo Naroda,* 172, 5 Oct. 1917, p.4; *Ekho derev.* 2, p.14; *Prof. dvizh. v 1917g.,* p.154.
141 I.A. Baklanova, *Rabochie Petrograda v period mirnogo razvitiya revolyutsii* (Leningrad, 1978), pp.94–5.
142 *Fab. zav. kom.,* pp.36, 57.
143 *Ibid.,* p.344.
144 N.P. Payalin, *Zavod im. Lenina* (Moscow, 1933), pp.364, 378.
145 *Oktyabr'skaya revolyutsiya i fabzavkomy,* vol.1 (Moscow, 1927), pp.117, 238.
146 *Ibid.,* p.260.
147 Stepanov, *Rabochie Petrograda,* p.111.
148 *Delo Naroda,* 55, 19 May 1917, p.4.
149 *Revolyutsiya 1917g.: khronika sobytii,* vol.2, ed. N. Avdeev (Moscow, 1923), pp.173–4, 180.
150 *Delo Naroda,* 125, 12 Aug. 1917, p.1.
151 *Kontorskii Trud,* 2, Nov. 1917, p.12.
152 *Bor'ba,* 1, pp.7–9.
153 D. Antoshkin, *Ocherk dvizheniya sluzhashchikh v Rossii* (Moscow, 1921), p.70.
154 *Prof. dvizh. v 1917g.,* pp.346–7.
155 *Ibid.,* pp.347, 349.
156 *Fab. zav. kom.* pp.446–7.
157 Gaza, *Putilovets na putyakh,* p.106.
158 *Fab. zav. kom.,* pp.460–4.
159 *Rabochii kontrol' v promyshlennykh predpriyatiyakh Petrograda, 1917–18gg.* (Leningrad, 1947), p.138.
160 *Istoriya obuvnoi fabriki Skorokhod* (Leningrad, 1969), pp.161–2.
161 *Rab. kontrol',* p.72.
162 *Golos Chertezhnika,* 3, 1 Oct. 1917, p.5.

NOTES TO CHAPTER 6

1 V.I. Selitskii, 'Nekotorye voprosy bor'by petrogradskikh rabochikh za kontrol' nad proizvodstvom v period mirnogo razvitiya revolyutsii', *Istoriya rabochego klassa Leningrada,* issue 2 (Leningrad, 1963); M.L. Itkin, 'Nekotorye funktsii rabochego kontrolya v period podgotovki vooruzhennogo vosstaniya', *Rabochii klass i rabochee dvizhenie v Rossii v 1917g.*

2 Z.V. Stepanov, 'K voprosu o rabochem kontrole nad proizvodstvom i raspredeleniem', *Istoriya SSSR*, 4 (1968), 225–8. For further discussion of this problem, see T.A. Ignatenko, *Sovetskaya istoriografiya rabochego kontrolya i natsionalizatsii promyshlennosti v SSSR, 1917–67gg.* (Moscow, 1971), pp.203–5.

3 V.I. Lenin, *Selected Works*, vol.1 (London, Lawrence and Wishart, 1947).

4 P. Avrich, *The Russian Revolution and the Factory Committees* (Columbia University, Ph.D., 1962), Ch.2.

5 W. Rosenberg, 'Workers and Workers' Control in the Russian Revolution', *History Workshop*, 4 (1978), 92.

6 Avrich, *The Russian Revolution and the Factory Committees*, pp.92–3; see also, P. Avrich, 'The Russian Factory Committees in 1917', *Jahrbücher für Geschichte Osteuropas*, 2 (1963), 161–82.

7 *Ibid.*, p.110.

8 P. Avrich, 'The Bolsheviks and Workers' Control', *Slavic Review*, 22, no.1 (1963), 54.

9 J.L.H. Keep, *The Russian Revolution: a study in mass mobilisation* (London, Weidenfeld, 1976), p.89.

10 F.I. Kaplan, *Bolshevik Ideology and the Ethics of Soviet Labour* (London, Owen, 1969), pp.128–9. In referring to 'a type of cooperative association,' Kaplan is here citing Lozovskii's description of workers' control.

11 P. Kropotkin, *Fields, Factories and Workshops Tomorrow* (London, Allen and Unwin, 1974).

12 J. Juillard, *Fernand Pelloutier et les origines du syndicalisme d'action directe* (Paris, Editions du Seuil, 1971); F.F. Ridley, *Revolutionary Syndicalism in France* (Cambridge University Press, 1970); P. Stearns, *Revolutionary Syndicalism and French Labor* (New Brunswick, N.J., Rutgers University Press, 1971).

13 B. Pribicevic, *The Shop Stewards' Movement and Workers' Control, 1910–22* (Oxford University Press, 1959); M. Derber, *The American Idea of Industrial Democracy* (Urbana, University of Illinois Press, 1970), pp. 56–9.

14 P. Avrich, *The Russian Anarchists* (Princeton University Press, 1971).

15 A. Berkman, *The Russian Tragedy* (Orkney, Cienfuegos, 1976); G.P. Maximoff, *Syndicalists in the Russian Revolution* (n.p, n.d. [1978]).

16 Voline, *The Unknown Revolution, 1917–21* (Detroit, Black and Red, 1974).

17 *Golos anarkhista*, 1, 21 Nov. 1917. An anarchist, Gorelik, wrote that 'anarchist workers were too weak in ideas and numbers to have much effect', cited by V.V. Komin, *Anarkhizm v Rossii* (Kalinin, 1969), p.145.

18 One should note that in Spain the success of anarchism derived entirely from its organisational strength. In Andalusia in the last third of the nineteenth century the anarchists successfully merged trade-union organisation with communal organisation in order to pit the power of the *pueblo* against the latifundists and wine-growing bourgeoisie. After the First World War the anarcho-syndicalist CNT owed its success largely to organisational flexibility, linked to strategic perspicuity. See T. Kaplan, *The Anarchists of Andalusia, 1868–1903* (Princeton University Press, 1977); J. Romero Maura, 'The Spanish Case', *Anarchism Today*, ed. J. Joll and D. Apter (London, Macmillan, 1971).

19 S.N. Kanev, *Oktyabr'skaya revolyutsiya i krakh anarkhizma* (Moscow, 1974), p.54.
20 *Ibid.*, p.73.
21 B.I. Gorev, *Anarkhizm v Rossii* (Moscow, 1930), p.124.
22 This was not true of anarcho-syndicalists. At the Izhora works they 'took every measure to ensure that actions by workers have an organised and not a sectional character'. *Golos truda*, 20, 25 Nov. 1917, p.4.
23 *Oktyabr'skaya revolyutsiya i fabzavkomy*, vol.1 (Moscow, 1927), pp.70–1.
24 *Ibid.*, pp.215, 233.
25 *Ibid.*, vol.2, pp.184, 186.
26 *Novaya Zhizn'*, 6 Jan. 1918, p.4.
27 Voline, *Unknown Revolution*, p.175.
28 Rosenberg, 'Workers' Control', p.95.
29 L.S. Gaponenko, *Rabochii klass Rossii v 1917g.* (Moscow, 1970), p.225.
30 D.A. Kovalenko, 'Bor'ba fabrichno-zavodskikh komitetov Petrograda za rabochii kontrol' nad proizvodstvom (mart–oktyabr' 1917g.)', *Istoricheskie Zapiski*, 61 (1957), p.80.
31 *Okt. rev. i fab.*, vol.1, p.82.
32 *Ibid.*
33 *Ibid.*, p.165–6.
34 *Natsionalizatsiya promyshlennosti i organizatsiya sotsialisticheskogo proizvodstva v Petrograde, 1917–20gg.*, vol.1 (Leningrad, 1958), p.34.
35 *Ibid.*, p.266.
36 V.I. Selitskii, *Massy v bor'be za rabochii kontrol'* (Moscow, 1971), p.42.
37 N.P. Payalin, *Zavod imeni Lenina, 1857–1918* (Moscow, 1933), pp.378–9.
38 Z.V. Stepanov, *Rabochie Petrograda v period podgotovki i provedeniya oktyabr'skogo vooruzhennogo vosstaniya* (Moscow, 1965), pp.114–5.
39 M.I. Mitel'man, *1917 god na Putilovskom zavode* (Leningrad, 1939), p.141.
40 *Novyi Put'*, 3–4, 1 Dec. 1917, p.25.
41 Selitskii, *Massy v bor'be*, p.43.
42 *Rabochii kontrol' v promyshlennykh predpriyatii Petrograde*, vol.1 (Leningrad, 1947), p.57.
43 *Ibid.*, p.43.
44 *Krasnyi Arkhiv*, 103 (1940), 108.
45 *Revolyutsionnoe dvizhenie v iyule: iyul'skii krizis* (Moscow, 1959), p.352.
46 *Okt. rev. i fab.*, vol.2, pp.76–80.
47 *Trudorezina*, 15, 29 July 1917, p.1.
48 Stepanov, *Rabochie Petrograda*, p.116.
49 *Ibid.*
50 *Ibid.*, p.117.
51 Avrich, 'Bolsheviks and Workers' Control', p.62.
52 Kaplan, *Bolshevik Ideology*, p.97.
53 O. Anweiler, *The Soviets: The Russian Workers', Peasants' and Soldiers' Councils, 1905–21* (New York, Random House, 1974), p.127.
54 *Okt. rev. i fab.*, vol.1, p.95.
55 The left-wing Menshevik D. Dallin admitted to the conference that industrialists were deliberately cutting back production. *Ibid.*, p.106.
56 *Ibid.*, p.95.

57 The much-depleted Menshevik cell at the Aivaz works in November bewailed the 'pernicious delusion that it is possible for workers to alleviate the economic chaos and protect the working masses from the effects of the rising cost of living and imminent unemployment simply by their own efforts'. *Plamya*, 1, 24 November 1917, p.4.

58 See Cherevanin's resolution to the Third Trade-Union Conference, *Tret'ya vserossiiskaya konferentsiya professional'nykh soyuzov* (Moscow, 1927), pp.450–2.

59 'Tezisy dlya agitatorov i propagandistov', Central Committee of SR party, no.9, 1918 (n.p.).

60 See resolution on factory committees passed by the third congress of the SRs. *Delo Naroda*, 64, 2 June 1917, p.2.

61 *Znamya Truda*, 13, 6 Sept. 1917, p.4.

62 *Volya Truda*, 2, 12 Sept. 1917, pp.2–3.

63 *Okt. rev. i fab.*, vol.1, p.94.

64 Bill Shatov's famous characterisation of the trade unions at the First National Congress of Trade Unions in January 1918. *Pervyi vserossiiskii s"ezd professional'nykh soyuzov* (Moscow, 1918), p.101.

65 V.I. Lenin, *Polnoe Sobranie Sochinenii*, 5th ed., vol.32 (Moscow, 1962), p.438.

66 Lenin, *Pol. sob. soch.*, vol.34 (Moscow, 1962), p.175.

67 *Ibid.*, p.161.

68 Lenin, *Pol. sob. soch.*, vol.31 (Moscow, 1962), p.168.

69 *Listovki petrogradskikh bol'shevikov, 1917–20gg.*, vol.3 (Leningrad, 1957), p.40.

70 *Okt. rev. i fab.*, vol.1, p.70.

71 *Ibid.*, pp.107–9.

72 Lenin, *Pol. sob. soch.*, vol.35 (Moscow, 1962), p.63.

73 *Ibid.*, p.148.

74 *Okt. rev. i fab.*, vol.2, pp.217–63.

75 *Ibid.*, p.124.

76 *Ibid.*, pp.170–1.

77 *Ibid.*, p.186.

78 *Tret'ya konferentsiya*, pp.482–4.

79 *Shestoi s"ezd RSDRP(6)* (Moscow, 1958), pp.261–3.

80 Lenin, *Pol. sob. soch.*, vol.32, pp.139–62; compare Larin's critique of the draft programme *Rabochii Put'*, 31, 8 Oct. 1917, p.2.

81 In this belief, Lenin was at odds with Gramsci, theorist of the Italian factory councils, who envisaged proletarian state power growing up *on the basis of* workers' power in the factories, and who saw the struggle for workers' control as growing naturally into a contestation for state power. On this point, as on many others, it was Bordiga, not Gramsci, who was closer to Lenin. It is also worth noting in this connection that Gramsci saw the Italian councils as the (potential) equivalent of the Russian soviets. He believed that the forms of the proletarian state must be councils based on production. In Russia, however, it was the factory committees which were based on production, whereas the soviets were organised on a territorial basis (though largely elected on a production

basis). Gramsci rejected Bordiga's call for territorially-based organisation, since he believed that it was as *producers*, that the working class would make communism. See A. Gramsci, *Political Writings, 1910–20*, (London, Lawrence and Wishart, 1977).

82 *Vospominaniya o Lenine*, vol.2 (Moscow, 1969), p.416; L. Trotsky, *History of the Russian Revolution*, vol.2 (London, Sphere, 1967), p.303.

83 V. Perazich, *Tekstili Leningrada v 1917g.* (Leningrad, 1927), pp.28–9.

84 *Leningradskie tekstilya*, 6–7 (1927), 9.

85 Perazich, *Tekstili Leningrada*, p.28.

86 *Istoriya Leningradskoi obuvnoi fabriki Skorokhod* (Leningrad, 1969), p.134.

87 B. Shabalin, *Krasnyi Treugol'nik, 1860–1935* (Leningrad, 1938), p.158.

88 *Professional'noe dvizhenie v Petrograde v 1917g.*, ed. A. Anskii (Leningrad, 1928), p.271.

89 *Petrogradskie bol'sheviki v oktyabr'skoi revolyutsii* (Leningrad, 1957), pp. 45–5.

90 *Ibid.*, p.55); I.G. Tomkevich, *Znamya oktyabrya* (Leningrad 1972), p.33.

91 *V ogne revolyutsionnykh boev*, vol.1 (Moscow, 1967), pp.131–2.

92 They were chairmen, respectively, of the factory committees at the Gun, Langenzippen, Duflon, Soikin, Putilov, Skorokhod and Siemens-Halske works.

93 I.I. Gaza, *Putilovets na putyakh k oktyabryu* (Moscow, 1933), p.85.

94 *Izvestiya raionnogo komiteta Petrogradskoi Storony*, 1, July 1917, p.3.

95 *Istoriya fabriki Skorokhod*, p.172.

96 *Fabrichno-zavodskie komitety Petrograda*, ed. I. Mints (Moscow, 1979), pp.573–4.

97 *Rabochii*, 6, 29 Aug. 1917, p.4.

98 *Rabochii Put'*, 22, 28 Sept. 1917, p.4.

99 *Rab. Put'*, 20, 26 Sept. 1917, p.4.

100 B.M. Freidlin, *Ocherki istorii rabochego dvizheniya v 1917g.* (Moscow, 1967), p.158.

101 *Pravda*, 79, 11 June 1917, p.4.

102 *Oktyabr'skoe vooruzhennoe vosstanie v Petrograde* (Moscow, 1957), p.118.

103 Perazich, *Tekstili Leningrada*, p.92.

104 *Rab. Gazeta*, 54, 12 May 1917, p.4; *Delo Naroda*, 99, 13 July, 1917, p.4.

105 *Rab. Put'*, 14, 19 Sept. 1917, p.4.

106 See the constitutions of the Gun works committee of July and August: *Rab. kontrol' v prom. pred.*, vol.1, pp.124–5; *Okt. rev. i fab.* vol.1, pp.67–8.

107 *Narodnoe khozyaistvo*, 11 (1918), 7.

108 Stepanov, *Rabochie Petrograda*, p.113.

109 *Okt. voor. vosst. v Pet.*, pp.92, 103–4, 110, 135; *Revolyutsionnoe dvizhenie v sentyabre* (Moscow, 1961), pp.259, 292, 311.

110 *Okt. voor. vosst. v Pet.*, pp.92, 96, 99, 125, 133.

111 *Rev. dvizh. v iyule*, pp.352–3.

112 *Pravda*, 178, 3 Nov. 1917, p.4.

113 Len. gos. ist. arkhiv (LGIA), f.1477, op.3, d.1, 1.66.

114 *Rev. dvizh. v sentyabre*, pp.329–30.

115 Pankratova, *Fabzavkomy v bor'be*, pp.226–7. The first conference of factory committees in Moscow called for 'democratic' control of the

factory committees, though the second in October called for workers' control. Most of the resolutions which called for state control in Petrograd were passed before the autumn. See, for example, the resolution of the seventh district of the Putilov works which, as late as the end of July, expressed support for the Coalition government and called for state control of the economy. *Zemlya i Volya*, 103, 30 July 1917, p.3.

116 *Putilovets v trekh revolyutsiyakh* (Leningrad, 1933), pp.364–5.
117 *Okt. voor. vosst. v Pet.*, p.91.
118 *Znamya Truda*, 32, 30 Sept. 1917, p.3.
119 *Golos Truda*, 3, 25 Aug. 1917, p.3.
120 *Okt. rev. i fab.*, vol.2, pp.179–81.
121 *Golos Truda*, 4, 1 Sept. 1917, p.4; *Proletarii*, 9, 23 Sept. 1917, p.4.

NOTES TO CHAPTER 7

1 *Torgovo-Promyshlennaya Gazeta*, 213, 1 Oct. 1917, pp.1–2.
2 *Delo Naroda*, 176, 10 Oct. 1917, p.1; *Rab. Gazeta*, 143, 26 Aug. 1917, p.2; Z.V. Stepanov, *Rabochie Petrograda v period podgotovki i provedeniya oktyabr'skogo vooruzhennogo vosstaniya* (Moscow, 1965), pp.143–4.
3 *Delo Naroda*, 160, 21 Sept. 1917, p.4; *Rab. Put'*, 18, 23 Sept. 1917, p.4.
4 *Rabota soyuza muchnykh izdelii i osnovanie soyuza pishchevikov 1917 god* (Leningrad, 1927), p.16.
5 Stepanov, *Rabochie Petrograda*, p.144.
6 *Ekonomicheskoe polozhenie Rossii nakanune velikoi oktyabr'skoi sotsialisticheskoi revolyutsii*, part 1 (Moscow, 1957), p.225.
7 P.V. Volobuev, *Proletariat i burzhuaziya Rossii v 1917g.* (Moscow, 1964), pp.302, 306.
8 *Ekon, pol.*, part 1, p.166.
9 *Izvestiya*, 63, 11 May 1917, p.1.
10 *Izvestiya*, 65, 13 May 1917; *Izvestiya*, 68, 17 May 1917.
11 R.P. Browder and A.F. Kerensky, *The Russian Provisional Government*, vol.1 (Stanford University Press, 1961), p.745.
12 *Ibid.*, p.739.
13 *Ibid.*, pp.740, 746; *Ekon. pol.*, part 1, pp.209, 537–8; Volobuev, *Proletariat i burzhuaziya*, p.338.
14 Cited by Volobuev, *Proletariat i burzhuaziya*, p.205.
15 *Ibid.*
16 *Ibid.*, pp.294–5.
17 *Materialy po statistike truda Severnoi oblasti*, issue 1 (Petrograd, 1918), 18.
18 *Ibid.*
19 I.I. Gaza, *Putilovets v trekh revolyutsiyakh* (Leningrad, 1933), pp.340–1.
20 *Ibid.*, p.340.
21 *Delo Naroda*, 62, 31 May 1917, p.4.
22 *Revolyutsionnoe dvizhenie v mae–iyune* (Moscow, 1959), pp.280–1.
23 *Pravda*, 64, 24 May 1917, p.4.
24 *Pravda*, 65, 25 May 1917, p.4; *Pravda*, 68, 28 May 1917, p.4; *Pravda*, 93, 29 June 1917, p.4; *Delo Naroda*, 66, 4 June 1917, p.4.

25 See the resolution from the Aivaz workers, *Pravda*, 92, 27 June 1917, p.4.
26 Stepanov, *Rabochie Petrograda*, p.99.
27 *Ibid.*; *Rab. Put'*, 7, 10 Sept. 1917, p.3.
28 Stepanov, *Rabochie Petrograda*, p.100.
29 *Ibid.*
30 *Metallist*, 3, 1 Oct. 1917, p.16.
31 *Fabrichno-zavodskie komitety Petrograda: Protokoly*, ed. I.I. Mints (Moscow, 1979), pp.336, 342, 349, 378, 391.
32 N.P. Payalin, *Zavod imeni Lenina, 1857–1918* (Moscow, 1933), p.397.
33 *Fab. zav. Kom.*, pp.91, 95, 593.
34 *Oktyabr'skaya revolyutsiya i fabzavkomy*, vol.2 (Moscow, 1927), pp.35–6.
35 *Pravda*, 65, 25 May 1917, p.3; *Pravda*, 71, 2 June 1917, p.3; *Delo Naroda*, 58, 26 May 1917, p.4; *Vestnik professional'nykh soyuzov*, 2, 15 Sept. 1917, p.10.
36 *Professional'noe dvizhenie v Petrograde v 1917g.* (Leningrad, 1928), p.123.
37 *Metallist*, 4, 18 Oct. 1917, p.10.
38 *Metallist*, 5, 9 Nov. 1917, p.3; *Rab. Put'*, 10, 14 Sept. 1917, p.3.
39 Stepanov, *Rabochie Petrograda*, p.140.
40 *Ibid.*, p.143.
41 *Ibid.*, p.142.
42 *Ibid.*
43 Gaza, *Putilovets v trekh rev.*, pp.386–7; M.I. Mitel'man et al., *Istoriya Putilovskogo zavoda, 1908–17gg.*, 4th edn (Moscow, 1961), p.142.
44 Gaza, *Putilovets v trekh rev.*, pp.386–91; *Rab.Put'*, 32, 10 Oct. 1917, p.4.
45 *Fab. zav. kom.*, pp.490–3.
46 Stepanov, *Rabochie Petrograda*, p.146.
47 *Fab. zav. kom.*, pp.267–311.
48 *Golos Rabotnitsy*, 5–6, 17 June 1917, p.14.
49 Stepanov, *Rabochie Petrograda*, p.141.
50 V.I. Selitskii, *Massy v bor'be za rabochii kontrol'* (Moscow, 1971), p.195.
51 *Rabochii kontrol' v promyshlennykh predpriyatiyakh Petrograda, 1917–18gg.*, vol.1 (Leningrad, 1947), p.71.
52 N. Dmitriev, 'Petrogradskie fabzavkomy v 1917g.', *Krasnaya Letopis'*, 2 (23) (1927), 82.
53 *Rab. kontrol' v prom. pred.*, p.108.
54 *Novyi Put'*, 1–2, 15 Oct. 1917, pp.9–10.
55 'Materialy k istorii rabochego kontrolya nad proizvodstvom', *Krasnyi Arkhiv*, 103 (1940), 109.
56 *Raionnye sovety v Petrograde v 1917g.*, vol.2 (Moscow, 1965), pp.184–6.
57 *Ibid.*, pp.249, 259, 263.
58 *Revolyutsionnoe dvizhenie v iyule* (Moscow, 1959), pp.342–3.
59 *Delo Naroda*, 69, 8 June 1917, p.4.
60 Stepanov, *Rabochie Petrograda*, p.135; *Okt. rev. i fab.*, vol.1, p.148; A.M. Pankratova, *Fabzavkomy v bor'be za sotsialisticheskuyu fabriku* (Moscow, 1923), p.245.
61 'Iz istorii bor'by za rabochii kontrol'', *Krasnyi Arkhiv*, 69–70 (1935), 138–58; *Okt. rev. i fab.*, vol.1, p.146.
62 *Revolyutsionnoe dvizhenie v sentyabre* (Moscow, 1961), pp.284–5.

63 Stepanov, *Rabochie Petrograda*, p.136.
64 Volobuev, *Proletariat i burzhuaziya*, pp.266, 269.
65 *Rab. kontrol v prom. pred.*, pp.179, 181–3, 190; Stepanov, *Rabochie Petrograda*, p.151.
66 Browder and Kerensky, *The Provisional Government*, vol.1, p.723. The allusion is to a speech by P.P. Ryabushinskii, the textile magnate, who warned the Congress of Trade and Industry that 'the bony hand of hunger and national destitution will seize by the throat the friends of the people'.
67 Stepanov, *Rabochie Petrograda*, p.151.
68 *Okt. rev. i fab.*, vol.2, pp.18, 27–8.
69 Stepanov, *Rabochie Petrograda*, p.152.
70 *Ibid.*; *Rab. Put'.*, 31, 8 Oct. 1917, p.4.
71 *Rab. Put'.*, 7, 10 Sept. 1917, pp.3–4.
72 *Torgovo-promyshlennaya Gazeta*, 213, 1 Oct. 1917, p.1.
73 *Okt. rev. i fab.*, vol.1, p.186.
74 *Trudy pervogo vserossiiskogo s"ezda delegatov rabochikh zavodov, portov i uchrezhdenii Morskogo Vedomstva* (Petrograd, 1917), protocol 4.
75 *Ibid.*
76 *Ibid.*, protocol 10.
77 M. Fleer, 'Putilovskii zavod v 1917–18gg.', *Bor'ba Klassov*, 1–2 (1924), 294.
78 Gaza, *Putilovets v trekh rev.*, pp.386–91.
79 *Ibid.*, p.398.
80 *Vserossiiskaya tarifnaya konferentsiya soyuzov metallistov* (Petrograd, 1918), pp.15–20.
81 *Oktyabr'skoe vooruzhennoe vosstanie v Petrograde* (Moscow, 1957), p.127.
82 *Okt. rev. i fab.*, vol.2, pp.173–5.
83 *Ibid.*, p.188.
84 M.L. Itkin, 'Tsentral'nyi sovet fabzavkomov Petrograda v 1917g.', *Oktyabr'skoe vooruzhennoe vosstanie v Petrograde* (Moscow, 1980), p.179.
85 Stepanov, *Rabochie Petrograda*, p.29.
86 V.Z. Drobizhev, *Glavnyi shtab sotsialisticheskoi promyshlennosti* (Moscow, 1966), p.54.
87 *Oktyabr'skaya revolyutsiya i fabzavkomy*, vol.1 (Moscow, 1927), p.132.
88 *Ibid.*, p.79.
89 *Ibid.*, p.135.
90 *Ibid.*, p.136.
91 *Metallist*, 12 (1922), 64–5.
92 *Vsesoyuznyi soyuz metallistov v resolyutsiyakh i postanovleniyakh s"ezdov i konferentsii*, vol.1 (Moscow, 1927), pp.104–5.
93 *Tret'ya konferentsiya professional'nykh soyuzov* (Moscow, 1927), p.12.
94 *Ibid.*, pp.76–88.
95 *Ibid.*, pp.484–5.
96 *Ibid.*, p.388,
97 *Okt. rev. i fab.*, vol.1, p.229.
98 *Ibid.*, p.233.
99 *Ibid.*, p.231.

100 *Ibid.*, p.233.
101 *Ibid.*, vol.2. pp.189–93.
102 *Ibid.*, p.193.
103 *Ibid.*, pp.189, 193.
104 *Ibid.*, p.193.

NOTES TO CHAPTER 8

1 S.G. Strumilin, 'Problemy ekonomiki truda', *Izbrannye proizvedeniya*, vol.1 (Moscow, 1963), pp.72–3.
2 *Torgovo-Promyshlennaya Gazeta*, 84, 25 April 1917, p.2.
3 *Vserossiiskii uchreditel'nyi s''ezd rabochikh metallistov* (Petrograd, 1918), p.87.
4 J.A. Banks, *The Sociology of Social Movements* (London, Macmillan, 1972).
5 C. Tilly, *From Mobilisation to Revolution* (Reading, Mass., Addison-Wesley, 1978), Ch.3.
6 Cited by A. Pankratova, *Fabzavkomy Rossii v bor'be za sotsialisticheskuyu fabriku* (Moscow, 1923), p.152.
7 *Novyi Put'*, 1–2, 14 Jan. 1918, p.4.
8 *Vestnik obshchestva zavodchikov i fabrikantov*, 5, 10 June 1917, p.3.
9 *Rab. Gazeta*, 1, 6 March 1917, p.2.
10 *Izvestiya*, 33, 6 April 1917, p.2.
11 *Rabotnitsa*, 1–2, 10 May 1917, p.12.
12 *Rabotnitsa*, 7, 19 July 1917, p.14.
13 *Pravda*, 83, 15 June 1917, p.4.
14 V. Perazich, *Tekstili Leningrada v 1917g.* (Leningrad, 1927), p.71.
15 *Ibid.*
16 *Ibid.*, pp.74–5.
17 Z.V. Stepanov, *Rabochie Petrograda v period podgotovki i provedeniya oktyabr'skogo vooruzhennogo vosstaniya* (Moscow, 1965), pp.34, 50.
18 T.I. Shatilova, *Ocherk istorii leningradskogo soyuza khimikov, 1905–18gg.* (Leningrad, 1927), pp.10, 54; S. Volin, *Deyatel'nost' men'shevikov v profsoyuzakh pri sovetskoi vlasti* (New York, 1962), p.29.
19 Perazich, *Tekstili Leningrada*, p.35.
20 *Ibid.*, p.51; *Professional'noe dvizhenie v Petrograde v 1917g.*, ed. A. Anskii (Leningrad, 1928), pp.123, 143.
21 *Okt. rev. i fab.*, vol.2, pp.217–31.
22 *Trudorezina*, 1, 22 April 1917, p.4.
23 LGIA, f.1182, op.1, d.96, 1.17.
24 LGIA, f.1186, op.4, d.16, 1.39.
25 N.D. Karpetskaya, *Rabotnitsy i velikii oktyabr'* (Leningrad, 1974), p.59.
26 *Tret'ya konf. prof. soyuzov*, pp.425–6, 456–8.
27 *Vestnik prof. soyuzov*, 2, 15 Sept. 1917, p.5.
28 *Okt. rev. i fab.*, vol.2, p.192.
29 *Rabotnitsa*, 4, 30 May 1917, p.6.
30 *Golos kozhevnika*, 4–5, 1 Dec. 1917, p.23.
31 *Ekho derevoobdelochnika*, 3, 12 Dec. 1917, p.13.
32 *Petrogradskii rabochii*, 1, 1 Feb. 1918, p.20.
33 *Rab. Gazeta*, 61, 20 May 1917, p.3.

34 *Pravda*, 64, 24 May 1917, p.4; *Delo Naroda*, 60, 28 May, 1917, p.4.
35 T. Trenogova, *Bor'ba petrogradskikh bol'shevikov za krest'yanstvo v 1917g.* (Leningrad, 1946), p.78; *Krasnaya Letopis'*, 2 (23) (1927), 55–6.
36 G. Dryazgov, *Na puti k komsomolu* (Leningrad, 1924), pp.36–63.
37 A.Ya. Leikin, 'Oktyabr'skoe vooruzhennoe vosstanie i molodezh', in *Oktyabr'skoe vooruzhennoe vosstanie v Petrograde*, sb. stat. (Moscow, 1980), p.236; V.M. Startsev, *Ocherki po istorii Petrogradskoi krasnoi gvardii i rabochei militsii* (Moscow, 1965), p.265.
38 Dryazgov, *Na puti k komsomolu*, pp.31–2.
39 A.N. Atsarkhin, *Pod bol'shevistskoe znamya: soyuzy rabochei molodezhi v Petrograde v 1917g.* (Leningrad, 1958), pp.76–7.
40 Dryazgov, *Na puti k komsomolu*, pp.31–2; Atsarkhin, *Pod bol. znamya*, pp.67, 114.
41 Atsarkhin, *Pod bol. znamya*, p.121.
42 *Yunyi Proletarii*, 1, 11 Nov. 1917, p.19; *Novaya Zhizn'*, 143, 3 Oct. 1917, p.4.
43 Dryazgov, *Na puti k komsomolu*, pp.31–2.
44 Atsarkhin, *Pod bol. znamya*, p.115.
45 LGIA, f.1278, op.1, d.84, 1.12.
46 Atsarkhin, *Pod bol. znamya*, p.116.
47 *Ibid.*, p.114.
48 *Ibid.*, p.67.
49 *Metallist*, 2, 19 Feb. 1918, pp.8–9; *Golos kozhevnika*, 10–11, 15 April 1918, p.18.
50 R.H. Turner and L.M. Killiam, *Collective Behaviour*, 2nd edn (Englewood Cliffs, N.J., Prentice-Hall, 1972), Chs.5–6.
51 E.J. Hobsbawm, *Labouring Men* (London, Weidenfeld, 1964) pp.15–22.
52 *Tret'ya konferentsiya prof. soyuzov*, pp.446–7.
53 *Metallist*, 12 (1922), p.63; *Ekho derevoobdelochnika*, 3, 12 Dec. 1917, p.13.
54 *Ekho derevoobdelochnika*, 2, 19 Oct. 1917, p.12.
55 *Metallist*, 1–2, 17 Aug. 1917, p.19.
56 *Ibid.*
57 *Ekho derevoobdelochnika*, 2, p.11.
58 *Ibid.*
59 *Proletarskii prizyv*, 4, 20 Sept. 1917, p.4; *ibid.*, 6, 27 Dec. 1917, p.4.
60 *Tkach*, 1, Nov. 1917, p.28; *Prof. dvizh. v Petrograde*, pp.116–30.
61 *Metallist*, 1–2, 17 Aug. 1917.
62 *Tkach*, 1, 1917, p.28.
63 *Pravda*, 25, 6 April 1917, p.3.
64 *Prof. dvizh. v Petrograde*, p.125.
65 *Metallist*, 7, 16 Dec. 1917, p.2.
66 *Delo Naroda*, 121, 8 Aug. 1917, p.1.
67 *Revolyutsionnoe dvizhenie v sentyabre* (Moscow, 1961), p.267.
68 A.A. Sviridov, 'Fabrichno-zavodskie komitety kak forma organizatsii piterskikh rabochikh v 1917g.', *Uch. zapiski Len. gos. ped. int.*, vol.298 (1971).
69 *Ibid.*
70 *Okt. rev. i fab.*, vol.1, pp.25, 31, 241.
71 *Ibid.*, p.241.

72 *Ibid.*, p.30.
73 *Ibid.*, p.33.
74 *Ibid.*, p.240.
75 M. Ferro, *October 1917* (London, Routledge, 1980), Ch.7.
76 *Ibid.*, p.194.
77 For a detailed critique see my review article in *Soviet Studies*, vol.30, no.3 (1981), pp.454–9.
78 *Fabrichno-zavodskie komitety Petrograda v 1917g.* (Moscow, 1979), pp.220, 222.
79 *Ibid.*, pp.311–12.
80 *Ibid.*, p.350.
81 *Ibid.*, pp.355–7.
82 LGIA, f.1186, op.4, d.16, 1.2.
83 *Fab. zav. kom.*, p.540.
84 *Ibid.*, p.574.
85 *Rabochii*, 6, 29 Aug. 1917, p.4.
86 *Oktyabr'skoe vooruzhennoe vosstanie v Petrograde* (Leningrad, 1948), p.34.
87 M. Weber, *Economy and Society*, vol.3 (New York, Bedminster, 1968), Ch.11.
88 A symbol of the bureaucratic aspect of factory committee practice was the use of the ubiquitous rubber stamp on all documents which emanated from the committees.
89 S.N. Eisenstadt, 'Bureaucracy and Bureaucratisation', *Current Sociology*, 7 (1958), 102.
90 R. Hyman, 'The Politics of Workplace Trade Unionism', *Capital and Class*, 8 (1979), 61.
91 *Rabotnitsa*, 11, 18 Oct. 1957, p.15.
92 *Golos kozhevnika*, 6–7, 25 Jan. 1918, p.18.

NOTES TO CHAPTER 9

1 *First Decrees of Soviet Power*, ed. Yu. Akhapkin (London, Lawrence and Wishart, 1970), pp.36–8.
2 A.V. Venediktov, *Organizatsiya gosudarstvennoi promyshlennosti v SSSR*, vol.1 (Leningrad, 1957), pp.82–5.
3 *Dekrety sovetskoi vlasti*, vol.1 (Moscow, 1957), pp.77–85; V.I. Lenin, *Polnoe sobranie sochinenii*, 5th edn, vol. 35 (Moscow, 1962), pp.30–1.
4 J.L.H. Keep, *The Debate on Soviet Power: minutes of the All-Russian Central Executive Committee of Soviets* (Oxford University Press, 1979), p.318.
5 *Ibid.*, pp.124–5.
6 *First Decrees of Soviet Power*, pp.36–8.
7 S.N. Kanev, *Oktyabr'skaya revolyutsiya i krakh anarkhizma* (Moscow, 1974), p.165.
8 *Novyi Put'*, 3–4, 1 Dec. 1917, pp.25–6.
9 *Natsionalizatsiya promyshlennosti v SSSR, 1917–20gg.*, ed. I.A. Gladkov (Moscow, 1954), p.76.
10 *Ibid.*, pp.77–84.
11 D.L. Limon, 'Lénine et le contrôle ouvrier', *Autogestion*, 4 (1967), 83–5.

12 *Novaya Zhizn'*, 19, 26 Jan. 1918, p.3.
13 Lenin, *Pol. sob. soch.*, vol.35, p.448.
14 E.H. Carr, *The Bolshevik Revolution*, vol.2 (London, Pelican, 1965), pp.79–80.
15 A. Pankratova, *Fabzavkomy Rossii v bor'be za sotsialisticheskuyu fabriku* (Moscow, 1923), pp.386–91.
16 A. Lozovskii, *Rabochii Kontrol'* (Petrograd, 1918), p.21.
17 *Ibid.*, p.21.
18 *Ibid.*, p.20.
19 *Ibid.*, p.23.
20 *Novyi Put'*, 1–2, 14 Jan. 1918, p.4.
21 *Ibid.*
22 Lozovskii, *Rab. Kontrol'*, p.24.
23 *Ibid.*, pp.24–5.
24 See the conference of metalworkers' delegates on 20 December 1917. *Rabochii kontrol' v promyshlennykh predpriyatiyakh Petrograda, 1917–18gg.*, vol.1 (Leningrad, 1954), p.244.
25 Venediktov, *Org. gos. prom.*, pp.94–5.
26 *Metallist*, 1, 11 Jan. 1918, p.2.
27 *Pervyi vserossiiskii s"ezd professional'nykh soyuzov* (Moscow, 1918), p.69.
28 *Ibid.*, p.338.
29 *Ibid.*, S. Volin, *Deyatel'nost' men'shevikov v profsoyuzakh pri sovetskoi vlasti* (New York, 1962), p.35.
30 *Novyi Put'*, 3, 21 Jan. 1918, p.8.
31 *Pervyi s"ezd prof. soyuzov*, p.69.
32 *Vestnik Truda*, 3, 1921, p.11.
33 *Resolyutsii vserossiiskikh konferentsii i s"ezdov professional'nykh soyuzov* (Petrograd, 1919), p.92.
34 P.A. Garvi, *Professional'nye soyuzy v Rossii v pervye gody revolyutsii, 1917–21* (New York, 1958), p.32–4.
35 *Pervyi s"ezd prof. soyuzov*, p.82; *Professional'nyi Soyuz*, 1, Feb. 1918, pp.11–13.
36 Carr, *The Bolshevik Revolution*, vol.2, pp.220–9; R. Daniels, *The Conscience of the Revolution* (Cambridge, Mass., Harvard University Press, 1960), Ch.5.
37 *Metallist*, 2, 19 Feb. 1918, pp.3–4.
38 *Oktyabr'skaya revolyutsiya i fabzavkomy*, ed. P.N. Amosov, vol.1 (Moscow, 1927), p.190.
39 *Vserossiiskaya tarifnaya konferentsiya soyuzov metallistov* (Petrograd, 1918), p.7.
40 *Metallist*, 6, 30 Nov. 1917, pp.3–6.
41 *Metallist*, 1, 11 Jan. 1918, p.14.
42 *Novyi Put'*, 3, 1918, pp.12.
43 *Ibid.*
44 A.V. Krasnikova, *Na zare sovetskoi vlasti* (Leningrad, 1963), p.68.
45 *Pervyi s"ezd prof. soyuzov*, p.235.
46 *Ibid.*
47 *Ibid.*, p.240.
48 *Ibid.*, p.229.
49 *Novyi Put'*, 3, 1918, pp.1–2.

50 *Ibid.*
51 *Noyvi Put'*, 4–5, 25 Feb. 1918, p.13.
52 *Novaya Zhizn'*, 19, 26 Jan. 1918, p.3.
53 *Metallist*, 2, 1918, p.5; *Metallist*, 3, 23 March 1918, p.15.
54 *Prof. Soyuz*, 1, 1918. The quotation is of the purported dying words of Emperor Julian the Apostate (Theodoret, *Historia Ecclesiae*, vol.III, 20).
55 Cited by Pankratova, *Fabzavkomy v bor'be za sots. fabriku*, pp.298–9.
56 See the resolution of the Sixth Party Congress. *KPSS v resolyutsiyakh* (Moscow, 1954), pp.376–9. Soviet historians generally argue that the Bolshevik government planned to carry out full-scale nationalisation from the first. In 1956 V.P. Nasyrin was heavily reprimanded for denying this. See V.P. Nasyrin, 'O nekotorykh voprosakh sotsialisticheskogo preobrazovaniya promyshlennosti v SSSR', *Voprosy Istorii*, 5 (1956), 90–9; Venediktov, *Org. gos. prom.*, p.187.
57 *Kommunist*, 3, 16 May 1918; Carr, *The Bolshevik Revolution*, vol.2, pp.83–8; 95–105.
58 See, for example, Yu. Boyarkov's article in *Vestnik Metallista*, 4–6, 1918.
59 *Natsionalizatsiya promyshlennosti i organizatsiya sotsialisticheskogo proizvodstva v Petrograde, 1917–20gg.*, compiler M.V. Kiselev, vol.1 (Leningrad, 1958), p.7.
60 *Ibid.*, p.167.
61 *Istoriya sotsialisticheskoi ekonomiki SSSR*, vol.1 (Moscow, 1976), p.117.
62 *Novyi Put'*, 1, 1918, pp.33–5.
63 *Ibid.*, *Novyi Put'*, 6–7, 1918, pp.26, 31.
64 *Nats. prom. i org. sots. proizvodstva*, vol.1, pp.186–91.
65 *Ibid.*
66 *Novyi Put'*, 1, 1918, pp.33–5.
67 *Novyi Put'*, 4–5, 1918, p.13.
68 Carr, *The Bolshevik Revolution*, vol.2, p.104.
69 *Novyi Put'*, 4–5, 1918, p.14.
70 Lenin, *Pol. sob. soch.*, vol.35, p.198.
71 V.I. Lenin, *Pol. sob. soch.*, 5th edn, vol.34 (Moscow, 1962), p.320.
72 V.I. Lenin, *Pol. sob. soch.*, 5th edn., vol.36 (Moscow, 1962), p.199.
73 *Ibid.*
74 *Kommunist*, 1, 20 April 1918, pp.12–16; *Kommunist*, 2, 27 April 1918, pp.5–17.
75 *Theses of the Left Communists (1918)* (Glasgow, Critique pamphlet, 1977), p.18.

NOTES TO CHAPTER 10

1 *Pervyi vserossiiskii s"ezd professional'nykh soyuzov* (Moscow, 1918), p.200.
2 V.Z. Drobizhev, *Glavnyi shtab sotsialisticheskoi promyshlennosti* (Moscow, 1960), p.54.
3 Cited by A. Lozovskii, *Rabochii kontrol'* (Petrograd, 1918), p.98.
4 Cited by V.Z. Drobizhev, *Stroitel'stvo organov upravleniya promyshlennosti v SSSR v 1917–18gg.*, candidate dissertation (Moscow University, History Faculty, 1957), p.107.

5 A.V. Venediktov, *Organizatsiya gosudarstvennoi promyshlennosti v SSSR*, vol.1 (Leningrad, 1957), p.137.
6 *Krasnyi Arkhiv*, 103 (1940), 124–5.
7 A. Pankratova, *Fabzavkomy Rossii v bor'be za sotsialisticheskuyu fabriku* (Moscow, 1923), pp.245–6; *Nationalizatsiya promyshlennosti i organizatsiya sotsialisticheskogo proizvodstva v Petrograde, 1917–20gg.*, vol.1 (Leningrad, 1958), p.200.
8 LGIA, f.1182, op.1, d.96, 1.88.
9 N.P. Payalin, *Zavod imeni Lenina* (Moscow, 1933), pp.401–2.
10 *Ibid.*, pp.404–5.
11 *Ibid.*
12 *Ibid.*, pp.406–7; *Nats. prom. i org. sots. proizvodstva*, vol.1, pp.53–5.
13 G. Tsyperovich, *Petrogradskie profsoyuzy v oktyabre 1917g.* (Moscow, 1927), p.48. For a discussion of the attitudes of Russian engineers at this time see K.E. Bailes, *Technology and Society under Lenin and Stalin* (Princeton University Press, 1978), pp.22–3.
14 Lozovskii, *Rab. kontrol'*, pp.93–4.
15 *Kontorskii Trud*, 3–4, Dec. 1917, p.4.
16 Lozovskii, *Rab. kontrol'*, p.95.
17 Venediktov, *Org. gos. prom.*, vol.1, p.141.
18 *Kontorskii Trud*, 2, Nov. 1917, p.15.
19 *Oktyabr'skii perevorot*, ed. A.A. Popov (Petrograd, 1918), p.399.
20 *Kontorskii Trud*, 2, p.15.
21 *Putilovets v trekh revolyutsiyakh*, ed. I.I. Gaza (Leningrad, 1933), pp.413–14.
22 *Leningradskie Tekstilya*, 6–7 (1927), 10.
23 *Golos Truda*, 3 Nov. 1917, p.1.
24 Cited by Drobizhev, *Stroitel'stvo organov upravleniya*, p.115.
25 *Ibid.*
26 V. Perazich, *Tekstili Leningrada v 1917g.* (Leningrad, 1927), p.80.
27 *Tkach*, 2, Dec. 1917, p.15.
28 Drobizhev, *Glavnyi shtab sots. prom.*, p.98.
29 *Ibid.*
30 *Rabochii kontrol' v promyshlennykh predpriyatiyakh Petrograda, 1917–18gg.*, vol.1 (Leningrad, 1947), pp.254–5.
31 Venediktov, *Org. gos. prom.*, pp.157–8; *Spisok Fabrichno-zavodskikh predpriyatii Petrograda* (Petrograd, 1918), p.20.
32 *Nats. prom. i org. sots. proizvodstva*, vol.1, pp.34–5.
33 *Ibid.*
34 *Rab. kontrol' v prom. pred.*, pp.230–1.
35 *Natsionalizatsiya promyshlennosti v SSSR, 1917–20gg.*, ed. I.A. Gladkov (Moscow, 1954), p.96.
36 *Nats. prom. i org. sots. proizvodstva*, vol.1, pp.68–9.
37 *Rab. kontrol' v prom. pred.*, p.279.
38 *Ibid.*, p.316; *Spisok fab. zav. pred.*, p.26.
39 *Rab. kontrol' v prom. pred.*, pp.230–1.
40 *Pravda*, 16, 21 Jan. 1918, p.4.
41 *Rabochii Put'*, 36, 14 Oct. 1917, p.4.

42 *Nats. prom. i org. sots. prom.*, vol.1, pp.61–2.
43 *Ibid.*
44 *Ibid.*, p.135.
45 *Nats. prom. v SSSR*, pp.350–2.
46 V.P. Milyutin, *Sovetskoe ekonomicheskoe razvitie Rossii v diktature proletariata* (Moscow, 1918), p.85.
47 *Trudy pervogo vserossiiskogo s"ezda sovetov narodnogo khozyaistva* (Moscow, 1918), p.92.
48 Drobizhev, *Glavnyi shtab sots. prom.*, p.99. Most Soviet historians reject the view of nationalisation as a spontaneous process from below, and argue that it was planned government policy. See Venediktov, *Org. gos. prom.*, vol.1, p.193.
49 *Nats. prom. i org. sots. proizvodstva*, vol.1, p.xii.
50 Drobizhev, *Glavnyi shtab sots. prom.*, p.100.
51 *Spisok fab. zav. pred.*
52 M.N. Potekhin, *Pervyi sovet proletarskoi diktatury* (Leningrad, 1966), p.253.
53 Venediktov, *Org. gos. prom.*, vol.1, pp.201–2.
54 Potekhin, *Pervyi sovet*, p.253.
55 Venediktov, *Org. gos. prom.*, vol.1, p.145.
56 *Ibid.*, pp.313–6.
57 S.A. Oppenheim, 'The Supreme Economic Council, 1917–21', *Soviet Studies*, 30, no.1 (1973), pp.14–15.
58 *Trudy pervogo s"ezda sovnarkhoz.*, pp.259–60; 339–59.
59 Drobizhev, *Glavnyi shtab*, p.121.
60 *Materialy po statistike Petrograda*, issue 1 (Petrograd, 1920), p.45.
61 *Natsionalizatsiya promyshlennosti i organizatsiya sotsialisticheskogo proizvodstva v Petrograde, 1917–20gg.*, vol.2 (Leningrad, 1960), p.vii.
62 *Pravda*, 25, 14 Feb. 1918, p.4.
63 *Pravda*, 24, 31 Jan. 1918, p.4; A.I. Vdovin and V.Z. Drobizhev, *Rost rabochego klassa SSSR, 1917–40gg.* (Moscow, 1976), p.77.
64 *Materialy po statistike truda*, issue 6 (Petrograd, 1919), p.35.
65 *Nats. prom. i org. sots. proizvodstva*, vol.1, p.194.
66 *Materialy po statistike truda Severnoi oblasti*, issue 1, (Petrograd, 1918), p.19.
67 *Materialy po statistike truda*, issue 5 (Petrograd, 1919), p.33.
68 *Ibid.*, p.43.
69 *Krasnyi Treugol'nik na putyakh oktyabrya* (Leningrad, 1927), p.19.
70 *Mat. po stat. truda Sev. obl.*, issue 1, p.18.
71 Vdovin and Drobizhev, *Rost rab. klassa*, p.77.
72 *Mat. po stat. truda*, issue 6, p.38.
73 This was the view of M.I. Gil'bert, 'K voprosu o sostave promyshlennykh rabochikh SSSR v gody grazhdanskoi voiny', *Istoriya proletariata SSSR*, 3 (1934) and *ibid.*, 1 (1935); and also of the Left SR, I.Z. Shteinberg, in an article in *Znamya Truda*, 213, 16 May, 1918, p.1.
74 O.I. Shkaratan, 'Izmeneniya v sotsial'nom sostave fabrichno-zavodskikh rabochikh Leningrada, 1917–18gg.', *Istoriya SSSR*, 5 (1959), p.24.
75 *Mat. po stat. truda Sev. obl.*, issue 1, p.18.
76 Z.V. Stepanov, *Rabochie Petrograda v period podgotovki i provedeniya oktyabr'skogo vooruzhennogo vosstaniya* (Moscow, 1965), pp.28–9; V.V.

Anikeev, 'Svedeniya o bol'shevistskikh organizatsiyakh s marta po dekabr' 1917g.', *Voprosy Istorii KPSS*, 2 (1958), p.134 gives a figure of 49,478 for Petrograd and the surrounding area.

77 A.V. Krasnikova, *Na zare sovetskoi vlasti* (Leningrad, 1963), p.133; *Statistika truda*, 1–4 (1919), 14–15.

78 L.M. Kleinbort, *Istoriya bezrabotitsy v Rossii, 1857–1919* (Moscow, 1925), p.288.

79 *Ibid.*

80 *Ibid.*

81 *Novaya Zhizn'*, 50, 24 March 1918, p.4; *Pravda*, 58, 26 March 1918, p.2.

82 *Petrogradskaya Pravda*, 66, 4 April 1918, p.2.

83 I.I. Gaza, *Putilovets na putyakh k oktyabryu* (Moscow, 1933), p.118.

84 *Putilovets v trekh revolyutsiyakh*, pp.428–9.

85 *Nats. prom. i org. sots. proizvodstva*, vol.2, p.36.

86 *Ibid.*

87 *Nats. prom. v SSSR*, p.654.

88 *Nats. prom. i org. sots. proizvodstva*, vol.2, p.170.

89 M. Lur'e, *Trudovaya povinnost' i rabochii kontrol'* (Petrograd, 1918), p.9.

90 S.G. Strumilin, 'Problemy ekonomiki truda', *Izbrannye proizvedeniya*, vol.3 (Moscow, 1964), p.361.

91 Cited by J. Bunyan, *The Origin of Forced Labor in the Soviet State, 1917–21* (Johns Hopkins University Press, Baltimore, Md., 1967), pp.20–1.

92 *Vestnik professional'nykh soyuzov*, 1, 4 May 1918, p.18.

93 *Nats. prom. i org. sots. proizvodstva*, vol.2, p.xvi; *Metallist*, 5, 22 May 1918, p.9.

94 M. Dewar, *Labour Policy in the USSR, 1917–28* (London, Royal Institute of International Affairs, 1956), p.28.

95 *Nats. prom. i org. sots. proizvodstva*, vol.2, p.171.

96 In the factories where piece-rates were reintroduced successfully, such as the Nevskii shipyard, the Carriage Construction works, the Putilov shipyard and the Ekval' works, they had a very healthy effect on productivity. *Ibid.*, pp.178–82.

97 On 20 October 1920 a conference of Petrograd metalworkers agreed 'as an experiment' to introduce piece-rates for a period of six months, this time without any limit on earnings. Henceforward piece-rates took root throughout industry. *Ibid.*, pp.227–8.

98 *Petrogradskaya Pravda*, 110, 30 May 1918, p.2.

99 *Vestnik profsoyuzov*, 2, 15 June 1918, p.20.

100 *Petrogradskaya Pravda*, 154, 21 July 1918, p.5.

101 *Nats. prom. i org. sots proizvodstva*, vol.2, p.32.

102 See the decree of the Council of Trade Unions of the Northern oblast' of late 1918 (*Rab. kontrol' v prom. pred.*, pp.457–8) and the ARCTU decree of August 1918 (cited by Pankratova, *Fabzavkomy v bor'be*, pp.268ff.). It should not be assumed that the more radical style of control died in 1918. Attempts continued during the Civil War to resurrect it, not only by the factory committees, but by some local *sovnarkhozy* and even trade unions. See B. Bor'yan, 'Rabochii kontrol', 1917–21', *Vestnik Truda*, 10–11 (1921), p.28.

103 'Chrezvychainoe sobranie upolnomochennykh fabrik i zavodov Petro-grada: Protokoly', *Kontinent*, 2 (1975), pp.389–90; *Novaya Zhizn'*, 60, 23 March 1918, p.4.
104 *Novyi Den'*, 16, 12 April 1918, p.4.

NOTES TO CONCLUSION

1 B.H. Moss, *The Origins of the French Labor Movement* (Berkeley, University of California Press, 1976); M.P. Hanagan, *The Logic of Solidarity* (Urbana, University of Illinois Press, 1980); E.P. Thompson, *The Making of the English Working Class* (London, Penguin, 1963); I. Prothero, *Artisans and Politics in early nineteenth-century London* (London, Methuen, 1979); D. Geary, 'The German Labour Movement, 1848–1919', *European Studies Review*, 6 (1976), 297–330.
2 J.P. Courtheoux, 'Naissance d'une conscience de classe dans le prolétariat textile du Nord, 1830–70', *Revue économique*, 8 (1957), 114–39.
3 V. Bonnell, 'Trade Unions, Parties and the State in Tsarist Russia', *Politics and Society*, 9, no.3 (1980), 299–322.
4 P. Kropotkin, *Memoirs of a Revolutionist* (New York, Grove Press, 1970), p.32.
5 G. Plekhanov, *Russkii rabochii v revolyutsionnom dvizhenii* (Geneva, 1892), p.15.
6 M. Ferro, *October 1917* (London, Routledge, 1980), p.179–80.
7 Even by the winter of 1917–18, the objectives of the workers who took temporary control of their factories in Petrograd cannot be described as 'syndicalist'. Compared to Yugoslavia since 1958, and especially since the 1970s, where the self-management bodies take, in theory at least, a wide range of decisions concerning what will be produced, and how revenue will be spent, the aspirations of the Petrograd committees were far more centralist and state-oriented. Similarly, one has only to compare the limited experiment in workers' self-management in Petrograd to the genuinely syndicalist collectivisation of industry by the CNT in Catalonia in October 1936, to see how different it was. There ownership of the workplaces passed into the hands of the unions, and the economy was managed in a federal rather than centralised manner. See G. Hunnius, *Workers' Control* (New York, Vintage, 1973); I. Adizes, *Industrial Democracy: Yugoslav Style* (New York, Macmillan, 1971); B. Denitch, *The Legitimation of a Revolution* (New Haven, Conn., Yale University Press, 1976); G. Shabad, 'Strikes in Yugoslavia: implications for industrial democracy', *British Journal of Political Science*, 10 (1980); R. Fraser, *The Blood of Spain* (London, Penguin, 1981), pp.213–36.
8 *Novyi Put'*, 6–8, 25 March 1918, p.2.
9 V.I. Lenin, *Polnoe sobranie sochinenii*, vol.36 (Moscow, 1962), p.300. The following account of Lenin's thinking at this time is based on: J. Rancière, *La leçon d'Althusser* (Paris, 1974); C. Claudin-Urondo, *Lenin and the Cultural Revolution* (Brighton, Harvester, 1977); U. Santamaria and A. Manville, 'Lenin and the Problem of Transition', *Telos*, 27 (1976), 79–96.
10 Lenin, *Pol. sob. soch.*, vol. 36, pp.173–4.

11 *ibid.*, p.189.

12 M. Brinton, *The Bolsheviks and Workers' Control, 1917–21* (London, Solidarity, 1970), p.42.

13 As usual it was Trotsky who attempted to make a virtue out of this particular shortcoming. In *Terrorism and Communism* (1920), he argued: 'The dictatorship of the proletariat is expressed in the abolition of private property in the means of production, in the supremacy over the whole Soviet mechanism of the collective will of the workers, and *not at all* in the form in which economic enterprises are administered' [my emphasis].

14 C. Bettelheim, *Class Struggles in the USSR: first period, 1917–23* (Brighton, Harvester, 1977), p.42.

15 P. Corrigan et al, *Socialist Construction and Marxist Theory* (London, Macmillan, 1978), pp.3–4; R. Williams, *Marxism and Literature* (Oxford University Press, 1977), pp.90–4. Compare the defence of technological determinism in G.A. Cohen, *Karl Marx's Theory of History* (Oxford, Clarendon, 1978).

16 K. Marx, *Capital*, vol.1 (London, Penguin, 1976), pp.928–9.

17 K. Marx and F. Engels, *The German Ideology* (New York, International, 1970), p.56.

Bibliography

I. ARCHIVES

Leningrad State Historical Archive (LGIA)

fond 1229	Factory Inspectorate of Petrograd guberniya
fond 1333	Company Accounts of the Cable Works
fond 1357	Petrograd Metal Works
fond 1278	Kersten knitwear factory
fond 416	Baltic works: proceedings of conciliation committee
fond 1304	Baltic works: works committee
fond 1477	1835 Gas Light Company
fond 1182	Nevskaya footwear factory
fond 1186	Pechatkin paper mill
fond 1296	Petrograd Arsenal

2. NEWSPAPERS

i. The Petrograd Socialist Press, 1917–18

Name	Organ of
Delo naroda	Central Committee of SR party
Den'	Right-wing Mensheviks
Edinstvo	Plekhanov's supporters
Golos anarkhista	Anarchists
Golos bunda	Central Committee of the Jewish Bund
Golos rabotnitsy	Menshevik paper for working women
Golos sotsial-demokrata	SD Internationalists
Golos truda	Anarcho-syndicalists
Izvestiya	EC of Petrograd Soviet
Izvestiya raionnogo komiteta Petrogradskoi Storony	Menshevik party committee of Petrogradskaya district
Kommuna	Anarchists
Kommunist	Left Communists

Narodnoe slovo	Popular Socialists
Novyi den'	Right-wing Mensheviks
Partiinye Izvestiya	Menshevik internal organ
Petrogradskaya pravda	North-West oblast' bureau of Central Committee and Petrograd guberniya committee of Bolshevik party
Petrogradskii rabochii	SR (centre)
Plamya	Menshevik
Pravda	Central Committee of Bolshevik party
Rabochaya gazeta	Central Committee of Menshevik party
Rabotnitsa	Bolshevik paper for working women
Shchit	Central Committee of Menshevik party
Trud i volya	Trudoviks
Volya naroda	Right SR's
Volya Truda	SR Maximalists
Yunii proletarii	Socialist Union of Young Workers
Zemlya i volya	Petrograd oblast' committee of SRs
Znamya Truda	Left SR's

ii. The Petrograd Trade-Union Press, 1917–18

Name	*Organ of*
Bor'ba	Industrial and commercial *sluzhashchie*
Ekho derevoobdelochnika	Wood workers
Golos chertezhnika	Draughtsmen
Golos kozhevnika	Leatherworkers
Gudok	Railway workers of Petrograd–Moscow junction
Kontorskii trud	Clerical workers
Metallist	Metalworkers
Mysli zheleznodorozhnika	Railway workers of Nikolaev line
Nabat	Foodworkers
Nashe slovo	Catering workers
Novyi put'	Central Council of Factory Committees
Pechatnik	Printers
Pischebumazhnik	Paperworkers
Pochtovo-Telegrafnyi tribun	Post-Office employees
Professional 'nyi Soyuz	Menshevik trade-union journal
Professional'nyi Vestnik	All-Russian Council of Trade Unions
Proletarii igly	Needleworkers
Proletarskii prizyv	Glassworkers
Rabochii kooperator	Workers' consumer-cooperatives
Rabotnik vodnogo transporta	Waterway employees
Revolyutsionnyi pechatnik	Internationalist printers
Stroitel'	Construction workers
Tkach	Textile workers
Trud	Predecessor to *Rabochii kooperator*
Trudorezina	Rubber workers (mainly the Triangle Works)

310 Bibliography

Vestnik aptechnogo truda	Pharmacy employees
Vestnik kustarnoi promyshlennosti	Bureau of All-Russian Congresses of Artisans
Vestnik metallista	Provisional Central Committee of national metalworkers' union
Vestnik professional'nykh soyuzov	Petrograd Council of Trade Unions
Zerno pravdy	Predecessor to *Nabat*
Zhizn' farmatsevta	Predecessor to *Vestnik aptechnogo truda*

iii. Miscellaneous

Gazeta vremennogo rabochego i krest'yanskogo pravitel'stvo
Izvestiya soveta s"ezdov predstavitelei promyshlennosti i torgovli
Malen'kaya gazeta/Narodnaya gazeta (extreme right wing)
Petrogradskaya gazeta
Torgovo-promyshlennaya gazeta
Vestnik petrogradskikh obshchestva zavodchikov i fabrikantov
Vestnik vremennogo pravitel'stva

3. PRIMARY SOURCES

Akhapkin, Yu. (ed.) *First Decrees of Soviet Power*, London, Lawrence and Wishart, 1970
Belkin, G. 'Iz istorii bor'by za rabochii kontrol'', *Krasnyi Arkhiv*, 21–3 (69–70) (1935) 138–58.
Browder, R.P. and Kerensky, A.F. *The Russian Provisional Government*, 3 vols., Stanford University Press, 1961.
Bunyan, J. and Fisher, H.H. *The Bolshevik Revolution, 1917–18*, Stanford University Press, 1934.
Bunyan, J. *The Origin of Forced Labor in the Soviet State, 1917–21*, Baltimore, Md., Johns Hopkins Press, 1967.
'Chresvychainoe sobranie upolnomochennykh fabrik i zavodov Petrograda', *Kontinent*, 2 (1975), 385–419.
Dekrety sovetskoi vlasti, vol.1, Moscow, 1957.
Deyateli revolyutsionnogo dvizheniya v Rossii: bio-bibliograficheskii slovar', vol.5, issues 1–2, Moscow, 1931, 1933.
Deyateli SSSR v oktyabr'skoi revolyutsii, supplement to vol.41, Granat encyclopedia, 7th ed., Moscow, n.d.
Ekonomicheskoe polozhenie Rossii nakanune velikoi oktyabr'skoi sotsialisticheskoi revolyutsii, parts 1 and 2, Moscow, 1957.
Fabrichnaya-zavodskaya promyshlennost' v period 1913–18gg., *Trudy Ts.S.U.*, vol.26, issue 1–2, Moscow, 1926.
Fabrichno-zavodskie komitety Petrograda: protokoly, ed. I.I. Mints, Moscow, 1979.
Fleer, M.G. 'Putilovskii zavod v 1917–18gg.', *Bor'ba klassov*, 1–2 (1924).
Geroi Oktyabrya: biografii aktivnykh uchastnikov oktyabr'skogo vooruzhennogo vosstaniya, Leningrad, 1967.
'Iz istorii bor'by za rabochii kontrol'', *Krasnyi Arkhiv*, 69–70 (1935), 138–58.

'Iz istorii krasnoi gvardii Petrograda', *Istoricheskii Arkhiv*, 5 (1957), 119–45.

Kanun Revolyutsii: deyatel'nost' rabochego predstavitel'stva pri Tsentral'nom Voenno-Promyshlennom Komitete, ed. E. Maevskii, Petrograd, 1918.

Keep, J.L.H. *The Debate on Soviet Power: minutes of the All-Russian Central Executive Committee of the Soviets*, Oxford University Press, 1979.

KPSS v resolyutsiyakh, Moscow, 1954.

Lenin, V.I. *Polnoe sobranie sochinenii*, 5th edn., vols.27, 30, 31, 32, 33, 34, 35 and 36, Moscow, 1962.

Leningradskie rabochie v bor'be za vlast' sovetov, Leningrad, 1924.

Lin'ko, G. 'Rabochee dvizhenie na fabrike Kenig v 1917g.', *Krasnyi Arkhiv*, 58 (1933), 133–40.

Listovki petrogradskikh bol'shevikov, vol.3, Leningrad, 1957.

'Materialy k istorii rabochego kontrolya nad proizvodstvom,1917–18gg.', *Krasnyi Arkhiv*, 6 (1940), 106–29.

Materialy k uchetu rabochego sostava i rabochego rynka, Petrograd, 1916.

Materialy ob ekonomicheskom polozhenii i professional'nom organizatsii peterburgskikh rabochikh po metally, St Petersburg, 1909.

Narvksaya zastava v 1917g., v vospominaniyakh i dokumentakh, Leningrad, 1960.

Natsionalizatsiya promyshlennosti i organizatsiya sotsialisticheskogo proizvodstva v Petrograde, 1917–20gg., vols.1 and 2, compiler M.V. Kiselev, Leningrad, 1958 and 1960.

Natsionalizatsiya promyshlennosti v SSSR, 1917–20gg, sbornik dokumentov, ed. I.A. Gladkov, Moscow, 1954.

Oktyabr'skaya revolyutsiya i fabzavkomy, parts 1 and 2, ed. P.N. Amosov et al., Moscow, 1927.

Oktyabr'skii perevorot: fakty i dokumenty, ed. A.A. Popov, Petrograd, 1918.

Oktyabr'skoe vooruzhennoe vosstanie v Petrograde 1917g., sbornik dokumentov i materialov, Leningrad, 1948.

Oktyabr'skoe vooruzhennoe vosstanie v Petrograde, vospominaniya aktivnykh uchastnikov, Leningrad, 1956.

Perepiska sekretariata TsK RSDRP (b) s mestnym partiinym organizatsiyami mart–oktyabr', 1917g., Moscow, 1957.

Pervyi legal'nyi komitet Peterburgskogo komiteta RSDRP(b): sbornik materialov i protokolov zasedanii za 1917g., Moscow, 1927.

Pervaya rabochaya konferentsiya fabrichno-zavodskikh komitetov, Petrograd, 1917.

Pervyi vserossiiskii s"ezd professional'nykh soyuzov, 7–14 yanvarya 1918g., Stenograficheskii otchet, Moscow, 1918.

Petrogradskii Sovet rabochikh i soldatskikh deputatov: protokoly zasedanii, Moscow, 1925.

Professional'noe dvizhenie rabochikh khimikov i stekol'shchikov, 1905–18gg., ed. Yu.K. Milonov, Moscow, 1928.

Profsoyuzy SSSR: dokumenty i materialy v 4 tomakh, vol.1, ed. I. Borshchenko, Moscow, 1963.

Putevoditel' po rezolyutsiyam vserossiiskikh s"ezdov i konferentsii professional'nykh soyuzov, ed. Yu.K. Milonov, Moscow, 1924.

Putilovets v trekh revolyutsiyakh, ed. I.I. Gaza, Leningrad, 1933.

Pyat' let: soyuz rabochikh kozhevnikov, 1917–22, Moscow, 1922.

Rabochee dvizhenie v gody voiny, ed. M.G. Fleer, Moscow, 1925.

Rabochee dvizhenie v Petrograde v 1912–17gg., dokumenty i materialy, Leningrad, 1958.
Rabochee dvizhenie v 1917g., ed. V.L. Meller and A.M. Pankratova, Moscow, 1926.
Rabochii kontrol' v promyshlennykh predpriyatiyakh Petrograda 1917–18gg., vol.1, Leningrad, 1947.
Raionnye sovety Petrograde v 1917g.: protokoly, vols. 1–3, Moscow, 1964–6.
Resolyutsii vserossiiskikh konferentsii i s"ezdov professional'nykh soyuzov, ed. G. Tsyperovich, Petrograd, 1919
Revolyutsiya 1917 god: khronika sobytii,
  vol.1, yanvar'–aprel', ed. N. Avdeev, Moscow, 1923.
  vol.2, aprel'–mai, ed. N. Avdeev, Moscow, 1923.
  vol.3, iyun'–iyul', ed. V. Vladimirova, Moscow, 1923.
  vol.4, avgust–sentyabr', ed. V. Vladimirova, Moscow, 1924.
  vol.5, oktyabr', ed. K. Ryabinskii, Moscow, 1926.
  vol.6, oktyabr'–dekabr', I.N. Lyubimov, Moscow, 1930.
Rukovodyashchie materialy i postanovleniya Tsentral'nogo Komiteta vserossiiskogo soyuza rabochikh metallistov, issue 3, Moscow, 1924.
Sed'maya (aprel'skaya) vserossiiskaya i petrogradskaya obshchegorodskaya konferentsiya RSDRP(b), 1917g., Moscow, 1934.
Shestoi s"ezd RSDRP(b), avgust 1917g.: protokoly, Moscow, 1958.
Soyuz stroitel'nykh rabochikh SSSR: sbornik materialov, Leningrad, 1926.
Spisok fabrichno-zavodskikh predpriyatii Petrograda, Petrograd, 1918.
Spisok fabrichno-zavodskikh zavedenii goroda Sankt-Peterburga, St Petersburg, 1914.
Statisticheskie dannye Petrograda, Petrograd, 1916.
Statisticheskii sbornik po Petrograda i Petrogradskoi gubernii, Petrograd, 1922.
Statisticheskii sbornik za 1913–17gg. (*Trudy Ts.S.U.*), vol.7, issue 1, Moscow, 1921; issue 2, Moscow, 1922.
Svod otchetov fabrichnykh inspektorov za 1909g., St Petersburg, 1910.
Svod otchetov fabrichnykh inspektorov za 1910g., St Petersburg, 1911.
Svod otchetov fabrichnykh inspektorov za 1911g., St Petersburg, 1912.
Svod otchetov fabrichnykh inspektorov za 1912g., St Petersburg, 1913.
Theses of the Left Communists (1918), Glasgow, Critique pamphlet, 1977.
Tret'ya vserossiikaya konferentsiya professional'nykh soyuzov, 3–11 iyunya, 1917g., Stenograficheskii otchet, Moscow, 1927.
Trudy pervogo vserossiiskogo s"ezda delegatov rabochikh zavodov, portov i uchrezhdenii Morskogo Vedomstva, Petrograd, 1917.
Trudy pervogo vserossiiskogo s"ezda sovetov narodnogo khozyaistva, 25 maya–4 iyunya 1918g., Moscow, 1918.
Velikaya oktyabr'skaya sotsialisticheskaya revolyutsiya: dokumenty i materialy:
  Revolyutsionnoe dvizhenie v Rossii v aprele, Moscow, 1958.
  Revolyutsionnoe dvizhenie v Rossii v mae–iyune, Moscow, 1959.
  Revolyutsionnoe dvizhenie v Rossii v iyule, Moscow, 1959.
  Revolyutsionnoe dvizhenie v Rossii v avguste, Moscow, 1959.
  Revolyutsionnoe dvizhenie v Rossii v sentyabre, Moscow, 1961.
  Revolyutsionnoe dvizhenie v Rossii nakanune oktyabr'skogo vooruzhennogo vosstaniya, Moscow, 1962.
  Oktyabr'skoe vooruzhennoe vosstanie v Petrograde, Moscow, 1957.

Vserossiiskaya tarifnaya konferentsiya soyuzov metallistov: protokoly, Petrograd, 1918.

Vserossiiskii uchreditel'nyi s"ezd rabochikh metallistov, Petrograd, 1918.

Vsesoyuznyi soyuz metallistov v rezolyutsiyakh i postanovleniyakh s"ezdov, konferentsii i plenumov TsK, part 1, Moscow, 1927.

Vtoroi s"ezd RSDRP(b): protokoly, Moscow, 1959.

4. SECONDARY AND OTHER WORKS

Adibek-Melikyan, E.A. *Revolyutsionnaya situatsiya v Rossii nakanune oktyabrya*, Erevan, 1967.

Adizes, I. *Industrial Democracy: Yugoslav Style*, New York, Macmillan, Free Press, 1971.

Althusser, L. *For Marx*, London, Penguin, 1969.

Aluf, A. *Profsoyuzy v oktyabr'skoi revolyutsii*, Moscow, 1927.

   Bol'shevizm i men'shevizm v professional'nom dvizhenii, Moscow, 1926.

   Professional'noe dvizhenie v Rossii: fevral'–oktyabr' 1917g., Moscow, 1926.

Andreev, A. *Sovety rabochikh i soldatskikh deputatov nakanune oktyabrya*, Moscow, 1967.

Anikeev, V.V. 'Svedeniya o bol'shevistskikh organizatsiyakh s marta do dekabr' 1917g.', *Voprosy Istorii KPSS*, 2 (1958), 126–93; 3(1958), 96–168.

Antonov, N. *Dva goda diktatury proletariata v metallopromyshlennosti Petrograda*, Petrograd, 1920.

Antoshkin, D. *Ocherk dvizheniya sluzhashchikh v Rossii*, Moscow, 1921.

Anweiler, O. *The Soviets: the Russian Workers', Peasants' and Soldiers' Councils, 1905–21*, New York, Random House, 1974.

Arbuzova, A. 'Oktyabr' 1917g. na Petrogradskom Trubochnom zavode', *Krasnaya Letopis'*, 6 (1932), 175–8.

Atkinson, D., Dallin, A. and Lapidus, G. *Women in Russia*, Stanford University Press, 1977.

Atsarkin, A.N. *Pod bol'shevistskoe znamya. Soyuzy rabochei molodezhi v Petrograde v 1917g.*, Leningrad, 1958.

Avrekh, A.Ya. *Stolypin i tret'ya duma*, Moscow, 1968.

Avrich, P. 'The Bolsheviks and Workers' Control', *Slavic Review*, 22, no.1 (1963), 47–63.

   The Russian Anarchists, Princeton University Press, 1971.

   'The Russian Factory Committees in 1917', *Jahrbücher für Geschichte Osteuropas*, 11(1963), 161–82.

   The Russian Revolution and the Factory Committees (Columbia University, Ph.D.), 1961.

Badaev, A.E. *The Bolsheviks in the Tsarist Duma*, London, 1932.

Bailes, K.E. 'Alexei Gastev and the Soviet Controversy over Taylorism', *Soviet Studies*, 29, no.3(1977), 373–94.

   Technology and Society under Lenin and Stalin, Princeton University Press, 1978.

Baklanova, I.A. and Stepanov, Z.V. 'Rabochie-metallisty Petrograda v dni velikogo oktyabrya', in *Oktyabr'skoe vooruzhennoe vosstanie v Petrograde*, Moscow, 1957, 62–105.

Baklanova, I.A. 'K voprosu o militarizatsii truda v period pervoi imperialisticheskoi voiny', in *Rabochii klass i rabochee dvizhenie v Rossii, 1861–1917*, Moscow, 1966, 304–13.
   Rabochie Petrograda v period mirnogo razvitiya revolyutsii (mart-iyun'), Leningrad, 1978.
Balabanov, M. *Ot 1905 k 1917g.*, Moscow, 1927.
   Ocherki po istorii rabochego klass v Rossii, parts 2 and 3, Moscow, 1925–6.
Banks, J.A. *The Sociology of Social Movements*, London, Macmillan, 1972.
Bastiony revolyutsii, vol.1, Leningrad, 1957.
Bater, J.H. *St. Petersburg: Industrialisation and Change*, London, Edward Arnold, 1976.
Berkman, A. *The Russian Tragedy*, Orkney, Cienfugos, 1976.
Berlin, P.A. *Russkaya burzhuaziya v staroe i novoe vremya*, Moscow, 1922.
Bernshtein-Kogan, S. *Chislennost', sostav, i polozhenie peterburgskikh rabochikh*, St Petersburg, 1910.
Bertrand, C. *Revolutionary Situations in Europe, 1917–22*, Montreal, Interuniversity Centre for European Studies, 1977.
Bettelheim, C. *Class Struggles in the USSR: first period, 1917–23*, Brighton, Harvester, 1977.
Biblikov, Yu., Malyshkin, V. and Shalaeva, E. *Profsoyuzy do velikoi oktyabr'skoi revolyutsii, 1907–17gg.*, Moscow, 1957.
Binshtok, V.I. and Kaminskii, L.S. *Narodnoe pitanie i narodnoe zdorov'e*, Moscow, 1929.
Bonnell, V. 'Trade Unions, Parties and the State in Tsarist Russia', *Politics and Society*, 9, no.3 (1980), 299–322.
Borisov, G. and Vasil'ev, S. *Stankostroitel'nyi zavod imeni Sverdlova*, Leningrad, 1962.
Bor'yan, B. 'Rabochii kontrol' 1917–21gg.', *Vestnik truda*, 10–11 (1921), 29–40.
Braverman, H. *Labor and Monopoly Capital*, New York, Monthly Review Press, 1974.
Brik, K. 'Organizatsiya soyuza metallistov v 1917g.', in *Professional'noe dvizhenie v Petrograde v 1917g.*, Leningrad, 1928, 116–30.
Brinton, M. *The Bolsheviks and Workers' Control*, London, Solidarity, 1970.
Brody, D. (ed.) *The American Labor Movement*, New York, Harper and Row, 1971.
Brown, G. *Sabotage: a study in industrial conflict*, Nottingham, Spokesman, 1977.
Bry, G. *Wages in Germany, 1871–1945*, Princeton University Press, 1960.
Buchanan, H.R. 'Lenin and Bukharin on the Transition from Capitalism to Socialism: the Meshchersky controversy, 1918', *Soviet Studies*, 28, no.1 (1976), 66–82.
Buiko, A.M. *Put' rabochego: zapiski starogo bol'shevika*, Moscow, 1934.
Bulkin F. A. *Na zare profdvizheniya: istoriya peterburgskogo soyuza metallistov, 1906–14gg.*, Leningrad, 1924.
Bulkin, F. *Soyuz metallistov, 1906–18gg.*, Moscow, 1926.
Burdzhalov, E.N. *Vtoraya russkaya revolyutsiya*, Moscow, 1967.
Burgess, K. *The Challenge of Labour: Shaping British Society, 1850–1930*, London, Croom Helm, 1980.

The Origins of British Industrial Relations, London, Croom Helm, 1975.

Buzinov, A. *Za Nevskoi zastavoi*, Moscow, 1930.

Carr, E.H. *The Bolshevik Revolution*, vols.1 and 2, London, Pelican, 1965.

Chamberlin, W.H. *The Russian Revolution*, 1917–21, vols.1 and 2, New York, Universal Library, 1965.

Chauvier, J.-M. 'Contrôle ouvrier et "autogestion sauvage" en Russie', *Revue des pays de l'Est*, 1 (1973), 71–100.

Chermenskii, E.D. *Fevral'skaya burzhuazno-democraticheskaya revolyutsiya 1917g. v Rossii*, Moscow, 1959.

Clark, M. *Antonio Gramsci and the Revolution that Failed*, New Haven, Conn., Yale University Press, 1977.

Claudin-Urondo, C. *Lenin and the Cultural Revolution*, Sussex, Harvester, 1977.

Clegg, H., Fox, A. and Thompson, A.F. *A History of British Trade Unionism*, Oxford, Clarendon Press, 1964.

Cohen, G.A. *Karl Marx's Theory of History*, Oxford, Clarendon Press, 1978.

Collins, D.M. 'A note on the numerical strength of the Russian Red Guards in October 1917', *Soviet Studies*, 24, no.3, 1972.

Comfort, R. *Revolutionary Hamburg*, Stanford University Press, 1966.

Corrigan, P., Ramsay, H. and Sayer, D. *Socialist Construction and Marxist Theory*, London, Macmillan, 1978.

Courtheoux, J.P. 'Naissance d'une conscience de classe dans le prolétariat textile du Nord, 1830–70', *Revue économique*, 8 (1957), 114–39.

Crisp, O. *Studies in the Russian Economy before 1914*, London, Macmillan, 1976.
'Labour and Industrialisation in Russia', *Cambridge Economic History of Europe*, vol.7, part 2, Cambridge University Press, 1978, 308–415.

Daniels, R.V. *The Conscience of the Revolution*, Cambridge, Mass., Harvard University Press, 1960.
Red October: The Bolshevik Revolution of 1917, New York, Scribners, 1967.

Davidenko, A.I. 'K voprosu o chislennosti i sostave proletariata Peterburga v nachale XXv.' in *Istoriya rabochego klassa Leningrada*, issue 2, Leningrad, 1963, 92–112.

Davidovich, M. *Peterburgskii tekstil'nyi rabochii v ego byudzhetakh*, St Petersburg, 1912.

Demidov, V.A. 'Zemlyacheskie organizatsii i ikh rol' v bor'be bol'shevistskoi partii za soyuz rabochego klassa s trudyashchimsya krest'yanstvom v period podgotovki oktyabrya', *Uchenye zapiski Len. gos. ped. in-ta im. Gertsena*, 175 (1958).

Denitch, B. *The Legitimation of a Revolution: the Yugoslav Case*, New Haven, Conn., Yale University Press, 1976.

Derber, M. *The American Idea of Industrial Democracy*, Urbana, University of Illinois Press, 1970.

Devlin, R.J. *Petrograd workers and workers' factory committees in 1917* (State University of New York, Binghampton, Ph.D.), 1976.

Dewar, M. *Labour Policy in the USSR, 1917–28*, London, Royal Institute of International Affairs, 1956.

Dmitriev, N. 'Petrogradskie fabzavkomy v 1917g.', *Krasnaya Letopis'*, 2 (23) (1927), 62–100.

Dobrotvor, N. 'Massovoe rabochee dvizhenie ot fevralya k oktyabryu', *Istorik-marksist*, 4–5 (1932), 37–71.

Dorovatovskii, P. *Soyuz rabochikh narodnogo pitaniya i obshchezhitii: ocherk istorii leningradskoi organizatsii, 1905–18gg.*, Leningrad, 1928.

Soyuz transportnykh rabochikh: ocherk istorii leningradskoi organizatsii, 1905–18gg., Leningrad, 1927.

Drobizhev, V.Z. *Glavnyi shtab sotsialisticheskoi promyshlennosti*, Moscow, 1966.

Drobizhev, V.Z. *Stroitel' stvo organov upravleniya promyshlennosti v SSSR* (Moscow University, History Faculty, candidate dissertation), 1957.

Drobizhev, V.Z., Sokolov, A.K. and Ustinov, V.A. *Rabochii klass Sovetskoi Rossii v pervyi god proletarskoi diktatury*, Moscow, 1975.

Drulovic, M. *Self-Management on Trial*, Nottingham, Spokesman, 1978.

Dryazgov, G. *Na puti k komsomolu*, Leningrad, 1924.

Dublin, T. 'Women, Work and Protest in the Early Lowell Mills', *Labor History*, 16, no.1 (1976), 96–116.

Egorova, A.G. *Profsoyuzy i fabzavkomy v bor' be za pobedu oktyabrya*, Moscow, 1960.

Partiya i profsoyuzy v oktyabr'skoi revolyutsii, Moscow, 1970.

El'nitskii, A. *Istoriya rabochego dvizheniya v Rossii*, part 2, Moscow, 1924.

Engels, F. 'Socialism, Utopian and Scientific', *Marx-Engels Selected Works*, London, Lawrence and Wishart, 1968.

Ermanskii, O.A. *Iz perezhitogo (1887–1921gg.)*, Moscow, 1927.

Eroshkin, M.K. *The Soviets in Russia*, New York, 1919.

Falkus, M. *The Industrialisation of Russia, 1700–1914*, London, Macmillan, 1972.

Ferro, M. *The Russian Revolution of February 1917*, London, Routledge, 1972.

October 1917, London, Routledge, 1980.

'The Birth of the Soviet Bureaucratic System', *Reconsiderations on the Russian Revolution*, ed. R.C. Elwood, Slavica Publishers Inc., Columbus, Ohio, 1976, 100–32.

Fitzpatrick, S. *The Commissariat of Enlightenment: Soviet Organisation of Education and the Arts under Lunacharsky*, Cambridge University Press, 1970.

Fleer, M.G. *Peterburgskii komitet bol' shevikov v gody imperialisticheskoi voiny 1914–17gg.*, Leningrad, 1927.

Rabochee dvizhenie v Rossii v gody imperialisticheskoi voiny, Leningrad, 1926.

Florinsky, M.T. *The End of the Russian Empire*, New York, Collier, 1961.

Foster, J. *Class Struggle in the Industrial Revolution*, London, Methuen, 1974.

Frantishev, I.M. *Leningradskie krasnostroiteli*, Leningrad, 1962.

Fraser, R. *The Blood of Spain*, London, Penguin, 1981.

Freidlin, B.M. 'Dekret o rabochem kontrole', *Istorik-marksist*, 5 (1933).

Ocherki istorii rabochego dvizheniya v 1917g., Moscow, 1967.

'Petrogradskii sovet professional'nykh soyuzov v 1917g.', *Materialy po istorii profsoyuzov*, 2 (1924), 286–94.

Freysinnet, M. *Le processus de déqualification-surqualification de la force de travail*, Paris, 1974.

Friedmann, G. *Industrial Society*, Glencoe, Illinois, Free Press, 1955.

Ganelin, R.Sh. and Shepelev, L.E. 'Predprinimatel'skie organizatsii v

Petrograde v 1917g.' in *Oktyabr'skoe vooruzhennoe vosstanie v Petrograde, sb. stat.*, Moscow, 1965.

Gaponenko, L.S. *Rabochii klass Rossii v 1917g.*, Moscow, 1970.

Garvi, P.A. *Professional'nye soyuzy v Rossii v pervye gody revolyutsii 1917–21*, New York, 1958.

Gaza, I.I. *Putilovets na putyakh k oktyabr'yu*, Moscow, 1933.

Geary, D. 'Radicalism and the worker: metalworkers and revolution, 1914–23', in *Society and Politics in Wilhelmine Germany*, ed. R.J. Evans, London, Croom Helm, 1978, 267–86.

'The German Labour Movement, 1848–1919', *European Studies Review*, 6 (1976), 297–330.

Genkina, E.V. 'Fevral'skii perevorot' in *Ocherki po istorii oktyabr'skoi revolyutsii*, vol.2, Leningrad, 1927.

Gerbach, V.V. and Kuznetsov, K.A. *Rabochie-baltiitsy v trekh revolyutsiyakh*, Leningrad, 1959.

Gerschenkron, A. *Economic Backwardness in Historical Perspective*, Cambridge, Mass., Harvard University Press, 1962.

'Problems and Patterns of Russian Economic Development', *The Transformation of Russian Society*, ed. C. Black, Cambridge Mass., Harvard University Press, 1960, 42–72.

Gessen, V.Yu. *Trud detei i podrostkov v fabrichno-zavodskoi promyshlennosti Rossii ot XVIIv. do oktyabr'skoi revolyutsii*, Moscow, 1927.

Geyer, D. 'The Bolshevik Insurrection in Petrograd', *Revolutionary Russia*, ed. R. Pipes, Cambridge Mass., Harvard University Press, 1968, 164–79.

Gil'bert, M. 'K voprosu o sostave promyshlennykh rabochikh SSSR v gody grazhdanskoi voiny', *Istoriya Proletariata*, 3 (19) (1934), 28–37; 1 (21) (1935), 149–71.

Gimmer [Sukhanov, N.] 'K kharakteristike rossiiskogo proletariata', *Sovremennik*, 4 (1913), 321–30.

Gimpel'son, E.G. *Velikii oktyabr' i stanovlenie sovetskoi sistemy narodnogo khozyaistva, 1917–1920gg.*, Moscow, 1977.

Gindin, I.F. 'Russkaya burzhuaziya v period kapitalizma, ee razvitie i osobennosti', *Istoriya SSSR*, 2 (1963), 57–80; 3 (1963), 37–60.

Glickman, R. 'The Russian Factory Woman, 1880–1914', in *Women in Russia*, ed. D. Atkinson and G. Lapidus, Stanford University Press, 1977, 63–83.

God russkoi revolyutsii, sb. stat., Moscow, 1918.

Goodey, C. 'Factory Committees and the Dictatorship of the Proletariat', *Critique*, 3 (1974), 27–47.

Goodrich, C. *The Frontier of Control*, London, Pluto, 1975, orig. edn 1920.

Gordienko, I. *Iz boevogo proshlogo, 1914–18gg.*, Moscow, 1957.

Gordon, M. *Workers before and after Lenin*, New York, 1941.

Gorev, B.M. *Anarkhizm v Rossii*, Moscow, 1930.

Gorsen, P. and Knödler-Bunte, E. *Proletkult: System einer Proletarischen Kultur*, Band 1, Stuttgart, 1974.

Gorz, A. 'Technology, technicians and class struggle', in *The Division of Labour*, ed. A. Gorz, Brighton, Harvester, 1976.

Gramsci, A. *Political Writings, 1910–20*, London, Lawrence and Wishart, 1971.

Grave, V. *K istorii klassovoi bor' by v Rossii v gody imperialisticheskoi voiny*, Moscow, 1926.

Grinevetskii, V.I. *Poslevoennye perspektivy russkoi promyshlennosti*, Moscow, 1918.

Grunt, A.Ya. *Moskva – 1917: revolytsiya i kontrrevolyutsiya*, Moscow, 1976.

Gusev, K.V. *Krakh melkoburzhuaznykh partii v SSSR*, Moscow, 1966.

Krakh partii levykh eserov, Moscow, 1963.

Gvozdev, S. *Zapiski fabrichnogo inspektora*, Moscow, 1911.

Haber, S. *Efficiency and Uplift: Scientific Management in the Progressive Era, 1890–1920*, Chicago University Press, 1964.

Haimson, L.H. (ed.) *The Mensheviks from the Revolution of 1917 to the Second World War*, Chicago University Press, 1974.

'The Problem of Social Stability in Urban Russia', *Slavic Review*, 23, no.4 (1964), 619–42; 24, no.1 (1965), 1–22.

Hanagan, M.P. *The Logic of Solidarity: Artisans and Industrial Workers in Three French Towns, 1871–1914*, Urbana, University of Illinois Press, 1980.

Hasegawa, T. *The February Revolution in Petrograd 1917*, Seattle, Washington University Press, 1981.

'The Problem of Power in the February Revolution of 1917 in Russia', *Canadian Slavonic Papers*, 24, no.4 (1972), 611–33.

Haupt, G. and Marie, J.-J. *Les Bolcheviks par eux-mêmes*, Paris Maspero, 1969.

Hinton, J. *The First Shop Stewards' Movement*, London, Allen and Unwin, 1973.

Hobsbawm, E.J. *Labouring Men*, London, Weidenfeld, 1965.

Hosking, G.A. *The Russian Constitutional Experiment*, Cambridge University Press, 1973.

Hunnius, G. (ed.) *Workers' Control*, New York, Vintage, 1973.

Hyman, R. *Industrial Relations: a Marxist Introduction*, London, Macmillan, 1975.

'The Politics of Workplace Trade Unionism', *Capital and Class*, 8 (1979), 54–67.

Ignatenko, T.A. *Sovetskaya istoriografiya rabochego kontrolya i natsionalizatsii promyshlennosti v SSSR, 1917–67gg.*, Moscow, 1971.

Iroshnikov, M.P. *Sozdanie sovetskogo tsentral'nogo gosudarstvennogo apparata: oktyabr' 1917–yanvar' 1918.*, Leningrad, 1967.

Istoriya leningradskogo soyuza rabochego poligraficheskogo proizvodstva, 1904–7, vol.1, Leningrad, 1925.

Istoriya leningradskoi obuvnoi fabriki Skorokhod, Leningrad, 1969.

Istoriya rabochego klassa Rossii 1861–1900gg., Moscow, 1972.

Istoriya rabochikh Leningrada, vol.1, Leningrad, 1972.

Istoriya sotsialisticheskoi ekonomiki SSSR: Sovetskaya ekonomika v 1917–20gg., vol.1, Moscow, 1976.

Itkin, M.L. 'Tsentral'nyi sovet fabzavkomov Petrograda v 1917g.' in *Oktyabr'skoe vooruzhennoe vosstanie v Petrograde, sbornik statei*, Moscow, 1980, 172–181.

'Tsentry fabrichno-zavodskikh komitetov v 1917g.', *Voprosy Istorii*, 2 (1974), 21–35.

Ivanov, B. *Po stupen'yam bor'by: zapiski starogo bol'shevika*, Moscow, 1934.

Ivanov, L.M. 'Samoderzhaviya, burzhuaziya i rabochie', *Voprosy Istorii*, 1 (1971), 81–96.

'Preemstvennost' fabrichno-zavodskogo truda i formirovanie proletariata v Rossii', in *Robochii klass i rabochee dvizhenie v Rossii, 1861–1917*, Moscow, 1966, 58–140.

Ivanov, N.Ya. *Velikii oktyabr' v Petrograde*, Leningrad, 1957.

Johnston, R.J. *Peasant and Proletarian*, Leicester University Press, 1979.

Jones, G. Stedman, 'Class Struggles in the Industrial Revolution', *New Left Review*, 90 (1975), 45–69.

Juillard, J. *Fernand Pelloutier et les origines du syndicalisme d'action directe*, Paris, Seuil, 1971.

Kabo, E. *Pitanie russkogo rabochego do i posle voiny*, Moscow, 1926.

Kanatchikov, S. *Iz istorii moego bytiya*, Moscow, 1926.

Kanev, S.N. *Oktyabr'skaya revolyutsiya i krakh anarkhizma*, Moscow, 1974.

Kaplan, F.I. *Bolshevik Ideology and the Ethics of Soviet Labour*, London, Peter Owen, 1969.

Kaplan, T. *The Anarchists of Andalusia, 1868–1903*, Princeton University Press, 1977.

Karpetskaya, N.D. *Rabotnitsy i velikii oktyabr'*, Leningrad, 1974.

Katkov, G. *Russia 1917: the February Revolution*, New York, Harper and Row, 1967.

Kats, A. 'K istorii primiritel'nykh kamer v Rossii', *Vestnik Truda*, 10 (1923), 185–97.

Keep, J.L.H. *The Russian Revolution: a study in mass mobilisation*, London, Weidenfeld, 1976.

Khain, A. *Proidennyi put': soyuz masterovykh i rabochikh zheleznodorozhnogo petrogradskogo uzla v 1917–19gg.*, Moscow, 1925.

Khodeev, M. *Vserossisskii professional'nyi soyuz rabochikh i sluzhashchikh syvazi*, Moscow, 1921.

Kir'yanov, Yu. I. 'Vliyanie pervoi morovoi voiny na izmenie chislennosti i sostava rabochikh Rossii', *Voprosy Istorii*, 10 (1960), 89–101.

Kleinbort, L.M. *Ocherki rabochego intelligentsii: teatr, zhivopis', muzika*, vol.2, Petrograd, 1923.

Kleinbort, L.M. *Istoriya bezrabotitsy v Rossii 1857–1919gg.*, Moscow, 1925.

Koenker, D.G. *Moscow Workers in 1917*, vols.1 and 2 (University of Michigan, Ph.D.), 1976.

'Urban Families, Working-Class Youth Groups and the 1917 Revolution in Moscow', in *The Family in Imperial Russia*, ed. D.L. Ransel, Urbana, University of Illinois Press, 1978, 280–304.

Kokhn, M.P. *Russkie indeksy tsen*, Moscow, 1926.

Kollontai, A. *Rabotnitsa za god revolyutsii*, Moscow, 1918.

Komin, V.V. *Anarkhizm v Rossii*, Kalinin, 1969.

Kovalenko, D.A. 'Bor'ba fabrichno-zavodskikh komitetov Petrograda za rabochii kontrol' nad proizvodstvom', *Istoricheskie Zapiski*, 61 (1957), 66–111.

Kovalenko, D.A. *Oboronnaya promyshlennost' sovetskoi Rossii v 1918–20gg.*, Moscow, 1970.

Krasil'nikov, S. 'Syvaz'Leningradskogo rabochego s zemlei', *Statisticheskoe Obozrenie*, 4 (1929), 107–10.

Krasnikova, A.V. *Na zare sovetskoi vlasti*, Leningrad, 1963.

Krasnyi Treugol'nik na putyakh oktyabrya, Leningrad, 1929.

Kritsman, L. 'O russkoi revolyutsii', *Vestnik sotsialisticheskoi akademii*, 1 (1924), 55–67.

Kropotkin, P. *Fields, Factories and Workshops*, London, Allen and Unwin, 1974.

Memoirs of a Revolutionist, New York, Grove Press, 1970.

Krupskaya, N. *Memories of Lenin*, London, Panther, 1970.

Krupyanskaya, V.Ya. 'Evolyutsiya semeino-bytovogo uklada rabochikh', in *Rossiiskii proletariat – oblik, bor'ba, gegemoniya*, Moscow, 1970, 217–89.

Kruze, E.E. and Kutsentov, D.G. 'Naselenie Peterburga' in *Ocherki istorii Leningrada*, vol.3, Moscow, 1956.

Kruze, E.E. *Polozhenie rabochego klassa Rossii v 1900–14gg.*, Leningrad, 1976.

Peterburgskie rabochie v 1912–14gg., Moscow, 1961.

Krylova, I.I. 'K voprosu o statistike stachek petrogradskikh rabochikh v gody pervoi mirovoi voiny', in *Iz Istorii imperializma v Rossii*, Moscow, 1959, 414–33.

Larin, Yu. *Krest'yane i rabochie v russkoi revolyutsii*, Petrograd, 1919.

Laue, T. von 'Russian peasants in the factory, 1892–1904', *Journal of Economic History*, 21 (1961), 61–80.

'Russian labour between field and factory', *California Slavic Studies*, 3 (1964), 33–65.

Laverychev, V.Ya. *Tsarizm i rabochii vopros*, Moscow, 1972.

Lee, D. 'Skill, craft and class: a theoretical critique and a critical case', *Sociology*, 15, no.1 (1981), 56–78.

Leiberov, I.P. *Na shturm samoderzhaviya: petrogradskii proletariat v gody pervoi mirovoi voiny i fevral'skoi revolyutsii*, Moscow, 1979.

'Petrogradskii proletariat v gody pervoi mirovoi voiny', in *Istoriya rabochikh Leningrada*, vol.1, Leningrad, 1972, 461–511.

'Stachechnaya bor'ba petrogradskogo proletariata v period mirovoi voiny', in *Istoriya rabochego klassa Leningrada*, issue 2, Leningrad, 1963, 156–86.

Sverzhenie tsarizma, Leningrad, 1964.

Leiberov, I.P. and Shkaratan, O.I. 'K voprosu o sostave petrogradskikh promyshlennykh rabochikh v 1917g.', *Voprosy Istorii*, 1 (1961), 42–58.

Leiken, A.Ya. 'Oktyabr'skoe vooruzhennoe vosstanie i molodezh'' in *Oktyabr'skoe vooruzhennoe vosstanie v Petrograde. Sbornik statei*, Moscow, 1980, 235–41.

Lepse, I. 'Piterskie metallisty v oktyabre', *Metallist*, 17 (1922).

Leskova, L.I. 'Kollektivnye dogovory rabochikh s predprinimatelyami v 1905–07gg. kak istoricheskii istochnik' in *Rabochii klass i rabochee dvizhenie v Rossii*, Moscow, 1966, 345–57.

Levin, I.D. 'Rabochie kluby v Peterburge, 1907–14gg.', *Materialy po istorii professional'nogo dvizheniya v Rossii*, 3 (1924), 88–111; 4(1924), 200–26.

Liebman, M. *Leninism under Lenin*, London, Cape, 1975.

Limon, D.L. 'Lénine et le contrôle ouvrier', *Autogestion*, 18–19 (1970), 65–109.

Littler, C. 'Understanding Taylorism', *British Journal of Sociology*, 29, no.2 (1978), 185–200.

Loginova, S.E. 'Partiya bol'shevikov – organizator revolyutsionnogo tvorchestva mass v reshenii prodovol'stvennoi problemy v period podgotovki oktyabrya', *Uchenye zapiski Len. universiteta* 259, seriya istoricheskikh nauk, vyp. 31 (1959), 63–85.

Longley, D. 'Divisions in the Bolshevik party in March 1917', *Soviet Studies*, 24, no.2 (1972), 61–76.

Lozovskii, S.A. *Rabochii kontrol'*, Petrograd, 1918.

Lubasz, H. (ed.) *Revolutions in Modern European History*, New York, Macmillan, 1976.

Lukes, S. *Power: a radical view*, London, Macmillan, 1974.

Lur'e, M. *Petrogradskaya krasnaya gvardiya (fevral' 1917–fevral' 1918g.)*, Leningrad, 1938.

Trudovaya povinnost' i rabochii kontrol', Petrograd, 1918.

Lyashchenko, P.I. *History of the National Economy*, New York, Macmillan, 1949.

Maier, C. *Recasting Bourgeois Europe*, Princeton University Press, 1975.

Malakhovskii, V. *Iz istorii krasnoi gvardii: krasnogvardeitsy Vyborgskogo raiona 1917g.*, Leningrad, 1925.

Markus, B.L. 'K voprosu o metodakh izucheniya sotsial'nogo sostava proletariata SSSR', *Istoriya proletariata*, 2 (1930), 23–71.

Marx, K. and Engels, F. *The German Ideology*, ed. C.J. Arthur, New York, International, 1970.

Marx, K. *Capital*, vol.1, London, Penguin, 1976.

Maura, J. Romero, 'The Spanish Case', in *Anarchism Today*, ed. J. Joll and D. Apter, London, Macmillan, 1971, 60–83.

Maximoff, G. *Syndicalists in the Russian Revolution*, reprint 1978 (n.p.).

Mel'gunov, S.P. *The Bolshevik Seizure of Power*, Santa Barbara, Clio, 1972.

Michels, R. *Political Parties*, New York, Macmillan, Free Press, 1968.

Milligan, S. 'The Petrograd Bolsheviks and Social Insurance, 1914–17', *Soviet Studies*, 20, no.3 (1969), 369–74.

Milyutin, V. *Sovetskoe ekonomicheskoe razvitie Rossii v diktature proletariata*, Moscow, 1918.

Natsionalizatsiya promyshlennosti, oktyabr'skii perevorot i diktatura proletariata, Moscow, 1919.

Mints, I.I. *Istoriya velikogo oktyabrya*, vols. 1–2, Moscow, 1967–8.

Mints. L.E. *Okhod krest'yanskogo naseleniya na zarabotki*, Moscow, 1925.

Mitel'man, M.I. *1917 god na Putilovskom zavode*, Leningrad, 1939.

Mitel'man, M., Glebov, V. and Ul'yanskii, A. *Istoriya Putilovskogo zavoda, 1908–17gg.*, 4th edn, Moscow, 1961.

Monds, J. 'Workers' Control and the Historians', *New Left Review*, 97 (1976), 81–100.

Montgomery, D. *Workers' Control in America*, Cambridge University Press, 1979.

Moskovskaya Zastava v 1917g., Leningrad, 1959.

Moss, B.H., *The Origins of the French Labor Movement: the Socialism of the Skilled Workers, 1830–1914*, Berkeley, University of California Press, 1976.

Munting, R. 'Outside earnings in the Russian peasant farm: the case of the Tula province, 1900–17', *Journal of Peasant Studies*, 3 (1976), 428–46.

Murzyntseva, S.V. 'Bor'ba rabochikh voennykh predpriyatiyakh Peterburga v 1910–14gg.', *Vestnik Len. gos. universiteta*, 1967, *seriya ist. yazyk, lit*, no.14, 63–75.

'Iz istorii ekonomicheskogo polozheniya rabochikh na predpriyatiyakh voennogo i morskogo vedomstv v 1907–14gg. v Peterburge', *Uchenye zapiski Len. gos. universiteta, seriya ist. nauk*, 32 (1959), no.270, 217–40.

Nasyrin, V.P. 'O nekotorykh voprosakh sotsialisticheskogo preobrazovaniya promyshlennosti v SSSR', *Voprosy Istorii* 5 (1956), 90–9.

Naumkin, V.G. 'Na izhorskom zavode nakanune fevral'skoi revolyutsii', *Krasnaya Letopis'*, 1 (40) (1931).

Naumov, G. *Byudzhety rabochikh goroda Kieva*, Kiev, 1914.

Netesin, Yu.N. 'K voprosu o sotsial'no-ekonomicheskikh kornyakh i osobennostyakh "rabochei aristokratii" v Rossii', in *Bol'shevistskaya pechat' i rabochii klass v Rossii*, Moscow, 1965, 192–211.

Nevskii, V. *Ocherki po istorii RKP(b)*, vol.1, Leningrad, 1927.

Ocherk istorii leningradskogo soyuza derevoobdelochnikov za 1917–18gg., Leningrad, 1927.

Ocherki po istorii oktyabr'skoi revolyutsii, ed. M.N. Pokrovskii, 2 vols., Moscow, 1927.

Oktyabr' v Petrograde, sb. stat., ed. O.A. Lidak, Leningrad, 1933.

Oktyabr'skoe vooruzhennoe vosstanie: semnadtsatyi god v Petrograde, 2 vols., ed. S.N. Valk, Leningrad, 1967.

Ol'khovaya, L.V. 'Rabochaya kooperatsiya kak forma organizatsii proletariata' in *Rossiiskii proletariat: oblik, bor'ba, gegemoniya*, Moscow, 1970, 256–70.

Oppenheim, S.A. 'The Supreme Economic Council, 1917–21', *Soviet Studies*, 25, no.1 (1973), 3–27.

Pankratova, A. *Fabzavkomy i profsoyuzy v revolyutsii*, Moscow, 1927.

Fabzavkomy Rossii v bor'be za sotsialisticheskuyu fabriku, Moscow, 1923.

Papernikov, Ya. S. *Ocherk po istorii leningradskogo soyuza rabochikh kozhevnikov*, Leningrad, 1930.

Payalin, N.P. 'Putilovskii zavod v 1917g.', *Krasnaya Letopis'*, 3 (48) (1932), 165–88; 4 (49) (1932), 113–36; 5–6 (50–9) (1932), 135–73.

Zavod imeni Lenina, 1857–1918, Moscow, 1933.

Pazhitnov, K.A. *Polozhenie rabochego klassa v Rossii*, vols. 2 and 3, Leningrad, 1924.

Perazich, V. *Tekstili Leningrada v 1917g.*, Leningrad, 1927.

Petrogradskie bol'sheviki v oktyabr'skoi revolyutsii, Leningrad, 1957.

Petrogradskie bol'sheviki v trekh revolyutsiyakh, ed. N.Ya. Ivanov, Leningrad, 1966.

Pinchbeck, I. *Women Workers in the Industrial Revolution*, London, Frank Cass, 1969.

Pinezhskii, E. *Krasnaya gvardiya*, 2nd edn, Moscow, 1933.

Pipes, R. *Social Democracy and the St. Petersburg Labour Movement*, Cambridge, Mass., Harvard University Press, 1963.

Plekhanov, G. *Russkii rabochii v revolyutsionnom dvizhenii*, Geneva, 1892.

Pollard, S. *The Genesis of Modern Management,* London, Edward Arnold, 1959.
Pospielovsky, D. *Russian Police Trade Unionism,* London, Weidenfeld, 1971.
Potekhin, M.N. *Pervyi sovet proletarskoi diktatury,* Leningrad, 1966.
Poulantzas, N. *Classes in Contemporary Capitalism,* London, New Left Books, 1975.
   State, Power and Socialism, London, New Left Books, 1978.
Pribicevic, B. *The Shop Stewards' Movement and Workers' Control,* Oxford, Blackwell, 1959.
Professional'noe dvizhenie v Petrograde v 1917g. ed. A. Anskii, Leningrad, 1928.
Professional'nye soyuzy SSSR 1905–17–27, v proshlom i nastoyashchem, Moscow, 1927.
Prokopovich, S.N. *Byudzhety peterburgskikh rabochikh,* St Petersburg, 1909.
Prothero, I. *Artisans and Politics in early nineteenth-century London,* London, Methuen, 1979.
Rabinowitch, A. *Prelude to Revolution: the Petrograd Bolsheviks and the July 1917 Uprising,* Bloomington, Indiana University Press, 1968.
   The Bolsheviks Come to Power, New York, Norton, 1976.
Rabochie Leningrada v bor'be za pobedu sotsializma, Moscow, 1963.
Rabochie Rossii v epokhu kapitalizma, Rostov, 1972.
Rabochii klass i rabochee dvizhenie v Rossii, 1861–1917gg., Moscow, 1966.
Rabochii klass i rabochee dvizhenie v Rossii v 1917g., Moscow, 1964.
Rabota soyuza muchnykh izdelii i osnovanie soyuza pishchevikov – 1917 god, Leningrad, 1927.
Rancière, J. *La leçon d'Althusser,* Paris, 1974.
Rashin, A.G. 'Demobilizatsiya promyshlennogo truda v Petrogradskoi gubernii za 1917–18gg.', *Materialy po statistike truda,* Petrograd, issue 5 (1919).
Rashin, A.G. *Formirovanie rabochego klassa Rossii,* Moscow, 1958.
   'Gramotnost' i narodnoe obrazovanie v Rossii v XIXv. i nachale XXv.', *Istoricheskie zapiski,* 37 (1951), 28–80.
   Naselenie Rossii za 100 let (1811–1913gg.), Moscow, 1956.
Revolyutsionnyi Petrograd god 1917, Leningrad, 1977.
Ridley, F.F. *Revolutionary Syndicalism in France,* Cambridge University Press, 1970.
Rigby, T.H. *Lenin's Government: Sovnarkom, 1917–22,* Cambridge University Press, 1979.
Rimlinger, G.V. 'Autocracy and Factory Order', *Journal of Economic History,* 20 (1960), 67–92.
Rosenberg, W.G. 'Workers' control on the railroads', *Journal of Modern History,* 49, no.2 (1977), D1181–D1219.
   'Workers and workers' control in the Russian Revolution', *History Workshop,* 5 (1978), 89–97.
Rossiiskii proletariat: oblik, bor'ba, gegemoniya, Moscow, 1970.
Rowbotham, S. *Hidden from History,* London, Pluto, 1977.
Rozanov, M.D. *Obukhovtsy,* Leningrad, 1965.
Rozenfeld, Ya.S. and Klimenko, K.I. *Istoriya mashinostroeniya SSSR,* Moscow, 1961.
Ruban, N.V. *Oktyabr'skaya revolyutsiya i krakh men'shevizma,* Moscow, 1968.

Ryabov, N.F. *My s Vyborgskoi storony*, Moscow, 1961.

Sablinsky, W. *The Road to Bloody Sunday*, Princeton University Press, 1976.

Santamaria, U. and Manville, A. 'Lenin and the Problem of Transition', *Telos*, 27 (1976), 79–96.

Schneider, E. *Industrial Sociology*, New York, McGraw Hill, 1957.

Schneiderman, J. *Sergei Zubatov and revolutionary Marxism*, Ithaca, Cornell University Press, 1976.

Schwarz, S.M. 'Fabrichno-zavodskie komitety i profsoyuzy v pervye gody revolyutsii' in R.P. Browder and A.P. Kerensky, *The Provisional Government*, Stanford University Press, 1961, pp.724–6.

The Russian Revolution of 1905, Chicago University Press, 1967.

Scott, J.W. and Tilly, L. *Women, work and the family*, New York, Holt, Rinehart and Winston, 1978.

Selitskii, V.I. *Massy v bor'be za rabochii kontrol' (mart–iyun' 1917g.)*, Moscow, 1971.

'Nekotorye voprosy bor'by petrogradskikh rabochikh za kontrol' nad proizvodstvom v period mirnogo razvitiya revolyutsii', *Istoriya rabochego klassa Leningrada* (Leningrad), 2 (1963).

Semanov, S.N. *Peterburgskie rabochie nakanune pervoi russkoi revolyutsii*, Moscow, 1966.

Serebrovskii, A.P. *Revolyutsiya i zarabotnaya plata rabochikh metallicheskoi promyshlennosti*, Petrograd, 1917.

Sergeev, N.S. *Metallisty: istoriya Leningradskogo Metallicheskogo zavoda im. XXII s"ezda KPSS*, vol.1, Leningrad, 1967.

Sestroretskii instrumental'nyi zavod imeni Voskova, 1721–1967gg., Leningrad, 1968.

Seton-Watson, C. *Italy: from Liberalism to Fascism, 1870–1925*, London, Methuen, 1967.

Shabad, G. 'Strikes in Yugoslavia: implications for industrial democracy', *British Journal of Political Science*, 10 (1980), 293–315.

Shabalin, B. *Krasnyi Treugol'nik, 1860–1935*, Leningrad, 1938.

Shapovalov, A.S. *V bor'be za sotsializm*, Moscow, 1957.

Shatilova, T.I. *Fabzavkomy i profsoyuzy v 1917–18gg.*, Moscow, 1927.

Ocherk istorii leningradskogo soyuza khimikov, 1905–18gg., Leningrad, 1927.

Shepelev, L.E. 'Predprinimatel'skie organizatsii v Petrograde v 1917g.' in *Oktyabr'skoe vooruzhennoe vosstanie v Petrograde*, Moscow, 1957.

Shishkin, V.F. *Velikii oktyabr' i proletarskaya moral'*, Moscow, 1976.

Shkaratan, O.I. 'Izmeneniya v sotsial'nom strukture fabrichno-zavodskikh rabochikh Leningrada, 1917–28gg.', *Istoriya SSSR*, 5 (1959), 21–38.

Problemy sotsial'noi struktury rabochego klassa SSSR, Moscow, 1970.

Shkaratan, O.I. and Vakzer, A.Z. 'Razvitie sotsialisticheskogo otnosheniya k trudu: rabochie Leningrada v 1917–24gg.', *Uchenye zapiski Len. gos. ped. inst. im. Gertsena* 165, (1958).

Shlyapnikov, A. *Kanun semnadtsatogo goda*, part 2, Moscow, 1922.

Semnadtsatyi god, Moscow, vol.1, 1923; vol.2, 1925; vol.3, 1927; vol.4, 1931.

Shuster, N.A. *Peterburgskie rabochie v 1905–07gg.*, Leningrad, 1976.

Sidorov, K. 'Rabochee dvizhenie v Rossii v gody imperialisticheskoi voiny 1914–17gg.', in *Ocherki po istorii oktyabr'skoi revolyutsii*, vol.1, ed. M.N. Pokrovskii, Leningrad, 1927.

Skocpol, T. *States and Social Revolutions*, Cambridge University Press, 1979.

Smirnov, A.S. 'Zemlyacheskie organizatsii rabochikh i soldat v 1917g.', *Istoricheskie zapiski*, 60 (1957), 86–123.

Smith, S.A. 'Craft Consciousness, Class Consciousness: Petrograd 1917', *History Workshop*, 11(1981), 33–56.

'Bolshevism, Taylorism and the Technical Intelligentsia: the Soviet Union, 1917–41', *Radical Science Journal*, 13 (1983), 3–27.

Sobolev, G.L. *Revolyutsionnoe soznanie rabochikh i soldat Petrograda v 1917g: period dvoevlastiya*, Leningrad, 1973.

Sostav fabrichno-zavodskogo proletariata SSSR, ed. A.G. Rashin, Moscow, 1930.

Spriano, P. *The Occupation of the Factories*, London, Pluto, 1975.

Startsev, V.M. *Ocherki po istorii Petrogradskoi krasnoi gvardii i rabochei militsii*, Moscow, 1965.

'Ustavy rabochei krasnoi gvardii Petrograda', in *Voprosy istoriografii i istochnikovedeniya istorii SSSR*, Moscow, 1963, pp.177–221.

Stearns, P. *Lives of Labor: Work in a Maturing Industrial Society*, New York, Holmes and Meier, 1975.

Revolutionary Syndicalism and French Labor, New Brunswick, N.J., Rutgers University Press, 1971.

Stearns, P. and Mitchell, H. *Workers and Protest: the European Labor Movement, the Working Classes and the Origins of Social Democracy, 1890–1914*, Itasca, Illinois, Peacock, 1971.

Stepanov, Z.V. *Rabochie Petrograda v period podgotovki i provedeniya oktyabr'skogo vooruzhennogo vosstaniya*, Moscow, 1965.

'K voprosu o rabochem kontrole nad proizvodstrom i raspredeleniem, *Istoriya SSSR*, 1 (1967), 232–4.

'Voprosy chislennosti i struktury rabochikh Petrograda v 1917g.', in *Rabochii klass i rabochee dvizhenie v Rossii v 1917g.*, Moscow, 1964.

Stinchcombe, A. 'Bureaucratic and Craft Administration of Production', *Administrative Science Quarterly*, 4 (1958–60), 168–87.

Strumilin, S.G. 'Obshchii obzor severnoi oblasti', *Materialy po statistike truda Severnoi oblasti*, issue 1 (1918).

'Sostav proletariata Sovetskoi Rossii v *1917–19gg.*' in *Dva goda diktatury proletariata*, Moscow, 1919.

'Problemy ekonomiki truda', *Izbrannye proizvedeniya*, vol.3, Moscow, 1964.

'Statistika i ekonomika', *Izbrannye proizvedeniya*, vol.1, Moscow, 1963.

Zarabotnaya plata i proizvoditel'nost' truda v russkoi promyshlennosti, 1913–22gg., Moscow, 1923.

Sukhanov, N.N. *The Russian Revolution*, ed. J. Carmichael, Oxford University Press, 1955.

Sviridov, A.A. 'Fabrichno-zavodskie komitety kak forma organizatsii piterskikh rabochikh v 1917g.', *Uchenye zapiski Len, gos. ped. inst. im. Gertsena*, 298 (1971), 68–104.

'Piterskie rabochie v bor'be za ukreplenie soyuza s bedneishim krest'yanstvom vo vremya podgotovki oktyabr'skogo vooruzhennogo vosstaniya', *Uchenye zapiski Len. gos. ped. inst. im. Gertsena*, 131 (1957), 39–63.

'Proletariat Petrograda v bor'be za rabochii kontrol' v period organizatsii shturma (sentyabr' – oktyabr' 1917g.), *Uchenye zapiski Len. gos. ped. inst. im. Gertsena*, 102 (1955), 3–30.

Tanyaev, A. *Ocherki dvizheniya zheleznodorozhnikov v revolyutsii 1917g. (fevral' – oktyabr')*, Moscow, 1965.

Thompson, E.P. *The Making of the English Working Class*, London, Penguin, 1963.

'Time, Work Discipline and Industrial Capitalism', *Past and Present*, 38 (1967), 56–97.

Tikhanov, A. *Vserossiiskii soyuz rabochikh poligraficheskogo proizvodstva*, Moscow, 1921.

'Rabochie-pechatniki v gody voiny', *Materialy po istorii professional'nogo dvizheniya v Rossii*, 3 (1925).

'Rabochie-pechatniki v 1917g.', *Materialy po istorii professional'nogo dvizheniya*, 4 (1925).

Tilly, C. *From Mobilisation to Revolution*, Reading, Mass., Addison-Wesley, 1978.

Timofeev, P. *Chem zhivet zavodskii rabochii*, St Petersburg, 1906.

Tokarev, Yu.S. *Narodnoe pravotvorchestvo nakanune velikoi oktyabr'skoi sotsialisticheskoi revolyutsii (mart–oktyabr' 1917g.)*, Moscow, 1965.

Tomkevich, I.G. *Znamya oktyabrya*, Leningrad, 1972.

Touraine, A. *L'évolution du travail ouvrier aux usines Renault*, Paris, Centre nationale de la recherche scientifique, 1955.

Trenogova, T. *Bor'ba petrogradskikh bol'shevikov za krest'yanstvo v 1917g.*, Leningrad, 1946.

Trotsky, L. *History of the Russian Revolution*, London, Sphere Books, 1967.

Problems of Everyday Life, New York, Pathfinder, 1973.

Terrorism and Communism, Ann Arbor, University of Michigan Press, 1961.

Tseitlin, D.A. 'Fabrichno-zavodskie komitety Petrograda v fevrale-oktyabre 1917 goda', *Voprosy Istorii*, 11 (1956), 86–97.

Tsybul'skii, V.A. 'Rabochie Sestroretskogo zavoda v 1917g.', *Istoriya SSSR*, 4 (1957), 141–54.

Tsyperovich, G. *Petrogradskie profsoyuzy v oktyabre*, Moscow, 1927.

Turner, H.A. *Trade Union Structure and Growth*, London, Allen and Unwin, 1962.

Turner, R.H. and Killiam, L.M. *Collective Behaviour*, Englewood Cliffs, N.J., Prentice-Hall, 1972.

Uslovye byta rabochikh v dorevolyutsionoi Rossii, Moscow, 1958.

Vasenko, A. *Za 100 let (1840–1940): k stoletiyu len. gos. bumazhnoi fabriki im. Volodarskogo*, Leningrad, 1940.

V boyakh: sbornik vospominanii posvyashchennykh geroicheskoi bor'be vasileostrovtsev, Leningrad, 1932.

Venediktov, A.V. *Organizatsiya gosudavstvennoi promyshlennosti v SSSR*, vol.1, Leningrad, 1957.

Vinogradov, V. 'Krasnaya gvardiya Petrogradskogo metallicheskogo zavoda', *Krasnaya letopis'*, 2 (23) (1927).

V ogne revolyutsionnykh boev: sbornik vospominanii starykh bol'shevikov-piterstsev, vol.1, Moscow, 1967; vol.2, Moscow, 1971.

Volens, N. 'Zarabotnaya plata i rabochee vremya petrogradskikh tekstil'shchikov v yanvare i iyule 1917g.', *Materialy po statistike truda Severnoi oblasti*, 3 (1919).

Volin, S. *Deyatel'nost' men'shevikov v profsoyuzakh pri sovetskoi vlasti*, New York, Inter-University Project on the History of the Menshevik Movement, no.13, 1962.

Voline, *The Unknown Revolution 1917–21*, Detroit, Black and Red, 1974.

Volobuev, P.V. 'Leninskaya ideya rabochego kontrolya i dvizhenie za rabochii kontrol' v marte-oktyabr' 1917g.', *Voprosy Istorii KPSS*, 6 (1962), 39–55.

Proletariat i burzhuaziya Rossii v 1917g., Moscow, 1964.

Vovchik, A.F. *Politika tsarizma po rabochemu voprosu v predrevolyutsionnyi period, 1895–1904gg.*, L'vov, 1964.

Vyborgskaya Storona: iz istorii bor'by rabochego klassa za pobedu velikoi oktyabr'skoi revolyutsii: sbornik statei i vospominanii, Leningrad, 1957.

Ward, B. 'Wild Socialism in Russia', *California Slavic Studies*, 3(1964), 127–48.

Weber, M. *Economy and Society*, vol.3, New York, Bedminster, 1968

White, J.D. 'Moscow, Petersburg and the Russian Industrialists: a reply to Ruth Amende Roosa', *Soviet Studies*, 24, no.3 (1973), 414–20.

Wildman, A. *The Making of a Workers' Revolution*, Chicago University Press, 1967.

Williams, G.A. *Proletarian Order*, London, Pluto, 1975.

Williams, R. *Marxism and Literature*, Oxford University Press, 1977.

Wright, E.O. 'Class Boundaries in Advanced Capitalist Societies', *New Left Review*, 98 (1976), 3–41.

Za 20 let: k dvatsatiletiyu soyuza metallistov, ed. V. Rabinovich, Leningrad, 1926.

Za god, sbornik statei, Petrograd, 1918.

Zagorsky, S.O. *State Control of Industry in Russia during the war*, New Haven, Conn., Yale University Press, 1928.

Zavlyalov, S. *Istoriya izhorskogo zavoda*, vol.1, Leningrad, 1934.

Zelnik, R.E. *Labor and Society in Tsarist Russia: the Factory Workers of St. Petersburg*, Stanford University Press, 1971.

'Russian Bebels: an introduction to the memoirs of Semen Kanatchikov and Matvei Fisher', *Russian Review*, 35, no.3 (1976), 249–89; 35, no.4(1976), 417–47.

'Russian Workers and the Revolutionary Movement', *Journal of Social History*, 6, no.2 (1972–3), 214–36.

Zlokazov, G.I. *Petrogradskii sovet rabochikh i soldatskikh deputatov v period mirnogo razvitiya revolyutsii (fevral'-iyun' 1917g.)*, Moscow, 1969.

Index

Kerensky government: *continued*
Coalition Government; Labour,
Ministry of
Kersten knitwear factory: wages, 117;
women workers, 198, 235–6;
workers' opposition to re-
instatement of administrative
personnel, 56; youth committee, 198
Kharkov, collective wage contracts in,
120
Koenig mill: penalties to improve labour
discipline, 90–1; women workers
present list of 'requests' to director,
69–70
Kokhn, M.P., 45
Kollontai, Alexandra, 194–5, 236
Kolokol'nikov, P.N., 170, 181
Kolovich, anarchist militant, 235
kompaniya, typesetters working in, 33
Konovalov, A.I., 76, 171
Kornilov, General L.G., 112, 113, 180; *see
also* Kornilov rebellion
Kornilov rebellion, 112, 115, 162
Kostelovskaya, textile union delegate to
sovnarkhozy congress, 241
Kotlov, 211
Kotov, 235
Kozhevnikov textile mill, political com-
position of factory committee, 160
Kozitskii, V.N., 161, 294 n.92
Kresty jail raid, 143
Kronstadt sailors, strikes in protest
against threatened execution of, 49,
51
Kropotkin, Peter, 142, 143, 255
Kuskova, E. D., 109
Kuznetsov works, resolution on workers'
control, 165

Labour, Ministry of: arbitrates in metal
contract negotiations, 123, 125, 126;
averts strike by *sluzhashchie*, 135; and
demands for sequestration, 179, 236;
programme of social reform, 170–1;
refuses loan to Brenner works, 148;
see also Skobelev circulars
Labour and Light group, 97
labour discipline: Bolshevik dilemma
over, 264; breakdown of, 88–90,
246–9; factory committees and, 90–
2, 155, 247–8, 251; Lenin's attitude
to, 261; trade unions and, 247, 248,
249, 250, 251; in tsarist factories,

37–8; *see also* absenteeism;
drunkenness; theft
labour exchanges, 76, 244, 247
labour movement, Russian, compared
with West, 28–9, 59, 64–5, 103–4,
109, 133, 253, 254, 285 n.11,
land-ownership by workers, 17–19
Langenzippen works: extent of workers'
control, 165, 166–7, 176–7, 231–2;
political composition of factory
committee, 161, 162; re-election of
factory committee, 205, 251; strikes,
53; workers' resolution on Skobelev
circulars, 180–1
Larin, Yu., 92, 158, 184, 248
Latvian workers, 23, 96, 191
Law on factory committees (23 Apr
1917), 78–9
leather industries: attitude of employers
to workers' control, 231; size of
workforce, 10; wage differentials,
131; women employed in, 25;
working hours, 44; young workers,
25; *see also* leatherworkers' union
leatherworkers' union, 69, 201, 217;
cooperation with CCFC, 220;
political affiliations of board, 115;
professional sections, 202; size of
membership, 105, 200; women
workers, 133, 194
Lebedev, N.I., 111
Lebedev factory: and Skobelev circular,
180; workers' takeover of, 178, 179
Left Communists, 229
legislation, industrial, 37, 38, 76, 78–9,
170, 188
Leiberov, I.P., 21, 22, 23, 49, 50
Lenin, V.I.: attitude to factory
committees, 159; and Bolshevik
seizure of power, 144; calls for return
to one-man management, 228, 241,
251, 261; and cultural level of
workers, 95, 98; and economics/
politics dichotomy, 2–3, 140; favours
centralised state regulation of
economy, 150, 223, 226–7; stance on
workers' control, 153–6, 209–10,
213, 225–6, 227, 228, 259; strategy
for transition to socialism, 260–2
Leontiev Mills: political affiliations of
factory committee, 160; strike
activity at, 53
Lepse, I.I., 161, 294 n.92

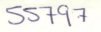
55797

Printed in the United Kingdom
by Lightning Source UK Ltd.
136442UK00001B/141/A

9 780521 316187